D0899149

The Critique of Ultra-Leftism in China, 1958-1981

William A. Joseph

The Critique of Ultra-Leftism in China, 1958-1981

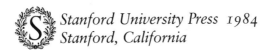 *Stanford University Press 1984*
Stanford, California

Stanford University Press
Stanford, California
© 1984 by the Board of Trustees of the
Leland Stanford Junior University
Printed in the United States of America
ISBN 0-8047-1208-5
LC 83-42832

12-11-84

To the memory of
my father, Howard R. Joseph, and
my mother, Myra I. Joseph

And to my aunt, Rosabel K. Brown

Acknowledgments

I must begin by thanking my wife, Sigrid Bergenstein. Over the years, I have drawn greatly on her knowledge and experience of China. She has truly been a partner to me in the Long March from dissertation to book, and without her support this project would not have been completed.

I am also particularly grateful to John Wilson Lewis of Stanford University. It was John Lewis who first enticed me into the world of Chinese studies when I was an undergraduate at Cornell University during the early years of the Great Proletarian Cultural Revolution. He later served as my adviser in graduate programs at Stanford and supervised the writing of the doctoral dissertation on which this book is based. I owe a very special thank-you to Harry Harding, previously of Stanford and now with the Brookings Institution, who also served as one of my dissertation advisers and subsequently provided encouragement for revising the dissertation for publication. Both John Lewis and Harry Harding were the sources of much enlightenment and inspiration to me during my years of training as a sinologist and as a political scientist. My intellectual and personal debt to them extends far beyond the pages that follow.

The other members of my doctoral examination committee at Stanford—Alexander Dallin, Victor Li, and Lyman Van Slyke—helped me refine the dissertation version of this study with their thoughtful comments and questions. Maurice Meisner provided a thorough and insightful reading of the manuscript and offered useful suggestions for clarifying, elaborating, and reorganizing. Roderick MacFarquhar commented on the chapters on the Great Leap Forward and called my attention to several points that needed reworking.

Hsiao-ti Falcone introduced me to word-processing while she

was the computer consultant at Wellesley College and greatly facilitated communications with the publisher and the typesetter. Barbara Sindriglis, Cathryn Entner, Carol Mazzarella, Kerry Walk, and Lori Martin all contributed to the typing of the manuscript at various stages.

I am grateful to York University and Wellesley College for gainful employment and intellectual stimulation during the completion of the dissertation and the preparation of the book. The Committee on Faculty Awards of Wellesley College provided generous support for work on the manuscript.

Finally, I would like to thank Stanford University Press, especially Jess Bell for his confidence in this project and his guidance in seeing the book through to publication. John Feneron was a most able and amiable production editor, and Shirley Taylor did a magnificent job of editing and polishing the text.

Although this book is in many ways the product of the "collective wisdom" of many individuals, I of course take full responsibility for the presentation and interpretation of the material.

W.A.J.

Contents

A Note on Romanization

Romanization of Chinese names, terms, phrases, and titles used in this book is given in Pinyin, the official system of transliteration in the People's Republic of China. The only exceptions are in cited titles of and quotations from certain English-language sources that use the Wade-Giles system. Excerpts from translation sources (e.g., *Survey of the China Mainland Press*) published before the adoption of the Pinyin system have been changed to Pinyin for the sake of consistency. The capital of the People's Republic of China is referred to as Peking throughout the text except in footnotes where Beijing is used after the cited source adopted the Pinyin spelling (e.g., *Beijing Review*, Beijing Domestic Service). The following are the most frequent cases where Wade-Giles may appear in the book; the Pinyin equivalent is given in parentheses:

Chang Ch'un-ch'iao	(Zhang Chunqiao)
Ch'en Po-ta	(Chen Boda)
Chengchow	(Zhengzhou)
Chiang Ch'ing	(Jiang Qing)
hsia-fang	(xiafang)
Hua Kuo-feng	(Hua Guofeng)
Kwangtung	(Guangdong)
Lin Piao	(Lin Biao)
Mao Tse-tung	(Mao Zedong)
P'eng Teh-huai	(Peng Dehuai)
Tachai	(Dazhai)
Teng Hsiao-p'ing	(Deng Xiaoping)
Tsinghua University	(Qinghua University)
Wang Hung-wen	(Wang Hongwen)
Wang Tung-hsing	(Wang Dongxing)

The Critique of Ultra-Leftism in China, 1958-1981

I

The Revolutionary Looking Glass

> Now, if you'll only attend, Kitty, and not talk so much, I'll
> tell you all my ideas about Looking-glass House. First,
> there's the room you can see through the glass—that's just
> the same as our drawing room, only the things go the
> other way.　　　　　　　　　*Through the Looking Glass*

On January 25, 1981, a special tribunal of China's Supreme People's Court pronounced final judgment on Mao's widow, Jiang Qing, and nine codefendants who had been charged with an assortment of counterrevolutionary crimes committed during the Great Proletarian Cultural Revolution of 1966–76.[1] The written judgment summarizing the case and imposing the sentences found the defendants guilty of carrying out "conspiratorial activities for the purpose of seizing supreme power of the Party and the state."[2] These activities, which included the political and physical persecution of veteran cadres and intellectuals as well as attempts to foment armed rebellion and stage a coup d'état, were said to constitute "criminal offenses" under the laws of the People's Republic of China. The document further stated that the duty of the Court had been to consider only the crimes of the accused and not "other problems of the defendants that do not fall into the category of criminal offenses."[3]

The "other problems" mentioned in passing in the Court's judgment referred to political errors committed by Jiang Qing and her close associates, known as the Gang of Four, and the followers of Lin Biao, China's one-time defense minister who had perished in a plane crash in Outer Mongolia in 1971 after allegedly masterminding a plot to assassinate Mao Zedong. The propaganda surrounding the two-month long trial of the so-called "Jiang Qing and Lin Biao counterrevolutionary cliques" frequently stressed that the radical socio-economic policies and the ultra-Left political line espoused by the defendants during the Cultural Revolution, however erroneous and harmful to China's development, were not matters of

criminal culpability and were therefore not subject to court proceedings. As China's Chief Procurator declared in a report an-
nouncing the completion of the pretrial investigation, "We are pre-
paring to start the public prosecution of the counterrevolutionary
crimes [committed] by the cliques of Lin Biao and Jiang Qing which
violated the law. The prosecution will not concern their mistakes in
work, which include mistakes in [political] line." [4]

The distinction drawn between the political errors and the criminal offenses of those on trial was more than a rhetorical device to
obscure the workings of a "show" trial or to add an ex post facto
justification to the incarceration of the losers in a power struggle
within the Party leadership. Rather, this distinction was a logical
corollary of a far-reaching critique of ultra-Leftism as a deviant
trend in China's socialist development that unfolded after the arrest
of the Gang of Four in October 1976. One of the chief characteristics of Chinese politics in the early post-Mao era was the effort of
the Deng Xiaoping regime to attribute many of the problems of the
first decades of Communist rule to Leftist deviations in ideology,
policy, and leadership technique. One of the most serious charges
against the ultra-Left concerned the way in which the Party radicals
had turned principled differences among comrades into matters of
violent ideological confrontation. Disagreements over policy had
often been interpreted by the ultra-Leftists as manifestations of
class struggle to the point where purge and persecution became the
predominant modes of handling inner-Party disputes. The radicals
made no distinction between political errors and criminal acts: political errors *were* criminal acts in that they were seen as antagonistic contradictions between the "people" and their enemies bent on
destroying the revolution.

With the overthrow of the Gang of Four and the consolidation of
power by Deng Xiaoping, the Chinese leadership quickly took steps
to reduce the antagonism that had marked inner-Party struggle during the reign of the radicals, since political stability was necessary in
the interests of the broad goal of rapid economic modernization.
One important ingredient of the attempt to redefine the nature and
scope of inner-Party struggle was a strong and repeated assertion
that counterrevolutionary crimes and political errors should be
analytically distinguishable from one another and must not be
treated in an indiscriminate manner as was done during the Cultural Revolution.

It was such a distinction that was applied in the case of the Gang of Four and the followers of Lin Biao, who were ostensibly tried not for their political mistakes or erroneous ideas but only for their actual counterrevolutionary crimes. The public record of the trial shows that the charges against the accused were, in fact, limited to the persecution of political opponents, coup plans, and machinations designed to disrupt the Party and seize or consolidate power.[5] No mention was made of ultra-Leftism at any point in the trial because, according to the logic of the differentiation between counterrevolution and political error, ultra-Leftism itself was not a crime.

But in a broader sense, ultra-Leftism has, indeed, been on trial in China since the death of Mao and the arrest of the Gang of Four. The radical ideas and policies that dominated the political landscape of the People's Republic from the Great Leap Forward through the Cultural Revolution stand indicted and condemned for bringing untold harm to the Chinese people. Mao's successors have expended as much time, energy, and political capital on exorcising the Leftist ghosts of the past as they have on building their own program for modernizing China. Yet the critique of ultra-Leftism through which this ideological exorcism has been performed is not simply a phenomenon of post-Mao politics. Its roots go far back in the history of the Chinese Communist movement, and the outcomes of several earlier campaigns against ultra-Leftism created influential precedents for the criticism of the Gang of Four. This study investigates the way in which the Chinese Communists have attempted to analyze and rectify Leftist deviations in the theory and practice of their movement after Liberation. It also examines how and why such critiques of ultra-Leftism became the focus of severe political conflict and controversy within the Party leadership.

Values, Power, Politics, and Revolution

People commit themselves to political combat for many different reasons. Some seek to further personal ends, such as ego gratification or wealth, through political movements and the instruments of government. Others are drawn to politics in the pursuit of more noble causes. Public testimony alone is not a reliable guide for identifying what motivates political activism. Outward adherents of similar value schemes or ideologies may be motivated by vastly differing mixtures of narrow personal concern and broader social commitment. The dynamics of raw power struggles are often obfuscated by admirable rhetoric and utopian visions, and no account of political action is complete without acknowledging the complex interplay of power conflict and value conflict that informs the world of politics. To see politics only as the quest for selfless social goals is naïve; but to reduce politics to a Hobbesian struggle motivated solely by brutish instincts and selfish ends is to deprive political life of all but its most profane meaning. Politics is rarely just a contest for power. It is often a struggle between different views of how society should be organized, how resources should be distributed, and how authority should be exercised. In other words, the heart and much of the heat of politics emerge from the conflict of values; and politics is the process by which that value conflict is resolved or managed.[6]

A revolution is a particular kind of political conflict. It is, as Charles Tilly suggests, "an extreme condition of the normal political process" in which contention for power and influence is an ongoing fact of life; what distinguishes a revolutionary situation is the existence of "multiple sovereignty" when competing groups exercise control over different sectors of society and offer "effective, competing, mutually exclusive claims" as to who should rule the polity as a whole.[7] The objective of the revolutionaries is to resolve the "multiple sovereignty" into a singular sovereignty in which they replace the existing government as the prevailing power in the polity; the objective of the government is to resist this assault on its authority and legitimacy. Both sides are locked in a contest for the control of territory and for the allegiance of the population.

Furthermore, a revolution is, above all, the effort to induce a profound transformation of a society by discrediting old values and inculcating new ones.[8] Violent, extra-legal mass action, commitment to the realization of a more humane society, and a thorough restructuring of the dominant systems of stratification are all important aspects of revolutionary change as a political phenomenon.[9] But underlying these characteristics is the elemental fact that a revolution is a clash between contradictory and antagonistic world views and conflicting value schemes. Certainly the hope and fear that are aroused by both revolution and counterrevolution attest to the concrete factors of power, wealth, and status that are at stake in these movements. But the material realities of a revolutionary situation do not diminish the significance of the value conflict that is at the heart of the battle between contenders for power. It is only by appreciating the value dimension of such struggles that we can begin to comprehend the magnitude, the passion, the uncompromising nature, and the unpredictability of those rare political events we can truly call revolutions.

As a subtype of politics, a revolutionary movement also contains an internal dynamic of value conflict. Revolutionaries may agree on the necessity of overthrowing the *ancien régime* and establishing a new order; but they may have very different ideas about the means by which the old order is to be brought down and over the exact nature of the society that is to replace it. In many ways, the value conflict inherent in this sort of political contention within a revolutionary movement may be as severe and as irreconcilable—and as momentous in its implications for society and history—as the dynamic that inspired the initial challenge to the old regime. Witness the conflicts between the Levellers and the Cromwellians in the English revolution, the Girondins and the Jacobins in France, the Bolsheviks and the Mensheviks in the Russian Social Democratic Labor Party, and the advocates of rural revolt and those favoring urban insurrection in the early years of the Chinese Communist Party—to mention only a few of the internal political struggles that shaped the destinies of the "Great Revolutions." [10]

This book is a study of value conflict within a revolutionary movement. It is also a study of the relationship between value conflicts and power struggles within a revolutionary party. It is a description and analysis of one aspect of the protracted controversy within the Chinese Communist Party over the nature and direction of socialist development in post-Liberation China. More particularly, it is an examination of the reaction of some Party leaders to certain trends in China's post-Liberation history that they believed might steer the revolution into failure through economic dislocation, political turmoil, and social disaffection. These trends were, in turn, seen as symptomatic of serious ideological deviations falling into the broad category of "ultra-Leftism" (*jizuozhuyi*). This was an evaluation that rested on certain assumptions by the critics of ultra-Leftism—assumptions not shared, naturally, by those being criticized, who regarded their policies not at all as ultra-Left but as the embodiment of deeply held convictions about the process of socialist construction in China. To the ultra-Left, their critics were guilty of Rightist errors that, if unchecked, would lead to the abandonment of the mandate to build a truly revolutionary society. The conflict between political actors holding divergent perspectives on the nature of socialism in China has been the major force that has shaped Chinese politics in the last two decades.[11] An important objective of this study is to clarify the operation and impact of that force by examining in detail the actions and views of one of the parties in the conflict, the critics of the ultra-Left.

The Meaning of Ultra-Leftism

The terms "Left" and "Right" acquired their political meaning in the context of the French revolution.[12] At that time (1789–91) the Constituent Assembly, which had been formed to govern the new Republic, divided over the issues of the royal veto, the structure of the legislature, and the nature of the franchise. One side wanted to maintain the authority of the crown by an absolute veto, to preserve some of the rights of the aristocracy by having a nonelected upper house, and to limit the scope of popular sovereignty by imposing tax and property qualifications for voting. Their opponents demanded a more far-reaching assault on the remnants of feudalism and called for no royal veto, a single-chamber legislature in which all power rested with elected representatives, and the abolition of all restrictive qualifications (other than sex) on the franchise. A third grouping preferred compromise on all these issues.[13]

As this debate proceeded in the Assembly, those who advocated the royal veto and associated positions were seated on the right side of the legislative chamber (from the vantage point of the presiding officer) and their opponents were seated on the left, with the advocates of compromise appropriately situated in the center. Thus, the confluence of political argument and physical arrangement came to reflect, in David Caute's words, "the most fundamental cleavage in modern society, a conflict of principle, attitude, and policy."[14] The Left came to be associated not only with demands for more radical change but also with the pursuit of popular sovereignty and greater social and economic equality. The Right was inextricably connected with the defense of the status quo and the preservation of special privilege.

Given this political distinction, it was only natural that the growing socialist and communist movements of the late eighteenth and early nineteenth centuries would adopt for themselves the nomenclature of the Left. Leftism was seen as symbolic of the commitment to the goal of a classless society, while Rightism came to be ascribed to those perceived as opponents of this ineluctable trend of history; furthermore the labels Left and Right became points of reference in determining ideological deviations *within* the revolutionary movement.[15]

Rightism came to signify the ideological orientation of those ostensible socialists and communists whose penchant for compromise or "reformism" diluted their revolutionary commitment to the point of ineffectiveness. Such deviations to the Right took the form of "revisionism" and "opportunism," with the former denoting tampering with the fundamental principles of Marxism and the latter political sin attributed to those who sacrificed the long-range objectives of the revolution to short-term, personal interests. On the other hand, those who were seen as driven by an excess of revolutionary fervor to engage in irresponsible action or espouse unworkable policies were deemed to be guilty of deviations to the Left. Rightism of any stripe was, by definition, anathema to the cause of the socialist revolution; but to preserve the sanctity of the term Left as embodying the correct orientation of the movement in its march toward the classless society, deviations derived from a stance too radical for the times were designated as "Left," with quotation marks used to set the deviant apart from the true Left. The term "ultra-Left" was invoked to designate the most extreme manifestations of these deviations.[16] In this study, I shall for the most part dispense with the quotation marks for the sake of simplicity and shall use the terms Left and ultra-Left more or less interchangeably.[17]

Thus, the objective meaning of Left and Right in their original contexts as indicators of behavior reflecting distinct political values was merged with use of the terms as more subjective categories to classify and denigrate political opponents. The subjective nature of this function of the labels Left and Right resulted from the fact that the standard used to test revolutionary correctness versus deviation was dependent on the values of the person or party doing the labeling. What one side perceived as deviant and destructive to the revolutionary cause was what their opponents held to be the correct tactic, strategy, or policy for ensuring the continued success and progress of socialism. Left and Right became highly relative terms, which shifted meaning according to the historical situation and the changing power alignments within the revolutionary movement, and through the mix of objective and subjective meanings, they became important lexical weapons for both profound value conflict and petty factionalism in all domestic socialist parties and in the international communist movement during the twentieth century.

The relativity of the terms Left and Right in changing historical circumstances is illustrated by the recent convergence in Soviet and Chinese views of the political history of the People's Republic of China. Since the days of Stalin the Soviet party has viewed the Chinese Communist movement as heretical because of its reliance on a peasant base and its unorthodox revolutionary tactics. The Great Leap Forward and the Great Proletarian Cultural Revolution confirmed the Soviet perception of Maoism as a particularly virulent form of ultra-Leftism.[18] The Chinese Communists, of course, rebuffed this view as an indication of the Rightist, revisionist nature of Soviet ideology.

Since the death of Mao, the distance that separates Soviet and Chinese definitions of ultra-Leftism and revisionism has shrunk markedly. The official line of the Chinese Communist Party now also regards the Great Leap and the Cultural Revolution as manifestations of the ultra-Left trend that dominated China's politics between 1958 and 1976. Furthermore, the Chinese no longer use the term revisionism to refer to the domestic situation in the Soviet Union and now define the essence of the contradiction between the two nations as resulting from the USSR's "hegemonic" foreign policy. This change in attitude does not indicate a return to a Soviet model of development but rather seems to suggest the desire of the current Chinese leadership to eradicate the influence of ultra-Leftism in their own ranks and to remove the term revisionism from use in the domestic political vocabulary. As a result, the Chinese view of what constitutes concrete manifestations of ultra-Leftism in ideology and policy-making politics has changed dramatically in the early years of the post-Mao era.

Despite this rather loose way of affixing the label of ultra-Leftism in the politics of communist parties, the term nonetheless retains a certain definite connotation in the context of Marxism-Leninism. In fact, it is one conclusion of this study that the core meaning of the term ultra-Leftism has remained remarkably consistent throughout the vagaries of political struggle that have characterized the internal history of the Chinese Communist Party. The next chapter will elaborate in some detail the component errors that make up the composite deviation referred to as ultra-Leftism. For now, I shall only offer some general comments on the use of the term in this book.

In his 1937 essay, "On Practice," Mao Zedong gave one of the most concise definitions of Right and Left deviations within the revolutionary movement. After affirming that a revolutionary must, at all times, attune political action to the concrete realities of the historical moment and not let subjective preferences or preconceptions obscure the objective demands of the situation at hand, he continued:

It often happens, however, that thinking lags behind reality; this is because man's cognition is limited by numerous social conditions. We are opposed to die-hards in the revolutionary ranks whose thinking fails to advance with changing objective circumstances and has manifested itself historically as Right opportunism. These people fail to see that the struggle of opposites has already pushed the objective process forward while their knowledge has stopped at the old stage. This is characteristic of the thinking of all die-hards. Their thinking is divorced from social practice, and they cannot march ahead to guide the chariot of society; they simply trail behind, grumbling that it goes too fast and trying to drag it back or turn it in the opposite direction.

We are also opposed to "Left" phrase-mongering. The thinking of "Leftists" outstrips a given stage of development of the objective process; some regard their fantasies as truth, while others strain to realize in the present an ideal which can only be realized in the future. They alienate themselves from the current practice of the majority of the people and from the realities of the day, and show themselves adventurist in their action.[19]

Thus, the common denominator of Left and Right errors was, in Mao's terms, "the breach between the subjective and the objective, [and] the separation of knowledge from practice."[20] Aside from these similar epistemological origins, both types of error were seen as having similar results in that they each seriously compromised the revolution. As Mao put it twenty years later, "In terms of damage to the revolutionary cause, to be on the 'Left' is no better than to be on the Right and should therefore be resolutely corrected."[21]

Although recognizing some congruence in the origins and impact of Left and Right deviations, Marxist analysts have regarded them as two qualitatively different phenomena. Rightism, owing to the influence of regressive or bourgeois ideology, reflects a less than wholehearted commitment to revolutionary change. Ultra-Leftism implies that one's values are, in theory, consistent with the ultimate goals of the revolution; however, the actions of ultra-Leftists are judged to be seriously out of phase with the material and ideologi-

cal realities of the times and therefore undermine rather than enhance the revolutionary cause. As Michael Waller states it, ultra-
Leftists are those who persist in "chasing after the desirable in
obviously inauspicious circumstances."[22] They are, in a word, impatient revolutionaries.

In communist politics, Left and Right errors reflect departures
from a "correct" line as determined by the "scientific" application
of dialectical materialism to the solution of problems and affirmed
through the process of democratic centralism within the revolutionary party.[23] The "party line" refers to the "overall assessment" of a
particular situation and the derivative practical measures (tactics,
strategies, policies) for achieving the most pressing tasks of the moment.[24] The "general line" denotes the "essential formula for solving the principal contradiction of a given historical period."[25]
Therefore, a major task of party leadership is to identify the principal contradiction of the moment, arrive at a general line for its resolution, and disseminate correlative party lines for attacking specific
problems. A line (general or party) also includes particular ideological components (values) as well as concrete policy formulations.

In theory, a line must always be correct because it is "scientifically" derived.[26] But this does not preclude aberrant incidents of
deviation to either the Left or the Right on the part of individuals
charged with implementing the line. Such erroneous tendencies and
appropriate rectification measures are to be expected in the course
of revolutionary practice. In fact, as John Lewis has pointed out,
Chinese Communist doctrine in particular "stresses errors and tensions," an emphasis that "stems from the Party's preoccupation
with mistakes and deficiencies."[27] This preoccupation, in turn, reflects the leadership's determination not to let individual deviations
subvert the implementation of the correct line.

However, the line itself can become the source of fundamental
conflict within the revolutionary movement. In a process similar to
Tilly's definition of a revolution as a situation in which a polity is
faced with the dilemma of "multiple sovereignty," a revolutionary
movement can be confronted with a "plurality of Party lines" when
the proponents of contending lines claim a monopoly on correctness and damn their opponents as deviants of the Right or Left.[28]
Such has been the history of the international communist movement from Bakunin's split with Marx and Engels in the 1870's
through Yugoslavia's challenge to Soviet hegemony in the late

1940's and the emergence of the Sino-Soviet schism in the 1950's and 1960's.[29] This situation of a "plurality of Party lines" also characterizes an important aspect of the evolution of contemporary Chinese politics through the Cultural Revolution. The Chinese Communist Party has for decades described such a situation as involving "line struggle" (*luxian douzheng*), which is the conflict between "different policy programs whose purpose is to set guidelines for movement towards quite different types of regime."[30] In other words, the line struggle is symptomatic of deep-seated value conflict within the Party leadership.

I am primarily concerned in this study with the question of ultra-Leftism as part of the process of line struggle rather than with more commonplace Leftist deviations within the context of an overall "correct" line. What I shall describe in the cases that follow is one important component of conflict in the Chinese Communist Party that resulted from irreconcilable value differences and the derivative policy preferences among leadership groups. The task here is to elaborate the efforts of the critics of the ultra-Left to mount a political offensive against a line they believed to be injurious to the development of socialism in China. The use of the term ultra-Leftism is based solely on the critical perspective of one of those groupings concerning the line espoused by their opponents. The attribution of deviance is that of the critics and is not intended at any point to convey a political judgment on the part of the author.

Approach and Assumptions

The focus of this study, then, is the *critique* of ultra-Leftism as it has developed in Chinese politics since 1958. By a critique of ultra-Leftism I mean the process in which public attention is concentrated on alleged Leftist line errors as a source of dysfunction in China's socialist construction; this process incorporates some combination of media *criticism* and policy *rectification*. As will become evident in the case studies, the particular blend of criticism and rectification that developed at different stages in each case had an important bearing on the evolution of the critique over twenty-plus years; for now, it is sufficient to point out that these two ingredients are related, but distinguishable characteristics of the process I call the critique of ultra-Leftism.

If one objective of this study is to illuminate the "*two*-line struggle" that has dominated Chinese politics since the mid-1950's, what justification is there for concentrating on the perspective of just *one* side (the critics of the ultra-Left) and not giving the other protagonists in the conflict their say? There are two major reasons for this approach.

First, the perspective of the critics of the Right has already been the subject of extensive analysis.[31] By and large, those within the Party leadership who were the targets of the Cultural Revolution have been treated in the literature from a "passive" point of view: they have been seen as the defenders of a particular line that posited a certain model of development geared more toward economic growth than toward equality and revolutionary change and also embodied their own interest in maintaining and extending the power of a bureaucratic and technocratic elite.[32] They have also been cast as victims of the radical dynamic of the Chinese revolution who were swept away in the mass movement of the Cultural Revolution only to regain power in a coup d'état in October 1976.[33] But this group not only was the defender of a particular line; they also had a logical case against the line represented by their opponents in the Party and had, at several points, attempted a political offensive against that line. In other words, those who were pushed aside in the fury of the Cultural Revolution (and who hold the preponderance of power in post-Mao China) had developed a coherent critique of what they judged to be a disastrous ultra-Left trend in China's post-Liberation development. This critique evolved from a fundamental value conflict as well as from more particularistic considerations of power politics. That the history and impact of this critique of ultra-Leftism has been more or less ignored as a vital element in Chinese politics since 1958 is certainly understandable given the myopia induced in both Chinese propaganda and Western scholarship by the events of the Cultural Revolution. An important objective of this study is to offer a corrective to this analytical myopia by telling the story of an important part of the two-line struggle that has hitherto been relatively neglected.

The great significance of the critique of ultra-Leftism in Chinese politics since the death of Mao provides a second rationale for focusing on this one aspect of the two-line struggle. It is evident to any observer of contemporary events in China that since the downfall of the Gang of Four the Party leadership has undertaken a massive effort to reverse the policies and discredit the ideology of the

Cultural Revolution. In part, this effort has taken the form of a pervasive critique of ultra-Leftism in which the line allegedly pushed by Lin Biao and the Gang has come under sustained political attack. The critique has developed to the point where the ultra-Left is now said to have held sway in the Party for the best part of two decades (1957–76) and to have brought the People's Republic to the brink of political and economic disaster. Nearly all the problems in China's development since the anti-Rightist campaign of 1957 are traced to the influence of this ultra-Left trend. The campaign against the ultra-Left that has emerged in the first years of the post-Mao era is to some extent due to the precedents set by earlier critiques. The present description and analysis of these precedents are meant to put the current critique into a historical perspective that can help us understand the motives, actions, and value preferences of the new regime, for to grasp the full significance of the direction China has taken in recent years, it is as essential to understand the current leadership's "negative" evaluation of a substantial portion of China's history since Liberation as it is to detail the "positive" content of the policies and ideology espoused by Deng Xiaoping and his associates. In other words, the critique of ultra-Leftism is as important a part of what has happened in China since Mao's death as the drive to develop the Chinese economy known as the Four Modernizations.[34]

Several interrelated assumptions are embodied in the approach taken here to the study of Chinese politics. The first was implicit in earlier comments concerning the relevance of values to the understanding of political life. Such values are particularly important in analyzing a self-consciously ideological system that is committed to the revolutionary transformation and rapid modernization of society.[35] We shall assume an ideology to consist of an internally logical set of values that defines the relationship between human beings and their physical and social environments, prescribes the boundaries of acceptable and expected behavior, and posits a model of the ideal society. These values give coherence to all social life and direction to political action; they are also, as argued earlier, one source of political conflict.

The second assumption of this study is that the central actors in contemporary Chinese politics take ideology and doctrine very seriously and that the policy preferences they express reflect their ideological and doctrinal orientations. The analysis herein assumes that the pivotal struggles that have engulfed the Chinese leadership in the period under discussion have been much more than what one analyst has called "a dramaturgy of left-and-right" masking the fact of sheer power politics; the case studies that follow suggest strongly that the policy changes and shifts in political lines in the years since 1958 have hardly been limited to "minute variations" within a commonly accepted value scheme.[36]

On the contrary, the two-line struggle that this study seeks to elucidate was the product of a profound value conflict within the Party leadership over the very nature of socialism in China.[37] This clash of values was reflected in disputes over concrete matters of policy in particular areas such as education, material incentives, and health;[38] it also resulted ultimately in the evaporation of any common ideological ground (other than the use and manipulation of certain words and symbols) between proponents of the two lines. The cleavage was so deep that it juxtaposed widely different interpretations of the basic principles of Marxism-Leninism and led to diametrically opposed versions of the meaning and validity of Mao Zedong Thought. To put it in Franz Schurmann's terms, the value conflict we are describing infected both the "pure ideology" (the "world view" based on Marxism-Leninism) and the "practical ideology" (the "rational instruments for action" based on Mao Zedong Thought) that had once been vaunted as the great unifying force of the Chinese Communist Party.[39]

Furthermore, we assume that this value conflict has had profound consequences not only for Chinese elite politics but also for China's overall development. Again, as Schurmann points out, one important function of a revolutionary ideology is to replace the value structure of the system that has been overthrown and to provide a basis for the legitimacy of the new order.[40] The line struggle that dominated the Chinese Communist Party between the Great Leap Forward and the arrest of the Gang of Four reflected a fundamental conflict over the basis of legitimacy in socialist China. Mao regarded this conflict as a manifestation of the contradiction between proletarian and bourgeois ideologies and the embodiment of the struggle of opposites that would keep the revolution from stagnating and ossifying. But the line struggle also made the Party prone to rampant factionalism, induced widespread alienation and cynicism among the population, and deflected attention from the pressing tasks of economic and political development. True, the deep and protracted nature of this value conflict gave the Chinese revolution a sense of dynamism, but it did much to undermine the "consensus, community, legitimacy, organization, effectiveness, [and] stability" of the system; in other words, it contributed as much to "political decay" in China as it did to "continuing the revolution under the dictatorship of the proletariat."[41] This is a legacy that the current leadership of China must deal with; and one objective of this study is to describe how the political struggles surrounding the critique of ultra-Leftism contributed to the creation of that legacy.

Finally, we assume that the terms Left and Right have an objective meaning as tools of analysis for Chinese politics despite their subjective use as derogatory labels in political warfare.[42] We assume that they have some validity other than as a "rhetorical device for explaining and justifying leadership purges."[43] The terms Left and Right can be empirically associated with different ideological orientations and policy packages—that is, they are indicative of sharply diverging political lines.

The distinction between these lines is usually made in terms of "radical" versus "moderate" or "revolutionary" versus "pragmatic" alliances within the Chinese leadership, radical and revolutionary being those who put priority on socio-economic equality or continuing transformation of relations of production, moderate and pragmatic being those who favor economic modernization and expansion of the forces of production.[44] These distinctions are, of course, gross oversimplifications that in some ways obscure rather than clarify the differences between conflicting political lines, but they are at least a useful point of reference for dramatizing the deep conflict over the correct path for China's development that has permeated the Party leadership.

Here too, however, one must bear in mind the relative nature of Left and Right (or radical and moderate) as descriptive terms for understanding Chinese politics. Certainly the post-Mao leadership would reject the label of Rightism to describe their political line; they would designate themselves as the representatives of the *true* Left (in the Marxist-Leninist sense of being the ones following the line that best assures the future of the revolution). The Gang of Four, on the other hand, would scoff at the label ultra-Left applied to their line and would roundly condemn the Rightist nature of the current regime. Therefore, though we can confidently use Left and Right as shorthand terms for describing objective ideological and policy preferences as they relate to one another, we must not lose sight of the relativity of these terms when used as political labels.

A few words should be said about the rationale for choosing the three case studies that form the body of this book. These cases cover the following periods: (1) the Great Leap Forward (1958–61), (2) the aftermath of the death of Lin Biao throughout the time when Lin was being criticized in the media under the rubric "Swindlers like Liu Shaoqi" (1971–73), and (3) the criticism campaign against the Gang of Four as it unfolded following their purge in October 1976. The first two cases encompass times when the ultra-Left line is said by the post-Mao leadership to have dominated the Chinese Communist Party; the final case falls in the period after the removal of the most visible and vocal ultra-Leftists from the Party leadership. These three periods were also ones when the critique of ultra-Leftism itself became an issue of serious political controversy within the leadership, with one group seeking to expand the critique while another sought to stop, deflect, or limit it. Together, these cases form a continuing process in which the outcome of each in turn greatly affected the development of the critiques that followed. This is particularly apparent in the way in which the pattern of the critique of the Great Leap Forward shaped the handling of the issue of ultra-Leftism during the next twenty years. In a sense, then, this study presents a single case divided into three related episodes rather than three strictly comparable cases.

The choice of these three cases is not meant to imply that there have not been other incidents of reaction against alleged ultra-Left deviations in the years since the founding of the People's Republic. A truly comprehensive study of the critique of ultra-Leftism in China's contemporary political history would have to contain analyses of the effort to correct Leftist errors in the Land Reform campaigns of the late 1940's and early 1950's;[45] the "antiadventurist" campaign launched to curtail the excesses of the cooperativization movement of 1955–56;[46] the reaction to the "anarchy" of Red Guards judged by the Center to have gone to extremes in carrying out the mandate of the Cultural Revolution to seize political power from those "party persons in authority taking the capitalist road";[47] and the 1967–68 suppression of the "ultra-Left conspiracy" of the so-called "May 16 Group" that had sought to "drag out the handful of capitalist-roaders in the army," take control of the Foreign Ministry, and launch a broad-sided attack on Zhou Enlai and his associates in the State Council.[48] All these incidents are of interest to our subject of inquiry, but they can be considered as secondary phenomena in the evolution of the critique of ultra-Leftism because they never developed into a coherent attempt to criticize or rectify an ultra-Left *line*. The three cases that I have singled out for detailed study are the major episodes in the critique of ultra-Leftism in Chinese politics and are quite worthy of analysis on their own.

Objectives

I have already made reference to the most important objective of this study: to examine the critique of ultra-Leftism as a key aspect of the fundamental value conflict that has shaped elite politics and socialist development in China since 1958. Before elaborating some of the major questions that will have to be answered, let me first state clearly what the analysis that follows will *not* attempt to do.

First, it will not concentrate on individual political personalities. Certain actors, such as Peng Dehuai, Zhou Enlai, Deng Xiaoping, and Zhang Chunqiao, will necessarily appear frequently in the discussion of the political contention surrounding the critique of ultra-Leftism, and inferences concerning their ideological preferences cannot be avoided. Nonetheless, the association between these individuals and a particular political line is only an incidental aspect of the topic at hand, and no effort will be made to elaborate the political complexion of any single actor. Only in the case of Mao Zedong are we really concerned with the role of an individual; and our concern is with the important impact that the Chairman had on the evolution of the critique rather than with trying to "prove" whether he himself can be classified more appropriately as an ultra-Leftist or a critic of the ultra-Left.

Likewise, this is not a study of factionalism in Chinese politics. The value conflict that is of interest here did contribute to the appearance of identifiable leadership alignments based on personal ties, ideological affinities, and common political objectives. The discussion of the conflict between groups I identify as the Cultural Revolutionaries and the Veteran Revolutionaries in the period 1971–73 and between the "Whatever" and the "Practice" factions in the period 1976–80 argues that informal political alliances had a very important impact on the development of the critique of ultra-Leftism in those two periods. Beyond that, however, I shall not attempt to elaborate the origins, structures, or functions of these alliances as separate phenomena. Furthermore, contrary to the factional view of Chinese politics, this study takes the position that these groupings were motivated more by distinct value preferences than by raw power considerations.[49]

Third, this study will not offer a "meta-critique" of the critique of ultra-Leftism—that is, it will not seek to test the validity of that critique against the historical record as Lowell Dittmer did in his study of the Cultural Revolution criticism of Liu Shaoqi and the alleged "capitalist road."[50] The inquiry here is a first step in understanding the Chinese perspective on ultra-Leftism; future efforts may well be directed at ascertaining the objectivity of the post-Mao leadership's evaluation of the impact of an ultra-Left line on China's socialist development.[51]

Fourth, as should be obvious, this is not a study of ultra-Leftism per se, and it will not deal directly with the question of the political or sociological origins of radical trends within revolutionary movements or with the operation of an ultra-Left line in power. Its focus is not the so-called ultra-Left periods in Chinese political history but the ex post facto critiques of those periods. There is some important overlap between the two, especially in the case of the Great Leap Forward, but the emphasis will always be on the latter period: the *retreat* from the Great Leap rather than the specifics of the Leap itself; the period *after* the fall of Lin Biao rather than Lin Biao in power; and the first years of the *post*–Gang of Four era rather than the details of the Gang's ascendancy. It need hardly be said that an analytic discussion of the workings of ultra-Leftism in practice would fit into a comprehensive meta-critique that I have defined as beyond the scope of this study.

There are four central questions in this study.

1. How has the critique of ultra-Leftism developed over the last two decades? What pattern, if any, has emerged in the evolution of the critique? How do we explain the circuitous unfolding of the critique in its various stages? What is the relationship between the different episodes of the critique?

In exploring these questions, we shall be concerned with the ways in which the critique itself became the object of serious political struggle within the Chinese Communist leadership. It is in this line of inquiry that we find the link between value conflict and power politics that was emphasized earlier in this discussion. Chapters 3, 5, and 6 detail the political dynamics of the critique in the three different cases, and therefore focus most directly on these questions.

2. What have been the major complaints of the critics of the ultra-Left? What are the major issues raised in the critique of ultra-Leftism? In what ways is an ultra-Left line seen as bringing harm to China's socialist development? In what ways is ultra-Leftism judged to deviate from the principles and practice of Marxism–Leninism–Mao Zedong Thought? Is there any continuity in the issues or themes raised by the critiques of ultra-Leftism in the different periods under discussion?

In elaborating the content of the critique, we are seeking to elucidate the generic problem of ultra-Leftism; although the focus of this study is the Chinese Communist Party, the observations and conclusions are relevant to the analysis of similar phenomena in other socialist movements.[52] Chapters 2, 4, and 7 will discuss and analyze the issues involved in the critique of ultra-Leftism.

3. What was the role of Mao Zedong in the evolution of the critique of ultra-Leftism? In what ways did the political actions of Chairman Mao and the ideological influence of Maoism affect efforts to criticize or rectify Leftist trends in the Party? What has been the effect of the current critique of the ultra-Left line on the retrospective evaluation of Mao Zedong's contributions to the Chinese revolution?

4. Finally, what has been the function of the critique in Chinese politics? How do the critiques fit in with the overall pattern of Chinese politics since 1958? What role does the latest episode of the criticism and rectification of Leftist deviations play in shaping the post-Mao political environment? What implications does the critique of ultra-Leftism hold for the future of Chinese politics?

Ultra-Leftism vs. Revisionism: The Looking Glass War

When the Cultural Revolution destroyed the illusion of unity in China's leadership, some Western sinologists undertook to show that the origins of the "two-line struggle" between Mao Zedong and Liu Shaoqi could be traced back to the pre-Liberation history of the Chinese Communist movement. Thus, the conflict that erupted in the mid-1960's between "Chairman Mao's revolutionary line" and the "revisionist line" of the "capitalist roaders" was seen as the culmination of long-seething contradictions that had grown out of the divergent experiences and roles of various leaders in the struggle for national power.[53] Other research was directed at elaborating the content and context of Mao's criticism of the "revisionist line" and the process of his struggle against the bureaucrats and institutions that he thought embodied that line.[54] These efforts greatly enriched our perspective on the Cultural Revolution by making that cataclysmic event comprehensible as more than just a naked contest for power.

But this explanatory work also abetted the emergence of a *one*-sided view of the *two*-line struggle that obscured an important aspect of the complexity of the conflict involved in the Cultural Revolution. This view was one-sided in the sense that, although it took full account of the origins and implications of Mao's critique of revisionism, it did not offer a corresponding understanding of the countercritique of ultra-Leftism.

Even before the Cultural Revolution, some observers had presciently described the dynamic introduced into Chinese politics by the pursuit of the often contradictory socialist goals of revolution (progressive changes in the relations of production and the superstructure) and modernization (growth and development of the forces of production).[55] These conflicting priorities were translated into the two-line struggle of the Cultural Revolution. But because of the inflamed rhetoric and one-sided division of power that characterized Chinese politics in the late 1960's, it was relatively easy to follow the revolution line's critique of the modernization line as "revisionist"; however, it was not nearly so obvious that those favoring modernization as the priority in socialist development had just as coherent a critique of the revolution line as "ultra-Leftist."[56]

Put another way, each line in the two-line struggle also had two dimensions, one of affirmation and one of criticism. We have had a good understanding of both the affirmative dimension (the Great Leap and the Cultural Revolution) and the critical dimension (the critique of revisionism) of the revolution line; we have also had a fairly clear grasp of the affirmative aspect of the modernization line. What has been missing has been an appreciation of the critical dimension of the modernization line, that is, the critique of ultra-Leftism.

The two-line struggle as manifest in the Cultural Revolution and, indeed, throughout the history of the Chinese Communist movement, has truly been a "looking glass war."[57] Deviance has always been in the eye of the critic. What has been denounced by some as an erroneous line threatening the very life of the revolution was precisely the line that others held to be the only path to victory for socialism in China. This mirror-image aspect of the two-line struggle in Chinese politics may seem obvious; but it is not so obvious that our view of that struggle has largely been from only one side of the mirror. It is an important purpose of this study to slip, like Alice, "through the looking glass" to see what is on the other side. But unlike Alice, what we shall discover there is not a world of make-believe but the reality of deep ideological conflict that has shaped Chinese Communist politics for more than thirty years.

2

The Critique from Marx to Mao

> What childish innocence it is to present one's own impatience as a theoretically convincing argument!
>
> Engels (1874)

It would be an exaggeration to claim that ultra-Leftism is a major theme in the writings of Karl Marx, Friedrich Engels, Vladimir Lenin, or Mao Zedong. But it would not be stretching either the letter or the spirit of their works to say that each of them devoted enough attention to the problem of Left deviations in the socialist revolution to indicate that ultra-Leftism was a recurring and striking theme in the development of their respective political philosophies and programs. The purpose of this chapter is to survey the relevant writings of these "revolutionary teachers" (to use the Chinese expression, *geming daoshi*) in order to sketch out the ideological framework within which the critique of ultra-Leftism has occurred in Chinese Communist politics and to illustrate the striking continuity of subthemes in the criticism of Leftist deviations in the different historical contexts that shaped the evolution of Marxist theory.

The writings of Marx, Engels, Lenin, and Mao that deal with the question of ultra-Leftism are among their most explicitly political works.[1] Their comments on the subject generally appear in essays, letters, and speeches written either in direct response to or as ex post facto analysis of a challenge by a Left opposition to their leadership within the revolutionary movement. Although their views on the problem of ultra-Leftism are sometimes discussed on the plane of dialectical and historical materialism, the usual context is at the more practical level of revolutionary tactics, inner-party struggle, and policies for socialist construction. The maxim of materialist epistemology that theory should emerge from practice is certainly borne out in the way in which the critique of ultra-Leftism developed as part of the body of Marxism–Leninism–Mao Zedong Thought.[2]

Historical Context

The earliest comments by Marx and Engels on issues related to the themes of ultra-Leftism that we shall consider in this chapter occur in their criticism of the utopian socialists and the proponents of nonviolent anarchism.[3] The utopians, such as Fourier, Saint-Simon, and Owen, had provided the foundations for the socialist critique of industrial capitalism in the early nineteenth century and a blueprint for a more humane, communitarian society of the future. Their dissent was expressed politically as an appeal for peaceful social change based on a reasoned rejection by all people of good will of the sinister and unnatural forces of urbanization, industrialization, and centralization. They trusted the ultimate goodness of human nature to provide motivation for rectifying the injustices of capitalism; they also believed that farsighted individuals such as themselves could serve as the principal instigators and guides for the moral transformation of the human condition. The utopian vision was profoundly idyllic and agrarian; it reflected a preference for small-scale communities embodying the virtues of simple rural life and giving priority to agriculture as the means by which society would meet its needs and wants. This better world would also be an egalitarian one in which hierarchy and specialization were minimized and people worked and lived together naturally as social beings without the compulsion of political authority or economic incentive.

Marx and Engels criticized this view of the existing order and its correlative assumptions about the future as being "utopian" in the worst sense: unrealistic, other-worldly, fanciful, impractical. Though they shared much of the utopians' disgust for the miseries imposed by capitalism, they had no patience with the idealism and lack of scientific rigor that characterized the utopian approach to social criticism and political action. As Maurice Meisner has noted: "Although the utopian socialists were no less vigorous than the Marxists in condemning the social evils of capitalist industrialism, their critiques tended to be based more on moral judgements of the injustices of the new economic order than on any historical analysis of the nature and the function of the system."[4] In the view of Marx and Engels, the utopians erred because they devalued "all political, and especially all revolutionary action," preferring instead to paint "fantastic pictures of the future society" and to build "castles in the air." The result of such utopianism was "to deaden the class struggle and reconcile the class antagonisms"[5] and thus delay the advent of the true revolution.

The Marxists rejected the utopian vision of human development because it failed to recognize the historical inevitability of capitalism as a necessary step on the way to socialism and denied any special revolutionary role to the proletariat. Marx and Engels did not look upon the city and the factory as symptomatic in themselves of the degradation of humanity; rather they proclaimed that these forms of social organization that had been both created and defiled by capitalism could be transmuted into instruments for liberation once they had passed from the hands of the bourgeoisie into those of the proletariat. And, of course, it would be the task of the proletariat acting as a self-conscious and organized revolutionary class to grasp the historical moment offered by the full ripening of the contradictions of capitalism, seize power, and remake society in its own image.

The uncompromising antiauthoritarianism and extreme egalitarianism of many of the utopian socialists were an early manifestation of trends that would later be more explicitly identified with ultra-Leftism. The utopians also reflected the Leftist tendency to believe in the immediate realization of a more beneficent society without taking adequate account of the complex historical process involved in such a radical transformation; the crux of their error in this regard was, according to the Marxists, their blind faith in the power of human will as a motive force for social change and their naïve assumptions concerning the possibility of skipping or retreating from the stage of capitalism rather than incorporating its many redeeming features into the building of socialism.

The utopian socialists reached the height of their influence in the early nineteenth century and, according to Marx and Engels, represented only the premature revolutionary yearnings of "the proletariat in its infancy."[6] However, the rise of early anarchists like Pierre Joseph Proudhon (1809–1865) coincided with the coalescence of various elements of radical socialism into a coherent political movement.[7] The Proudhonists shared with the utopians a preference for socio-economic changes through persuasion and reason rather than violent class struggle. Yet their antistatism was more focused and vitriolic. The political activities of these "peaceful anarchists" within the First International (1864) can hardly be said to have constituted ultra-Leftism; indeed, they consistently opposed such anticapitalist measures as expropriation and socialization of the means of production as too extreme.[8] Quite correctly, Marx and Engels put Proudhon's philosophy into the category of "Conservative or Bourgeois Socialism" when drawing up their list of deviant trends within the working class movement.[9] Nevertheless, we can detect several elements in Proudhonism that link it with the problem of ultra-Leftism.

First, the Marxists were critical of the strong anarchist trend in Proudhon's theories and anticipated the influence this would have on some of the more militant antiauthoritarians within the International.[10] Secondly, they strongly objected to the emphasis that Proudhon and his followers put on the issue of distribution in both their critique of capitalism and their socialist vision.[11] The Proudhonists' principal complaint about capitalism was its injustice, which they believed was inherent in any system based on private property and wage labor; their political program demanded "a fairer distribution of the proceeds of labor."[12] The Marxists objected to this emphasis as embodying a deceitful hope of compromise between the proletariat and the bourgeoisie through minor economic concessions, which would only deflect the true mission of the working class to uproot capitalism in its entirety.

Even more, they objected to the the Proudhonists' view of socialism as more a matter of abolishing inequality rather than of radically restructuring society so as to unleash the forces of production and liberate human beings as producers. The Marxists believed that although socialism would certainly exterminate exploitation, it would not, as the Proudhonists hoped, usher in an era of social leveling; on the contrary, inequality in some form would remain for a long time even under socialism as a stimulus to productivity and a means of distribution. It is worth noting that Marx's most vehement statement concerning the persistence of such "bourgeois right" in the socialist mode of production was made in response to the Gotha Program of the German Social Democratic Party, which was heavily influenced by Proudhon's intellectual and political disciples.[13] Thus, we can observe in the Marxist denunciation of Proudhon a precursor of the struggle between those in the Chinese Communist Party who, more than one hundred years later, would argue that the primary task of socialism was to develop the forces of production and those, later condemned as ultra-Leftists, who would contend that distributive issues such as the elimination of all "bourgeois right" should be the animus of the socialist revolution.

The emergence of the exiled Russian revolutionary Mikhail Bakunin (1814–1876) as Marx's principal challenger for leadership of the European revolution in the 1860's reflected the rise of anarchism as a serious trend within the socialist movement.[14] Bakunin gradually came into irreconcilable conflict with the Marxists over the structure of authority within the International Workingmen's Association (IWA) and over the hypothetical organization of the revolutionary society that they were striving to achieve. Thus, the Bakuninists brought together the antiauthoritarianism of Proudhon and the utopianism of the early socialists in a new, virulent strain of revolutionary anarchism.

Marx and Engels believed that such anarchist positions as the demand for the abolition of all inheritance rights, the blanket refusal to participate in the bourgeois political process, and the indiscriminate use of terror undermined the socialist revolution from the extreme Left. But it was only after the anarchists set up a "secret organization" (the International Alliance of Socialist Democracy) within the IWA that Bakunin and his followers were expelled for conspiracy and sectarianism. Marx and Engels continued to struggle with the anarchists who had responded to their expulsion from the IWA in 1872 by establishing a series of rival organizations to spearhead their own political movement in Europe.[15] Many of the specific examples of the ideological critique of ultra-Leftism discussed below are drawn from Marx's and Engel's quarter-century-long diatribe against Bakuninism.

Lenin's contributions to the critique of ultra-Leftism can be divided into two stages, before and after the seizure of power. Prior to the Bolshevik seizure of power, Lenin devoted a good deal of attention to refuting what he saw as utopian and anarchistic trends among the radical opponents of the czarist regime. After the Revolution of 1917, he found it necessary to defend many aspects of his plan for socialist construction in Russia against charges of revisionism by a Left opposition within his own party. He also dealt with the problem of ultra-Leftism when offering tactical advice to non-ruling communist parties in Europe.

Lenin's early criticisms of Russian populism as an anti-czarist revolutionary movement were a harbinger of his later battles with the Left opposition.[16] He considered populism (or narodism) to be a variant of utopian socialism and rejected both its antimodern critique of capitalism and its rural egalitarian vision of the future society. Likewise, he denounced the subjectivist and voluntaristic character of the populist demands for immediate radical change, which considered "neither objective historical reality nor conditions of economic scarcity . . . as barriers to the achievement of socialism."[17]

With the growth of capitalism in Russia at the end of the nineteenth century, populism declined as a realistic revolutionary alternative, and Lenin turned his attention to the appearance of anarchist trends in the social democratic movement. When the Revolution of 1905 forced the czar to concede to certain democratic demands, Lenin found himself in conflict with those socialists who rejected any participation in the newly formed bourgeois-dominated parliament (the Duma) or trade unions. He condemned the Menshevik "New Iskra" Group and the "Otzovist" faction of the Russian Social Democratic Labor Party for their dogmatic advocacy of radical tactics for gaining power and for not understanding the complicated process of making a socialist revolution in a relatively underdeveloped country.[18]

Even before the triumph of the Bolshevik revolution, Lenin was engaged in a polemical debate that pitted his "social democratic" concept of the future socialist society against the more egalitarian prescriptions of the anarchists.[19] This struggle escalated after the establishment of the Soviet Union as Lenin found himself challenged by a Left opposition within the Communist Party that attacked his blueprint for constructing the new society.[20]

The first arena of conflict between Lenin and the Left concerned the negotiation and signing of the Brest-Litovsk Treaty of 1918 which ended Russian participation in World War I. The Left—including Bukharin—pressed for a continuation of the "revolutionary war" against German imperialism, whereas Lenin argued for compromise (and even territorial concessions) given the desperate economic and military situation facing the newborn Union of Soviet Socialist Republics.[21] Lenin gradually found himself trading charges and countercharges with the Left opposition literally up to the time of his death in 1924. Against accusations of elitism and authoritarianism, he defended his views on the imperative of maintaining a firm dictatorship of the proletariat under the leadership of a vanguard party in order to contain the forces of counterrevolution.[22] He also opposed the "anarcho-syndicalist" sentiment in the Party that advocated greater industrial democracy and decentralization in contrast to his own preference for a tightly controlled state-run economy.[23]

But it was Lenin's initiation of certain measures of "state capitalism" to resurrect the war-torn Russian economy that provoked the greatest opposition and elicited his most thorough political and ideological critique of ultra-Leftism.[24] Bukharin and others could not accept Lenin's rationale for a compromise with the bourgeoisie in the interest of national salvation and development. They considered his espousal of such policies as higher salaries for technicians and managers, hierarchical administrative systems in factories, and management-enforced disciplinary and efficiency regulations ("Taylorism") as tantamount to a betrayal of the socialist principles of the Bolshevik revolution. Lenin's denunciation of this opposition was expressed most trenchantly in his 1918 essay, "Left-Wing Childishness and the Petty-Bourgeois Mentality."[25] The themes of the class origins and ideological "immaturity" of the ultra-Left were developed more fully in his "political masterpiece," *Left-Wing Communism: An Infantile Disorder* (1920).[26] This work reviewed the history of struggles against Left deviations within the Bolshevik movement; it also contained Lenin's views on the absolute necessity for tactical flexibility in making a radical revolution and a searing indictment of the damage that dogmatism inflicted on the socialist cause.

Like Lenin, Mao's commentaries on ultra-Leftism fall into distinct pre- and post-power seizure stages. But, unlike Lenin, Mao's concern with Left deviations diminished after Liberation. Mao's major political struggles and much of his writing between 1927 and 1949 clearly centered on the problem of Left errors like dogmatism and adventurism in the Chinese Communist movement. However, beginning in the mid-1950's, he increasingly turned both the force of his political power and the focus of his critical attention to the Rightist dangers of revisionism and conservatism in the Party.

Mao's critique of ultra-Leftism was forged in the context of his opposition to the "three Left lines" that dominated the Chinese Communist Party at various intervals between 1927 and 1935.[27] A strong Left sentiment first grew in the Party as a reaction to what had been criticized as Right opportunism and "capitulationism" by one of the Party's founders (Chen Duxiu) in the aftermath of

Chiang Kai-shek's April 1927 coup against his Communist partners in the United Front. This sentiment blossomed into a full-fledged political line in late 1927 that led the Party in a direction of dogmatic emphasis on urban insurrection as the prime instrument of revolutionary strategy. This line was "virtually terminated" through inner-Party struggle by the spring of 1928 after a series of attacks on urban areas failed.[28]

By mid-1930, a Left trend was again emerging in the Chinese Party leadership as a result of an overly optimistic evaluation of the growing contradictions between Chiang Kai-shek and some of his warlord allies and also of the enormous influence of the Moscow-directed Comintern, which itself had undergone a "Leftward turn" in reaction to Stalin's domestic political struggles.[29] In China, this Left trend coalesced into the dominant line of the Communist Party under the leadership of Li Lisan, who resurrected the strategy giving priority to the seizure of large cities and repudiated Mao's increasing insistence that the key to China's social revolution lay in mobilizing the peasantry and establishing secure rural base areas.[30]

After military defeats at the hands of the Guomindang once more proved the inapplicability of the urban strategy to conditions in China, Li Lisan was criticized for his leadership errors, but his political line was not thoroughly analyzed, and it was not long before an ultra-Left trend reemerged within the Party. In early 1931, a group of Chinese students recently returned from Moscow took over the leadership. Headed by Wang Ming and Bo Gu, this new leadership deflected the criticism of Li Lisan's ultra-Leftism by portraying his errors as Rightist and attacking the laxity of earlier Party meetings and resolutions in failing to identify Right opportunism as the main danger to China's revolution. The maneuver forestalled the criticism of the Left errors committed under Li Lisan's leadership and allowed Wang Ming to establish his political hegemony within the Chinese Communist Party. Thus emerged the period of the "third Left line," which, according to Mao, consisted of "a programme that continued, revived, or developed the Li Lisan line and other 'Left' ideas in a new guise."[31]

The Wang Ming line held sway in the Party for four years. At first, Wang Ming and his followers maintained the policy of trying to seize key cities as a prelude to the imminent expansion of the socialist revolution in China. Even after successive military defeats led to the final abandonment of the urban strategy and the retreat of the Party center to the Jiangxi rural base area in late 1931, the Left leadership continued to labor under the assumption that the Chinese revolution was at a decisive stage and pressed for large-scale offensives against the growing Guomindang encirclement. They rejected Mao's advocacy of a protracted people's war involving guerilla tactics as a reflection of the Rightist error of "military conservatism." [32] When the Nationalist forces ultimately compelled the Communists to quit the Jiangxi Soviet and undertake the Long March in October 1934, the Left line was thoroughly discredited.

The Zunyi Conference, convened in January 1935 during the Long March, provided the forum at which Mao was able to rally sufficient support "to triumphantly put an end to the domination of the 'Left' line in the central leading body and to save the Party at this most critical juncture." [33] At Zunyi, Mao not only consolidated his political power within the communist movement but also won the first important vindication of his vision and strategy for the Chinese revolution. [34]

Even though the hegemony of the Left lines was broken after 1935, Mao continued to hammer away at any signs of ultra-Left deviations, particularly those that betrayed dogmatic approaches to the learning and application of Marxism-Leninism. [35] The 1942 Rectification Campaign that was launched to unify the Party around the emerging body of Mao Zedong Thought had as one of its explicit objectives the elimination of the residual influences of dogmatism and sectarianism that remained from the early Left lines. [36]

In terms of policy deviations, the major Left errors that commanded Mao's attention in the 1940's occurred in the implementation of land reform in the liberated areas. In these areas, over-enthusiastic cadres or the mobilized masses sometimes went beyond the strictures of the Party's generally moderate guidelines. Mao frequently had to warn against the use of excessive coercion and egalitarian trends in the distribution of the "fruits" of land reform. He was especially alarmed by the appearance of a "poor peasant line" that lumped middle peasants in the category of exploiters to be expropriated. Mao saw this as an erroneous Left trend that not only violated the spirit of the transitional period of the New Democracy, which rested on a broad-based united front against feudalism, but also threatened to undermine production by driving some of the countryside's most skillful farmers into political paranoia and economic passivity. [37]

After Liberation, Mao's essays and speeches continued for a time to reflect a concern that adventurism and commandism in implementing nationwide land reform and cooperativization were politically and economically counterproductive, but by the mid-1950's his dominant concern had clearly begun to shift to the dangers of conservatism and revisionism in the Party.[38] Though he was still cautioning against pursuing the socialist transformation with excessive haste and reminding his comrades that "to guard against the 'Left' deviation is Marxism,"[39] he was at the same time becoming increasingly worried that the Party, resting on the laurels of its victories, was beginning to lag behind the popular demand for accelerating the pace of transformation. Speaking of the popular upsurge in the cooperativization movement in 1955, he observed that many cadres were "tottering along like a woman with bound feet and constantly complaining, 'You're going too fast.'"[40]

By late 1956 and early 1957, the Party leadership was embarked upon its then muted, but eventually fateful struggle over the nature of the principal contradiction facing Chinese society in the next phase of its socialist development. Liu Shaoqi was a main proponent of a line that put as the major task the rectifying of the imbalance between the advanced relations of production and the backward forces of production (i.e., modernization). Mao firmly believed that the principal contradiction was still between the proletariat and the bourgeoisie (i.e., class struggle), even though the essence of that contradiction was now political and ideological rather than economic.[41] The debate on this matter contributed to the Chairman's growing conviction that "in the present circumstances, revisionism is more pernicious than dogmatism." "It is an important task for us to unfold criticism of revisionism on the ideological front now," he declared.[42] Clearly, he still upheld "bold advances" as the guiding principle of the socialist transformation.[43]

The setbacks of the Great Leap Forward of 1958–61 provided the context for Mao Zedong's last substantive contributions to the critique of ultra-Leftism. The excessive haste and lack of planning that characterized the establishment of the people's communes, the commandist approach of many cadres in the implementation of novel policies such as the communal mess halls and backyard steel furnaces, the extreme egalitarianism of the new income-distribution schemes, and the inflated expectations and targets of the economic planners all forced Mao to face up to the grave harm that ultra-

Leftism could bring to socialist development. But Mao's commentaries and self-criticisms on the errors of the Leap are interesting not only for the sharpness of his observations on the tragic results of idealism and adventurism but also for his strong reaffirmation of the overall correctness of the underlying principles and spirit of the Great Leap.[44] The broad consequences of the Leap forced him to recognize the enormous dangers of such deviations; yet his own ideological preferences led him to find much encouragement in the enthusiasm and boldness of the times.

The ramifications of the failure of the Great Leap strategy brought Mao into something of a political eclipse in the early 1960's, but during those years his concern with the growing threat of what he saw as revisionist trends within the Party hardened into a preoccupation that would ultimately motivate the Great Proletarian Cultural Revolution.[45] He was preoccupied not only with political developments within the Chinese Communist Party but also with the deepening ideological conflict between China and the Soviet Union. From that period on, Mao's comments on the problem of ultra-Leftism were minor and sporadic. Although he criticized the anarchist trends among certain Red Guard factions during the Cultural Revolution and sanctioned the purge of the extremist "May 16 Group," which had escalated the search for "capitalist roaders" in various state and army organizations beyond acceptable bounds, he never demonstrated any sustained concern that the general orientation of the movement was guilty of Leftist deviations.[46] Similarly, his comments on the Lin Biao affair and his warnings to the Gang of Four dealt almost exclusively with the sectarian and conspiratorial activities of these factions and hardly touched on the more fundamental issues involved in a true critique of ultra-Leftism; in other words, he criticized the "counterrevolutionary crimes" of Lin Biao and the Gang of Four, but not their ultra-Left political line.

In sum, Mao's approach to the question of Leftist deviations in China's revolution passed through several distinct stages. From 1927 to 1954, he expressed clear-cut political and ideological opposition to ultra-Left trends in the Party, which he viewed as the source of greatest danger to the success of the revolution. In the mid-1950's, he remained politically opposed to such deviations but began to waver in his thinking about how serious a threat ultra-Leftism posed to the socialist transformation of China in contrast to revisionism from the Right. During the Great Leap Forward, he almost completely abandoned his earlier concern that adventurism might sabotage the implementation of Party policy and exhibited instead a strong affinity for bold advances and revolutionary enthusiasm by masses and cadres alike. In the aftermath of the Leap and prior to the Cultural Revolution, Mao's attitude toward ultra-Leftism was rather ambiguous: though he seemed chastened by the disasters wrought by the strategy of Leaping Forward, he nonetheless displayed a growing ideological and political preoccupation with what he perceived as increasing trends toward conservatism in the Party and inequality in society. From 1965 until his death in 1976, he seemed rather oblivious to the problem of ultra-Leftism in China's socialist development but concentrated on efforts to "continue the revolution under the dictatorship of the proletariat" and combat the "restoration of capitalism" in China. These stages are essential for understanding Mao's contributions to the ideological context of the critique of ultra-Leftism to which we now turn. They also had an important bearing on the political context of the specific cases that form the core of this study.

Themes in the Critique of Ultra-Leftism

Dogmatism

The most pervasive theme in the Marxist critique of ultra-Leftism is the problem of dogmatism. Marx, Engels, Lenin, and Mao were all aware that the socialist cause could be damaged by revolutionaries who were rigid in their interpretation of doctrine and unwilling to adopt the tactical flexibility demanded by changing circumstances. Marx criticized the anarchists for blind adherence to the "eternal principles" of socialist revolution even when the actual result of such doctrinal fidelity was political or economic setback for the proletariat. He defended tactical compromises against what he mockingly referred to as the anarchists' charges of "the terrible crime of *lese-principle*" and caricatured the anarchist credo as proclaiming, "May our class be crucified, may our race perish, but may the eternal principles remain unstained!" [47]

Lenin was equally scathing in his attacks on dogmatists who refused to deviate under any circumstances from their hardened preconceptions of revolutionary strategy: "Anyone who is out to think up for the workers some kind of recipe that will provide them with cut-and-dried solutions for all contingencies, or promises that the policy of the revolutionary proletariat will never come up against difficult or complex situations, is simply a charlatan."[48] Mao, in the same spirit, scornfully dismissed Party cadres who sought in the ideology "a ready-made panacea which, once acquired, can easily cure all maladies."[49] Marxism-Leninism, he cautioned more than once, should be regarded not as a "lifeless dogma" but only as "a guide to action" that must be applied creatively to shifting circumstances.[50]

The "revolutionary teachers" often attributed the radicalness of the dogmatists' approach to politics and ideology to their lack of understanding of the objective situation and contrasted the simplicity of their formulations to the complexity of the actual world in which they sought to make revolution. Commenting on the unrealistic aspects of the anarchist program for building a revolutionary movement in Europe, Engels stated: "All these fine ultra-radical and revolutionary phrases merely serve to conceal the utter poverty of ideas and the most complete ignorance of the conditions in which the daily life of society is carried out."[51] Mao frequently criticized the Leftist tendency to apply dogmatically certain tenets of Marxism-Leninism, derived as they were from the European context, to the very different historical and social situation prevailing in China. Mao's observation that the "theory" behind the dogmatist line often consisted of isolated fragments of ideology simplistically "transported" out of context echoed the concern of his predecessors.[52] Engels attributed the popularity of Bakunin's variant of socialism to the fact that its essence could "be learned by heart in five minutes."[53] Lenin had also criticized such ideological reductionism by the Left when he accused his opposition of not bothering to analyze complex situations but instead merely "learning by heart and committing to memory revolutionary slogans."[54]

Marx, Engels, Lenin, and Mao all insisted that one of the most important qualities of a revolutionary leader was the ability to adjust to the changing conditions of the struggle and to forge compromises that could be used to turn otherwise disadvantageous circumstances to the benefit of the forces of revolution. Lenin, in his 1920 essay on Left-wing communism, warned that the dogmatic, "no compromise" approach to revolution was "like making a difficult ascent of an unexplored and hitherto inaccessible mountain and refusing in advance ever to make zig-zags, ever to retrace one's steps, or ever to abandon a course once selected and try others." Adaptability and flexibility were essential to the proletarian cause, and the critical task of the socialist revolutionary was to apply "the general and basic principles of communism . . . to the specific features in the objective development towards communism" in different places and times. And for the revolution to succeed, "It is necessary to link the strictest devotion to the ideas of communism with the ability to effect all the necessary practical compromises, tacks, conciliatory maneuvers, zig-zags, retreats, and so on." [55]

Because of their uncompromising approach, the dogmatists were prone to commit gross errors in devising tactics for the seizure of power and in drawing up specific measures for building the socialist society. But the doctrinaire communists demonstrated their own not inconsiderable disdain for certain of the policies favored by Marx, Engels, Lenin, and Mao that they thought violated the dictates of principle and conscience. Among the issues that Marx, Engels, and Lenin tangled over with the anarchists was the question of whether the proletariat and their political party should participate in bourgeois political processes and institutions as one means of improving their position and expressing their views. The anarchists argued that such participation only lent legitimacy to the bourgeois state and contaminated the purity of the ultimate objective of the proletariat to overthrow all the institutions of the existing order. Marx claimed that to engage in such an "abstention from politics" would deny the proletariat "every real method of struggle because all the arms to fight with must be taken from the existing society." He argued that the IWA could not reject participation in bourgeois politics just because "the inevitable conditions of this struggle do not unfortunately fit in with the idealist fantasies that these doctors of social science have deified under the name of Liberty, Autonomy, and Anarchy." [56]

Lenin reiterated this criticism when he defended the participation of the Russian Social Democratic Labor Party in the czarist-sanctioned Duma of 1905 against the opposition of the quasi-anarchist Otzovist faction. He rejected their accusations that the Social Democrats were engaged in Right opportunism by joining in the parliament and insisted that they were "utilizing the . . . Duma in a revolutionary Social Democratic way" as "an instrument for the socialist education and organization of the mass of workers." [57] Once he was in power, Lenin advised the nonruling communist parties of Germany and Britain to reject the position of antiparliamentary

Leftists, which he said reflected "intellectualist childishness, not the serious tactics of a revolutionary class." [58]

Marx, Engels, and Lenin had a running battle with the anarchists over the issue of authority within the revolutionary movement and in the revolutionary society of the future. The anarchists equated all manifestations of authority with bourgeois politics and demanded complete democracy in the communist International. Marx and Engels, to the contrary, defended the need for a structure of authority to insure coordination and discipline in the revolutionary party, and Engels, in a letter to a friend, specifically rejected the anarchist claim that a revolution, by its very nature, was an antiauthoritarian act:

I know nothing more authoritarian than a revolution, and when one's will is imposed on others with bombs and bullets, it seems to me an act of authority is being committed. . . . When I am told that centralization and authority are two things that should be condemned under all possible circumstances, it seems to me that those who say so do not know what a revolution is or are revolutionaries in name only. [59]

Similarly, Engels refuted the anarchist notion that socialist society could function without any hierarchical structures of authority. Referring to the question of future industrial organization, he declared that the very nature of large-scale, modern industry—be it capitalist or socialist—demanded authority, discipline, rules, and regulations. Even when the communist goal of the withering away of the state was achieved in the distant future, concentrated economic authority would still have to exist as a sine qua non of modern industry. In a classic essay on this question, Engels put his case this way:

. . . the material conditions of production and circulation inevitably develop with large-scale industry and large-scale agriculture, and increasingly tend to enlarge the scope of . . . authority. Hence it is absurd to speak of the principle of authority as being absolutely evil, and the principle of autonomy as being absolutely good. Authority and autonomy are relative things whose spheres vary with the various phases of the development of society. If the autonomists confined themselves to saying that the social organization of the future would restrict authority solely to the limits within which the conditions of production render it inevitable, we could understand each other; but they are blind to all facts that make the thing necessary, and they passionately fight the word. [60]

Lenin, likewise, denied the revolutionary correctness of the anarchists' unremitting antiauthoritarianism. He upheld his belief in the necessity for a vanguard party to lead the proletarian revolution against charges by the Left opposition that he was advocating a "revolution from above" rather than supporting a true mass movement.[61] The seizure of power did not, according to Lenin, negate the need for a vanguard party to exercise the "iron hand" of a dictatorship of the proletariat over the forces of counterrevolution in order to safeguard the fruits of victory.[62] He also rejected the suggestion of Bukharin and others that more economic authority be vested in individual industries and unions and the call of the "Workers' Opposition Group" within the Bolshevik Party for an elected "All Russian Congress of Producers" to run the national economy. Such "syndicalism," though seemingly very revolutionary, Lenin warned, would simply undermine the authority of the Party, induce anarchy in the economy, and aid the restoration of the bourgeoisie to power in Russia.[63]

Lenin also rebuffed accusations that his introduction of certain measures of "state capitalism" to salvage and reinvigorate the war-wrecked Russian economy represented a "deviation to the Right."[64] He castigated the Left communists for their insistence on "a most determined policy of socialization" as being dogmatic adherence to an idea that was entirely inappropriate in the circumstances in which the newly formed Soviet Union found itself.[65] Lenin believed that the socialist republic not only must make use of "first class capitalist experts" from the old regime (who were to be paid munificent salaries as an incentive to make their services available to the new government) but also must adapt appropriate lessons from the advanced state capitalism of Germany. Indeed, the existence of Soviet political power ensured that the forms of German technology and industrial expertise could be used to the benefit of the Russian proletariat. When the Left opposition objected, on principle, that it was "unbecoming" for socialist Russia to learn from bourgeois Germany, Lenin replied firmly: "Either they do not know the facts of life, do not see what actually exists and are unable to look truth in the face, or they confine themselves to comparing abstractly 'capitalism' with 'socialism' and fail to study the concrete forms and stages of the transition that is taking place in our country."[66]

Mao also found it necessary to uphold a policy of utilizing the national bourgeoisie after Liberation against pressures for a more rapid and forceful program of nationalization.[67] But his more dramatic confrontations with the Left came over the issues of land reform, the united front, and the peasant basis of his strategy for revolution in China. In each of these cases, Mao was accused of following a heretical line that violated fundamental Marxist principles; he, in turn, hung the label of dogmatism on those who opposed his policies.

According to Mao, Li Lisan and Wang Ming denied the necessity for a "shift in the center of gravity" of the Party's revolutionary efforts to the countryside following the crushing defeat of the urban revolution in 1927. They charged that such a shift would negate the proletarian essence of the socialist revolution, and continued to press for an emphasis on urban insurrection, industrial strikes, and large-scale military operations because such policies were more conducive to their conception of how *the* socialist revolution should unfold. In Mao's view, these tactics reflected "adventurism" and "putschism" and grew out of a doctrinaire approach that failed to take into account either the special historical context of the revolution in China or the objective balance between the forces of revolution and counterrevolution.[68]

With regard to the call for a second United Front between the Communists and the Guomindang to resist Japanese imperialism in the late 1930's, the Left preferred a policy of carrying on the social revolution and the national revolution simultaneously. Mao criticized this dogmatic refusal to compromise with the domestic enemy in the effort to muster all possible strength and resources against a common international foe. In his view, such a policy of "all struggle and no alliance" threatened to undermine fatally the revolutionary cause in China by dividing its forces along two fronts rather than focusing on the resolution of the principal contradiction.[69]

Mao also struggled against a dogmatist trend in the implementation of land reform in the liberated areas. On the one hand, he consistently opposed the doctrinaire "poor peasant line," which insisted on pursuing "pure" class policies and thus resulted in radical egalitarianism and the exclusion of many middle peasants from the distribution of the "fruits" of land reform. The advocates of this line also used excessive harshness in the treatment of landlords and rich peasants and engaged in the expropriation and suppression of small-scale rural capitalists whom Mao considered to be a "progressive" force in the overwhelmingly feudal countryside.[70] According to Mao, these Left deviations grew out of the dogmatic approach to policy implementation in the liberated areas that failed to appreciate the objective balance of rural class relations.[71] Further-

more, Mao, besides arguing vigorously against this poor peasant
line, also had to defend his own relatively moderate land reform
program against broadsides from the Left that he was pursuing a
"rich peasant line" that short-circuited the completion of the agrarian revolution through unprincipled compromises with the forces
of counterrevolution.[72]

In sum, Marx, Engels, Lenin, and Mao consistently criticized
those communists who eschewed tactical flexibility and political
compromise for the sake of adherence to certain cherished and abstract doctrines. In the view of these "revolutionary teachers," the
cause of socialism was threatened quite as much by being dashed
against the rigid wall of dogmatism as it was by the tendency to be
led down the path of Right opportunism.

Subjectivism

Marx, Engels, Lenin, and Mao were generally agreed that the
root cause of dogmatism was to be found in the propensity of some
radicals (especially those from a petty-bourgeois intellectual background) to base political action on their own preconceptions and
perceptions rather than on concrete investigation of the conditions
of society. This deviation was called "subjectivism" or "idealism"
because it reflected an imposition of the subjective ideals of the revolutionary onto the objective situation in which he or she was seeking to make revolution. The result of such subjectivism was that
certain revolutionary activities, though perhaps "correct" in a theoretical sense, were impractical because they were incompatible with
the material and ideological realities of the times.

Because of his special concern with the relationship between theory and practice, Mao paid particular attention to the political and
ideological errors that could result from a contradiction between
the subjective and objective approaches to revolution. Some radicals were prone to slip into dogmatism, he noted, because they did
"not proceed from an objective and comprehensive picture of the
balance of class forces, but [took] subjective wishes, impressions,
and empty talk for reality, [took] a single aspect for all aspects,
the part for the whole, and the trees for the forest."[73] Mao retro-
spectively criticized the urban strategy of the Left for its subjective
rationale that the socialist revolution in China was at a "decisive
stage" and that the victory of the proletariat was "imminent." The
ultra-Leftists, he said,

were forever dreaming that the struggles of the other masses in the cities would suddenly break through the enemy's severe repression and surge forward, erupt into armed insurrection in key cities, achieve "victory first in one or more provinces," and bring about a so-called nationwide revolutionary high-tide and nationwide victory; and *they made this dream the basis on which all their work was planned and organized.*[74]

Mao had pointed out in his essay "On Practice" (1937) that when "thinking lags behind reality" the result is likely to be Right opportunism. He then went on to warn against the opposite tendency of letting subjective desire obscure the limitations imposed by reality: "The thinking of the 'Leftists' outstrips a given stage of development of the objective process; some regard their fantasies as truth, while others strain to realize in the present an ideal which can only be realized in the future. They alienate themselves from the current practice of the majority of the people and from the realities of the day, and show themselves adventurist in their actions."[75]

In this passage, Mao succinctly delineated several specific problems connected with Left subjectivism: (1) *telescoped development,* the failure to observe the proper sequence of the stages of historical development; (2) *excessive voluntarism,* the belief that human will and motivation can overcome all objective impediments to historical change; (3) *fallacy of mass consciousness,* a false conception of the readiness of the masses to accept radical social change; (4) *adventurism,* a predilection for extreme tactics and programs in the pursuit of revolutionary goals. Let us examine each of these components in turn.

Telescoped development. Left subjectivism, as depicted in Marxism–Leninism–Mao Zedong Thought, often involves a mode of thinking or a program of action that compresses what should be separate stages of historical development. This telescoped view of development results when the ardent desire to hasten the realization of certain revolutionary goals blinds the activist to the temporal limits of human action and induces a striving for immediate ideological gratification. Engels captured the essence of this error when he remarked on the extremist nature of the political tactics of the French anarchists, the Blanquist Communards:

The . . . Blanquists are communists because they imagine that merely because *they* want to skip the intermediate stations and compromises, the matter is settled, and if "it begins" [the revolution] in the next few days— which they take for granted—and they take over power, "communism will be introduced" the day after tomorrow. If that is not immediately possible, they are not communists.[76]

Lenin and Mao defended the notion that the party of the proletariat should actively support the bourgeois democratic revolution against those who were urging unfettered social change that would result in the immediate establishment of a socialist society and the dictatorship of the proletariat. Lenin contended that the level of economic development and mass political consciousness in Russia in 1905 made "the immediate and complete emancipation of the working class impossible" and staunchly upheld his decision that the Social Democrats should participate in the Duma:

Replying to the anarchists' objections that we are putting off the socialist revolution, we say: we are not putting it off, but are taking the first step towards it. . . . Whoever wants to reach socialism by any other path than that of political democracy, will inevitably arrive at conclusions that are absurd and reactionary in the economic and political sense.[77]

Mao noted that many of the dogmatic policies pursued under the Li Lisan and Wang Ming lines reflected the error of subjectivism because they were singularly inappropriate to the concrete problems posed by China's stage of development in the 1930's. The ultra-Leftists committed grave mistakes that threatened the very life of the Party, Mao declared, because

they carried out a number of so-called "class line" policies *going beyond the democratic revolution*, for instance, a policy of eliminating the rich peasant economy and other ultra-Left economic and labour policies; a state policy in which no exploiter had any political rights; a policy of popular education in which its content stressed communism; an ultra-Left policy towards intellectuals; a policy of working among enemy troops to win over only the soldiers, but not the officers; and an ultra-Left policy on the suppression of counterrevolutionaries. Thus, *the immediate tasks of the revolution were distorted*, and the revolutionary forces were isolated, and the Red Army movement suffered setbacks.[78]

Another important manifestation of the Left subjectivist error of telescoped development was misjudging the nature and timing of the transition period after the seizure of power between the stages of capitalism, socialism, and ultimately communism. The ultra-Leftists were reproached for not taking sufficient heed of Marx's observation that any new society inevitably bears the "birthmarks" of the era from which it emerged and that such vestiges of the past cannot be swept away overnight.[79] The revolutionary regime must steer a delicate course between proper respect for the material and ideological constraints bequeathed by capitalism and feudalism and the urge to press ahead with the building of a socialist society. Left subjectivists believed that it was possible to abbreviate significantly the transitional period or refused to recognize the necessity of any transition at all; on the contrary, they were said to be driven by "the idea of giving immediate effect to the maximum program" for the realization of socialism or even communism.[80] This deviation might manifest itself either in attempting to implement policies that were premature for a given stage of development or in criticizing the policies of others as being insufficiently "progressive."

Lenin confronted the first aspect of the problem of telescoped development when he reprimanded those who were pressing for a more rapid program of nationalization and collectivization shortly after the Bolshevik revolution: "To attempt to practice today, to anticipate the future result of a fully developed, fully stabilized and constituted, fully comprehensive and mature communism would be like trying to teach high mathematics to a child of four."[81] Mao expressed similar sentiments when he analyzed the shortcomings of the radical communization in the early phases of the Great Leap Forward. The basic error of those times, he observed, was that many comrades (including himself) had advocated policies that reflected a subjective view of historical development that "mistakes socialism for communism."[82]

Several instances of the second manifestation of the subjective distortion of the stages of revolutionary change—the debunking of policies that the ultra-Left perceived as retrogressive—have already been noted in the discussion of dogmatism. Lenin commented that the anarchists' denunciation of parliamentary tactics as being insufficiently revolutionary reflected their "radically incorrect ideas of the course of social development," which made them "unable to take into account those peculiarities of the concrete political (and economic) situation in different countries which determines the specific significance of one or another means of struggle for a *given period of time*."[83] He defended parliamentarianism as a tactic for the proletariat that was entirely appropriate in certain circumstances and dismissed ultra-Leftists who "have naïvely mistaken subjective 'rejection' of a reactionary institution for its actual destruction by the combined operation of a number of objective factors." Although the dawning of the socialist revolution presaged the eventual disappearance of bourgeois parliaments, this goal would be reached only in the distant future: "Parliamentarianism has become 'historically obsolete.' That is true in the propaganda sense. However, everybody knows this is still a far cry from overcoming it in practice. . . . It is a glaring theoretical error to apply the yardstick of world history to practical politics." So, he concluded, "It is obvious that the 'Lefts' . . . have mistaken their desire, their politico-ideological attitude for objective reality. That is a most dangerous mistake for revolutionaries to make."[84]

Finally, the controversy over Lenin's introduction of certain measures of "state capitalism" to revitalize the ravaged Russian economy likewise caused him to analyze the way in which the ultra-Left's view of historical development led them to what were, in his opinion, thoroughly fallacious judgments on the correctness or incorrectness of specific policies. Answering the Lefts' ideological misgivings about his economic policies, he remarked, "It has not occurred to them that state capitalism would be *a step forward* as compared with the present state of affairs in our Soviet Republic."[85]

Excessive voluntarism. A second error of Left subjectivism closely related to telescoped development is that of excessive voluntarism, or the exaggeration of the extent to which human consciousness and action can overcome material and ideological obstacles to the revolution. Marx was referring to the inadequacy of just such a voluntarist approach to historical change when he reproved Bakunin for his total disregard of the economic preconditions for socialist revolution. He reminded the anarchists that the advent of socialism presupposed the development of capitalism and the emergence of an industrial proletariat. But Bakunin, he said,

understands nothing whatever about social revolution; all he knows about is the political phrases; its economic prerequisites do not exist for him. Since all the economic forms, developed or undeveloped, that have existed till now have included the enslavement of the worker (whether in the shape of the wage worker or the peasant, etc.) he presumes that a *radical revolution* is equally possible in all of them. . . . *The basis of Bakunin's social revolution is the will, and not the economic conditions.*[86]

Both Lenin and Mao were accused of being excessively voluntarist themselves in their efforts to make a "radical revolution" in countries that fell far short of the "economic prerequisites" Marx deemed necessary as a minimum basis for socialism. Maoism has especially been noted for its emphasis on the capacity of human beings to compensate for the deficiencies, imbalances, and impediments of the objective situation through concentrated will and effort.[87] Yet both Mao and Lenin often spoke of the importance of a thorough understanding of the material context of revolutionary activity, and they certainly recognized that there were definite limits to the scope of human action.

For example, in rebuking the ultra-Left faction among the German communists for their strident rejection of participation in bourgeois politics, Lenin warned that a "revolutionary mood" alone could not justify the adoption of tactics more radical than objective conditions would allow.[88] Mao, too, criticized the subjectivists in his own Party who denied the necessity of practical social investigation before embarking on a particular course of action; they had "no intention of seeking truth from facts," he said, but based their work on "sheer subjective enthusiasm" for the revolutionary cause.[89] In his self-criticism for the excesses of the Great Leap Forward, he admitted that the Party leadership's enthusiasm for communism had become "a little excessive" and had led to gross violations of the objective laws of development in the rush for rapid industrialization and large-scale communization.[90]

Fallacy of mass consciousness. One of the pivotal points of Marxist political analysis is the observation that potentially revolutionary classes are afflicted with what is known as "false consciousness."[91] This thesis states that part of the proletariat is lured into complacency, conservatism, or even counterrevolution by a misplaced sense of their own material stake in preserving the bourgeois system. Ironically, one of the hallmarks of the subjectivism of the ultra-Left, according to Marxism–Leninism–Mao Zedong Thought, is the tendency to underestimate the objective reality of this false consciousness among a vast majority of the populace. Rather, Left subjectivists assume that the level of mass political consciousness is as high as their own and that the masses are, therefore, receptive to and eager for the most radical program for revolution. This error may be called the fallacy of mass consciousness.

It was in this vein that Marx attacked Bakunin's call for an immediate abolition of all inheritance rights as one step in dismantling the juridical basis of socio-economic inequality. Marx argued against including this demand in the platform of the International because he believed that most people, whatever their class, still placed great hope in the prospect of being able to pass on their property to their children; far from being in accordance with the desire of the masses, a policy that advocated the denial of inheritance rights would "not be a serious act, but a foolish measure, rallying the whole peasantry and the whole small middle class round the reaction."[92]

Lenin, despite being a staunch advocate of the vanguard party, was even more blunt in exposing the fallacy of mass consciousness to which some revolutionaries fell victim. Referring to the anarchists' claim that parliamentary politics was "obsolete" as a revolutionary tactic, he cautioned his fellow communists that they "must not sink to the level of the masses. . . . But at the same time you must soberly follow the actual state of class consciousness and the preparedness of the entire class (not only of its communist vanguard) and of all the working people (not only of their advanced elements)."[93]

Mao was particularly concerned about the way in which the critical areas of cultural and propaganda work often reflected the perspective of those with the most heightened consciousness rather than the true attitudes and aspirations of the masses. What was needed, instead, was fidelity to the mass line, which meant staying in tune with the current thinking of the workers and peasants. One of Mao's clearest statements on this dilemma is worth quoting at length:

All work done for the masses must start from their needs and not from the desire of any individual, however well-intentioned. It often happens objectively that the masses need a certain change, but subjectively they are not yet conscious of the need, not yet willing or determined to make the change. In such cases we should wait patiently. We should not make the change until, through our work, most of the masses have become conscious of the need for the change and are willing and determined to carry it out. Otherwise we shall isolate ourselves from the masses. Unless they are conscious and willing, any kind of work that requires their participation will turn out to be a mere formality and will fail. . . . We should not be impetuous; impetuosity leads only to failure. This is true in any kind of work, and particularly in the cultural and educational work the aim of which is to transform the thinking of the masses. There are two principles here: one is the actual needs of the masses rather than what we fancy they need; and the other is the wishes of the masses who must make up their own minds instead of our making up their minds for them.[94]

One of the major themes in Mao's criticism and self-criticism of the ultra-Left tendencies of the Great Leap Forward, sometimes expressed in graphic language, was the way in which the Party's "communist" policies frequently ran smack into the stone wall of

peasant efforts to defend their private material interests. Such peasant "particularism" took the form of bitter resistance to egalitarian
policies (such as the rural mess halls and distribution according to
need rather than labor) and the requisition without compensation
of private plots, tools, and trees for communal use. In his series of
speeches at the Zhengzhou Conference in early 1959, the Chairman
defended this peasant "particularism" and chastised himself and
his comrades for considering only their own preferences in policy
formulation and implementation and neglecting the disposition of
the masses. "It is very dangerous to want only communism," he
warned, "and not particularism. . . . [T]o want communism alone
just won't work."[95]

This manifestation of the fallacy of mass consciousness in which
the vanguard ignores the relatively low level of popular ideology
generally expresses itself politically as "commandism." Cadres are
guilty of commandism when they force the masses to participate in,
or at least acquiesce in, policies that the people do not truly support
or understand. But there are times when the momentum of the revolution breaks through the barrier of false consciousness and reveals to the masses their true stake in making revolution; when this
happens, a variant deviation may occur that can be called "Left tailism." "Tailism," in the Marxist lexicon, usually refers to a Rightist
deviation that results when the leadership falls behind and even
tries to impede the legitimate demands of the people for further or
more rapid revolutionary change.[96] "Left tailism" describes a situation in which members of the vanguard party do not adequately re-
strain the masses from engaging in extreme measures to secure
something that might be an immediate gain but could have harmful
consequences in the long run. By failing to act as a curb on mass
passions, the Party ignores its duty as the most farsighted segment
of the proletariat—not because it misunderstands the popular
mood as in the case of the mass consciousness fallacy, but because it
gives in to the popular mood too easily. For example, in the implementation of land reform, Mao criticized some local cadres for
"doing everything as the masses want it done" and therefore failing
to serve as a brake on extremist tendencies in land distribution and
the handling of the cases of landlords and rich peasants.[97]

Adventurism. The ideological certitude that is part of the imped-
imenta of dogmatism and subjectivism is apt to give rise to rashness
in the choice of tactics and the timing of political action. The con-

viction that they hold a monopoly on the "truth" impels ultra-Leftists to press ahead frenetically in the effort to achieve their revolutionary goals as directly as possible without regard to any objective limitations. Mao, speaking of just such "adventurism" in the cooperativization movement of 1955, compared rash political action to inducing prematurely the labor of a pregnant woman:

As the old Chinese sayings go, "When a melon is ripe, it falls off its stem," and "When water flows, a channel is formed." We should act in accordance with specific conditions and achieve our aims naturally instead of forcing their attainment. Take childbirth for instance. It requires nine months. If, in the seventh month, the doctor should exert pressure and force the child out, that would not be good, that would be a "Left" deviation. If, on the other hand, the unborn child is already nine months old and very much wants to come out and yet you don't allow it, that would be a Right deviation.[98]

In addition to this tendency for adventurism in the pursuit of positive revolutionary objectives, Left subjectivists were also criticized for becoming afflicted with a pervasive negativism that led them to engage in acts of wanton destruction against the old regime and its remnants. In other words, they were both cocksure in their appraisal of what must be done to consolidate gains for the cause of socialism and blindly determined in their attacks against what they judged to be the targets of the revolution.

Marx and Engels condemned the terrorist tactics of the anarchists, using words that sound much like those that would be used more than one hundred years later in the criticism of the "smashers, grabbers, and looters" who were followers of the Gang of Four's ultra-Left line. In the anarchist program, they pointed out, "the economic and political struggle of the workers for their emancipation is replaced by the universal pan-destructive acts of heroes of the underworld. . . . In a word, one must let loose the street hooligans suppressed by the workers themselves."[99] Lenin, in a similar vein, remarked that the anarchists wanted only to destroy the bourgeois state and had no positive program to replace it with something better. This approach, he said, reflected "the tactics of *despair*, instead of a ruthlessly bold revolutionary effort to solve concrete problems while taking into account the practical conditions of the mass movement."[100] In sum, the "revolutionary teachers" criticized the ultra-Left for their adventurism in the quest both to build the new society and to destroy the old.

Sectarianism

Marx, Engels, Lenin, and Mao agreed that one of the most politically destructive offshoots of dogmatism and subjectivism was the
appearance of extreme sectarian trends within the revolutionary
movement. The doctrinal certainty with which the ultra-Leftists ap-
proached the practice of revolution was seen as highly conducive to
the emergence of sharp factional divisions in the party. This Left
sectarianism was apparent sometimes in the proclivity of the Left to
stick together tightly in pursuit of a particular version of the revolutionary "truth" and sometimes in an expressed antagonism toward
those whom they called heretics or counterrevolutionaries.

Marx and Engels often took up the subject of the sectarian activities of the Bakuninists within the International Workingmen's
Association. They impugned the anarchist Alliance of Socialist Democracy that had been formed by Bakunin as a lobby within the
IWA as a "parasite body," which fomented "internal quarrels" that
severely weakened the revolutionary movement.[101] Although they
found Bakunin's philosophy abhorrent, Marx and Engels contended that the real source of their irreconcilable difference with
the anarchist lay not so much in divergent principles as in his un-
forgivable and unrelenting provocation of "open warfare within
our ranks."[102] The die of antagonism that ultimately led to the expulsion of Alliance members from the IWA was cast when Bakunin,
frustrated by the rejection of his anarchist program, turned from
open and principled debate to "indirect means" to further his position. "The main result of the Bakuninists' action," Engels wrote,
"has been to create a split in our ranks. Nobody opposed their special dogma, but they were not content with that and wanted to
command and impose their doctrines on all our members."[103]

Mao was especially apprehensive of the organizational impact of
the conspiratorial tendencies of the ultra-Left. The factionalism of
Li Lisan and Wang Ming had been particularly destructive to the
revolutionary movement because it had "created a sectarianism
which alienated the masses within the Party . . . as well as one
which alienated the masses outside the Party."[104] Sectarianism also
undermined one of the cornerstones of Mao's revolutionary strategy, the united front. The ultra-Left refused to recognize the necessity of "uniting all those who can be united" in the effort to resolve
the principal contradiction in a given period of time (e.g., to unite

with the Guomindang to defeat Japanese imperialism) and pre-ferred, instead, for the sake of principle, to carry on the struggle on all fronts simultaneously. The Rightist error would have been to ad-vocate "cooperation and expansion [of the united front] that are unconditional in character," whereas the Leftist mistake was to maintain an uncompromising "closed-doorism" that put class and doctrinal purity above the imperative of tactical flexibility.[105]

The complaint that Left sectarians espoused policies and engaged in politics that emphasized struggle and conflict to an exaggerated degree is an important theme in the Marxist critique of ultra-Leftism. Mao often decried the Left's predilection for "ruthless struggles" within the Party and for dealing "merciless blows" against comrades who had made a few mistakes in thinking or work style.[106] In one essay, he neatly summed up the ideological ori-gins of the misguided use of class struggle by the ultra-Left:

Those with a Rightist way of thinking make no distinction between ourselves and the enemy and take the enemy for our own people. They regard as friends the very persons whom the broad masses regard as enemies. Those with a "Left" way of thinking magnify the contradic-tions between ourselves and the enemy to such an extent that they take cer-tain contradictions among the people for contradictions with the enemy and regard as counterrevolutionaries persons who are actually not counter-revolutionaries.[107]

That sort of mishandling of contradictions among the people turned nonantagonistic differences into life-and-death struggles and drove a wedge deep into the heart of the revolutionary movement. Marx and Engels characterized as "a holy inquisition" the Bakunin-ists' inflammatory accusations against those within the IWA who disagreed with the anarchist approach.[108] Rather than accept some diversity of views on how to achieve the common goal of socialist revolution, the Bakuninists concluded that the nonanarchist mem-bers of the leading bodies of the IWA (especially Marx and Engels) were simply "reactionaries."[109]

Mao's strictures against Li Lisan and Wang Ming were much like those of Marx and Engels against Bakunin—that they were fractur-ing Party unity with their "factionalist policy towards cadres" who dissented from their line. In a striking parallel with what would be-come one of the central themes of the critique of the Gang of Four's ultra-Left line, Mao took note of what he considered to be some of the most serious errors of Li and Wang:

[They] indiscriminately branded [as counterrevolutionaries] all Party comrades who found the wrong line impracticable and who therefore expressed doubt, disagreement or dissatisfaction, or who did not actively support the wrong line or firmly carry it out; they stigmatized these comrades with such labels as "Right-opportunism," "the rich peasant line" . . . "the line of conciliation" . . . [and] waged "ruthless struggles" against them and dealt them "merciless blows," and even conducted inner-Party struggle against them as if they were dealing with criminals and enemies.[110]

Their sectarianism turned the very people who should have been at the forefront of the revolutionary movement into "struggle objects": "The factionalists did not regard veteran cadres as valuable assets of the Party; instead they attacked, punished and dismissed from the central and local organizations large numbers of veteran cadres who were experienced in work and had close ties with the masses, but were uncongenial to the factionalists and unwilling to be their yes-men."[111]

Mao interspersed his catalogue of the injustices done by the ultra-Leftists to the veteran cadres with a comment on how the sectarians had promoted young supporters to positions of responsibility and authority for which they had insufficient experience. He complained that, in addition to their persecution of veteran Party members, the Left leadership did not "give proper education of new cadres nor handle their promotions seriously . . . instead they rashly promoted new cadres and cadres from outside who lacked working experience and close ties with the masses, but were congenial with the factionalists and were merely their blind followers and yes-men."[112] This point presages the post-Mao criticism of many of the followers of the Gang of Four as "helicopters" who rose rapidly to power during the Cultural Revolution because of their adherence to the ultra-Left line rather than on account of any true merit or skill.

Mao's handling of the recurring problem of inner-Party sectarianism took an interesting turn at the Party's Eighth National Congress in August 1956. There, he argued that it would be wrong to deny Li Lisan and Wang Ming (who were still relatively active members of the Party) election to the Eighth Central Committee because of their past ultra-Left errors. Denouncing sectarian tendencies within the Party, Mao asked rhetorically:

Why would we make a mistake if we had not elected [to the Seventh Central Committee] those who had erred? Because it would have meant that we were following their example. Their procedure was to reject anyone once labeled by them as an opportunist, regardless of whether or not he had actually made mistakes. If we had followed this procedure, we would have been following their line, the Wang Ming line or the Li Lisan line. . . . The inner-Party relations they cultivated were such that they rejected without exception all those who had made mistakes and those who had waged struggles against them or denounced them as opportunists.[113]

Origins of Ultra-Leftism

The "revolutionary teachers" consistently ascribed the origins of both Left and Right deviations to the residual influence of "petty bourgeois" ideology in the revolutionary ranks. This influence derived principally from the social relations engendered by the small-scale production that was still an important aspect of the transitional society, especially among the peasantry. Speaking of the material circumstances that gave rise to petty-bourgeois deviations in the socialist movement, Lenin made this point: "Economic relations which are backward or which lag behind in their development constantly lead to the appearance of supporters of the labour movement who assimilate only certain aspects of Marxism, only certain parts of the new world outlook in general and the bourgeois-democratic world outlook in particular."[114] Although this petty-bourgeois ideology could be manifest as Right opportunism and conservatism,[115] it also took the form of ultra-Leftism. As Lenin put it, the petty-bourgeoisie, desirous of rapid change and a radical improvement in their own precarious situation, "easily goes to revolutionary extremes, but is incapable of perseverance, organization, discipline and steadfastness." Such "petty-bourgeois revolutionism" may seem to be a dedicated enemy of the capitalist order, but it is, in fact, socialism's "enemy within the working class movement" because "in all essential matters, [it] does not measure up to the conditions and requirements of consistently proletarian class struggle."[116]

Another source of petty-bourgeois ideology conducive to ultra-Leftism was attributed to the presence of large numbers of intellectuals in the socialist movement. These intellectuals, according to Mao, tended to be highly subjective in their approach to revolution because they were "divorced from production" and had only "book knowledge," which gave them merely a partial understanding of and stake in the complex process of socialist revolution and construction.[117] Mao welcomed intellectuals into the movement and suggested that they could "gradually become proletarian in their ideology through Marxist-Leninist education . . . and steeling in mass revolutionary struggles," but he added a caution: "Party members with a petty-bourgeois revolutionary character have joined the Party organizationally, but they have not yet joined the Party ideologically or have not yet done so fully and are often liberals, reformers, anarchists, Blanquists, etc. in the guise of Marxist-Leninists." [118] Therefore, unless the proletarian party actively transformed its petty-bourgeois members, the petty-bourgeoisie would usurp power and remold the Party in their own image.

The potential for ideological corruption by intellectuals was a particular danger for the Russian and Chinese parties, which were seeking to make a socialist revolution in underdeveloped countries without a large industrial proletariat. But Marx and Engels were also aware of the danger of such a distortion of the proletarian movement even in the more highly developed situation in Western Europe in the late nineteenth century. Bakunin complained that the Marxists were seeking to impose a tyranny of intellectuals ("learned socialists") over the working class in the form of the dictatorship of the proletariat; Marx and Engels replied in kind that the reason the anarchist program had brought the revolutionary movement in Europe to the brink of disaster several times was that the anarchists were misled by the subjectivism of certain "misunderstood geniuses" who were sorely out of touch with the needs of the proletariat. [119]

In addition to the economic circumstances that might generate Left deviations, Marxism also touches on the political conditions conducive to ultra-Left trends in the socialist movement. The essential point of this criticism concerns the dialectical relationship between Left and Right deviations. For example, Lenin remarked how part of the proletariat was attracted to a more radical program for revolution when they saw the leaders of the socialist movement making too many unnecessary compromises with the bourgeoisie. "Anarchism," he wrote, "was not infrequently a kind of penalty for the opportunist sins of the working class movement. The two monstrosities complement each other." [120]

In a variation on the same theme, Mao noted that a Left line tended to emerge in the midst of a struggle against Rightist errors. In such situations, not only did some Party members overcompensate for Rightist deviations of the past, but the more extreme elements in the Party could well dominate the leadership when the forces of moderation were paralyzed by the highly charged ideological milieu of rectification and criticism campaigns against Rightism. Mao applied this analysis to the rapid growth of the "Left sentiment" in the Party under Li Lisan in 1927. This trend had first appeared at the "Emergency Meeting" of the Party leadership in August 1927 to rectify Chen Duxiu's Rightist mistakes, which were blamed, in part, for the situation leading up to the Guomindang massacre of communists in Shanghai the previous April. This meeting, Mao observed, had been essentially correct in struggling against Chen's Right opportunism, "but in combatting Right errors, the meeting paved the way for 'Left' errors" in that the corrective policies that it condoned prompted serious adventurism, commandism, and sectarianism, which became the dominant line of the Party by late 1927.[121]

The resurgence of a Left trend within the Party was also more likely to occur if there had been inadequate analysis of earlier Leftist deviations. Mao noted that the appearance of the Wang Ming line had been made much easier by the fact that the Third Plenary Session of the Sixth Central Committee (September 1930) "failed to examine the ideological essence of the Li Lisan line thoroughly and to correct it."[122] Only through comprehensive criticism and analysis could cadres be brought to "a full ideological understanding" of the true nature of erroneous lines and in that way be prepared to guard against their recurrence.[123]

Left and Right deviations were also depicted as developing in certain distinct policy situations. Mao observed that Left errors tended to appear in circumstances that could be manipulated according to the extremist predilections of the dogmatists. For instance, Left errors were more likely during times of heightened antagonism and conflict between the proletariat and the bourgeoisie (e.g., after the collapse of the first United Front in April 1927); when the Red Army was achieving rapid victories; or when the masses had been mobilized and aroused to begin a program of land reform. In contrast, the possibility of Rightist deviations increased when the United Front was intact, following military defeats, or in areas where the agrarian revolution had yet to unfold.[124]

Motivations of Ultra-Leftists

Marx, Engels, Lenin, and Mao also considered the question of the motives of their political opponents on the Left, and the consistency with which they attributed rather benevolent intentions to many of the proponents of an ultra-Left line is in striking contrast to the thoroughly sinister character they ascribed to those deemed to have committed Rightist errors. Ultra-Leftists were seen as having carried a good idea or a basically correct policy to extremes, whereas the Rightists were usually depicted as conscious lackeys of the bourgeoisie who were determined to subvert the revolutionary movement.

For all their profound disdain for Bakunin's anarchist philosophy and his political tactics, Marx and Engels had to acknowledge that certain aspects of his program (such as atheism, opposition to the right of inheritance, and the call for the "abolition of the state") reflected essentially progressive inclinations. The problem was that the legitimacy of these revolutionary objectives was negated by the anarchists' counterproductive insistence on their immediate realization.[125]

Lenin, on several occasions, spoke benignly of the good intentions of those who advocated a position he considered to be ultra-Left. Responding to the anarchists who were calling for a general boycott by all soldiers of proletarian origin against fighting in intra-bourgeois wars, he suggested a more discriminating analysis of each situation and approvingly quoted Karl Kautsky as saying, "The idea of a military strike sprang from good motives, it is noble and full of heroism, but it is heroic folly." [126] And, although he ardently disagreed with the dogmatic antiparliamentarians, he still commented that such anarchists "are among the best, most honest and sincerely revolutionary members of the proletariat" who "have become enemies of Marxism only through misunderstandings." [127] Lenin found the revolutionary temper of the anarchists "highly gratifying" and instructed other Marxists "to learn to appreciate and support it for, in its absence, it would be hopeless to expect the victory of the proletarian revolution." [128] He recognized the ultimate bankruptcy of the anarchist approach but left no doubt that he thought kindly of their motives when he concluded that "the cause of the revolution may well be harmed by certain errors that those who are most devoted to the cause of revolution are about to commit or are committing." [129]

Mao, following his own instructions for dealing with line errors in the Party—"Treat all questions analytically; do not negate everything"—argued that the ultra-Left had been wrong in "the political tactics, the military tactics, and the cadres policy" that they had adopted; but in other important aspects "such as opposing Chiang Kai-shek and carrying on the Agrarian Revolution and the struggle of the Red Army there was no dispute between ourselves and the comrades who committed errors."[130]

By the mid-1950's, Mao's writings clearly indicate that he was becoming increasingly preoccupied with the danger of revisionism in the Party. But in the wake of the excesses of the rural collectivization and communization campaigns, he was prompted to speak out against the trends toward adventurism and dogmatism in policy implementation. Yet his essays and speeches of that period show a relatively conciliatory attitude toward those comrades (including himself) who had made Leftist errors. In an article, "Things Are Beginning to Change," which set the tone for the anti-Rightist campaign of mid-1957, Mao acknowledged that although dogmatism had been a problem in the recent past, for the most part, the dogmatists "are staunch and steadfast and devoted to the Party and the country, only their approach to problems shows a 'Left' one-sidedness." In contrast, those who exhibited Right opportunist tendencies "pose the bigger danger because their ideas are a reflection of bourgeois ideology inside the Party."[131] It was true that Left errors could damage the revolutionary cause; nonetheless, the major criticism must, at that stage of China's development, be aimed at revisionism, because revisionism, unless checked, would surely rot the revolutionary ranks through the spread of bourgeois ideas, whereas the energy and enthusiasm of the ultra-Leftists could well turn into a positive force for building socialism:

When dogmatism turns into its opposite, it becomes either Marxism or revisionism. Our Party's experience shows that there have been many instances of dogmatism turning into Marxism but very few of dogmatism turning into revisionism, because *the dogmatists represent a proletarian school of thought* tainted with petty-bourgeois fanaticism. In some cases what is attacked as "dogmatism" is in fact mistakes in work. In other cases what is attacked as "dogmatism" is in fact Marxism itself. . . . Real dogmatists think that it is better to be on the "Left" than on the Right, and they have a reason—*they want revolution.*[132]

This formulation clearly depicted dogmatism and its associated Left deviations as a contradiction among the people, whereas revisionism and its derivative Rightist deviations were cast irrevocably into the realm of antagonistic contradictions between the people and the enemies of the revolution. This evaluation—and the policies and politics that grew out of it—had an enormous impact on the way in which the critique of ultra-Leftism developed in China after 1957.

In analyzing the Left excesses of the Great Leap Forward, Mao continued to reveal a forgiving attitude toward those guilty of adventurism. He conceded that the Party leadership had been overly exuberant in pushing communization, but then offered the excuse that "[If] we have taken a little too much [from the peasants], then we should make it clear that it was [done with] the good intention of building socialism."[133] In rebuffing criticism of the Leap, Mao argued that, whatever the problems, the "masses still support us," and the enthusiasm of the activists who had been responsible for some of the excesses in implementation must be treasured. "There is a bit of petty-bourgeois fanaticism," he admitted, "but not all that much." And then he queried his audience of Party leaders:

How should we look upon such enthusiasm for communism? Shall we call it petty-bourgeois fanaticism? I don't think we can put it that way. It's a matter of wanting to do a bit more . . . a bit faster . . . We must not pour cold water on this kind of broad mass movement. We can only use persuasion and say to them: Comrades, your hearts are in the right place. When tasks are difficult, don't be impatient. Do things step by step.[134]

Mao's conversations with Red Guard leaders in Peking in July 1968 further revealed the Chairman's generally forgiving attitude toward Left deviations.[135] His remarks certainly convey displeasure and even a sense of disappointment at the factional violence that had come to plague the Red Guard movement, but the general tone of his strictures to the zealous young rebels is rather like that of a loving father's lecture to his naughty children; there is an unmistakable note of encouragement ("We are sympathetic with your side," Mao proclaims at one point near the end of the dialogue),[136] and the gist of his ruminations is to reaffirm the basic correctness of the Cultural Revolution and the role of the Red Guards in the onslaught against revisionism.

One final perspective from Marx and Engels concerning the motives and intentions of ultra-Leftists must be mentioned here because of its special relevance to the critique of the Gang of Four. Whereas Lenin and Mao often seemed forgiving toward their opponents on the Left, Marx and Engels were unrelenting in their scorn for Bakunin. This antagonism reflected their conclusion that Bakunin's political program was subordinate to his unmitigated personal ambitions. In a letter to a friend in New York, Marx wrote: "To Mr. Bakunin doctrine . . . was and is a secondary matter— merely a means to his personal self-assertion. Though a non-entity as a theoretician, he is in his element as an intriguer." [137] Marx and Engels were convinced that the ultimate aim of the anarchist pro- gram was to establish Bakunin's personal dictatorship over the pro- letarian movement, and they thought Bakunin's advocacy of com- plete freedom was only a trick to mask his lust for power. Their scornful summation of Bakunin's line was that it espoused "anarchy at the bottom, discipline at the top" under the command of an amorphous, but all-powerful "Committee" with himself at the head. [138]

The distinction Marx and Engels made between the anarchists' erroneous political line and the unsavory political deeds and mo- tives of Bakunin and his followers anticipates a key part of the post- Mao critique of the Gang of Four. In both cases, an important dif- ferentiation was drawn between the ultra-Left nature of the errant line and the counterrevolutionary activities of the leading propo- nents of that line. One recalls Engels' remark, cited earlier, that the compelling reason for the expulsion of the Bakuninists from the IWA was not their "special dogma" but their factionalism, which split the International. [139] A strikingly similar rationale would be ap- plied to explain how the Gang of Four's conspiracies rather than their ultra-Left line were the ultimate cause of the irreconcilable contradiction between them and the Party. [140]

Objective Results of Ultra-Leftism

Although the "revolutionary teachers" recognized the positive aspects of the subjective motivations of many followers of an ultra-Left line, they were also alert to the objective harm that Left deviations could bring to socialism. As Mao put it: "in terms of damage to the revolutionary cause, to be on the 'Left' is in no way better than to be on the Right and should therefore be resolutely corrected." [141]

Ultra-Leftism's ultimate consequences for the revolution were ob- vious at the outset, in the harmful effect it had on the implemen- tation of party policies, for the dogmatism and extremism of the ultra-Left ensured the failure of otherwise sound ideas. Lenin issued a stern warning against such excesses: "Communists must exert every effort to direct the working class movement and social devel-

opment along the straightest and shortest road to the victory of Soviet power and the dictatorship of the proletariat on a worldwide
scale. But it is enough to take one step farther—a step that might
seem to be in the same direction—and truth turns into error." [142]

Engels, too, in his analysis of the failure of the revolt in Spain in
1873, noted how the anarchists' insistence on untainted working
class autonomy for each of their new small "states" had caused a
"fragmentation and isolation of the revolutionary forces which enabled the government troops to smash one revolt after another."
The result of the dogmatic adherence to what the Bakuninists proclaimed to be "a principle of supreme revolutionary wisdom" was
the defeat of the Spanish rebellion and the delivery of the proletariat over to a repressive regime. [143] And Mao, in his time, vividly
predicted the tragic consequences that extremism could have for
implementing a basically correct policy like cooperativization:

Is there any possibility of "Left" deviation? It is entirely possible. If the
leadership does not pay attention to the conditions of development or to
mass awareness, if it lacks overall planning and does not realize targets by
stages and by groups, if it favors quantity to the neglect of quality or loses
control, then "Left" deviationist mistakes will certainly occur. And these
will certainly make people cry out, cattle cry out, pigs cry out. After crying
out, there will be death, dead people, dead cattle, dead pigs. [144]

The observation that ultra-Leftism results in driving people away
from the socialist cause is another recurrent theme in the critique.
Engels argued that the Bakuninists' vociferous opposition to reli-
gion and the rights of inheritance alienated the very people who
should be rallied to the banner of revolution and would "drive
away a vast number of members [of the International] and . . . divide instead of uniting the European proletariat." [145]

By distorting the socialist program and fomenting discord within
the revolutionary movement, the ultra-Leftists also objectively
strengthened the bourgeoisie. The anarchists, Engels exclaimed,
should be expelled from the IWA because their activity "paralyzes
the action of the International against the enemies of the working
class [and] serves admirably the middle class and the govern-
ments." [146] Lenin reiterated this criticism when he condemned Leftist opposition to his idea of the vanguard party as "tantamount to
disarming completely the proletariat in the interests of the bourgeoisie." [147] Furthermore, the dogmatism of the ultra-Left was criti-

cized by Mao as indirectly serving the ruling capitalist class, by fostering "blind obedience and docility" in the Party and by "treating the working class as a flock of sheep blindly following a few initiated leaders." [148] In another criticism of the Bakuninists, one that again foreshadowed a charge against the Gang of Four, Marx and Engels wrote that the anarchists' rejectionist attitude toward state education had the practical effect of depriving the proletariat of the intellectual and technical skills that could be well used in the interests of the socialist revolution. Bakunin, they said, "preaches the cult of ignorance to young Russians under the pretext that modern science is merely official science (Can one imagine an official mathematics, physics, or chemistry?)." [149]

The views and policies of the ultra-Left were seen as being ironically *retrogressive* in their impact on the course of historical development. Utopian socialism (and its later variant, Russian populism) was criticized by the Marxist-Leninists for the antimodern bent of its critique of capitalism and for its pastoral vision of the future society. Engels and Lenin both remarked on the way in which the anarchist prescription for socialist industrial organization without any hierarchy or centralization reflected a backward-looking orientation. "Wanting to abolish authority in large-scale industry," Engels wrote caustically, "is tantamount to wanting to abolish industry itself, to destroy the power loom in order to return to the spinning wheel." [150] Lenin reaffirmed this point when he criticized anarcho-syndicalist views of "the economic foundations of the future society." In contrast to the "progressive" centralization advocated by the revolutionary Social Democrats, "anarchist production," he observed, "would mean retrogression to obsolete techniques, to the old form of enterprise." [151]

Finally, the "revolutionary teachers" believed that one of the most detrimental ways in which ultra-Leftism jeopardized the revolution and aided the bourgeoisie lay in the fact that extremism severely discredited the public image of socialism. Engels felt that the rash actions and terrorist tactics of the anarchists would only lend credence to the view that the proletarian movement inherently involves "innumerable atrocities, without which the Philistines of all nationalities cannot imagine a workers' uprising." [152] Lenin caught the essence of this unintended consequence of ultra-Leftism: "The surest way of discrediting and damaging a new political (and not

only political) idea is to reduce it to an absurdity on the plea of de-
fending it. For any truth, if 'overdone' . . . if exaggerated, or if carried beyond the limits of its actual applicability, can be reduced to
an absurdity, and is even bound to become an absurdity under these
conditions." [153]

Summary

Despite the great differences in the historical and cultural contexts in which Marx, Engels, Lenin, and Mao were involved as political actors and philosophers, the themes and issues they raised in
their comments on Left deviations in the socialist revolution dis-
play a remarkable continuity. As will be seen in the case studies that
follow, many of the problems that the "revolutionary teachers"
confronted appear again in the contemporary Chinese critique of
ultra-Leftism.

According to Marxism–Leninism–Mao Zedong Thought, ultra-
Leftism most frequently emerges from petty-bourgeois ideology,
which finds particularly fertile ground in the movement to make a
socialist revolution under conditions of material and ideological
underdevelopment. The strength of such a deviant ideology and the
political tendencies that grow out of it are compounded when the
revolutionary movement is led by intellectuals who have, at best, a
tenuous relationship with the classes they endeavor to lead and mobilize. Some ultra-Leftists are prone to subjectivism, dogmatism,
and sectarianism because their "good intentions" to "make revolution" are not tempered by a sober analysis of the complex interaction between opportunities for and constraints on political action
inherent in any given historical moment; others are led to adopt an
extreme revolutionary stance because of "evil motives" in which a
lust for power becomes entangled with the promulgation of a radical political program. The activities of both elements may come together in a single ultra-Left line, though it is important to distinguish between those who pursue such a line out of a sincere but
misguided commitment to revolutionary objectives and those who
use the line cynically as an instrument of counterrevolution and
conspiracy. Nevertheless, whatever the origins of the line or the motivations of its adherents, ultra-Leftism has serious consequences
for the fate of the revolution. Not only does ultra-Leftism under-

mine the policies of the revolutionary movement by rash action and tactical inflexibility; it also discredits socialism in the eyes of the masses by associating socialist programs with extremism, violence, and material dislocation. Ultimately, the Marxist critique argues, ultra-Leftism serves to bolster the cause of the bourgeoisie as surely as do deviations to the Right within the revolutionary ranks.

3
The Origins of the Incomplete Critique

> Grain scattered on ground,
>   potato leaves withered.
> Strong young people have left
>   to smelt iron, only children
>   and old women reaped the crops.
> How can they pass the year?
> Allow me to appeal for the people.
>
> Peng Dehuai (1959)

The critique of ultra-Leftism first became an issue of serious political contention in post-Liberation China during the Great Leap Forward of 1958–61.[1] Although the critique of the Leap developed in circumstances quite different from those of the subsequent cases we shall examine, it nevertheless established a precedent that fundamentally shaped the conduct and context of future attempts to criticize and rectify Left errors.[2] This case study is not intended to provide a comprehensive examination of the policy-making process of the period or to undertake an evaluation of the rationality of the Great Leap strategy in relation to China's developmental problems of the late 1950's; neither will it shed any new light on the political alignments within the Chinese Communist Party elite as they emerged during this period. These tasks have been adequately dealt with elsewhere.[3] Rather, the purpose here is, first of all, to examine the Leap from the perspective of the evolution of the political struggle that emerged in the Party leadership as a result of the effort to correct the imperfections in the strategy of Leaping Forward.

Secondly, the chronological review of the period 1958–61 in this chapter will explore the reasons for the divergence between the thorough rectification of Great Leap policies and the almost complete lack of critical analysis of the line that produced the Leap in the first place. When the Great Leap finally fizzled and was abandoned in late 1961–early 1962, there was a consensus within the Party that the movement had brought on economic and political chaos for reasons other than natural disasters and the withdrawal of Soviet technical aid. Yet the political line that culminated in the Leap was never critically analyzed despite the almost complete reversal in the early 1960's of all the major policies associated with that line.

Moderate Innovation, High Tide, and First Retreat

The hyperenthusiastic, "full-steam-ahead-to-communism" approach to economic and social change that is often said to be the defining characteristic of the entire Great Leap period in fact lasted only a few months. The brief "high tide" of the Leap was preceded by an opening phase of relatively modest objectives and moderate methods and followed by downward-trending stages that were characterized by significant cumulative reductions in the scope of the movement, which ended in the full-scale retreat of the early 1960's.

The preliminary stage of the Great Leap Forward unfolded during the first half of 1958.[4] In March of that year, the National People's Congress endorsed a huge increase in the tempo of China's economic development: substantial increases were projected for the production of steel (19 percent), electricity (18 percent), and coal (17 percent) over the 1957 levels. These objectives set in motion an almost uncontrolled escalation of industrial targets that mounted throughout the spring, and several innovative measures designed to complement and facilitate the new economic drive were also begun. Among the most important measures were steps toward further decentralization of enterprise management, mass mobilization efforts to develop local industry and irrigation projects, strengthened Party supervision of economic planning, and a revitalized and extended "downward transfer" (*xiafang*) program to move higher-level personnel to subordinate units in order to enlarge the local pool of administrative and technical skills.[5]

When the Second Session of the Eighth Party Congress met in May to give formal approval to the launching of the Leap Forward, China was clearly embarked upon a bold effort to realize an unprecedented rate of economic growth. In his keynote speech to the meeting, Liu Shaoqi summed up the goals of this undertaking:

Now the people everywhere are full of confidence in the forward leap in production; they are determined to further speed up socialist construction. They are eager to remove the obstacles placed in their way by technical and cultural backwardness. In view of the basic victory of the socialist revolution already achieved on the economic, political, and ideological fronts, the Central Committee of the Party and Comrade Mao [Zedong] consider that the time is ripe to set new revolutionary tasks before the Party and the people, that now is the time to call for a technical revolution and, along with it, a cultural revolution.[6]

Liu's speech emphasized the development of the forces of production as the primary mission of the Leap; yet he also elaborated the call for a "cultural revolution" as part of the movement: "The present task is to effect a thorough and systematic readjustment in the relationships between people, rooting out the capitalist and feudal survivals of bygone days and building completely socialist relations . . . in every walk of life."[7] From its inception the Leap was clearly intended to be a comprehensive program to forge a qualitatively new development strategy for the People's Republic.

Nevertheless, this first stage of the Great Leap Forward can fairly be called a period of *moderate* innovation, not only in relation to the more radical policies that followed but also in terms of the nature of the basic objective of the Leap at this time. Liu's speech and all the policy pronouncements of the inaugural phase of the Great Leap referred to the goal of achieving a Leap Forward in *socialist* construction. Only in the late summer of 1958 did the emphasis shift to heralding the Leap as a transition to *communism*.[8] The early months of the Leap did, indeed, represent a fundamental departure from former practice and establish the context in which the subsequent "high tide" could occur, and the distinction between these two phases of the Leap should not be drawn too sharply. Yet it is important to note the fact that in its initial design, the Great Leap Forward was not seen as instrumental to the impending advent of a truly communist society. It was the escalation in the objectives, expectations, and policy packages associated with the Leap as a transition to communism—not just the inflation of economic targets or the turn to mobilization politics—that brought on the most serious problems in China's new development strategy.

Only in the late summer of 1958 did the transition to *communism* and the revolutionization of the *relations* of production become the dominant themes of the Leap. This shift of emphasis was reflected in the Beidaihe Resolution of the Central Committee issued on August 29, 1958, which officially sanctioned the nationwide establishment of rural people's communes. Although the Resolution maintained a cautious air on the timing of the transition, its message was straightforward: "Communism in China is no longer a remote future event. We should actively use the form of the people's communes to explore the practical road of transition to communism."[9]

There seems little doubt that the impetus for many of the most innovative policies of the Great Leap sprang from the grass roots;[10] but the Center bears clear responsibility for escalating the tone and tempo of the transformation, and it was the Beidaihe Resolution that marked the real start of a movement in which even the "sprouts of communism" were said to be bursting forth throughout the country. By October 1958 more than 90 percent of China's peasant households had been reorganized into communes that were enormous in scale and comprehensive in function; the scope of public ownership had been vastly expanded and the arena of private economic activity in the countryside drastically circumscribed; and a semi-supply system in which distribution of grain and other daily necessities was based on need rather than according to labor had been instituted in many areas.[11] These changes clearly represented a dramatic elevation of the level of socialization in the rural sector. But the media took this transformation one step further by heralding the communes as the harbinger of the imminent transition to communism; it also castigated those who expressed reservations about the speed of ideological and material changes then occurring in China.[12]

The Debate over Bourgeois Right

In the midst of the elated optimism about the transition to communism, an interesting—though seemingly insignificant—incident occurred that hinted at the possibility of China's new direction and the critique of ultra-Leftism being already a contentious issue within the leadership during the "high tide" of the Great Leap Forward. The particular cast of characters involved in this incident also indicates that the ideological battle lines for the political showdown of the 1970's were already being drawn in late 1958.

This incident centered around an article that first appeared in an issue of *Jiefang* (Liberation), the journal of the Shanghai Party committee; the author was Zhang Chunqiao, at the time a minor local theoretician but later a major figure of the Cultural Revolution and one of the radical leaders labeled as the "Gang of Four" after their arrest in October 1976. Zhang's article was a ringing endorsement of the egalitarian supply system of distribution and a virulent condemnation of the bourgeois nature of all wage schemes that allocated income according to labor or rank.[13] The emphasis of his argument was on the necessity to restrict actively all manifestations of "bourgeois right"—patterns of inequality resulting from differentials in income, status, or authority—in socialist society in order to keep up the momentum of the transition to communism.

The political tensions surrounding the publication of this article by Zhang Chunqiao were revealed in a "confession" extracted a decade later, in 1968, by Red Guards from Wu Lengxi, the editor of the nationally distributed Party newspaper *Renmin ribao* (People's Daily).[14] In this "Confession," Wu stated that Zhang's article was republished in *Renmin ribao* in October 1958 on the personal orders of Mao Zedong, who wanted to stimulate public discussion of persisting contradictions in the income distribution system. An editorial note by Chairman Mao accompanying the article said that, despite being "one-sided in some respects," Zhang's views were "in the main correct."[15] Wu Lengxi added that the "basic ideas" in Zhang's article had been voiced by Mao at the Beidaihe Conference in August 1958; we also know, from other sources, that the Chairman had expressed support for the rapid expansion of a supply system during a subsequent tour of people's communes.[16]

Zhang's article set off a heated debate in the media on the question of the persistence of inequality in socialist society. The issue at stake was how quickly such "bourgeois right" could be eradicated and replaced with more egalitarian modes of distribution.[17] Toward the end of 1958, Deng Xiaoping—then General Secretary of the Party—called a meeting to summarize the main points of this debate. Presumably, his objective in doing so was to set the ideological guidelines for Party policy on the rapidly expanding supply system in the communes, which was causing such difficulties as a decline in labor motivation and the wasting of resources. Deng and Hu Qiaomu (a leading Party propagandist of the 1950's who was purged during the Cultural Revolution and rehabilitated to a position of prominence in the post-Mao era) both delivered speeches warning against the premature abolition of "bourgeois right" in the form of the wage system and attacked the trend toward "petty-bourgeois egalitarianism" (i.e., ultra-Leftism in distribution policy). Deng even went so far as to argue that the wage system was less costly to the state than the supply system—a cold, economic calculation concerning a "sprout of communism" that probably did not sit well with Zhang and other ardent supporters of the Great Leap Forward.[18]

Zhang was assigned the task of producing a summary of this meeting on the distribution system. However, being displeased with the tone set by Deng and Hu, he did not write the report. According to Wu's account, Mao accepted this political stalemate, but later expressed dissatisfaction with the ideological compromise it reflected.[19]

This incident was a foreboding of the conflicts of the 1970's that pitted leadership groups including Zhang Chunqiao and Deng Xiaoping against one another. As in 1958, diverging views on the issue of bourgeois right in socialist society played a key role in the struggles growing out of the Cultural Revolution. And the debate of 1958 must have had an effect in propelling these two groups toward irreconcilable ideological antagonism.

The First Retreat

By late October of 1958 problems of economic dislocation and peasant dissatisfaction had become manifest enough to compel the leadership to convene a series of central level meetings to take stock of the situation and begin remedial action. The Wuhan Resolution, which emanated from one of these meetings in late November–early December, signaled the start of the first retreat from the Leap.[20]

The Wuhan Resolution reaffirmed the positive aspects of the commune movement and called for "an even bigger leap forward" in 1959; thus, in many ways, it continued to feed the inflated expectations of the times. For instance, it still expressed the hope of a rather unrealistic timetable for the modernization of the economy and made frequent references to the continued growth of "the elements of communism" such as the supply system and the communal mess halls as an important objective of the Leap Forward. However, it also called for a period of "educational work, overhaul, and consolidation, that is, the work of checking up on the communes," in the following months.[21]

Besides outlining the framework for a certain modicum of administrative reorganization, the Resolution also considered such problems as the excessive communization of private property, the disincentive effects of egalitarianism, the disruption of the commodity exchange system in the national economy caused by the trend toward self-reliance (indeed, autarky) in the communes, and the commandist tendencies of certain cadres who were eager to push the Leap to ever greater heights. Furthermore, even though the Wuhan Resolution maintained that the purpose of the Leap was to "lay the foundation of material and spiritual conditions for the transition from socialism to communism," it also firmly cautioned that "every Marxist must soberly realize that the transition is a fairly long and complicated process and that throughout this entire process society is still socialist in nature." [22] The Resolution also explicitly deflated the notion enunciated at Beidaihe that the basic change in the system of ownership in the countryside that was a precondition for a communist society could be achieved in a mere three or four years, though its own projection, that the development of the rural economy to a point where such a change of ownership was practicable would only "take fifteen, twenty or more years to complete," [23] was still a very ambitious one for such an undertaking.

Altogether, the Wuhan Resolution indicated an ambivalent evaluation of the Great Leap Forward by the Party leaders. It clearly maintained the ideals of the Leaping Forward strategy on the one hand while, on the other, recognizing the necessity to correct the most blatant excesses of the "high tide." As the launching of the Leap had reflected the relatively unified position of the leadership on the need for new directions in China's development, so, too, did this initial retreat proceed with near-unanimity at the top. [24]

Over the next few months, the "checking up" process revealed even more serious problems in the people's communes than those the leadership had been aware of. While the upper levels of the Party had been elaborating the finer points of the distinction between the "two transitions" (the transition from collective ownership to ownership by the whole people and the transition from socialism to communism) by the addition of qualifying statements and modifying clauses in central directives, the rural economy was plunging into increasingly worse straits and mass resistance to Leap policies was mounting. [25] The seriousness of the situation prompted the convening of an enlarged session of the Politburo at Zhengzhou in late February and early March of 1959. This conference condoned further administrative changes in the commune structure and transferred most production and distribution functions to the brigade, thus significantly reducing the authority of the higher levels in guiding critical aspects of rural life.

Mao gave several speeches at Zhengzhou in which he dealt at length with the increasingly obvious malfunctioning of the Great Leap program.[26] The Chairman aimed his most pointed remarks at the middle-level cadres who had gone to extremes in implementing commune policies, and he spoke bitingly of the "gust of communist wind" that swept the commune movement in the late summer and autumn of 1958—a "wind," he said, that was stirred up by those well-intentioned but overzealous cadres who were carried away by their desire to hasten the transition to communism. As a result of their zealousness, income leveling was enforced between richer and poorer teams, an excessively large proportion of collective production was earmarked for accumulation (especially for capital construction) rather than distribution, and the resources of lower levels and individuals were requisitioned for communal use without compensation. Even if carried out in the name of communism, these practices were equivalent to "banditry," and if they were not corrected they would drive people away from the cause of the revolution.[27] The Chairman even voiced a passionate defense of the "particularism" of peasants who resisted such incursions from above by hiding a part of their production.[28]

Mao's remarks at Zhengzhou were also peppered with self-criticism and criticism of his colleagues at the Center. He took responsibility for being "adventurist" in his own estimation of mass enthusiasm for rapid socialist transformation and admonished those at the highest levels who jeopardized the material interests of the peasants by their pursuit of revolutionary objectives.[29] Even prior to Zhengzhou, Mao had acknowledged that the leaders who had been responsible for setting the goals of the Great Leap (including himself) had been woefully ignorant of the concrete problems of economic construction. Reflecting upon the terrible vengeance that reality could wreak upon those who sought to defy its inherent restraints by will power and desire alone, Mao mused that he and his comrades had been "Like a child playing with fire, without experience, knowing pain only after getting burned. In economic construction . . . we declared war on the earth, unfamiliar with strategy or tactics. We must frankly admit such defects and errors."[30]

Despite these self-criticisms, Mao repeatedly reaffirmed both the general idea and the specific policies of the movement. He characterized the enthusiasm and activism of the basic-level cadres as highly valuable, even if somewhat excessive at times.[31] Referring to the wanton expropriation of private property and the commune's requisitioning without compensation of labor and implements belonging to the teams, he commented: "If we have taken a little too much, then we should make it clear that *it was done with the good intention of building socialism.*"[32] In evaluating the Great Leap, he said in one speech, "the relationship between our achievements and shortcomings . . . is like the relationship between nine of the ten fingers and the one remaining finger"; the main problem had been the work style of the cadres charged with implementing policy, though this problem had resulted in part from the fact that "the Center didn't produce concrete instructions earlier, so that lower level cadres didn't take hold of the situation properly."[33] Nonetheless, Mao argued, despite all the difficulties and turmoil of the past months, the peasants were still basically in support of the overall purpose and direction of the Leap: "After going through this kind of process of adjusting and consolidating the people's communes, our unity with the masses will be even closer."[34]

The signals emanating from Mao's speeches at Zhengzhou were highly ambiguous, conveying both affirmation and criticism of the "high tide" of the Great Leap Forward. The political implications of this ambiguity were perhaps best caught by the Chairman's seemingly contradictory use of the label "Right opportunism" in relation to those seeking to correct the excesses of the times. On the one hand, in the midst of his defense of peasant resistance to the "communist wind," he declared that he would himself "hold firmly to Right opportunism and carry it through right to the end and . . . right to the point of being expelled from the Party."[35] On the other hand, he had earlier cautioned those who considered the defects of the Leap as grounds for abandoning the whole program that their evaluation was "completely mistaken."[36] He reaffirmed the basic spirit and intent of the Beidaihe Resolution on the "superiority" of the people's communes as a vehicle for the transition to communism and added the warning: "If doubts appeared regarding such a fundamental question, that would just be completely in error and would constitute Right opportunism."[37]

In retrospect, Mao's message seemed to be: rectification of cadre work style was necessary to correct the Leftist excesses of the Leap,

but challenging the underlying line of the movement was unacceptable (a distinction that Peng Dehuai failed to heed a few months
later). Thus, the Chairman's use of the term "Right opportunist" to
describe his own opposition to the "communist wind" was rather
tongue-in-cheek, while his invocation of the same label as a warning to those who questioned the sagacity of the Leaping Forward
strategy was of deadly serious intent.

Whatever the subtleties of Mao's thinking at the time, the general thrust of the Party policy of readjustment that began with the
Wuhan Resolution and that was reconfirmed by the Zhengzhou
meetings invited a more searching examination of the origin of the
problems of the Great Leap Forward. The period from early 1959
through mid-1959 saw not only a turn toward various measures
designed to rectify specific policy errors, but also an upsurge in
criticism of many of the ideological assumptions that were judged
by some to have lent rationale to the "high tide" of the Leap. In the
first six months of 1959, we can detect the beginnings of a *comprehensive critique* of ultra-Leftism that incorporated both rectification of concrete policy problems and critical analysis of the line that
gave rise to those problems.[38]

During this period, the media devoted considerable space to criticism of the danger posed to China's socialist development by such
problems as a faulty understanding of the complexity of the transition to communism, the disparaging of the proper role of material
incentives under socialism, and the illusion that egalitarianism was
a reflection of revolutionary ideology. There was a corresponding
de-emphasis on mass mobilization as the cornerstone of China's development strategy, as well as an expression of greater faith in cautious planning and the role of technical expertise, and some skepti-
cism concerning pervasive Party leadership in economic units.[39] All
in all, many of the key ideas of the Leap were being critically scru-
tinized at the same time substantive policy readjustments were being made.

Although Mao supported the efforts to rectify policy and work
style, he does not appear to have been quite convinced of the value
of more far-ranging criticism of the Leaping Forward strategy that
was unfolding through the first half of 1959. At the Seventh Plenum
of the Eighth Central Committee held in Shanghai in April 1959,
Mao and Peng Dehuai were already at odds over the extent and
cause of the difficulties in the communization movement.[40] The

leadership—which up to that point had been relatively unified in both Leaping and Retreating—now was splitting over the very issue of the scope of the critique of ultra-Leftism. This split would culminate in the showdown between Mao and Defense Minister Peng at the Lushan Plenum in the summer of 1959.

From "Communist Wind" to "Right Opportunism"

The Party meetings held at Lushan, Jiangxi Province, in July and August of 1959 have been viewed by both Western observers and the post-Mao Chinese leadership as a major turning point in the political history of the People's Republic. They are seen as the first incident of high-level inner-Party conflict over policy and ideology, which set the scene for the line struggle that fueled the Cultural Revolution.[41] From the perspective of this study, the Lushan Plenum marked the end of whatever efforts were being made by those with growing doubts about the Great Leap Forward to expand their criticisms into a comprehensive critique of the line behind that movement.

The conflict between Mao and Peng at Lushan involved several issues.[42] Differences over the relationship between professional development of the People's Liberation Army along the lines of a Soviet military model and increasing politicization (including Party control and army participation in various facets of socialist construction other than military work) had been brewing for some time.[43] Although military issues do not appear to have been on the agenda at Lushan or to have been raised as part of Peng's criticisms of the Great Leap, they obviously played an indirect role in heightening the antagonism between the Chairman and the Defense Minister. Furthermore, Peng's critical view of the impact of the Leap was partly shaped by his alarm at the morale and supply problems that economic dislocations were having on the army under his command. He was also distressed that growing Soviet disdain for China's innovative (or to their view, heretical) development strategy might jeopardize his hopes for modernizing the military with Russian assistance.

Peng and his supporters were also deeply disturbed by the character of Mao's personal leadership, which they thought was drifting toward highly individualistic and arbitrary methods.[44] In particular, they were angry about the way in which the program of the Great

Leap had been formulated without adequate discussion, planning, or experimentation. When this matter came up at Lushan, Mao is known to have reacted bitterly against the charges that he had violated his own cherished principles of democratic centralism and the mass line.[45]

Yet whatever part these and other issues (including Peng's alleged "illicit" contacts with Soviet leaders concerning his dismay about the Leap) had in shaping the events at Lushan, it is clear that Peng's criticisms of the Great Leap Forward were central to the conflict. The main point of his dissent as expressed in his remarks at the preparatory small group discussions for the central meeting and later in his "Letter of Opinion" to Mao was that ideological subjectivism had led to a failure to appreciate fully the constraints imposed upon China's development alternatives by the material realities of the times.[46] Subjectivism, he said in his "Letter of Opinion," had led to the implementation of unworkable policies (like the hasty construction of the communes and rampant egalitarianism in distribution) and to "the habit of exaggeration" in both the delineation of objectives and the evaluation and reporting of results. These errors were counter to "the style of seeking truth from facts that the Party had formed over a long period of time," and it was because of them that the Party had lost the support of the masses.[47] Peng's concluding remarks struck at the very heart of the Great Leap:

In the view of some comrades, putting politics in command could be a substitute for everything. They forgot that putting politics in command was aimed at raising the consciousness of labor, insuring improvement of products in both quantity and quality, and giving full play to the enthusiasm and creativeness of the masses in order to speed our economic construction. Putting politics in command is no substitute for the economic principles, still less for the concrete measures in economic work. Equal importance must be attached to putting politics in command and the effective measures in economic work; neither should be overstressed or neglected.[48]

Peng suggested that the setbacks caused to China's socialist construction by the Leap far outweighed the benefits derived from the new strategy. In his view, the Party had suffered from a serious case of "petty-bourgeois fanaticism," which had caused the disastrous turn to the Left.

Peng's complaints were couched in tones of respect for Mao and at least paid lip service to the basic policies of the preceding year; furthermore the content of Peng's criticisms did not go much beyond many of Mao's own comments concerning the problems of the Great Leap.[49] Nevertheless, the Chairman's reaction was to accuse the critics of the Leap of being "Right opportunists" who were launching a "frantic attack against the Party."[50] While admitting that there had been some serious difficulties in the commune movement and that the leadership had displayed a lack of understanding of complex economic problems, Mao put most of the blame on problems of implementation by commune-level cadres. He vigorously defended the ideals and basic program of the Leap and contended that most of the excesses of the "high tide" had been corrected in the period since the Zhengzhou Conference. "There is no more 'communist wind' blowing," he proclaimed, "there is no more equalization [of richer and poorer teams], transfer [of resources between levels without compensation] or appropriation [of team funds by the commune]. There is no more pompous exaggeration. At the moment, the problem is not to oppose the 'Left,' but to oppose the Right."[51]

Mao's interpretation of the criticism of the Leap was that it was simply a reflection of a major line struggle within the Party that had been incited by certain members who disliked the mass movement method of socialist construction. He demanded that the Central Committee choose between his leadership and the alternative offered by Peng and his supporters.[52] The Chairman was able to rally the support of almost the entire Party leadership, who were unwilling to accept both the domestic and international consequences that a refutation of Mao would have had for the legitimacy of the Chinese revolution and backed Mao regardless of their feelings about the validity of Peng's criticisms.[53] The Lushan Plenum thus ended with a resolution condemning the "anti-Party clique headed by Peng Dehuai" and a communiqué reaffirming the general line of the Great Leap Forward and proclaiming that the principal danger to socialism in China was "the emergence of Right opportunist ideas among some cadres" at various levels of leadership.[54]

After Lushan, some adjustments of Great Leap policies were, in fact, made to forestall a repeat of earlier trends of false reporting of economic results, to bolster the production functions of the lower levels, and to spur individual productivity by increasing the percentage of collective income destined for distribution rather than accumulation.[55] But, in general, the immediate post-Lushan period can be characterized as a "Second Leap Forward."[56] The last quarter of 1959 and the first half of 1960 witnessed a renewal of some of the more radical policies of Leaping Forward. For instance, there was an intensified drive to establish rural communal mess halls and *urban* people's communes, even though these were two areas in which particular difficulties had been experienced in 1958–59. Also, Mao's endorsement in March 1960 of the "Constitution of the Anshan Iron and Steel Company" with its emphasis on mass movements, Party leadership, and nonbureaucratic structures of enterprise management clearly gave a shot in the arm to the "politics in command" approach to socialist development that Peng had challenged at Lushan.[57]

Moreover, the confrontation between Mao and Peng at Lushan was followed by an intense campaign against Right opportunism, which lasted until the end of 1959.[58] This campaign included extensive media criticism of such Rightist ideas as the denigration of mass movements in general and of the achievements of the Great Leap in particular. Disciplinary measures (to the point of purges and personal vilification) were carried out at the lower levels against cadres who had expressed opposition to Great Leap policies or had been too zealous in implementing the readjustments of the first half of 1959. Cautions against Leftist deviations like egalitarianism in distribution continued to be issued during the renewed Leap. But the weight of official criticism had clearly shifted to the danger that the Right posed to a big breakthrough in China's socialist development.

Retreat without Critique

When the "Second Leap Forward" ran into even worse economic difficulties and peasant resistance than the "high tide," the blame was initially focused on errors of implementation at the lower levels by "a few cadres who, although good-willed and well-intentioned, are inadequate in their ideological consciousness."[59] From mid-1960 through 1961, the so-called "five styles" or "five winds" (*wu feng*) became the target of a rectification campaign with a definite anti-Leftist tinge. This campaign was aimed at correcting the problems of the "communist wind" (egalitarianism), commandism, privilege seeking, blind direction of production without due regard for local conditions, and exaggeration of targets and results.[60] However, the criticism was directed only at problems of implementation; official propaganda consistently maintained the correctness of the original policies and ideals of the Great Leap Forward.[61] But as the problems in the economy mounted (compounded by unprecedented natural disasters and the precipitous withdrawal of Soviet technicians in mid-1960), a massive and final retreat from the Leap began.

Further readjustments of the communes were endorsed through the promulgation of an "urgent directive" on the rural situation (the "Twelve Articles") in November 1960 and the "Draft Regulations Concerning the Rural Communes" (the "Sixty Articles") in March 1961.[62] These documents stipulated greater autonomy for the team in matters of production and distribution, thereby further diluting the level of socialization in the countryside; they also sanctioned the reemergence of the private plots and rural free markets, which had been aggressively curtailed as vestiges of capitalism during the Leap. Similar adjustments were made on the industrial and educational fronts. By mid-1961 not only had the substance of the Great Leap Forward been completely reversed but even propaganda hailing its original ideals had ceased. The Party (with Mao's backing up until at least early 1962) was engaged in constructing a set of pragmatic policies designed to salvage the economy, assuage popular discontent, and establish a less radical framework for future development.[63]

Mao later came to view this new strategy as the breeding ground for rampant revisionism in the Party and the precursor to capitalist restoration in China as a whole. Whatever the objective merits of this evaluation, the period of the New Economic Policy—as the early 1960's are often called in a reference derived from Lenin's policies of the early 1920's to disengage from the radical measures of War Communism— constituted a profound break from the programs and priorities of Leaping Forward and led to the further fermentation of inner-Party antagonisms that would eventually culminate in the struggles of the Great Proletarian Cultural Revolution.

The focal point of this antagonism was what one analyst has referred to as "the widening gulf between Maoist ideology and Party practice in the policy process."[64] In other words, Mao became alarmed by what he perceived as the Rightist drift of the line that emerged from the efforts to pull the country out of the economic and social disasters of the late 1950's; at the same time many of the other top leaders became increasingly hardened in their conviction that the Great Leap Forward had proved the utter bankruptcy of the Chairman's ultra-Left perspective on socialist development. However, the critics of the Leap—restrained as they were by the political realities of the times—were unable (or unwilling) to undertake a campaign of public repudiation of the line that had engendered the Leap in the first place. Thus, the final retreat from the Great Leap Forward encompassed pervasive policy rectification without correlative line analysis, a process that we may term an *incomplete critique* of ultra-Leftism. The implementation of various policies to correct alleged Leftist errors does not in itself constitute a comprehensive critique; in our terms, to be truly comprehensive, a critique of ultra-Leftism must involve both policy rectification and a critical analysis of the line that gives rise to the refuted policies.

This is not to suggest that there was no public criticism of Leftist errors after Lushan. There was, in fact, some such criticism both in the second half of 1959 and in 1960–61; in particular, there were pointed criticisms of egalitarianism throughout the various phases of readjustment in the communes. Compared with the relatively broad campaign against ultra-Left tendencies in the first half of 1959, however, the later efforts were muted, to say the least. Most significantly, there was never any public denunciation or analysis of the Great Leap as a whole. In some ways, the myth of the correctness of the "Three Red Banners" of the Great Leap Forward, the general line for socialist construction, and the people's communes as an appropriate strategy for China's development in the later 1950's was maintained intact until the post-Mao era.

The incomplete critique of the Great Leap Forward certainly exacerbated simmering intra-elite antagonisms; it also, probably, spawned a good measure of public cynicism as the masses pondered the incongruity between policy rectification and official myth. We now turn to a consideration of why the critics of the Leap were never able to translate their disenchantment into a comprehensive critique of ultra-Leftism.

Why an Incomplete Critique?

It is clear that the relatively comprehensive critique of ultra-Leftism that was developing through the initial phase of retrenchment from the Leap in the first half of 1959 was turned aside by

Mao Zedong's actions at the Lushan meetings. But why was a comprehensive critique not revived after the dissipation of the "Second Leap Forward" in 1960–61?

First, Mao had made it crystal clear at Lushan that he simply would not tolerate a critique of the basic ideals of the Leap. Although the Chairman's power within the highest echelons of decision making may have been somewhat compromised by the failures of Leaping Forward, his influence was by no means negligible through the early 1960's. Despite the evidence that some of his comrades at the top sometimes bypassed or ignored Mao when it came to making concrete policy,[65] he still had the political wherewithal to block any moves toward a public or formal inner-Party repudiation of the line of the Leap as an ultra-Left deviation.

Second, Mao retained tremendous prestige within the Party rank and file and among the populace as a whole. Any critical analysis of the problems of 1958–60 would inevitably have reflected unfavorably on the Chairman's leadership and, by implication, tarnished the legitimacy of the Party as a whole. Furthermore, it was not as if Deng Xiaoping, Liu Shaoqi, Zhou Enlai, and others could claim to be entirely blameless in the formulation of Great Leap policy; they, too, had lent varying degrees of vocal and organizational support to the launching of the movement and had thus contributed to the radicalization of the political environment that had made the excesses of the "high tide" possible.

Third, the critics of the Leap may have been satisfied with the policy rectification measures of the retreat in the early 1960's and for that reason may not have felt any necessity for risking the type of ideological soul-searching that a thorough criticism of the line of the Leap would have entailed. They also may have expected that Mao had learned his lesson and would abide by his decision—made as early as February of 1958—to concentrate on the larger "questions of the direction, policy, and line of the Party and state"[66] and leave the detailed planning to those who were better versed in economic matters.

All in all, the critics of the Leap must have calculated that the political risks of a comprehensive public critique of the ultra-Left line that had caused so much hardship and discord far outweighed the possible benefits. Thus, they proceeded circumspectly when it came to analyzing what had gone wrong with the "Three Red Banners." For example, the fact that Peng Zhen, the mayor of Peking and a high-ranking Politburo member, ordered that an investigation into the origins of the problems of the Great Leap be carried out *in secret* in October 1961 attests to his fears of provoking Mao's wrath and stirring up public doubts about the wisdom of the Party's leadership.[67]

The Lushan Plenum was the major turning point in the evolution of the critique of the Great Leap Forward. Mao's vitriolic response to Peng Dehuai's criticisms of the Leap effectively stifled any deeper analysis of the line behind the "Three Red Banners." Why did Mao react as he did at Lushan?

The Chairman's actions at those meetings must be understood not only as a result of his confrontation with Peng at Lushan but also in the context of the criticism of the Leap that had been building up in the six or eight months prior to the Plenum. It was not so much the specific content of this criticism or the recommendations for various readjustments in Leap policies to which Mao objected— he had, in fact, voiced similar complaints and suggestions himself at Party meetings and in other forums through the first half of 1959. What seems to have riled Mao was the "tone and overall evaluation" of the critics of the Leap, which the Chairman interpreted as presaging a total refutation of his vision for China's development.[68] Mao accepted the necessity for a rectification of adventurist trends and "communist wind" work styles, but he bristled at Peng Dehuai's insinuation that the whole political line of the Great Leap was a product of "petty-bourgeois fanaticism" in the Party.

Mao's reaction at Lushan must also be placed in the context of his growing preoccupation through the 1950's with the problem of revisionism in the socialist revolution after the seizure of power. This problem had taken on added urgency in the late 1950's in connection with the Chairman's sharpened criticism of the domestic and foreign policies of the Soviet Union. The growing criticism of the Leap in the spring and summer of 1959 and the events at Lushan confirmed Mao's fears—only recently alerted by the "anti-adventurist" campaign undertaken in 1956 to curb the excesses of collectivization—that a rectification of Leftist tendencies threatened to "pour cold water" on the mass movement to build socialism and serve as a camouflage for a counterattack from the Right.

Therefore, in a reaction not unlike that of the Gang of Four a decade later in the aftermath of the death of Lin Biao, Mao acted to cut short a developing critique of ultra-Leftism. If developed to its logical conclusion, a critique of the Great Leap Forward would have constituted an unacceptable challenge to Mao's power within the Party and also to his deeply held ideological preferences concerning the direction of socialist construction in China.

The composite message of Mao's actions at Lushan was that Leftist errors in policy, no matter how severe the consequences, were not as serious a threat to socialism as Right opportunism, and therefore they should not be subjected to the same magnitude of public criticism. Mao's reaction to Peng also implied that the very attempt to criticize the Left was an act verging on counterrevolution. The practical result of this message was not merely the abrupt end to any possibility of a comprehensive critique of the Great Leap Forward but also a deflation of any concern with ultra-Left errors in both China's elite politics and mass political culture. It was made clear to the leaders at the top who may have been inclined to oppose Leftward drifts in policy that they were not to take any effective action; and at the same time, the officially espoused critical standards of Chinese political culture were sharply directed toward the dangers of revisionism, leaving ultra-Leftism unattended as a potential source of serious problems in socialist construction. Thus the background was set for the excesses of the Cultural Revolution, and as we shall see in subsequent cases, for the future development of the critique of ultra-Leftism in Chinese politics.

Conclusion

The chronology of events that shaped the development of the critique of ultra-Leftism in the Great Leap Forward can be divided into five phases. In its first phase, which lasted throughout the spring and early summer of 1958, the Leap was an ambitious attempt to forge a new path in China's development in order to remedy the problems caused by copying the Soviet model. Even though some of the economic targets set in this first phase were unrealistically high, the overall objective of the new program was still defined within the boundaries of *socialist* construction; it can therefore be termed a stage of moderate innovation.

The next stage, the "high tide" of the Great Leap Forward, lasted from the launching of the nationwide commune movement at the Beidaihe Conference in August 1958 through the end of that year. During this phase, not only was positive propaganda carried out to mobilize support for the Leap, but the anti-Rightist campaign that had begun in 1957 in the aftermath of the Hundred Flowers movement was extended to combat conservative tendencies among local cadres and the population in general. The defining characteristics of this phase were its emphasis on the Leap Forward as an effort to accelerate the transition to *communism* and its euphoric predictions as to the timetable for arrival in that utopia.

The Wuhan Resolution of December 1958 ushered in an initial period of consolidation and readjustment in response to the serious difficulties encountered in the administration of the new communes. This third phase involved both a process of "tidying up" in the people's communes and a concerted campaign against the Leftist trends of the "high tide." By the spring and summer of 1959 this campaign was showing signs of developing into a relatively comprehensive critique of ultra-Leftism that would incorporate both concrete policy rectification and critical line analysis. This nascent critique was curtailed by events at the Lushan Plenum in July and August 1959 when Mao's "victory" over Peng Dehuai led to a fourth phase, that of the "Second Leap Forward" and a renewed campaign against Right opportunism.

The beginning of the final phase of retreat was not clearly demarcated by a single central meeting or resolution but emerged gradually in late 1960 and early 1961 as the "Second Leap" floundered and then collapsed in the wake of severe economic dislocations, natural calamities, and the withdrawal of Soviet technical aid. In this period, which blossomed into the full-fledged New Economic Policy of the early 1960's, the Great Leap strategy was completely abandoned, but without any serious reevaluation of the ideology and political line of the Great Leap. It can therefore be characterized as an incomplete critique of ultra-Leftism. In contrast to the banging of propaganda drums that heralded the onset of the movement, the "Second Leap Forward" faded away with hardly a critical whimper.

This pattern of comprehensive and incomplete critique is important for understanding the political dynamics of the Great Leap Forward and its immediate aftermath. It is also essential for analyzing the roundabout development of the future efforts to criticize and rectify the ultra-Left trends that grew out of the Cultural Revolution.

4
The Critique of the Great Leap Forward

> . . . in dealing with questions of Party history we should lay stress not on the responsibility of certain individual comrades, but on the analysis of the circumstances in which the errors were committed, on the content of the errors, and on their social, historical, and ideological roots.
>
> Mao Zedong (1944)

The politically induced shift from a comprehensive to an incomplete critique of ultra-Leftism after the Lushan Plenum in mid-1959 effectively forestalled the development of a thorough analysis of the line of the Great Leap Forward. Nevertheless, in the course of dealing with the economic and social problems caused by the Leap many important issues were raised concerning the origins, content, and impact of Left deviations in China's socialist construction. This chapter elaborates some of these issues with regard to alleged manifestations of ultra-Leftism in ideology, leadership techniques and cadre work style, and concrete policy problems.[1] The examples cited in this catalogue of issues are drawn not only from the period of the most comprehensive critique of the ultra-Left errors of the Leap or from the words of its most fervent critics (such as Peng Dehuai). They are also taken from the post-Lushan phases of the Leap when substantive retrenchment did take place and from commentaries by Mao who, despite his general unyielding faith in the strategy of Leaping Forward, recognized the necessity of curbing the most extreme tendencies of the times.

Ideology

Socialism and the Transition to Communism

The concept and practice of the Great Leap Forward (at least after the Beidaihe Resolution of August 1958) were predicated on the assumption that China could reach the stage of true communism within a relatively short span of time. This belief rested, in turn, on a calculation that China as of 1958–59 had already completed, in the main, the fundamental tasks of socialist transformation and therefore contained (or with a burst of effort and enthusiasm quickly could attain) the requisite material and ideological conditions for undertaking the transition to becoming a communist society.

A number of considerations had led Mao and others toward such an optimistic calculation: China's generally impressive economic record since Liberation; the rapid and relatively smooth process of socialization in both industry and agriculture; the view that the anti-Rightist campaign of 1957 had succeeded in neutralizing the last pockets of resistance to the socialist revolution; and the apparent shift in the international balance of power in favor of the socialist camp as symbolized by the Soviet Union's launching of the world's first artificial satellite ("Sputnik") in late 1957.[2] The corollary to these positive assumptions was Mao's growing concern that without further increments in mass mobilization and continuous progress toward social and economic equality, the Chinese revolution faced the possibility of bureaucratization and retrogression. Therefore, a Great Leap Forward in the pace of China's socialist construction in order to hasten the realization of a communist society was not only deemed possible by Mao and many of his associates, but was also considered necessary to fulfill the Party's revolutionary mandate.[3]

The imminent accession to communism only became an explicitly pronounced goal of the Great Leap Forward with the locally generated, but centrally sanctioned, movement to establish the rural people's communes in the summer of 1958. In the initial call for the Leap Forward in his speech to the Second Session of the Eighth Party Congress in May 1958 Liu Shaoqi declared that the task ahead was "to build socialism by exerting our utmost efforts" and to turn China "in the shortest possible time into a great *socialist* country with a modern industry, modern agriculture, and modern science and culture."[4] Although he expressed confidence that China would be able "to catch up and surpass Britain within 15 years or less" on the industrial front and predicted that "within a very short historical period we shall certainly leave every capitalist country in the world far behind us," nowhere in his speech did Liu characterize the Leap as an effort to bring about an immediate transition to communism.[5]

The first official suggestion that the Leap was a movement that would "open a road on which our country can smoothly pass over from socialism to communism" was contained in a July 1958 *Hongqi* article by Chen Boda on the first commune experiments.[6] The Beidaihe Resolution of August 29, 1958, not only gave formal sanction to the people's communes but also directly linked their formation with a speedy realization of a communist society. Although cautioning that "at the present stage, our task is to build socialism" and that "the primary purpose of establishing the people's communes is to accelerate the speed of socialist construction," the Resolution also stated that "the purpose of building socialism is to prepare actively for the transition to communism." In conclusion, the Central Committee proclaimed that "the attainment of communism in China is no longer a remote future event. We actively use the form of the people's commune to explore the practical road of transition to communism."[7]

In fact, the Beidaihe Resolution merely gave expression to the mood of euphoria that had been building since the formation of the first communes in the spring. *Renmin ribao*'s confident prediction was typical of the current hopes for a full-fledged communist society:

China is moving forward at the speed of space flight. Not long ago, peasants in their fifties were worried that they might not last long enough to see the good days of communism. Now even octogenarians and nonagegenarians firmly believe that they will enjoy the happiness of communism. Indeed, some old men believe that they are already living in the communist age.[8]

What had happened was that the Beidaihe Resolution and the extensive propaganda surrounding its promulgation had dramatically radicalized the mood of the times by shifting the focus of policy from spurring a Great Leap Forward in socialist construction to bringing about a Great Leap Forward into communism. This distinction between "socialist construction" and "transition to communism" as the declared objective of the Leap was more than just an ideological abstraction; it also had a profound bearing on the attitudes and work style of cadres and the content of policy.

Through the months of the "high tide" of the Great Leap, the media constantly reinforced the notion that China was embarked upon the final stages of the transition to communism. But with the appearance of serious economic problems and popular discontent in the communes toward the end of 1958, the leadership was quick to identify overzealous assumptions about the relationship between the Leap and the transition to communism as the crucial ideological source of more concrete difficulties. Although the initial attempts to deflate expectations about the advent of communism merely amounted to a slight attenuation of the timetable for arrival in utopia,[9] there was still sustained criticism in late 1958 of those who were judged to have been "over-enthusiastic to communism with over-anxious demands" and had thereby brought about "adverse results" in the movement.[10]

Even when supporting the ideals of the Great Leap Forward, the press reiterated the importance of making a clear distinction between the stages of socialism and communism so as to avoid the unrealistic pursuit of communist goals of greater equality and less hierarchy from interfering with the principal task of socialism to achieve higher levels of production. A fundamental point in the critique of ultra-Leftism in the Great Leap was to remind cadres of the historical context in which they worked. There was no effort to deny that the ultimate goal of socialist construction was to reach the stage of communism or that socialism was a transitional period between capitalism and the classless and superabundant society of the future. The criticism was aimed at those who misjudged where China was in the spectrum of socialist development and therefore did not make an adequate distinction between "a great ideal and a realistic task . . . [and] between the work of today and the work of tomorrow."[11] Although the continued call to nurture the "elements of communism" during the socialist period may have confused some cadres about where to draw the line between "rashness" and "conservatism," the message to scale down expectations concerning the speed of the transition to communism was quite clear.[12]

To counter the ultra-Left perspective on the transition question, the media put great stress on comparing the objective situation of China in the late 1950's with the necessary conditions for entering communism. For example, communism presupposed "a foundation of modern, large [scale] production" with a majority of the population engaged in the industrial and service sectors of the economy; China, in contrast, was an overwhelmingly agrarian society characterized by "poverty and backwardness." Similarly, communism presumed "extremely rich supplies of social products" to guarantee the distribution of consumer goods according to need, not labor; since China still suffered from a great paucity of "social products," distri-

bution according to labor was necessary both to motivate productivity and to allocate scarce resources. On the ideological front, any
objective analysis of China *circa* 1958–59, it was argued, revealed
that "bourgeois ideology" remained "comparatively universal"
among the population and that the Chinese people on the whole
lacked the appropriate level of "consciousness and moral character" for establishing communist social relations. Politically, counterrevolution was still seen as a possibility, thus making "the elimination of the state's internal dictatorship function"—a prerequisite
for the communist goal of the "withering away" of the state—
unthinkable.[13]

In other words, the ultra-Left view of the Great Leap Forward
was criticized for not appreciating the fact that the transition to
communism presumed a very high level of economic and ideological development; the transitional stage was not the process of attaining those ends but was rather a ripening of communist values
and institutions reflecting material abundance and advanced social
consciousness consolidated during the period of socialist construction. Pervasive poverty and remnant bourgeois (to say nothing of
feudal) ideology were not the stuff of which a communist society
was made; the task of the socialist period was gradually to eliminate such conditions and to prepare the groundwork for the transition to communism.[14]

Uninterrupted Revolution vs. Revolution by Stages

Beneath the perception of the Great Leap Forward as the beginning of the transition to communism lay certain ideological assumptions concerning the general nature of historical change
that were also criticized as being ultra-Left. First, the notion that
socialist development was primarily characterized by a process of
"uninterrupted revolution" (*buduan geming*) was presented by the
critique as a one-sided view.[15] According to the theory of "uninterrupted revolution," socialist construction (and ultimately the transition to communism) was best promoted through continuous, progressive changes in social organization and values; these changes
were, in turn, to be propelled by the consciously induced fermentation of contradictions inherent in any stage of development. Furthermore, the theory held, a revolution that did not continue to develop to ever higher stages would stagnate and regress as various
interests became entrenched and resisted further efforts at revolu-

tionary change.[16] Mao himself had embraced the idea of "uninterrupted revolution" in a speech in January 1958 that was an early statement of Great Leap ideology. "I stand for the theory of permanent revolution," he declared. "In making revolution one must strike while the iron is hot—one revolution must follow another, the revolution must continually advance."[17] A concrete example of the application of "uninterrupted revolution" in the Chinese case was the compressed sequence of change in the countryside, in which the level of socialization rose from simple mutual-aid teams to complex communes in about six years.

The ultra-Left error in the Leap's quest to bring about a rapid transition to communism, the critique said, was to have ignored the dialectical complement of "uninterrupted revolution," namely "revolution by stages." This latter formulation dictated that each stage of development must be followed by a phase of consolidation, adjustment, and relaxation. Without such a break, people would become confused and exhausted; they needed time to catch their breath and acclimate themselves to the changed situation in their daily lives. A neglect of the necessity to observe the distinct stages in the revolutionary process also had severe consequences for policy making. If too many changes were introduced in rapid succession, the leadership at all levels would not have time to evaluate the effect of those changes through the mechanisms of popular response and cadre investigation. Planning would break down and mistakes would be compounded or exacerbated rather than corrected. Carried to an extreme, "uninterrupted revolution" was a violation of the mass-line technique of leadership—a theme to which we shall return shortly.

In sum, the ultra-Left error of overemphasizing the process of "uninterrupted revolution" led to a self-defeating pace of induced change as well as to the pursuit of policies that were incompatible with China's level of development. Rather than promote the continuation of the revolution, such an error distorted the policy process and alienated the masses.

Voluntarism vs. Materialism

A second assumption concerning the nature of social change that was challenged by the critique of ultra-Leftism in the Great Leap involved the relationship between objective and subjective factors as motivating forces in historical development. The error of exaggerating the power of human will to overcome material hindrances to rapid change—the so-called error of "voluntarism"—was criticized as another important ideological source of the problems of the Leap. The voluntarist perspective declared that "man is decisive" and that "so far as a revolutionary engaged in building socialism is concerned, teeming revolutionary fervor and the creative spirit of daring to think, to speak, and to act are the most fundamental things and constitute the great motive force of the Great Leap Forward." [18]

The critique of this view frankly posited that "being materialists, we must stick to the most fundamental theory of materialist theory—that objectivity is primary and subjectivity secondary." [19] Without totally negating the role of revolutionary determination and enthusiasm, the critique clearly acknowledged the constraints imposed on human action by the material reality of a particular stage of development:

The transition from socialism to communism is a course of objective historical development not influenced by the will of the people. After we have recognized and grasped the objective laws of development, we may develop our subjective capacity to accelerate the course of historical development. We cannot change these laws at random on our own subjective whims, nor can we bypass this historical development stage and leap into communism. [20]

Thus, cadres were warned that they could not simply rely on their own "revolutionary fervor" as a barometer for determining the pace and scope of social change; their work had to remain firmly rooted in respect for objective conditions. They had to recognize that, however great the enthusiasm for communism, China's material poverty severely limited the degree to which egalitarian distribution schemes could be implemented without damaging productivity, and that there were physical limits beyond which human beings and the soil could not be pushed no matter how fervent one's desire to achieve a big leap forward in yields per acre.

Relations or Forces of Production: Which Leads?

An offshoot of the criticism of the error of voluntarism was the debate over the connections between changes in the relations of production and growth in the forces of production. The latter refers primarily to the material factors of production (including human labor, machines, tools, raw materials, and natural resources);

growth in these forces denotes increased levels of output and productivity. The relations of production include the ownership of the means of production, the organization of labor, the distribution of the products of labor, and the class structure that emerges out of all these together; changes in the relations of production, in the context of socialist revolution, have to do with achieving higher levels of social and economic equality and overcoming various patterns of hierarchy and stratification.[21] The rule of thumb of orthodox Marxism is that changes in the relations of production are ultimately determined by the development of the forces of production. Maoism modified this "materialist determinism" by suggesting that, under certain circumstances, changes in the relations of production not only could precede growth in the forces of production but could actually serve as a stimulus for such growth.

In post-Liberation practice, this theoretical innovation was manifest in Mao's view that the best way to raise production and productivity in the countryside was to move ever onward to higher levels of socialization. The Great Leap Forward became another episode in the application of this logic: a breakthrough in the level of China's economic development needed to surpass the advanced capitalist countries and to prepare the way to communism could be achieved through a massive injection of enthusiasm and hard work and by inducing profound changes in the relations of production. Thus, the "high tide" of the Leap included great emphasis on raising the level of socialization in the countryside from ownership by the collective to ownership by the "whole people" and introducing more egalitarian systems of distribution. Much of the propaganda of the times stressed how such changes in the relations of production had led to a great upsurge in productivity in all sectors of the economy and were rapidly expanding the economic base on which to complete the transition to communism.[22]

A debate over the relationship between changes in the relations of production and growth in the forces of production had occurred several years earlier, in 1955–56.[23] At that time, the question was whether the transformation of the lower-level collectives should be carried out before the extensive mechanization of agriculture (and the increased level of industrialization that that presumed). In the aftermath of the first wave of economic dislocations caused by the Great Leap, the issue was raised once again as part of the effort to refute the theoretical underpinnings of what was seen as an ultra-

Left approach to China's development. The gist of the critique was that increments of social change out of phase with the level of China's productive forces would damage the economy, not induce growth. While upholding the importance of continuing social transformations, one journal clearly stated in March 1959 the case for the primacy of the material factors of development:

> . . . the change in the relations of production is conditioned by the development of the productive forces. The relations of production, if they fall behind the development of the productive forces, will hinder the growth of the productive forces. On the other hand, if the change in the relations of production is excessively above the level of the development of the productive forces (for instance, if the collective ownership of the rural people's communes is prematurely changed to all people's ownership) it will not conform with the law that the relations of production must correspond to the growth of the productive forces. If so, these relations of production cannot be changed and, moreover, chaos will be brought about due to the violation of the law of objectivity.[24]

The problems of the Leap were seen by its critics as reflecting the fact that the relations of production were not synchronized with the level of development in the forces of production; the readjustments of the commune system and other modifications in Great Leap policies can be viewed as efforts to restore the balance between these two components of socialist construction.[25]

Summary

The critique of ultra-Leftism challenged four ideological assumptions of the Great Leap Forward: (1) that the Leap was the beginning of a transition period that would bring the imminent realization of the communist society; (2) that China in 1958–59 was materially and ideologically prepared to undertake such a transition; (3) that subjective factors of mass enthusiasm and determination could more than compensate for any remaining hindrances to the transition to communism; (4) that transformation of the relations of production could promote greater levels of economic development, thereby consolidating the material basis necessary for the transition.

Clearly, the criticism of such ideological errors was full of intangibles. After all, there was no absolute standard for determining when the proper balance had been achieved between objective and subjective factors of historical change or when the relations of production corresponded to the forces of production. Indeed, the whole notion of socialism as a transition period between capitalism and communism was itself a rather imprecise yardstick for measuring ideological orientations; it could never be objectively determined whether one's actions should be based on due respect for the legacies of the past, the imperatives of the present, or the potentialities of the future. In the midst of such ambiguity, the claim of ideological error (whether ultra-Left or Right opportunist) could easily be manipulated to trap one's political opponents. This has, of course, happened frequently in contemporary Chinese politics, but the ideological questions raised by the critique of ultra-Leftism in the Great Leap Forward were prompted by the effort to probe the origins of very serious leadership and policy errors. That the criticism of these more concrete errors was swathed in an ideological critique reflected the judgment of some party leaders that the problems of the Leap resulted from a coherent, but erroneous, strategy of development (a line) and not merely from individual mistakes and minor deviations.

Leadership and Work Style

Leadership is the key variable in the Chinese Communist political process.[26] Just as good leadership is the vital link for ensuring the smooth and effective working of the political system, so, too, is poor leadership often identified as the source of policy failure. Without effective leadership there can be neither correct policy formulation nor correct implementation. At the heart of effective leadership in Chinese politics is the "mass line," which John Lewis has described as "the basic working method by which Communist cadres seek to initiate and promote a unified relationship between themselves and the Chinese population and thus to bring about the support and active participation of the people" in the policy process.[27] The mass line, therefore, serves as a mechanism through which leaders can stay in touch with the led in order to be more sensitive to their needs and opinions; it also provides a system for giving direction and inspiration to the people with the aim of achieving revolutionary objectives as defined by the Party. Operationally, the mass line involves the progressive cycling of the stages of *perception* (of popular views and objective conditions), *summarization* (of the gathered information), *authorization* (of general policy directives by higher levels), and *implementation* (of policy at the local level).[28] "Work style" (*zuofeng*) refers to the way Party and state cadres carry out their duties and responsibilities, especially the way they relate as leaders to the masses.[29] The unique Chinese Communist organizational methods of rectification and criticism/self-criticism were devised to remedy errors in cadre work style and to ensure that Party policy would not be undermined by the deviant actions of its own troops.[30]

There was general agreement among both the critics and the advocates of the Great Leap that Left deviations in cadre work style were responsible for many of the policy problems of the Leaping Forward strategy. However, the critics saw work-style errors as manifestations of a fundamentally wrong line, the origin of which lay in serious ideological errors at the Center; the advocates viewed the leadership shortcomings of the Leap as individual aberrations, which did not vitiate the overall validity of the strategy. Nevertheless, both critics and advocates showed great concern for the gross violations of the mass line by cadres seeking to implement various aspects of the Great Leap program.

The Political Environment of the Great Leap

One Chinese source attributed the ultra-Left errors in leadership during the Leap to certain conditions that are apt to creep up at any point in time, such as complacency among cadres whose egos become inflated as a result of rapid successes in achieving some goal, the pressure of arduous responsibilities, frustration over difficulties in carrying out tasks and meeting targets, and the prestige that cadres could exploit to impose their own will on the masses.[31] However, of greater interest to our study are the several factors that contributed to creating a political environment in China in 1958–59 that proved particularly conducive to what were denounced as Leftist errors in work style by lower-level cadres.

First, the ideological tempo of the times that heralded the Leap as the beginning of the transition to communism put enormous pressure on officials to show their true political colors through concrete action toward attaining that goal. *Zhongguo qingnian* (China Youth) implored its readers (mostly Communist Youth League activists) to be "ardent supporters of the sprouts of communism" that were bursting forth everywhere: "If you are sincere in your welcome of communism you must first demonstrate yourself as an ardent supporter when sprouts of communism appear now. . . . At the present moment the sprouts of communism have been growing like mushrooms. . . . This is the most opportune time for the test of communist consciousness of every one of our youth." [32] This same article went on to admit that the Great Leap in the autumn of 1958 was "developing at too fast a tempo" for some people; but it had encouragement for China's young people: "If we, fired with enthusiasm for the support of communism, determinedly listen to the words of the Party, toe the Party line, forget our narrow interests, discard individualism and opportunism, and firmly break with outmoded concepts, *we can catch up with the times.*" [33] Such appeals, repeated *ad infinitum* in the media during the "high tide" of the Leap, clearly put a premium on activism by both idealists and careerists that could easily spill over into extremism.

The tendency toward hyperactivism induced by the positive incentive to win praise through demonstrative allegiance to the goals of the Great Leap was compounded by the desire of cadres to avoid being labeled as conservative. The fear of such negative sanctions had been deeply instilled through the anti-Rightist campaigns that followed the Hundred Flowers Movement in mid-1957 and preceded the launching of the Leap in the first half of 1958, and the same fear as a source of Leftist errors in work style was revived during the "Second Leap Forward" in 1959–60, mainly as a result of the campaign against Right opportunism in the aftermath of the Lushan Plenum. [34] The best way to avoid accusations of being tainted with bourgeois inclinations was to make sure that one's actions could not, in any way, be interpreted as hampering the Leap Forward.

Another significant ingredient in the political environment of the Great Leap was the ambiguity and inconsistency of many of the directives emanating from the Center. For instance, the Beidaihe Resolution of August 1958, which marked the official start of the nationwide communization movement, reiterated the prevalence of the principle of income distribution according to labor and the system of collective ownership during the phase of socialist construction; but it allowed for implementation of more progressive policies of distribution according to need and ownership by the "whole people" in areas where "conditions permit." [35] Mao referred to this problem of vagueness in central directives several times in his speeches at the Zhengzhou Conference in February 1959. [36] Perhaps the lack of specific instructions was meant to allow room for adapting central policy to local conditions and changing circumstances, but at the commune level, cadres were more likely to make decisions out of enthusiasm for the transition to communism rather than on the basis of what conditions demanded. There was great incentive to show that one's locality was in the forefront of the movement and that conditions there clearly did permit the implementation of more advanced policies. Positive and negative motives for activism, together with the ambiguity of the message from the Center, thus created a situation in which "Left is better than Right" became a commonplace attitude among cadres uncertain which way to lean in carrying out policy.

Three systemic arrangements employed as part of the Great Leap strategy also contributed indirectly to Leftist tendencies among local cadres.[37] First, the process of political and economic decentralization that took place in 1957–58 to provide more scope for local initiative greatly attenuated the links between policy formulation and implementation;[38] given the environmental factors described above, such decentralization meant that local implementation often was more extreme than central formulation had intended.

Second, the downward transfer of cadres from higher to lower levels—the *xiafang* movement—was intensified in preparation for the Leap.[39] In addition to the ideological remolding of bureaucrats through closer contact with the masses, the objectives of the *xiafang* system were to streamline administrative structures and to infuse basic levels with the leadership skills needed to carry out the Great Leap program. But the *xiafang* movement also contributed to the ultra-Left trend in work style since a good portion of the sent-down cadres were likely to be "natural" activists who could be expected to approach the implementation of Leap policies with brimming enthusiasm. Other sent-down cadres looked upon their transfer to the lower levels as a demotion and were eager to win the approval of higher authorities who would ultimately determine the timing of their ascent back up the ladder of authority and prestige; therefore, they would feel compelled to exert special energy in carrying out directives from above.

Third, the Leap involved an increase in the relative power in various units of *Party* cadres who were entrusted to oversee the ideological drive that was to provide the motive power for the Leap.[40] The increased influence of the acknowledged "vanguard" elements (the Reds) and a corresponding decline in the authority of the inherently more cautious managers and technicians (the Experts) proved to be fertile ground for adventurist deviations in leadership.

In sum, there were several interacting ideological and political factors operating in the years of the Leap that enhanced the likelihood of Leftist errors in lower-level leadership. The various installments of readjustment and retreat in the Great Leap included important efforts to mitigate those conditions through criticism and rectification.

Rebuffing the "Five Winds"

The most extensive criticism of leadership errors during the Great Leap Forward involved repudiation of the so-called "five winds" (*wu feng*): the "communist wind" (*gongchanfeng*), commandism (*minglingzhuyi*), blind direction of production (*xiazhihui shengchan*), exaggeration (*fukua*), and privilege seeking by cadres (*ganbu teshu*).[41] The first four "winds" were clearly criticized as Leftist deviations; "privilege seeking" was a bureaucratic malaise evidenced in such Rightist errors as obtaining special access to material benefits, nepotism, and avoidance of participation in productive labor. Criticism of the four Leftist "winds" became an especially important theme in the various phases of retreat from the Great Leap Forward.

The "communist wind." This deviation was the target of sustained criticism by Mao in his speeches at Zhengzhou in early 1959. It referred to cadres who, for ideological reasons, attempted to implement policies too advanced for China's level of development; specifically, they were guilty of utopian assumptions about the relationship between the Leap and the transition to communism. The original use of the label "communist wind" denoted leadership errors in the realm of pushing ultra-Left economic policies under the rubric of "egalitarianism"; these types of errors will be discussed at length in the policy section below. But there were several other ways in which the "communist wind" affected the work style of cadres during the Leap.

For example, the "communist wind" cropped up in the ideological work of the times. In mid-1959, *Zhongguo qingnian*, which had earlier contributed to the radicalized political environment of the Leap through strident appeals to its readers to demonstrate their enthusiasm for communism by concrete action, criticized Youth League activists for holding such "immature opinions" as demanding "the elimination of individualism within three months" among all their peers and "100 percent conversion of League members into Party members within six months." The error of these activists was summed up as follows: "They want students to make faster progress and their motive is good. But this wish of theirs is subjective and unpractical and cannot be fulfilled. Those that think that ideological progress can be made by drawing a 'dead line' and laying down 'forcible regulations' are in fact negating the complexity and difficulty of ideological education work." [42]

The "communist wind" also appeared in a negative form in the tendency of some cadres to pursue ideological purity by expanding the scope of class struggle in their search for bourgeois elements who were retarding the transition to communism. One article admonished those who "make the method of class analysis absolute" and "indiscriminately put big hats [political labels] on everything." [43] Another article cautioned cadres that they must not make too liberal a use of the derogatory label "white flag" (i.e., bourgeois element) when criticizing individuals for ideological shortcomings:

The distinction between "red" and "white" is a solemn political problem to which we should give attention. If contradictions which do not arise from the two different ways [i.e., the proletarian and the bourgeois lines] are confused with contradictions which so arise, this will confuse people's minds and will also jeopardize our work of uniting and reforming the defective persons who still uphold socialism. . . . Of course some people are backward because they are affected by bourgeois thinking. However if they are not affected too deeply and if their individualist stink is not too unbearable, we should not brand them as "white flags." [44]

Although the criteria for determining levels of "bourgeois thinking" and "individualist stink" were left rather ambiguous, the intent of such criticism was clearly to get activists to pare down their doctrinal standards of judgment and to unite more and struggle less with others in all aspects of their work.

The "communist wind" reflected a particular failure in the stages of perception and summarization of the mass line. These stages are based on sustained "investigation and research" into local conditions and public opinion by basic-level cadres (perception) and the synthesis of facts and views gathered into a report to be passed onto higher levels as an aid in policy making (summarization). Cadres criticized for fanning the "communist wind" during the Leap violated these processes by letting subjective desire to hasten the transition to communism interfere with the perception of the objective situation in their localities; this, in turn, contaminated the content of their reports to superiors and in that way distorted the information on which policy was based. This type of ultra-Left deviation in work style is an example of the operation of what we referred to in chapter 2 as the "fallacy of mass consciousness": the tendency among those with a subjective and dogmatic approach to revolution to project their own "high" level of political awareness onto the masses and to substitute this projected consciousness for concrete investigation as a basis for determining the timing and content of new policies.

Mao was indirectly indicting this tendency in the Great Leap when he defended the peasants' efforts to conceal some of their resources from cadres who "wanted to communize things at a drop of the hat."[45] Activists had to remember, the Chairman pointed out, that peasants could only be convinced gradually of the wisdom of certain advanced communal policies. The Party—at the Center as well as on the lower levels—had made a serious miscalculation in estimating mass willingness to move rapidly to a higher stage of socialization:

Before the last Zhengzhou Conference [we] talked about the peasants' consciousness being high, a great army doing battle, and the communist style. But after the autumn harvest, [the peasants began] concealing production and dividing it among themselves. . . . Where had the communist style gone? Peasants are still peasants. That's just the way peasants are, and that's the way they should be. It's not possible to institute communism all at once. . . . [The problem] is that we demand too much.[46]

The vanguard Party had made the error of formulating policy on the basis of its own preconception about how a "revolutionary" class should act rather than on an accurate perception of the ideological and material realities of the times. In summarizing the sources of extreme egalitarianism in the commune movement, one article commented that many cadres had displayed the tendency to "take trees as forests" in thinking that the masses would quickly follow the towering example of the most progressive elements among them in embracing radical distribution schemes. "The Communist attitude towards labor and . . . property is frequently observed in our society," it noted, "but the consciousness of a few advanced persons does not amount to the consciousness of the whole people."[47]

Commandism. Closely related to the "communist wind" deviation was the problem of cadres who forced people to go along with Leap policies instead of trying to overcome their reluctance by showing them how the policies would benefit them. Cadres who truly believed that the transition to communism was imminent might easily lose patience with obdurate peasants and resort to simply issuing orders without soliciting mass opinions and mobilizing support. Reliance on ideological or physical coercion rather than persuasion constituted the error of "commandism." [48]

Commandism was a deviation in the implementation stage of the mass line. Rather than patiently winning popular acceptance for a new policy, cadres often rushed ahead to carry out the program. Violating the fundamental principle of voluntary compliance by railroading peasants into joining communal mess halls was a particularly widespread manifestation of the commandist approach to policy implementation during the Leap. The consequences of commandism were summed up as follows: "We may seem to have achieved certain results in a short period of time, [but] actually the fruits so borne are not so real, and often this may lead to damage to the relations between the cadres and the masses, undermine the activism of the broad masses, so that tasks which should have been realized will not be realized." [49] Even an inherently correct policy was destined to have adverse results if carried out by commandist means that negated the democratic aspects of the mass line.

The converse leadership error of "tailism" (*weibazhuyi*), which involved abdicating the Party's vanguard role of guiding mass action and "blindly following untutored popular demands," was also present in the breakdown of the mass line. [50] In December 1958 Mao criticized himself for letting his perception of the masses' desire for a better standard of living blind him to the objective realities of setting economic goals during the "high tide" of the Leap: "As for steel production, I had once favored producing 30 million tons next year. I have also had some second thoughts . . . In the past, I thought of 100 or 120 million tons in 1960 or 1962. At that time I was only concerned with the question of demand. I was worried over the problem of who would be using this steel, but did not think of the problem of whether it is possible." [51] Although Left "tailism" of this sort may have contributed to the problems of policy formulation at the Center during the Leap, the major contradiction in leadership style at the lower levels was clearly commandist in nature.

Blind direction. Commandism in agricultural work took the form of the error of "blind direction of production" by cadres with great zeal for the Leap Forward but little knowledge of practical farming matters. For example, one Party secretary who was determined to bring about a great surge in production insisted on the rapid transplanting of rice seedlings and disregarded as "conservative ideas" the advice of peasants that only phased sowing was appropriate under conditions in that locality. When the crop failed, this cadre was criticized for his commandist style of work and for disregarding the opinions of his subordinates and the masses.[52]

A related problem was the tendency of some overeager cadres to skip the experimental period and plunge at once into implementation of Leap policies on a wide scale. Local leaders who "neglected to always experiment first and rashly applied immature experience or even rashly popularized far and wide" policies that were untested were roundly criticized.[53] This error affected a broad range of policies in the communes, but it particularly applied to the incautious dissemination of new agricultural techniques that were expected to boost production quickly. The attitude that careful experimentation was a conservative approach to leadership apparently became rather prevalent in the radicalized political environment of the Great Leap. This view was explicitly refuted as part of the criticism of cadres who were alleged to have blindly led production. One article commented in June 1959:

There are people who think that the method of always experimenting first is not in conformity with the unfolding of large-scale mass movements and that because mass movements have to advance with the force of a torrent there is no room for meticulous experiments. . . . The things that must be popularized with the force of a torrent are the things which have been proven to be correct by the practice of the masses.[54]

Such statements reaffirmed a well-established work-style tradition of the Party that the popularization of a new course of action must proceed only after the culling of results from "typical experiments" had proved its validity in local conditions and its acceptability among the masses.

Another glaring example of the lack of experimentation and blind direction was the mass campaign to produce iron and steel. The backyard blast furnaces that were set up to meet the grossly unrealistic targets of the campaign proliferated throughout the countryside without due regard for objective conditions or possibilities. In this ill-planned, too hasty campaign, local resources were depleted, labor was misused, metal utensils were unnecessarily confiscated for smelting, and the steel that was produced was brittle and nearly useless.[55]

Blind direction and the failure to experiment also short-circuited the implementation phase of the mass line. Both deviations were said to have contributed significantly to the severe economic dislocations incurred during the Great Leap Forward.

Exaggeration. The "wind of exaggeration" took two forms during the Great Leap: gross inflation in the setting of production targets and false reporting of output allegedly achieved. Exaggeration became a rather widespread tendency among cadres at various levels for several reasons. Honest idealists might simply have been carried away with the ideological tempo of the Leap and really believed that the ambitious targets for production could be achieved by a mobilization of mass energy and enthusiasm. Others exaggerated targets and output as a way of impressing the higher levels with their full commitment to the Leap Forward and, sometimes, to make certain, in the vituperative anti-Rightist milieu, that they would not be accused of being conservatives. The idealist viewpoint was more indicative of a "pure" Left error in work style than the cynical and selfish motives of cadres who sought credit or shunned censure; yet the objective result of both was to stir up the "wind of exaggeration," which compounded the overall ultra-Left trend of the times.

Some of those who pushed for high targets apparently believed sincerely that increased quotas could in themselves serve as a stimulus for production, for they emphasized "the great active role played by high targets" and chided other cadres for being "satisfied with riding on an ass rather than a fleeting steed" in setting output goals for their units.[56] While cautioning against the promulgation of truly "inaccessible" targets, these optimists were confident that ambitious objectives could boost production by liberating both the communist consciousness and the physical energies of the masses.

The critics of this "theory" claimed that if targets were set too high, workers would become frustrated by their inability to reach the expected goals; or even if they could sometimes meet them, they would eventually become exhausted by having to work at a constantly high pitch and by being forced to forgo needed periods of rest in order to reach the targets.[57] High targets not only impaired the enthusiasm and energy of the people but also led to a neglect of quality in the pursuit of quantity and to inadequate maintenance of equipment in the quest for speed.[58]

Those who advocated the setting of consistently high targets were also reprimanded for overemphasizing the degree to which human action could surmount the limitation imposed by material reality. "How high or low targets should be set," one article remarked in mid-1959, "does not depend primarily on the subjective wish of man, but on objective possibilities."[59] Those who committed the error of exaggeration did not take sufficient account of the physical capacity of people, machines, and the environment to reach the high targets; they also deviated to the Left by neglecting material incentives and assuming that workers and peasants would exert themselves to the utmost and bear the increased workload merely out of love of communism. Reminding Party cadres that "setting plan targets is different from formulating political slogans," *Zhongguo qingnian* stressed that organizing production must, above all, be practical: "Political slogans only put forth the targets to be attained [in the distant future] . . . and impose no strict requirements in respect to time. Plan targets are different in that they impose strict requirements in respect to quantity, quality, cost as well as time within which the work is to be accomplished."[60]

The tendency of lower levels to exaggerate actual production figures (or, conversely, to hide poor results) was at least partly induced by the radical political environment of the Leap. Such exaggeration greatly impeded the vital communications function of the mass line by undermining the reliability of the information on which the higher levels depended for making effective decisions. The inaccurate data, in turn, distorted the summarization and authorization phases of the mass line since policy was predicated on faulty information from below; the enhanced expectations of the Center then resulted in increased pressure on lower levels to make yet another leap forward in production. Thus, the "wind of exaggeration" that became a serious leadership problem in the 1958–60 period fed a vicious cycle of malfunction in the mass line as it related to production.

Departmentalism

Another error in leadership that should be briefly noted was that of "departmentalism" (*benweizhuyi*). This was apparent in cadres who concentrated too much on maximizing the interests of their own localities and neglected the interests of the nation as a whole. This error is not, by nature, a manifestation of ultra-Leftism. In the early years of the People's Republic, for example, the problem was common in areas that were resisting integration into the newly unified political system.[61] At other times, it simply denotes resistance to central directives or the tendency of bureaucrats "to make their particular departments a little world of their own.[62] However, in the case of the Great Leap Forward, departmentalism was a direct offshoot of the deliberate policy of maximizing local initiative for development through extensive political and economic decentralization. This deviation fits into the context of this study because it was criticized for exacerbating Leftist tendencies in such policies as the commune movement and the campaign for the mass production of steel.

In February 1959 the policy of treating the nation as "one coordinated chessboard" was put forth in order to counter some of the trends toward excessive decentralization that had become pronounced during the "high tide" of the Leap.[63] Centralized leadership and local-level management must be coordinated; if they were not, it was warned, the result would be anarchy in planning and production. Mass enthusiasm and initiative were precious resources and must not be squelched, one authoritative article commented. However, it went on:

There are two sorts of enthusiasm. One conforms to the general line for building socialism, the sort of enthusiasm to run the whole country in the manner of a coordinated game. . . . The other sort of enthusiasm is to detach oneself from the general line for building socialism in violation of the principle of running the whole country in the manner of a coordinated game and to have regard for minor points to the disregard of the general situation. This sort of enthusiasm is in the nature of a blind action.[64]

This criticism was aimed as much at certain central planners who put "unrealistic" faith in local initiative as at lower-level cadres who had gone to extremes in interpreting the general policy of decentralization.

"Absolutists with Good Intentions"

Cadres alleged to be guilty of Leftist deviations in work style were said to be prone to "absolutism" (i.e., dogmatism) in their incomplete understanding of complex situations; they were criticized for being poor dialecticians when it came to dealing with the many contradictions inherent in socialist development.[65] This line of criticism always emphasized the error of thinking that revolutionary commitment could only be displayed by bold action; on the contrary, good leadership combined decisiveness and daring with sober analysis and a scientific attitude. As one commentator put it in June 1959, "To be bold in speaking and acting without being practical is to say silly things and do silly things and is as dangerous as a blind man riding a blind horse down a deep valley late in the night."[66] As a corrective to the subjective and dogmatic thinking that affected work style, cadres were reminded time and again of Mao's adage "to seek truth from facts"; they were urged to remember that correct action could only be based on concrete social investigation, not on preconceived notions of what was right or wrong for the revolution.[67]

However, the reprobation of cadres deemed to have committed Leftist errors in work style during the Great Leap Forward was almost always tempered by references to their sincere motives. The caveat in Mao's comment concerning the excesses of the early commune drive—"[If] we have taken a little too much, then we should make it clear that it was [done with] the *good intention* of building socialism"[68]—was frequently repeated in reference to lesser mortals who had also contributed to stirring up the "five winds."[69]

The connection between Left errors and good motives was carried a step further in the aftermath of the Lushan Plenum. The media not only shifted the focus of attention to the "frantic attack" by the Right opportunists as the major source of problems in the Leap, but also went to great lengths to refute the imputation of the critics of the movement that the Party's general line for socialist construction had fallen victim to a severe case of "petty-bourgeois fanaticism." During the "Second Leap Forward," a sharp distinction was made between such "fanaticism" and "revolutionary zeal." Some of the problems of the Leap were, it was admitted, due to the fact that "revolutionary zeal" had sometimes become divorced from "scientific analysis"; however, even then, such zeal reflected "the important power which several hundred million people are wielding in the construction of a new society" and had absolutely nothing in common with the much more reprehensible sin of "petty-bourgeois fanaticism."[70]

· In sum, the various ultra-Left work-style errors that were criticized during the Great Leap Forward had the combined effect of severely compromising all stages in the operation of the mass line. Because of the critical role of leadership in the policy process, such malfunctions would naturally have a detrimental impact on the concrete program of socialist construction. When the mass line broke down in the midst of a mobilization campaign with bold and innovative objectives like the Great Leap Forward, the consequences for policy were disastrous.

The Policy Dimension

The Origins of Policy Errors: Divergent Perspectives

In times when the Party leadership is relatively unified, the flow from formulation to implementation of central decisions moves smoothly, but when problems arise that cause serious malfunctions in the policy process, perceptions within the leadership as to the source (and hence the severity) of those problems often diverge sharply.

Some leaders may believe that the general line is correct and that the source of error is to be found in specific policies designed to achieve the objectives established by the line. Lower-level cadres are not to blame for policy errors since they have merely sought to execute faithfully the program sent down from above. Solutions to problems will be focused on policy adjustment and replacement; neither the line nor individual cadres will be subjected to rectification or criticism.

A second approach to policy malfunction would not only regard the line as correct but would also uphold the specific policies associated with that line as basically sound. This analysis would focus on ideological and work-style errors of *individual* leaders at the basic level as the source of policy problems. Rectification and criticism would be aimed principally at these individuals; if they change their behavior, policies can be salvaged and implemented as intended to realize the goals embodied in the line.

But some leaders might decide that the source of policy problems was in the formulation of the original line at the Center itself—that is, mistakes in work style and implementation on the lower levels are intertwined with, indeed caused by, a deviant line based on faulty ideological assumptions within the central leadership; similarly, erroneous policies are seen as the result of an erroneous line. In other words, this view of policy malfunction is *line*-focused, and the only effective remedy is an abandonment or pervasive modification of the misguided line.

For example, were the problems encountered in the process of establishing the rural people's communes in mid-1958 the result of wrongheaded notions concerning the nature of socialist development and the transition to communism that led to the promulgation of a thoroughly deviant (i.e., ultra-Left) line? Peng Dehuai, in his comments at the Lushan Plenum that the communes had been set up "too early," seemed to imply such a judgment on the wisdom of the basic line of the Great Leap Forward.[71] Or were only specific policies linked with the formation of the communes (e.g., the egalitarian modes of distribution, the mess halls, the backyard steel furnaces) mistaken while the commune movement as a whole was correct? Or were the problems of communization merely the result of leadership failures at the lower levels? Mao and other staunch supporters of the Leap tended toward these latter two views in their overall assessment of the strategy of Leaping Forward. Such divergent perspectives on the source of policy problems were at the heart of the political struggle within the Party during the Leap. The supporters of the Leap rejected a direct linkage between policy or work-style rectification and line criticism (i.e., a comprehensive critique of ultra-Leftism) precisely because they sought to prevent an attack on the fundamental values that had motivated the Leap in the first place.

The point here is that value conflict within a revolutionary leadership is manifest not only in contrasting development schemes or priorities but also in the divergence of opinion concerning the origins of policy errors and the scope of the perceived need for rectification and criticism. And, as the case of the Great Leap Forward shows, policy adjustment—no matter how far-reaching—can only be a temporary palliative to such value conflict since it leaves the most profound points of discord unresolved.

Nevertheless, the various efforts to readjust the specific components of the Great Leap program between 1958 and 1961 do offer an important perspective on the problem of ultra-Leftism in China's socialist development. In elaborating the content of these readjustments, the distinction will be made between policies that were rectified without criticism and policies in which rectification was linked to some measure of critical analysis. We shall look first at certain concrete aspects of the Leap that were dealt with by the method we have called an incomplete critique of ultra-Leftism and then move to policy issues that were subjected to a more comprehensive critique.

Specific Policy Issues: Incomplete Critique

Several of the most notable policies of the Great Leap simply "faded away" in the course of the retreat. For example, the rural mess halls, the urban communes, and the backyard steel furnaces all were abandoned without any effort to analyze or criticize the causes of their failure.[72] Yet the critics of the Leap would certainly have considered these experiments to be the reflection of an ultra-Left line since they represented an effort to realize communist ideals too soon and flew in the face of the objective constraints of the times. Similarly, the adjustment of the geographical size and functional scope of the rural communes in 1961–62 involved a tacit acknowledgment of serious Left errors in policy, although the origins of these problems were not explicitly criticized as such. The question of the appropriate scale of the people's communes can serve as an interesting example of a policy problem that went through a process of incomplete critique.

One of the most commonly acknowledged errors of the communization movement was the enormous size of the newly established political and economic units in the Chinese countryside.[73] The Beidaihe Resolution of August 1958 had offered rather ambiguous guidelines for determining the appropriate scale of the communes in their first incarnation. Although the Resolution proclaimed that "it is at present better to establish one commune to a township [*xiang*] with the commune comprising about two thousand peasant households," ample leeway was left for local variations. In sparsely populated areas, there might be several communes per *xiang*, the Resolution noted. In some regions, "several townships may merge and form a single commune comprising about six or seven thousand households, according to topological conditions and the needs for the development of production. As to the establishment of communes of more than 10,000 or even more than 20,000 households, we need not oppose them, but for the moment we should not take the initiative to encourage them."[74]

In practice, most local planners leaned toward the middle range of size alternatives. By the time the whole countryside had been communized and after the first round of readjustment in early

1959, the average commune was a multi-*xiang* creation comprising over 5,000 households.[75] This huge design overtaxed the administrative skills of the rural cadres charged with managing the new units; it also ran into the stone wall of village localism, which offered potent resistance against efforts to move various political and economic functions to a higher, more "progressive" level of decision making within the commune structure.[76]

One of the principal components of the 1961–62 retreat from the Leap was a great reduction in the size of the people's communes. The original 24,000 communes were subdivided into 74,000 units (averaging 1,600 households) with the result that the adjusted commune was generally equivalent to the old township.[77] Furthermore, most of the important production and distribution functions that had initially been vested in the commune authorities were delegated to the production team (a level equivalent to the former *lower*-level agricultural producers' cooperatives). In other words, the rural commune in 1962 was a mere shadow of the 1958 model, which had been heralded as an important vehicle for the transition to communism.[78]

The counterproductive scale of the original communes can be seen as the result of Left errors from several perspectives. First, it could be considered the product of leadership errors at the lower levels responsible for designing the structure of the communes in their particular locales. After all, the Beidaihe Resolution had stipulated (albeit with some ambiguity) a general size for the communes; therefore, local cadres had simply been carried away and were guilty of executing a central policy to an extreme without careful planning or experimentation.

If that assumption is correct, however, why was this Left deviation in work style not rectified sooner? The fact is that the prevailing powers at the Center did not recognize the large communes as a deviation; on the contrary, size was taken as an indication of progress in the Great Leap Forward, and the spontaneous generation of such all-encompassing units of rural life was perceived as a reflection of mass enthusiasm and preparedness for the transition to communism.

Second, the size of the communes could be analyzed as an offshoot of the radicalized political environment of the Great Leap. Local cadres were under the double pressure of having to prove their revolutionary stripe through zealous implementation of central directives and having to avoid the stigma of conservatism that might attach to caution or questioning. Sheer size therefore became a mark of success, and smallness was equivalent to the Rightist error of lagging behind the mass movement.[79] In this perspective, deviations in policy implementation were a direct result of a Leftist ideological error at the Center concerning the nature of the transition to communism and the attendant political pressures that were felt at the lower levels.

Finally, the size of the people's communes might have been part of a conscious attempt by both central and local planners to undermine the geographic bases of peasant particularism in order to hasten the revolutionary transformation of the countryside.[80] The new units would reorient and enlarge the world view that had for centuries limited rural life and provide the context for the inculcation of values more compatible with the goals of modernization and communism. If this was the intent of letting the communes leap over traditional marketing and socio-political structures, then a Left error could be ascribed to those leaders who believed that induced changes in the relations of production could break through the objective reality of village localism prior to a more profound ideological and material transformation of peasant life.

The above attributions of ultra-Left policy errors are entirely by inference. The process by which the communes were allowed to develop to a counterproductive size was never subjected to rigorous criticism. The principal document relating to the retreat from the Leap Forward in the countryside stipulated in great detail the adjusted communal structure designed to rectify the "high tide" model; but neither that document nor the propaganda surrounding its implementation in 1962 contained even the barest analysis of the line that had produced such problems in the first place.[81]

Specific Policy Issues: Comprehensive Critique

Despite general avoidance of broad examination of basic issues, there were some policy areas where a more or less comprehensive critique of ultra-Leftism did unfold during the Great Leap Forward. The most protracted critique of this nature concerned the problem of income distribution in a socialist society. Although the criticism of Leftist errors in distribution policy was most intense in the first half of 1959 (pre-Lushan), the problem of egalitarianism (*ping-junzhuyi*) remained a fairly constant theme throughout the various phases of leaping and retreating. Issues relating to distribution are also singled out here because they became an important part of the post-Mao critique of the line of Lin Biao and the Gang of Four and therefore illustrate the continuity of issues in the critique of ultra-Leftism in Chinese politics.

Chinese Communist ideology and its Marxist-Leninist antecedents have consistently been critical of tendencies within the revolutionary movement toward "absolute egalitarianism."[82] This term refers to efforts to eliminate all sources of material inequality (such as income differentials according to labor, skill, or status) and to divide the wealth of society on a straightforward per capita basis according to need; furthermore, such egalitarianism seeks the eradication of virtually all vestiges of private property and private economic activity. These objectives are seen as reflecting a utopian vision of socialism and are said to confuse the ending of inequality based on exploitation with a crude kind of leveling that is actually harmful to the material life of the people. Despite such longstanding ideological strictures against absolute egalitarianism, the "high tide" of the Great Leap brought forth pronounced tendencies in that direction which quickly became the focus of leadership concern.

The emphasis on the Leap as the beginning of the transition to communism created ideological pressure on cadres to implement policies to accelerate the advent of the new era. Therefore, nurturing "sprouts of communism" became a major priority of leadership work in the communes.[83] Among the "sprouts" most energetically cultivated were various egalitarian distribution schemes designed to destroy all manifestations of economic stratification and to speed the implementation of the communist credo, "From each according to his ability, to each according to his needs!"[84] There were three forms of egalitarianism in the people's communes: in the allocation of resources among the various levels (commune/brigade/team); in the income differentials permitted among units on the same level (mostly the teams); and in the distribution of material resources to individual peasant households. We shall consider the critique of each of these manifestations of egalitarianism in turn.

Appropriation without compensation. Allocation among levels in the commune structure became the subject of criticism when the higher authorities appropriated resources from below without adequate compensation. The tendency to move in this direction was induced by a combination of factors: the concentration of significant power at a newly created level of authority (the commune) charged with major tasks in capital construction but without a material base of its own; the designation of the brigade as the level of owner-ship of such assets as land, livestock, and fruit trees, and as the unit of accounting; and the spread of the notion that the team (i.e., the made-over traditional village) was a moribund unit of rural life not compatible with the transition to communism. These factors led to a "sucking up" of resources from the team, a process that could be rationalized as working in the interests of the larger collec-tive; this rationalization, in turn, obviated the need for compensat-ing the team for its appropriated resources. After all, team members were not really "losing" their resources but, in true communist fashion fitting the times, merely sharing them more equitably with the broader community; furthermore, they would continue to benefit, at least to some degree, from the use of those resources through their participation in the newly defined collective entity, the commune.

A similar trend appeared in the assignment of labor. Higher levels requisitioned manpower from the team to carry out various capital construction projects (irrigation, land reclamation, road building, etc.) without due consideration for the loss of income this would mean for individual households. The criticism and rectification of the problem of uncompensated transfer of resources and labor power between levels involved correcting erroneous notions about the nature of ownership in the people's communes.[85] Two interre-lated issues were at stake. The first was a reaffirmation that collec-tive ownership rather than ownership by the "whole people" was the primary form of control of the means of production in the rural economy. This meant that the allocation of resources derived from production (as well as chief responsibility for production planning) was to be retained by the unit that actually worked the land. Own-ership by the "whole people" (a euphemism for state control) meant, on the other hand, that all the fruits of production were subject to more centralized allocation as part of the state plan.[86]

One Left trend of the "high tide" of the Leap Forward was the extension of this latter, more "advanced" form of ownership from the industrial sector (where it had been in a dominant position since the mid-1950's) to agriculture. From the Wuhan Resolution (De-cember 1958) on, substantive attention was given to explaining why rural China was not yet prepared to adopt a system of ownership by the "whole people."[87] Materially, the production of the teams was not developed enough beyond subsistence to allow for more centralized capital accumulation without harming the living standards of most of the peasants; nor was the income profile of different teams and brigades equitable enough to permit more unified distribution by the commune without lowering the income levels of the better-off units. Ideologically, ownership by the "whole people" was said to violate objective conditions in the countryside because the vast majority of peasants did not yet trust such an abstract collectivity to satisfy their interests. This observation was a concession to the obvious unwillingness of peasants to cooperate with villages they had little personal contact with or that were traditional rivals.[88] As one article put it, those cadres who had sought to introduce ownership by the "whole people" in the communes "see the outstanding aspect of the new-born things, such as the growth in communist cooperation. However, they underrate or completely fail to see the transitional nature of ownership in the people's communes."[89]

The second aspect of the critique of uncompensated transfer concerned the issue of determining which level in the commune structure owned which resources and therefore had authority for their use and allocation. The resolution of this problem passed through successive stages, the first of which saw the brigade affirmed as the unit of ownership and distribution (functions that had been concentrated at the commune level during the "high tide"). By 1962, these powers had devolved to the team, as even the brigade turned out to be an unworkable level of collectivity on which to base economic life in the countryside.[90]

Leveling. Another manifestation of egalitarianism in relationships between economic units was the practice of redistributing resources among the teams or brigades in order to achieve a more equitable (or, in extreme cases, fully equal) standard of living throughout the commune. Such "leveling" was accomplished through centralizing accounting at a level higher than production so that all units were given equal consideration in the distribution process without regard to differences in natural endowments (e.g., better land), level of development, or amount of effort and available labor power.[91] Although such practices were initially seen as part of the Great Leap toward communism where need would outweigh labor as a determinant of resource distribution, they were eventually criticized for utopian assumptions concerning the relationship between individual productivity and material incentives during the socialist transition. The result of such utopianism was to encourage laziness rather than self-reliance in poorer units while drastically undermining enthusiasm for production in better-off teams and brigades.[92]

Both the equalization and transfer forms of egalitarianism were important themes in Mao's remarks at the Zhengzhou Conference concerning problems in the Great Leap. He likened such policies, which were theoretically intended to bring the peasants closer to the era of communism, to a situation in which "the pond is being drained in order to catch the fish."[93] The Chairman described the "communist wind" as "robbery in broad daylight," which expropriated the peasants' property without compensation as if they were landlords and capitalists.[94] In this context, he passionately defended the "particularism" of peasants who concealed part of their production in order to circumvent its appropriation by commune authorities. "It's very dangerous to want only communism and not particularism," Mao remarked. "We want communism and we also want particularism—to want communism alone just won't work. The peasants' concealing of production is excusable."[95] He cautioned commune cadres that any transfer of resources or labor power had to be done in accordance with the "law of exchange at equal value" in which the material interests of the lower levels and individual households were fully protected. Combining his penchants for piscine and scatological metaphors, the Chairman hammered home the objective reality of his view of the "law of value": "There isn't a thing in the world that doesn't involve exchanges; even man's struggle with the world involves exchange. For example, man eats and breathes, but he has to defecate and urinate and carry on the process of metabolism. . . . [This] is also exchange at equal value. Big fish eat small fish, small fish eat the big fish's shit."[96] Obviously, any attempt to negate such a fundamental law of nature when it came to distribution policy in the communes was a reflection of serious Left subjectivist thinking.

Micro-level egalitarianism: the supply system controversy. The micro-level manifestation of egalitarianism appeared when the newly formed communes moved quickly to institute a scheme of distribution in which grain and other daily necessities (such as cooking oil, firewood, and cotton cloth) were allocated to members at least partly on the basis of need rather than according to labor performed. This took the form of the "supply system," which varied by locality as to the percentage of income in kind to be received purely on a per capita basis.

The idea of the supply system seems to have sprung from the initiative of local cadres caught between feverish excitement over the transition to communism and the ambiguity of central directives.[97] The Beidaihe Resolution did not mention any form of supply system and recommended that there should be no precipitous alteration of the existing piecework arrangement in which distribution shares were figured according to a task-scaled rate multiplied by the total number of days (or hours) worked. However, the Resolution did mention that "Where conditions permit, the shift to a wage system may be made."[98] The agricultural wage system—in which peasants were guaranteed a set income not dependent on individual or collective output—was considered more progressive than the old workday system, mainly because it was less dependent on gross material incentives to labor and supposedly allowed less opportunity for competition between laborers. In addition, it was seen as an important step in bridging the gap between city and countryside—one of the essential preconditions for the transition to communism— since the trend toward a wage system was already gradually supplanting piece-rate compensation in industrial enterprises.

The shift from a workday to a wage system in the agricultural sector would have been a momentous change in itself. The rural wage system, in fact, proved unworkable on account of the weak material base of the Chinese countryside and was abandoned in the early 1960's. But once transforming the income distribution system became a goal of the Great Leap, the radicalized political environment led to an escalation in modes of distribution even beyond the agricultural wage system. The rush of communes to establish a supply system only "proved" more than ever the mass acceptance of communist values of distribution according to need and voluntary labor. This process was given a big push when one journal reported Mao's observation during an inspection tour in Anhui province in the fall of 1958: "Since one commune can put into practice the principle of rice without pay, clothing can also be had without pay in the future."[99]

By late 1958, the notion that the supply system should constitute the "basic portion" of distribution had become the rule rather than the exception in rural communes. Thus, most communes were apportioning peasant income by a ratio of 55 percent free supply to 45 percent according to labor-related criteria (in some combination of wages and workdays).[100] Although warnings were issued that a 100 percent supply system was still some way off, the general thrust of the "high tide" was to move steadily toward a purer communist system of distribution. As one article put it, "following the development of production and the elevation of ideological consciousness, the amount of supply should be gradually expanded. . . . Correspondingly, wages distributed according to labor should be reduced."[101]

Despite claims to the contrary by proponents of an extensive supply system, this "sprout of communism" had a disincentive effect on productivity similar to that caused by leveling. Another frequent problem was that many peasants rushed to take advantage of the communal cornucopia and literally ate themselves sick, engaged in hoarding, or invited relatives from areas with a less generous distribution system to partake of their bounty.[102]

The Wuhan Resolution, though it supported the use of a partial supply system, did make some attempt to reverse the trend toward micro-level egalitarianism:

. . . any negation of the principle of "to each according to his work" will tend to dampen the working enthusiasm of the people and is therefore disadvantageous to the development of production and the increase of social products, and hence to speeding the realization of communism. For this reason, in the income of commune members, the portion constituting the wage paid according to work done must occupy an important place over a long period and will, during a certain period, take first place. . . . In order to encourage the working enthusiasm of the people . . . the communes must strive gradually to increase the wages of their members, and for a number of years to come, must increase them at a rate faster than that portion of their income which comes under the heading of free supply.[103]

The Resolution also described attempts to realize a system of distribution based on need as "premature" and warned that "any attempt to enter communism by over-reaching ourselves when conditions are not mature is undoubtedly a utopian concept that cannot possibly succeed."[104]

The Wuhan Resolution was followed in early 1959 by a concerted campaign in the media to refute the purported link between egalitarianism and communism and reassert the legitimacy of material incentives in socialist society.[105] In language very similar to that used in the post-Mao critique of ultra-Leftism, the case was made that showing deep concern for the material interests of the masses was one of the most important tasks of socialist politics; forcing a false dichotomy between politics and economics was, it was claimed, a prime manifestation of Left adventurism.[106] Under the pressure of policy directives that accompanied this propaganda barrage, the supply system portion of rural distribution was gradually reduced throughout the subsequent phases of the retreat from the Leap Forward. By 1961–62, a revamped workday system similar to that which had prevailed prior to communization had become the dominant mode of rural distribution.[107]

The early stages of the Great Leap also involved speeding up the process of replacing piece-rate systems in the industrial sector with hourly or monthly wages.[108] However, there were those who felt that this progression from one form of distribution according to labor to another was not compatible with the accelerating transition to communism; thus, they urged the quick implementation of some type of urban free supply system. Acknowledging that some highly paid skilled workers might suffer a loss of income under a more egalitarian scheme of distribution, *Renmin ribao* claimed that almost all workers were so committed to the goal of reaching communism that they "will not . . . lose their labor enthusiasm just because of a little reduction in wages. On the contrary, they voluntarily do away with irrational high pay on the one hand and intensify production on the other."[109]

The critical response to this trend attacked the implicit assumption that people's "enthusiasm for communism" could be stimulated by reducing their standard of living. In fact, it was argued, just the opposite was true: the transition to communism was dependent on a growing abundance of social products that would provide a better material life for all; otherwise, people would be alienated from the revolution because they would come to associate communist ideals with being poor.[110]

The most virulent debate of this period was over the question of income distribution to cadres, especially those in the Party. We discussed in chapter 3 the political dynamics of this ideological debate, which centered around the October 1958 reprint in *Renmin ribao* of the article on "bourgeois right" by Zhang Chunqiao. This article was an all-out attack on the post-1949 wage system that had replaced the life of "military communism" and the free supply system in the pre-Liberation base areas. All types of wage systems, Zhang declared, were a bourgeois means of stimulating labor enthusiasm, which assumed that "socialism and communism can be bought like a piece of candy"; the old supply system had brought out the best in the Chinese people:

When the supply system was in force, millions upon millions of people fought an armed struggle for several decades, climbed snow-clad mountains, passing through grasslands, and undertook the 25,000 *li* Long March. Who ever received wages at that time? Can it be said that the victory in the anti-Japanese war, the liberation war, and the Resist-America, Aid-Korea war was won through the stimulation of wages? Each communist-minded person feels an insult when hearing such arguments.[111]

The basic point of Zhang's case for the supply system was that remnants of "bourgeois right" had to be constantly and consistently eradicated if socialist society were to continue its progress toward the ultimate goal of communism; concessions to wage systems—especially within the ranks of the Party—were a retrogression tantamount to revisionism.[112] Thus, positive support for a "sprout of communism" was combined with highly charged negative aspersions on the ideological complexion of anyone who dared question the sagacity of implementing a supply system at that stage of China's development.

The debate sparked by Zhang's article elicited substantial support for his stand on the issue of distribution in socialist society.[113] But many critical rejoinders also appeared in the press. For instance, Zhang was taken to task for not considering the vast differences between the demands of the present situation and those of the revolutionary war period. His critics argued that the gradual abolition of the supply system had not been "a result of attack by certain persons" or "the impact of bourgeois ideas." Rather, it had come about because of changing situations "under which the . . . supply system adapted to wartime could no longer fully meet the needs of the time."[114] For example, the task of administering production in the cities as well as in the countryside and the vast increase in bureaucrats, technicians, and managers needed after Liberation (including the need to "take over the working personnel of the old state system") necessitated the replacement of a free supply system based on conditions of grave scarcity and geared to highly committed revolutionary cadres. Only a less radical system of distribution could be counted upon to enlist the support required by the new regime. Any desire to hold to a notion that there was an inherent relationship between retention of the supply system and the building of socialism in China was deemed to be a mark of "petty-bourgeois egalitarianism." [115]

There was also substantial reaction to what was called Zhang's one-sided view of the proper role of "bourgeois right" during the period of socialist construction. One article proclaimed: "The Profitable Use of Surviving Bourgeois Right Is a Proletarian Right"— that is, when it is used to promote economic development for the benefit of society as a whole. [116] The inequality that resulted from the use of material incentives to stimulate labor enthusiasm was a remnant "bourgeois right" that had to be tolerated for the time being; the elimination of bourgeois right was contingent upon achieving a certain level of material and ideological development, not on subjective desire or political fiat. Issuing "an administrative order . . . to simply eliminate surviving bourgeois right . . . may seem revolutionary," one critic insisted, "but actually it is disadvantageous to the proletariat and is a hindrance to revolution." Distribution according to labor, on the other hand, "actually . . . is the most revolutionary principle . . . because it fits in with the social, political and economic conditions prevailing at the present stage and serves to combat economic exploitation, tighten up labor discipline, and stimulate one's labor enthusiasm." [117]

The seemingly abstract debate on the role of bourgeois right in socialist society did have an important impact on policy during the Great Leap Forward, not so much in this controversy over the supply system, which first raised the question, but in the subsequent development of programs that affected the scope of private economic activity in the rural areas. The policies concerning private plots, sideline domestic production, and rural free trade markets closely paralleled the pattern of leaping and retreating we have described in other issue areas. [118]

The ambiguity of the Beidaihe Resolution on the question of private economic activity once again led local cadres to communize the small portion of land that had previously been set aside for use by individual households and to proscribe the raising of pigs and other barnyard animals for consumption or sale by families. Cadres did this under the dual impetus of restricting "bourgeois right" in order to prevent the restoration of capitalism in the countryside and

of taking a big step toward a more completely communitarian society. In August 1959, emphasizing the point, a government order
shut down the traditional markets at which peasants sold or bartered some of the fruits of their private labor. The rationale for this
move was that commodity exchange of this sort was incompatible
with the surge toward communism both in its corrosive effects on
individual ideology and in its diversion of resources from allocation
for the collective good.

Within a short time, the economic consequences of these efforts
became abundantly clear. Peasants had responded by resistance
(such as slaughtering their pigs rather than allowing the commune
to take them over); the most productive sector of the rural economy
(in terms of the ratio between the percentage of land in private use
and the percentage of total output) had been undermined; and the
circulation of necessary commodities throughout the countryside
and to the cities broke down, creating grave imbalances. Through
1959 this trend was denounced as part of the "communist wind"
that had swept the rural areas in the "high tide" of the Great
Leap. At the same time, the positive role of the private sector was
lauded.[119]

The various versions of the regulations guiding the restructuring
of the communes in 1961–62 stipulated quite clearly that peasants
had the right to engage in and profit from private economic activity.[120] But the issue of an overly restrictive policy toward private
plots, sideline production, and the rural free market—and the correlative question of the scope of "bourgeois right" in socialist society—would emerge once again and become a major point in the
critiques of ultra-Leftism that grew out of the Cultural Revolution.

Conclusion

The economic and social problems of 1958–61 were so obvious
that there was common agreement in the Party leadership that the
Great Leap Forward had taken a disastrous turn to the Left. The
specific criticism and rectification of ultra-Left errors in ideology,
leadership, and policy that have been discussed in this chapter were
not themselves the source of dissension within the Party. Rather,
the most important differences arose over the question of what had
caused the Leap to lose its momentum. Was the Leap thrown off
course by *sui generis* Left errors by individual leaders at both the

Center and on the local levels? Or was the Great Leap, in itself, the product of an erroneous political line derived from totally fallacious assumptions about the nature of China's socialist development?

Mao's growing dissatisfaction with the direction taken by efforts to recover from the debacle of the Great Leap set the stage for the Cultural Revolution.[121] The future of China was also profoundly shaped by a divergence within the Party over the lessons to be learned from the experience of Leaping Forward. In essence, this divergence showed that there was an ultimately irreconcilable disagreement over the fundamental values of the Chinese revolution. This conflict would dominate politics in the People's Republic for the next two decades.

5
From Ultra-Left to Ultra-Right:
The Campaign against the
"Swindlers like Liu Shaoqi"

> When false Marxist swindlers pursue a revisionist, oppor-
> tunist line above, the evil wind of anarchism will go on
> the rampage and become a disaster below. Anarchism
> gains expression below, but its roots are high above.
>
> *Renmin ribao* (1972)

The decade between the collapse of the Great Leap Forward in
1961–62 and the death of Lin Biao, Chairman Mao's one-time
chosen "successor," in 1971 was one of the most momentous in the
history of the People's Republic of China. During this period, the
political conflicts and ideological antagonisms that had been brewing within the leadership of the Chinese Communist Party since
the mid-1950's erupted violently and new schisms appeared that
rocked China's whole political system. We can only highlight a few
of the features of this eventful decade that seem most relevant to the
central purpose of this study and provide helpful background for
understanding the case study that follows.

The early 1960's was a time when the attention of the Chinese
Communist Party was concentrated on undoing the damage
wrought by the Great Leap Forward and the "Three Hard Years" of
natural disasters that coincided with the retreat from the Leap.
Maurice Meisner, drawing on Crane Brinton's classic analysis of
the month in 1794 when Robespierre and the other radicals of the
French Revolution were overthrown by more moderate forces, has
characterized this period in China as one of "Thermidorean Reaction." [1] In the Chinese "Thermidor," power passed to those in the
Party "who were less interested in social change than in social stability, political order, and economic efficiency." [2] Consequently, bureaucratic and technocratic authority was emphasized and a host of
incentivist policies were introduced in agriculture and industry. [3]

Such measures did much to restore both order and productivity and to set China firmly on a course of more pragmatic economic development, but they also generated perceptible trends toward increasing socio-economic inequality and political hierarchy. These trends alarmed Mao and revived his fears of the possibility of a "bourgeois restoration" in China. The result of Mao's disquietude was, of course, his attack on the "capitalist roaders" in the Party, which culminated in the Great Proletarian Cultural Revolution.

In essence, the radical thrust in Chinese politics had been parried, but not disarmed, in the aftermath of the Great Leap Forward. Its resurgence in the form of the Cultural Revolution was not unrelated to the fact that the ultra-Leftist line of the Leap had never been subjected to a comprehensive critique even when its specific policies were discredited and its most vehement advocates politically neutralized. We can fairly say that although the critics of the ultra-Left held the balance of power in the early 1960's, they were not able or willing to use their position to scrutinize ultra-Leftism as a deviant ideology that posed a fundamental threat to socialist construction in China. The relative facility with which Mao was able to launch the Cultural Revolution can only be understood against the backdrop of the incomplete critique of the Great Leap Forward as described in the previous two chapters.

The Cultural Revolution was an enormously complex event that does not lend itself to easy generalizations. Nevertheless, Mao's actions in the movement revolved around three interrelated motives: to counter the trends toward bureaucratization and inequality through a mass assault on those in the Party he perceived as "taking the capitalist road" and on bourgeois ideology in general; to provide a transformative experience for China's youth who he felt needed to be shaken from the complacency of their relatively easy post-Liberation upbringing before they could truly become a worthy generation of "revolutionary successors"; and to engage in a power struggle with the Party cohort who had taken his self-imposed retreat from active policy making too seriously and had baldly ignored the Chairman's counsel.[4] From this mixture of motives emerged Mao's determination to rally a hodgepodge alliance of students, soldiers, disenchanted workers, and Party ideologues to join together in rebellion against the institutions and policies of the "Thermidor."

Of the many consequences of the Cultural Revolution, the one that most concerns us here and provides the bridge to the focus of this chapter was the rise of Lin Biao as a predominant figure in China's political system. Lin, a veteran military commander with a long and glorious record of service to the revolution, had succeeded Peng Dehuai as Defense Minister following the Lushan Plenum in 1959.[5] Through the early 1960's, he consolidated his control of the People's Liberation Army and became identified as one of Mao's chief political associates and ideological protégés. When the army emerged as a major component of the Maoist alliance in the Cultural Revolution, its commander, Marshal Lin, rode the radical tide of the movement to the pinnacles of power to become First Vice-Chairman of the Chinese Communist Party; in 1969 the Party constitution officially designated Lin as Mao's "close comrade-in-arms and successor." He eventually came into conflict with Mao over a variety of domestic and foreign policy issues, the most important of which was his reluctance to preside over a withdrawal of the army from active involvement in political affairs and to comply with the effort to rebuild the Communist Party as the center of power in the post-Cultural Revolution order.[6] This conflict escalated throughout much of 1970–71 and allegedly culminated in an attempt by Lin to mastermind the assassination of the Chairman as a prelude to a seizure of power. The authorized version of the case holds that Lin and his co-conspirators fled China by plane after their plotting was exposed and perished in a fiery crash on the steppes of Outer Mongolia on September 13, 1971.[7]

Lin's demise was followed by an extended period of official silence concerning his fate, all the more noticeable because of his obvious absence from the public scene and the omission of any reference to his person in the media. Gradually, however, the deposed "successor" came to be the indirect target of an extensive criticism campaign that provided a vehicle for a critique of ultra-Leftism aimed at the excesses of the Cultural Revolution. This critique and the political struggle that ensued from it are the subject of this chapter.

We are concerned here with the initial phase of the campaign to criticize Lin Biao. Chronologically, this phase begins with Lin's death in September 1971; it ends with the convening of the Tenth National Congress of the Communist Party of China in August 1973 and the start of the campaign to criticize Lin Biao and Confucius (*Pi Lin, Pi Kong*) shortly thereafter. This case focuses on the period when the critique of an "ultra-Left thought trend" (*jizuo sichao*) was a key part of the campaign against Lin Biao; it also describes the metamorphosis of the official interpretation of Lin's erroneous line from a denunciation of ultra-Leftism to a criticism of ultra-Rightism, a change that was induced by intense political struggle within the Party leadership over the proper evaluation of the Cultural Revolution. This metamorphosis was partly demarcated by a shift from criticizing Lin Biao indirectly under the rubric "Swindlers like Liu Shaoqi" to the open attack on the "Lin Biao clique" that began with Zhou Enlai's Political Report to the Tenth Party Congress. It should be noted, however, that this demarcation is not precise: the change from critiquing Lin's errors as ultra-Leftist in nature to portraying him as an ultra-Rightist was first set in motion within the framework of the campaign against the "Swindlers like Liu Shaoqi."[8]

Lin Biao *as an individual* is not the focal point of our discussion, though some inferences as to the nature of his political line will be drawn. No attempt will be made here to prove whether Lin Biao was, in fact, an ultra-Leftist, as claimed in the initial phase of the campaign against the "Swindlers" in 1971–72 and again in the post-Mao criticism of Lin and the Gang of Four, or whether his line was ultra-Rightist in nature, which was the dominant interpretation between 1973 and 1976. What is important here is that a critique of an ultra-Left trend in Chinese political life during the Cultural Revolution was linked with the criticism of Lin Biao following his "defeat" in the 1971 political showdown with Mao Zedong and that this critique was aborted in the process as the result of factional struggle at the highest levels of Party leadership.

The Campaign against the "Swindlers like Liu Shaoqi"

The first wave of criticism of Lin Biao that broke the official silence surrounding the fall of Chairman Mao's "close comrade-in-arms and successor" was tied into a campaign against unnamed "Swindlers of the Liu Shaoqi type" that had been featured in the Chinese media for several months prior to Lin's disappearance. The use of the term "Swindlers of the Liu Shaoqi type" (or "Swindlers like Liu Shaoqi") first appeared attached to a February 1971 *Hongqi* article in a "Brief Comment" (*duan ping*) calling for vigilance against "Wang Ming– and Liu Shaoqi–type sham Marxist political swindlers" (*Wang Ming, Liu Shaoqi yileide jiamakesizhuyide zhengzhipianzi*). In retrospect, it is clear that this formulation was aimed at Chen Boda, who had come under fire at the Second Plenum of the Ninth Central Committee held at Lushan in August and September of 1970.[9]

Chen Boda had been a close ideological and political ally of Mao Zedong since the days of the revolutionary struggle against the Guomindang.[10] Although Chen had played important roles in the formulation of major post-Liberation policy initiatives such as the collectivization of 1956–57 and the commune movement of 1958, he was catapulted to the heights of power in the turmoil of the mid-1960's when he became the editor of *Hongqi*, the Party theoretical journal, and co-chairman (with Jiang Qing) of the powerful Cultural Revolution Group, as well as one of only five members of the Standing Committee of the Politburo. His influence and political stature began to decline in 1969 as Mao sought to deescalate the tempo of the Cultural Revolution and start the process of reconstructing the Party. Lin Biao and Chen, who had been closely linked in propelling the Cultural Revolution, joined together to resist these efforts at consolidation and the corresponding increase in the power of Premier Zhou Enlai. The conflict between Lin and Chen, on the one hand, and Mao and Zhou, on the other, began at the Ninth Party Congress in April 1969 and burst out in the open at the Second Plenum of the Congress in mid-1970.[11]

Lin, Chen, and their allies among top-ranking army leaders directly challenged Mao and Zhou on several key issues at this plenum; when the challenge was rebuffed, Chen became the principal target of criticism not only for his sectarian activities within the Party but also as bearing major responsibility for the excesses of the Cultural Revolution. He was criticized for a variety of errors, including association with the "May 16 Group," which had been purged in 1967–68 for their ultra-Leftist assault on the Foreign Ministry, Zhou Enlai, and veteran army officers. Chen was also censured for his cynical manipulation of the cult of personality surrounding Mao and for his support of Lin's dogged attempts to reinstate the position of State Chairman (vacant since Liu Shaoqi's ouster) in China's constitution as a counterweight to Zhou's growing authority.[12] Chen abruptly dropped out of the political scene following this censure, and by early 1971 inner-Party criticism of him had expanded into a public media campaign of condemnation; however, Chen was not mentioned by name in this campaign and was attacked indirectly under the rubric "Swindlers like Liu Shaoqi." Mao later indicated that the criticism of Chen had been intended, in part, as a warning to Lin to cease his resistance to the shifts in the Party line on the Cultural Revolution.[13]

The campaign against the "Swindlers" reflected a contradictory assortment of charges concerning the nature and impact of Chen Boda's errors.[14] By inference, Chen was accused of ultra-Left errors such as advocating egalitarianism in rural policy and violating the socialist principle of distribution according to labor and of fomenting anarchy in industrial enterprises by negating the necessity for rational rules and regulations for enforcing worker discipline.[15] At the same time, the "Swindlers" also were criticized for a number of deviations that clearly fell more into the category of Rightist deviations, such as advocating "the dying out of class struggle" (*jieji douzheng ximielun*) and the "theory of productive forces" (*weishengchan lilun*), which allegedly neglected revolutionary social change in favor of economic development.[16] The anti-Rightist orientation of the criticism campaign was most clearly symbolized by linking the errors of the "Swindlers" with the name of Liu Shaoqi, the principal victim of the Cultural Revolution who had been depicted as "the number one Party person in authority taking the capitalist road." Thus, the criticism of Chen Boda in the period February–August 1971 displayed an ambiguity in the definition of the essence of his errors—a pattern that was to continue even after Lin Biao came to be included among those being attacked as "Swindlers like Liu Shaoqi." This ambiguity suggests that the political struggle over the critique of ultra-Leftism, which became a major issue within the Party leadership after Lin's death, had already been set in motion by late 1970 and early 1971. It also illustrates the difficulty that the Party had in disentangling itself from the obsessive concern with revisionism that had dominated the propaganda mill since the start of the Cultural Revolution.

Despite this ambiguity, the campaign against Chen Boda did have a definite anti-Leftist thread that reflected the effort to criticize and rectify the excesses of the Cultural Revolution. The formulation, "Wang Ming– and Liu Shaoqi–type sham Marxist political swindlers" made this implicit by evoking the name of Wang Ming, the archetypical "Left opportunist" in the pantheon of villains in early Party history. Other events also point to the fact that the criticism of Chen Boda was part of a larger assault on what was perceived by some as an ultra-Left trend. For example, in March 1971 Kuai Dafu, one of the most militant Red Guard leaders, was subjected to mass criticism at Qinghua University for his role in inciting violent confrontations on the campus in the early phase of the Cultural Revolution. Such violence was considered to be a reflection of the anarchism that resulted from the ultra-Left line spread by the "Swindlers." [17]

In the immediate aftermath of Lin Biao's attempted coup and death in September 1971, the criticism of the ultra-Left errors of the "Swindlers" intensified noticeably. Though for some months it was not apparent that the target of attack had been expanded to include Mao's one-time chosen successor, it seems clear in retrospect that Lin was lumped together with Chen Boda in the reporting of the latest line struggle within the Party and that the dominant character of his incorrect line was interpreted as ultra-Leftist. In other words, the vacillation that had been characteristic of the earlier phases of the campaign against the "Swindlers" stabilized in the direction of concentrating on the exposure and denunciation of their Leftist deviations. For example, the ghost of Wang Ming was again conjured up, [18] and a variety of issues was discussed in the media to illustrate the damage caused by "interference from the Left." There was sharp denunciation of the "ultra-Left thought trend" in such areas as the lack of labor discipline in industry and the entrenched resistance to the reassignment of veteran cadres purged during the Cultural Revolution. [19]

Traces of the vacillation over how to define the crimes of the "Swindlers" remained, however, so that even when ultra-Leftism was the clear target of the criticism, some attention was still given to the link between Left and Right deviations within the single counterrevolutionary line of all "Swindlers like Liu Shaoqi." This compression of different types of political errors into one wrong ideological line took the form of discussions of how and why the "Swindlers" had changed their tactics from "interference from the Right" to "interference from the Left" in their unrelenting efforts to sabotage socialism and undermine Chairman Mao's revolutionary line. "Swindlers like Liu Shaoqi" in socialist society, it was claimed, combined an "unchanging class nature" (bourgeois) with "ever-changing tactics" (sometimes Rightist, sometimes ultra-Leftist). [20] The implication of this combined Left/Right critique of the "Swindlers" was that the latest manifestation of the line struggle within the Party had been, at least tactically, ultra-Leftist. Because their

Rightist tactics had been exposed and discredited by the Cultural Revolution, the "Swindlers" had been forced to switch to the use of ultra-Left *means* as a camouflage for their goal of capitalist restoration in China. For instance, in regard to the role of science and technology during the socialist transition, Liu Shaoqi was said to have originally peddled such Rightist ideas as "technique first" and "the dictatorship of the technical authorities." When the Cultural Revolution unmasked and repudiated the fallacy of that line, the "Swindlers like Liu Shaoqi" (Chen Boda and Lin Biao) were said to have pushed the ultra-Left view that "technology is useless" in making revolution. Their purpose was alleged to have been "to frighten the proletariat into giving up [their] positions in science and technology" so the bourgeoisie could once again seize control.[21]

As an example of how class enemies changed their tactics in pursuit of their counterrevolutionary objectives, *Renmin ribao* related in some detail the history of the struggle of Yutian county in Hebei province against the local followers of the "Swindlers" all the way back to the Great Leap Forward.[22] The county made good progress in the Great Leap, it was claimed, until "Liu Shaoqi and his agents" pushed an ultra-Left line in policy toward pig raising (the county's main pursuit) by "shifting all pigs kept by commune members individually to collective raising," resulting in gross mismanagement leading to great economic loss. In the early 1960's, the "Swindlers" (again Liu) used the cover of the "Three Hard Years" to attack from the Right by pushing a policy under which collective pig farms were closed and all pigs allocated to individual households. Again, the result was great loss. When this policy was criticized during the Cultural Revolution, the collective economy was revitalized. However, people fell into complacency by the late 1960's and some "capitalist" practices began creeping up. In response, the "Swindlers" (this time Chen and Lin) were able to stir up an ultra-Left trend and pushed the county leadership once again to proscribe private pig breeding by raising the specter of revisionism. Again, the number of pigs dropped drastically, to the point where the fallacy of the ultra-Left line in pig raising was unmasked by the harm it caused to the material basis of socialism in the countryside and the income of individual peasant families. The local "Swindlers" were repudiated (in 1971) and a more balanced policy that supported both collective and private pig raising in proper dialectical relationship was implemented.

Despite the combination of charges of both Left and Right interference against the "Swindlers," the major thrust of the criticism and rectification at this time was clearly aimed at ultra-Leftism. This was reflected in the greater space and detail given to the exposure and criticism of Left errors in the media. There was also a clear implication that an ultra-Left trend was the most recent and immediate problem in Chinese political life in the aftermath of the first phases of the Cultural Revolution.

In late 1971, there was a backlash in the media by those within the Party leadership who wanted to deflate the growing critique of ultra-Leftism. For example, one attack on the line of the "Swindlers" in industrial development charged them with the Rightist sin of "replacing politics with technique": "Such a theory linking technological development with the realization of communism . . . is typical partisan, imperialist, revisionist, and reactionary talk. . . . To realize communism, the only road lies in persistent class struggle, persistent adherence to the proletarian dictatorship, and persistent continuous revolution under the proletarian dictatorship."[23]

Other counterattacks seeking to divert the criticism of ultra-Leftism accused the "Swindlers" of promoting such Rightist ideas as "students were more intelligent and adroit" than workers and peasants and pushing the "theory of productive forces," which denied the decisive role of social relations and the superstructure in socialist development.[24]

However, by early 1972, the balance in the struggle over the direction of the "Swindlers" campaign had shifted decisively toward those within the leadership who were in favor of vigorously pursuing the critique of the "ultra-Left thought trend." From January through mid-1972, a major offensive against ultra-Leftism was also carried on in the form of the beginnings of significant policy readjustments that were meant to undo the damage of the extreme Left line that had emerged out of the Cultural Revolution. Some of the most important of these early policy shifts were in the areas of industrial and agricultural affairs, especially with regard to management and distribution policies.[25] A series of national conferences on planning, public security, and science were held between the end of 1971 and the autumn of 1972 in which the "criticism of anarchism and the ultra-Left trend became an important issue."[26] In sum, a reaction against the ultra-Left trend did gain enough momentum in the first half of 1972 to be viewed as the dominant theme of both official criticism and concrete policy actions; thus, by mid-1972 a relatively comprehensive critique of ultra-Leftism aimed at the excesses of the Cultural Revolution was clearly unfolding.

The Struggle over the Critique

In the summer of 1972, there was a perceptible diminution of the public critique of ultra-Leftism in the media—whatever else might have been going on at national conferences or in policy-making circles. In August Zhou Enlai gave a speech chiding the staffs of *Renmin ribao* and other central propaganda organs for being lax in their exposure of problems related to the ultra-Left trend of recent years. Supposedly, Zhang Chunqiao and Yao Wenyuan then instructed the staff of *Renmin ribao* "not to be excessive" (*buyao guotou*) in their criticism of ultra-Leftism.[27] Apparently Zhou won this early round of the tug-of-war with the radicals, since the national media did show a brief upsurge in the criticism of ultra-Leftism—especially in agricultural policy—throughout the month.[28] The result of all this maneuvering was a complicated series of trends and countertrends in August and September 1972 as one group within the Party leadership pushed for a deepening of the critique of ultra-Leftism while another group sought to divert it.

The first group—which we may call the "Veteran Revolutionaries" because it consisted mostly of very senior cadres whose careers had been launched during the earlier days of the revolution—was headed by Zhou Enlai. This group had come to feel that an ultra-Left trend was the most serious problem in Chinese political life in the early 1970's and had to be thoroughly exposed, repudiated, and rectified. Of course, part of their reaction against what they labeled the ultra-Left trend lay in the fact that many of them had been victimized in the Cultural Revolution as Rightists; therefore a critique of ultra-Leftism also coincided with their newly reconstituted power base within the leadership following the demise of Lin Biao.

The second group—which we may call the "Cultural Revolutionaries" because it was made up mostly of younger cadres whose careers had blossomed during the Great Proletarian Cultural Revolution—had every reason to resist the growing criticism of the trends of recent years because it was a threat to both their core values (ideology) and their political position (power). This group was led by those who later came to be labeled the "Gang of Four"—though at this time (1972–73) the principal actors were Jiang Qing, Zhang Chunqiao, and Yao Wenyuan; Wang Hongwen was still operating in the wings during this phase of the struggle and did not really take his place on center stage until mid-1973.

In September 1972 numerous articles and broadcasts emanating mostly from the provincial media reflected an effort to direct the campaign against the "Swindlers" toward a revival of the anti-Rightist themes of "criticism of revisionism and rectification of work style" with a simultaneous downplaying of explicitly Leftist errors. This criticism of the "Swindlers' counterrevolutionary line" focused on their political ambitions and plots to usurp Party and state power.[29] The scant attention that was given to the ultra-Left errors of the "Swindlers" was limited to criticism of tactics, like "waving the red flag to defeat the red flag," that is, using radical slogans and programs cynically to undermine socialism. Several commentators stated emphatically that the "main orientation" of the criticism of the "Swindlers" had to be aimed at their revisionist objectives and, by implication, not at their ultra-Left tactics.[30] At this time, the theme of emphasizing the "Swindlers'" line as representing the interests of the landlord and capitalist classes also appeared.[31] This media effort to link the "Swindlers" with a decidedly Rightist position in the public mind was consistent with Central Committee documents on the Lin Biao case circulated as early as June 1972. For example, Central Committee Document No. 24 (1972) stressed Lin's attempted power seizure and plot to assassinate Mao and concluded: "The counterrevolutionary Lin Biao anti-Party clique is the proxy of the landlords, bourgeoisie, imperialists, revisionists, and reactionaries which have been overthrown in our Party."[32] Although this line of counterattack was itself blunted by another emphatic offensive against ultra-Leftism in late 1972, these themes anticipated the nature of the ultimately successful effort by the Cultural Revolutionaries to derail the critique of ultra-Leftism in 1973.

Apparently acting on the firm instructions of Zhou Enlai, who was displeased with this shift in emphasis in the criticism of the "Swindlers," *Renmin ribao* printed a series of major articles on the theme of anarchy and ultra-Leftism in the issue of October 14, 1972.[33] The lead article was entitled "Anarchism Is a Counterrevolutionary Tool of the False Marxist Swindlers." Citing heavily from Engels' essay "On Authority," the article attacked the "Swindlers" for sabotaging the major tasks and institutions of socialist construction by stirring up an anarchist trend among the masses:

During the Great Proletarian Cultural Revolution, Swindlers of the Liu Shaoqi type cunningly exploiting the dissatisfaction of the masses with the Right opportunist line, vigorously encouraged an ultra-"Leftist" thought trend which would have only democracy, but not centralism, only freedom, but not discipline. They declared that "the word of the masses is final" and "regulations and systems are useless," and loudly called for "smashing everything." Their purpose in so doing was to lead the struggle-criticism-transformation of the Great Cultural Revolution astray, utterly sabotage socialist labor discipline, wreck socialist production, and shake the economic base of the dictatorship of the proletariat at the foundation.[34]

Although this article dealt with the subject of ultra-Leftism more outspokenly than almost any previous criticism of the "Swindlers," it still analyzed ultra-Leftism as a tactical problem, rather than as a problem symptomatic of the persistence of an erroneous line within the Party, as in the case of the critique of revisionism:

The tactics of the Swindlers of the Liu Shaoqi type, when stripped of their mask, are to cover up their Rightist counterrevolutionary essence with the form of ultra-"Leftism." Verbally, they "utter the most Leftist, most revolutionary statements" to deceive others, but in reality they carry out downright rascally sedition; i.e., they carry out agitation by making use of the base instincts of man and the desire of small property owners to make a quick profit. By shouting such counterrevolutionary seditious slogans as "suspect everything" and "strike down everything" their purpose is to subvert the dictatorship of the proletariat.[35]

The second article in *Renmin ribao* was called "Firmly Uphold the Iron Discipline of the Proletariat—Some Understanding from a Reading of [Lenin's] 'Left-Wing Infantilism in the Communist Movement.'" This article stressed ways in which the teachings of Lenin could be of help "to further strengthen our regard for proletarian discipline, criticize the ultra-'Left' thought trend of anarchism spread by Swindlers of the Liu Shaoqi type, and more voluntarily implement Chairman Mao's revolutionary line."[36]

The third article was a synopsis of a pamphlet on Bakunin—"the father of anarchism"—prepared by the history department at Nanjing University. The article suggested that there was great contemporary relevance for understanding the "false Marxist swindlers" in studying Bakunin's writings and Marx's and Engels' responses to the anarchist movement in nineteenth-century Europe.

Following this series of articles, there was another noticeable spate of criticism of ultra-Leftist trends and anarchism in the official media. Particular emphasis was placed on rectifying ultra-Left tendencies in rural distribution,[37] the utilization of managers and technicians in industrial enterprises,[38] and education and intellectual policy.[39] For example, in late October, a symposium on education was held in Hunan specifically to criticize the ultra-Left tendency to put professional education work and politics in opposition to one another. The report on the proceedings of the symposium stressed the importance of classroom instruction in addition to practical work experience and political education and urged the restoration of "necessary rules and regulations" in schools, noting that instituting a revolutionary student-teacher relationship was not a license for anarchy in the classroom. The symposium cautioned its participants to be on guard against interference in educational work from both Right and Left, but "*in particular* the interference from extreme 'Left' ideas spread by Swindlers like Liu Shaoqi."[40]

According to a 1978 account, Jiang Qing, Zhang Chunqiao, and Yao Wenyuan were outraged by the revived onslaught against ultra-Leftism signified by the articles in the October 14 edition of *Renmin ribao*.[41] They allegedly masterminded a repudiation of the articles as "poisonous weeds" in the pages of *Wenhui Situation*, the internal staff organ of the Shanghai newspaper *Wenhui bao*.[42] Two numbers (November 4 and 24) of *Wenhui Situation* were specifically aimed at deflecting the mounting critique of ultra-Leftism. At the same time, relying largely on a "close ally" who held a top position at *Renmin ribao*, the Gang supposedly carried out "a campaign of suppression" at the newspaper in the last two months of 1972, after which "anarchism and the ultra-Left trend of thought once again became taboo for criticism."[43] The radicals' machinations at *Renmin ribao* spread into a generalized effort to "bludgeon people who mentioned opposing the 'Left'" and to "set the limits and tone of criticism" of Lin Biao by prohibiting any reference to Leftist deviations such as "voluntarism" and the theory that "politics can push everything aside."[44]

The Critique Aborted

The advent of 1973 saw the beginnings of the final phase in the year-long struggle over how to analyze and label the deviations of

Lin Biao *cum* "Swindlers like Liu Shaoqi." The December 1972 issue of *Hongqi* set the tone for the reformulation of the criticism of
the "Swindlers" that became dominant in the first few months of
the new year and signaled the beginning of the end of the critique of
ultra-Leftism. The *Hongqi* article was entitled "It Is Necessary to
Support and Develop Revolutionary New Things." The "Swindlers," the article declared, "have consistently been *ultra-Right* and
. . . the 'Left' phrases they uttered have been merely used to cover up
their Right essence. Even though they appeared as ultra-'Left' and
ultra-Right alternately, they did not depart from their aim; this is to
conspire to counter Chairman Mao's Marxist-Leninist line and to
push a revisionist line for the restoration of capitalism."[45] The article went on to a ringing advocacy of the Cultural Revolution reforms in education, hailing such innovations as "worker, peasant,
soldier students" and "open-door schooling"[46]—innovations that
had come under increasing attack during the critique of ultra-
Leftism in October and November.

The joint New Year's 1973 editorial of *Renmin ribao*, *Jeifangjun
bao*, and *Hongqi* frankly charged that the line of the "Swindlers"
was "a counterrevolutionary revisionist line": "In the new year, we
must continue to grasp firmly and well the task of prime importance—criticism of revisionism and rectification of the style of
work. In doing this, criticism of revisionism comes first and only
then rectification of work style."[47] Nothing was said about ultra-
Leftism or anarchism, which had been such conspicuous targets of
criticism in the preceding months. The implication of the editorial
was clearly that whatever problems might exist that could be labeled ultra-Leftist were no more than signs of overexuberance in
the implementation of correct policies (i.e., poor work style); the
main target of criticism should continue to be the problem that had
generated the need for the Cultural Revolution in the first place: revisionism from the Right.

During the first few months of 1973, the national and especially
the provincial media carried on a gradually escalating campaign to
promote the New Year's "directive" on the criticism of revisionism
and rectification of work style.[48] Not only did this media blitz portray the line of the "Swindlers" as ultra-Rightist, it also went to
great lengths to rebuff those who wished to continue criticism of
the ultra-Left trend. For instance, one provincial broadcast candidly
inquired: "What is the nature of the revisionist line of Swindlers

like Liu Shaoqi? *Some people say that it is ultra-Leftist. This is wrong.* The line of Swindlers like Liu Shaoqi is a counterrevolutionary revisionist line. It is ultra-Rightist."[49] Other articles and broadcasts suggested that continuing to criticize ultra-Leftism would facilitate the counterrevolutionary plots of the "Swindlers" and warned that the Party and the people must "prevent the emergence of an erroneous trend of diverting the main orientation of the struggle" away from the criticism of revisionism.[50] For example, the Party Committee of the Hunan Rubber Works criticized itself for being misled in just such a fashion:

At one time in the campaign to criticize revisionism and rectify the style of work, certain comrades in this work neglected to make a deep analysis of the nature and aim of the revisionist line of Swindlers like Liu Shaoqi, criticizing in isolation the fallacies spread by them in the economic sphere. They did not link criticism of the attempts of Swindlers like Liu Shaoqi to sabotage economic construction with all their crimes and political aims. As a result, they one-sidedly held that the reflection in the economic field of the revisionist line of Swindlers like Liu Shaoqi was ultra-Leftist. In this way, they could not carry out accurate and deep criticism in connection with reality, could not grasp the essence, and could not hit the vulnerable points.[51]

It will be recalled that one way of highlighting the ultra-Left content of the "Swindlers'" line was to link them with Wang Ming, the archetype of Left opportunism in Party history. Not only had all references to Wang Ming ceased by this time, but in early 1973, the switch to a clear designation of the "Swindlers'" essence as ultra-Rightist was reinforced by comparing them with such infamous Right opportunists as Chen Duxiu and Peng Dehuai.[52] One article went a step further by linking the "Swindlers" with Soviet revisionism: "We must realize that Swindlers like Liu Shaoqi and the renegades Kautsky and Khrushchev are jackals of the same lair, out and out revisionists, and renegades of the proletariat."[53]

Since the ultra-Left trend had been such a prime target of criticism in the earlier phases of the campaign against the "Swindlers," it could not be dropped inconspicuously. Various efforts were made to explain away the problem of ultra-Leftism as a matter of secondary concern. First, there was renewed emphasis on the old theme that ultra-Leftism had been purely a tactical ploy used by the "Swindlers" to confuse the vigilant masses and obscure the true Rightist nature of their line. The people were reminded to draw a clear distinction between main currents and secondary currents and were told that the "Swindlers'" ultra-Leftism was "the phenomenon, not the essence, the method, not the aim." [54]

A second effort to defuse the criticism of ultra-Leftism was the categorization of anarchistic and extremist tendencies at the lower levels as manifestations of less serious errors among the people in contrast to the outright counterrevolutionary aims of the "Swindlers." For example, one provincial newspaper acknowledged that the "Swindlers" had stirred up certain ultra-Left trends among the masses in order to create the necessary chaos for seizing power. It then went on to comment:

Ultra-Leftist things must be repudiated, the shortcomings and mistakes of the masses under the influence of nonproletarian ideology must be overcome. However, we must not confuse shortcomings and mistakes among the people with the revisionist line of Swindlers like Liu Shaoqi, nor substitute repudiation of the ultra-Left trend of thought for repudiation of the revisionist line of Swindlers like Liu Shaoqi. [55]

The implication of such statements was clear: ultra-Leftism should be treated as a reflection of nonantagonistic contradictions among the people, whereas the revisionist line of the "Swindlers" was an antagonistic contradiction between the people and their sworn enemy, the bourgeoisie. To focus criticism and rectification on the secondary trend of ultra-Leftism would only serve the interests of the bourgeoisie by distracting attention from exposing the counterrevolutionary objectives of the "Swindlers" in the Party.

A third maneuver was literally to turn earlier charges against the "Swindlers" on their head. In the effort to expose the "Swindlers'" Rightist essence, key ultra-Left errors formerly attributed to them were reinterpreted in such a way as to emphasize a Rightist aspect. For example, the anarchist slogan "Overthrow everything!," which had become popular in the Red Guard movement, was said to have implicitly meant overthrowing the *socialist* state and the dictatorship of the *proletariat* rather than a blanket renunciation of all authority. Similarly, "Politics can squeeze out everything else," which was alleged to have been the point of view held by the "Swindlers," was now seen to have implied that *bourgeois* politics should prevail in China. Finally, the "Swindlers" were acknowledged to have violated the proper dialectical unity between politics and production as charged in the critique of ultra-Leftism. But rather than having overemphasized politics to the detriment of production, as formerly charged, the accusation now was that they had advocated the old Liuist heresy of the "theory of the productive forces," which stressed the priority of economic growth over revolutionary social change in socialist development and thereby negated the imperative to keep proletarian politics in command in all policy matters.[56]

An attempt was also made at this time to obfuscate the critique of ultra-Leftism by mounting a strong defense of programs that had been the hallmark of the Cultural Revolution but were now under increasing attack in the campaign against the "Swindlers" as manifestations of the "ultra-Left thought trend." One broadcast declared, "To firmly grasp the struggle orientation for criticism of revisionism and rectification of the style of work, it is also necessary to fully recognize the fruits of the Great Proletarian Cultural Revolution."[57] The message here was not only to reaffirm the correctness of various radical policies but also to give more credence to the ultra-Rightist nature of the "Swindlers" by associating them with a betrayal of the Cultural Revolution.[58]

One of the principal arenas in which the struggle between the critique of ultra-Leftism and the defense of the Cultural Revolution became most intense was education. This struggle reached its height in mid-1973 with the appearance of the case of Zhang Tiesheng. Zhang had sat for the newly reinstituted university admission exams but had had very little time to prepare for them because he had been working in the countryside as a "sent-down" student. Therefore he handed in an almost blank exam paper on the back of which, it was said, he wrote a searing indictment of the examination system as a betrayal of the essence of the Cultural Revolution in education. Zhang was held up by the media as a model of a truly revolutionary student, and in the next few months became both a symbol and spokesman for the defense of the "fruits" of the Cultural Revolution.[59]

The case of Zhang Tiesheng was part of a larger offensive in 1973 against those who sought to correct what they perceived to be ultra-Left errors in education policy. An article by the "Education Revolution Group" at Fudan University in Shanghai—a school with close ties with the radicals—castigated "some comrades" who mistakenly analyzed the "Swindlers'" ultra-Right line in education as ultra-Left. The article charged that the "Swindlers" had "attempted to reverse the verdict on the revisionist education line they carried out for seventeen years before the Cultural Revolution," specifically by trying to undo innovative measures like the system of using political recommendations rather than examinations as the basis of university admissions. [60] Jürgen Domes has summarized the importance of this struggle as follows: "Here it is no longer a matter of factual debate over educational matters, but the beginning of a new and fundamental debate on the future internal political development of the People's Republic of China." [61] It is perhaps somewhat more accurate to portray the debate over education at this time as a manifestation of the contention between the Cultural Revolutionaries and the Veteran Revolutionaries that had been going on for some years, rather than the *beginning* of a *new* and fundamental debate. In a strict sense, it also proved to be much more than just a "debate"; it was, in fact, symptomatic of a life-and-death political struggle in the highest echelons of the Party.

The criticism of the "Swindlers'" line as ultra-Rightist in the first half of 1973 was noticeably unspecific. It dwelled almost exclusively on abstract attributes of the "Swindlers'" alleged revisionism. Even when a report emanated from a particular unit describing how the cadres and masses there finally came to realize the "Swindlers'" revisionist essence, very few details of the ultra-Right influence in that unit were given. In the same way, when these reports mentioned the ultra-Left tactics employed by the "Swindlers" to further their counterrevolutionary scheming, the discussion was usually limited to generalities such as the "Swindlers'" advocacy of the idea that "theory is useless" in education. [62] In other words, the metamorphosis of the "Swindlers'" erroneous line into a continuation of the struggle against revisionism that began in the Cultural Revolution appears a bit artificial and labored and stands in marked contrast to the much more concrete criticisms of the ultra-Left trend and anarchism made in 1971–72.

The Tenth Party Congress in August 1973 and the campaign to criticize Lin Biao and Confucius that began shortly thereafter formally signaled the total eclipse of the open critique of ultra-Leftism as an arena of struggle between the Veteran Revolutionaries and the Cultural Revolutionaries. Although both Lin Biao and Chen Boda were attacked by name for the first time in various speeches and documents emanating from the Congress, nothing was said that linked them to ultra-Left errors. On the contrary, Zhou Enlai's Political Report—which was the principal exposé of the alleged crimes of Lin and Chen—reaffirmed the then dominant designation of the "Swindlers'" line as ultra-Rightist and did not even mention ultra-Leftism as a tactical problem.[63] For example, early in the Report, Zhou stated that Lin and Chen

> were opposed to continuing the revolution under the dictatorship of the proletariat, contending that the main task after the Ninth Congress [April 1969] was to develop production. This was a refurbished version of the same revisionist trash that [Liu Shaoqi] and Chen [Boda] had smuggled into the resolution of the Eighth Congress [September 1956], which alleged that the major contradiction in our country was not the contradiction between the proletariat and the bourgeoisie, but that "between the advanced socialist system and the backward productive forces."[64]

It is impossible to read this part of Zhou's report without concluding that it reflects some sort of compromise (enforced or voluntary) between the Veteran Revolutionaries and the Cultural Revolutionaries.

Much of Zhou's invective against Lin was aimed at exposing his "counterrevolutionary conspiratorial clique," which sought to "usurp the supreme power of the Party and the state, thoroughly betray the line of the Ninth Congress, radically change the Party's basic line and policies for the whole historical period of socialism, turn the Marxist-Leninist Chinese Communist Party into a revisionist, fascist party, subvert the dictatorship of the proletariat, and restore capitalism."[65] The most candid analysis of Lin as an ultra-Rightist came in Zhou's charge that the Soviets had supported Lin in his revisionist schemes: "The Brezhnev renegade clique had impetuously voiced the common wish of the reactionaries and blurted out the ultra-Rightist nature of the Lin Biao anti-Party clique."[66]

The closest Zhou came to mentioning anything that might be even vaguely construed as a criticism of ultra-Leftism was the reference to the cynical use of the cult of personality around Mao by those like Lin "who never showed up without a copy of Quotations in their hand and never opened their mouths without shouting 'Long Live!' and who spoke nice things to your face but stabbed you in the back."[67] There are two other brief parts of the Political Report that could be interpreted as veiled criticisms of the ultra-Left trend. The first was Zhou's citation from Engels' "Letter to August Bebel" of October 1882 in which Engels said: "The development of the proletariat proceeds everywhere amidst internal struggles. . . . And when, *like Marx and myself, one has fought far harder . . . against the alleged socialists than against anyone else . . .* one cannot greatly grieve that the inevitable struggle has broken out."[68] This reference appears somewhat out of context with the rest of Zhou's attack on Lin, which relies heavily on exposing Lin's links with the landlords and bourgeoisie and their common interest in the restoration of capitalism in China.

The second reference that might be taken as an implicit criticism of ultra-Leftism was in Zhou's discussion of how the struggle against one erroneous tendency in the Party might cover up another latent erroneous tendency that would have to be confronted at some later date. After describing how Chen Duxiu's Right opportunism gave rise to Wang Ming's Left opportunism and how Wang Ming's Left deviation paved the way for his later turn to the Right, Zhou stated that "the struggle against Liu Shaoqi's revisionism covered Lin Biao's revisionism."[69] Although Zhou was careful not to label either Liu's or Lin's "revisionism," the subtle pairing of Right and Left deviations implied that the corollary (Right covers Left) was also true for the latest installment of the line struggle in the Party.

Despite what hindsight might allow us to read into Zhou's Political Report to the Tenth Party Congress, it is clear that the gist of the Report supported the current reinterpretation of the line of Lin Biao and the "Swindlers like Liu Shaoqi" as ultra-Rightist in essence. Following the Congress, events moved rapidly in a direction that reflected a consolidation of the position and influence of the Gang of Four (especially in the media, education, and cultural affairs) and established the framework for the ultimate showdown between the Cultural Revolutionaries and the Veteran Revolutionaries a few years later.

First, there was a near total cessation of attention to ultra-Leftism as a problem in China's socialist development. "Ultra-Left thought trend," "egalitarianism," "anarchism," and other code words that had been used in the past to criticize Left deviations almost completely disappeared from the continuing media campaign against Lin Biao. For example, the September 1973 issue of *Hongqi* featured several long articles in a section entitled "Continue to Carry Out Well the Criticism of Lin and Rectification of Work Style" devoted to repudiating the alleged crimes of the Lin Biao clique. Nowhere was there even the vaguest reference to ultra-Leftism or Left deviations.[70] The spearhead of the criticism of Lin was then clearly aimed at the ultra-Rightist line of this "bourgeois careerist, conspirator, counterrevolutionary double-dealer, renegade, and traitor."

Following this, in mid-September the campaign to criticize Confucius began. Almost from the start, this campaign was linked with the attack on Lin Biao, though it did not evolve into the full-blown Criticize Lin–Criticize Confucius (*Pi Lin Pi Kong*) Campaign until somewhat later.[71] The Lin-Confucius link—though it was eventually used as a vehicle by the Gang of Four for attacking Zhou Enlai—helped make the case for Lin's ultra-Right essence, since what could be more Rightist than Confucianism, the philosophical basis of Chinese feudalism?[72]

Finally, the Cultural Revolutionaries mounted an offensive in support of the "socialist newborn things," meaning the innovative policies of the Cultural Revolution, especially in education. For example, in the aftermath of the Tenth Congress, the press spoke glowingly of Zhang Tiesheng, the rebellious student from Liaoning, and lauded the "worker-peasant-soldier" pattern of university admission as the revolutionary trend of the day.[73] There were substantial modifications of Cultural Revolution reforms—for example, some exams continued to be given as a criterion for university admission despite the example of Zhang Tiesheng—but in broad outline, certainly, the trend in education presented by the media at this time was a clear reaffirmation of the Cultural Revolution policies.[74]

In short, by September 1973 the critique of ultra-Leftism was dead. The campaign against the "Swindlers like Liu Shaoqi," which had begun as an exposure of the ultra-Left trends in Chinese political life since the Cultural Revolution, had been transformed into a campaign of criticism against Lin Biao as another ultra-Rightist who not only sought to restore capitalism in China but also wished to turn back the wheel of history to an era guided by Confucian precepts condoning aristocratic rule.

Explaining the Aborted Critique

What factors operating in Chinese politics in 1971–73 explain the evolution of the critique of ultra-Leftism following the demise of Lin Biao? Why were the criticism and rectification of the excesses of the Cultural Revolution aborted in 1973 after developing into a relatively comprehensive critique of ultra-Leftism through much of 1972? We can better understand the unfolding of the campaign against the "Swindlers like Liu Shaoqi" by elaborating a few summary conclusions concerning the chronology of events that we have just described.

The campaign to criticize the "Swindlers like Liu Shaoqi" as it developed after Lin Biao's downfall in September 1971 became a struggle over the issue of whether ultra-Leftism should be criticized and rectified. This struggle was essentially a conflict between different opinions within the Party leadership on the question of whether there was or was not an "ultra-Left thought trend" in China's development. The struggle was between two groups within the Party leadership that we have called the Veteran Revolutionaries and the Cultural Revolutionaries. The Veteran Revolutionaries sought to use the criticism of the "Swindlers like Liu Shaoqi" as a forum for carrying out a thorough rectification of what was, they believed, a serious ultra-Left trend in Chinese political life that was causing great harm to China's socialist modernization. The Cultural Revolutionaries sought to defend and consolidate the "fruits" of the Cultural Revolution, which they believed to be the only effective remedy to China's drift down the "capitalist road" begun during the early 1960's. In other words, the Veteran Revolutionaries and the Cultural Revolutionaries differed profoundly on the question of the ideological basis of China's future development: what the former saw as an "ultra-Left thought trend," the latter considered to be the essence of the Chinese road to socialism.

Along with the ideological differences, critical power issues were also part of the struggle between these two groups. The Veteran Revolutionaries wanted desperately to resume their former position as a leading force in the Party and state apparatus. They hoped that by repudiating some of the excesses of the Cultural Revolution, they could bolster their contention that they had been unfairly purged and should be reinstated to help in the drive to remedy the long list of social, political, and economic problems facing the country. A critique of ultra-Leftism would also allow the Veteran Revolutionaries to gain some measure of vengeance against their tormentors. Conversely, the Cultural Revolutionaries were anxious to defend the "socialist newborn things" and the critique of the "capitalist roaders" in the Party since their claim to a share of power rested on the legitimacy of those two key aspects of the Cultural Revolution.

For very good reasons, the Cultural Revolutionaries were determined to derail the critique of ultra-Leftism that had emerged after the purge of Chen Boda and accelerated following the death of Lin Biao. The Gang of Four knew that the logic of the campaign against the "Swindlers like Liu Shaoqi" as it was evolving with its main focus on ultra-Leftism and anarchism in 1971–72 would ultimately implicate them, since they were so closely associated with the radical policies that were coming under assault. It was essential that they act forcefully and decisively in their efforts to forestall the growing critique of ultra-Leftism, for it not only attacked their core values to an unacceptable degree but also threatened their political survival.

The Cultural Revolutionaries were successful in curtailing and eventually stopping altogether the critique of ultra-Leftism in 1971–72. We can only speculate on some possible explanations that may have contributed to the outcome of the struggle over the critique of ultra-Leftism in 1971–73.

Did Mao intervene? At some point in the factional struggle, Mao could very well have stepped in to impose a resolution (as he supposedly did in the struggle between the same two groups over the succession to Zhou Enlai in January 1976 by resolving the issue in favor of a "compromise candidate" for Premier, Hua Guofeng). There are two possible reasons why Mao may have intervened: he could have been exasperated by the internecine squabbling within the highest echelons of the Party leadership and therefore sought to impose a settlement on the dispute by forging some sort of compromise between the factions; or he could have felt that the critique of ultra-Leftism as it developed in 1971–72 had gone too far and was beginning to challenge certain values and policies that he himself favored.[75] A precedent for the latter hypothesis can be found in Mao's handling of the Peng Dehuai affair at the Lushan Plenum in 1959: though the Chairman had himself criticized certain extreme Left tendencies of the "high tide" of the Great Leap Forward in 1958, he drew the line at the type of critical analysis of ultra-Leftism Peng was calling for in his letters and comments on the situation.

There is no evidence to suggest that Mao ever participated in or even supported the critique of ultra-Leftism as part of the campaign to criticize Lin Biao *cum* the "Swindlers." In fact, it can be inferred from the available documents that Mao was preoccupied from the start of his dispute with Lin over the latter's conspiratorial political activities rather than with his ideological deviations, Left or Right. For example, Mao's speeches to local cadres given on an inspection tour in August and September 1971—on the eve of his showdown with Lin—dealt with such themes as Lin's efforts to restore the position of State Chairman, his "surprise attacks" and "underground activities" (i.e., his factional maneuverings) at the 1970 Lushan Conference, and his cynical manipulation of the Mao cult. The speeches did not raise any points explicitly linking Lin Biao with the ultra-Left trend in the preceding years.[76]

Other internally circulated Central Committee documents concerning the Lin Biao case also support this contention. The distribution of Lin's alleged coup plan, "Outline of 'Project 571,'" for example, reinforces the view that Lin's essential sin was his conspiracy against the Chairman and the Party, not ultra-Leftism.[77] Such Central Committee documents as Nos. 61 (1971), 24 (1972), and 34 (1973), which cover the whole period when the struggle over how to label the "Swindlers" was unfolding, show a remarkable consistency in their interpretation of the most important issues in the Lin Biao case. These documents deal almost exclusively with the problems of conspiracy and factionalism in the Party and ignore matters relating to errors in political line.[78] If we can infer that the Central Committee documents were a fair reflection of Chairman Mao's own perception of the Lin Biao "problem," then the logical conclusion is that Mao never regarded the critique of ultra-Leftism that evolved in 1971–72 as essential to a repudiation of Lin Biao. On the contrary, he may very well have thought that such a critique was superfluous to the criticism of Lin and therefore called a halt to it when it seemed to be threatening his own ideological and policy preferences, to say nothing of his close political associates.

Was a compromise reached between the Veteran Revolutionaries and the Cultural Revolutionaries? Perhaps the conflict between these factions had reached such a level of acrimony and stalemate by late 1972 that both sides felt it in their interests (or were forced by Mao?) to accept some type of compromise that would put an end to the politicking and give the leadership as a whole a chance to turn its attention to more positive policy deliberations. A temporary cessation of the struggle would also let the two sides gather their forces for the ultimate struggle over the anticipated succession to Zhou and Mao. The compromise might have taken the form of a simple political trade-off, such as the Veteran Revolutionaries' agreeing to stop the critique of the ultra-Left trend in exchange for the Cultural Revolutionaries' agreeing to allow the rehabilitation of Deng Xiaoping in 1973. Or perhaps the compromise was reflected more in some sort of delineation of "spheres of influence" in certain policy areas between the factions, with the Veteran Revolutionaries exercising hegemony over economic affairs, science and technology, and cadre policy, while the Cultural Revolutionaries dominated the spheres of propaganda, culture, and education.

In general, the years 1974–75 can be characterized as a time when the explicit critique of ultra-Leftism ceased, but when there were definite continued efforts to correct what some perceived as excesses of the Cultural Revolution. These corrections were eventually labeled as attempts "to reverse the correct verdicts of the Cultural Revolution," which led, in turn, to the campaign to criticize Deng Xiaoping (*Pi Deng*) and the final confrontation between the Veteran Revolutionaries and the Cultural Revolutionaries in 1976. Thus, 1974–75 might be viewed as a hiatus reflecting a compromise or truce of sorts between periods of more intense struggle in 1971–73 and 1975–76.

Did the Cultural Revolutionaries simply outmaneuver their adversaries in gaining control of the media and propaganda organs, from which vantage point they could effectively defuse the critique of ultra-Leftism? There is some evidence for this hypothesis in the ex post facto official explanation of events of the last half of 1972, when the Gang of Four allegedly engaged in a number of behind-the-scenes manipulations at *Wenhui bao* and *Renmin ribao* to subvert the growing media criticism of the "ultra-Left thought trend" and anarchism.[79]

The most likely explanation is that, to one degree or another, all the above played a part in the ultimate outcome of the campaign to criticize the "Swindlers like Liu Shaoqi." With all the political ruptures caused by the Cultural Revolution and the Lin Biao affair, there must have been a strong desire for a period of relative stability and unity within the leadership and in China as a whole. A protracted effort to carry out a thorough critique of ultra-Leftism would have been a certain prescription for renewed factionalism at all levels of the system. Once the Veteran Revolutionaries had been assured that their claims for a voice in the post-Cultural Revolution order were being heeded and the radicals had shown their muscle in propaganda and cultural affairs, both sides were probably willing to settle for a political compromise on the very deep ideological differences that still divided them. Such a compromise was reflected in the fact that Deng Xiaoping's rehabilitation in August 1973 occurred simultaneously with the elevation of Wang Hongwen to the posts of first vice-chairman of the Party and member of the Standing Committee of the Politburo. Mao may well have been the instigator and engineer of this compromise, which effectively defused another round of intense inner-Party struggle, at least for the time being.

The critique of ultra-Leftism as it emerged in 1971–72 under the auspices of the Veteran Revolutionaries as part of the campaign to criticize the "Swindlers like Liu Shaoqi" was aimed principally at the surviving Cultural Revolutionaries and only secondarily at Lin Biao's past errors. Some scholars have argued that Lin was a leading advocate and staunch defender of the radical programs of the Cultural Revolution, but their evidence for linking him personally with those policies is thin.[80] Rather, it might be argued, on the basis of what we know about Lin's political activities in the 1960's and 1970's, that he was largely a political opportunist who supported whatever line and policies furthered his own power. One indication of this is the fact that the "Outline of 'Project 571'"—which was not only a detailed plan for the seizure of power but also a summary of Lin Biao's complaints about the political situation in China in 1970–71—is hardly a document that reflects an ultra-Left line.

Lin Biao became an extremely convenient and malleable target of criticism after his death. Almost in the same breath he could be accused of having committed all sorts of contradictory ideological or political errors, such as advocating both "politics can squeeze out everything else" and the "theory of productive forces," or the "theory that heroes make history" and the "theory that mass movements are naturally rational."[81] The mishmash of charges that were hurled against the "Swindlers like Liu Shaoqi" reflects, most importantly, the nature of the factional tug-of-war in 1971–73. But if Lin Biao really was in essence a political opportunist without any consistent Left or Right line, then the ease with which he could become a symbol of attack by both the Veteran Revolutionaries and the Cultural Revolutionaries becomes more believable.

Lin Biao was literally a dead issue by the time the critique of ultra-Leftism reached its height in 1972. There is ample reason to infer that the Veteran Revolutionaries had more immediate concerns than a posthumous excoriation of Mao's one-time chosen "successor" when they sought to promote a thorough criticism and rectification of Leftist line errors. In fact, most of the issues that emerged during the critique period we have described bear a much closer resemblance to the policy positions of the Gang of Four than to Lin's rather inconclusive political line. Therefore, it is likely that the critique of 1971–72 was directed at the Gang and that the critics of the ultra-Left were looking ahead to their confrontation with the Cultural Revolutionaries rather than backward at the sins of Lin Biao.[82]

This might also explain, in part, why Lin was not mentioned by name in public criticism until August 1973—after the radicals had been successful in having the label of ultra-Rightist pinned on him in the official interpretation of the case. If Lin was, in fact, basically a power-hungry conspirator, then it would be to the advantage of the Veteran Revolutionaries to keep Lin Biao as an individual out of the limelight in order not to detract from what they felt to be the more pressing task of a thorough critique of ultra-Leftism. It was much easier to attack the Cultural Revolutionaries covertly under the unspecific rubric "Swindlers like Liu Shaoqi" if the personality and personal history of Lin Biao could be kept out of the criticism and rectification campaign of 1971–72.

The true nature of the political link between Lin Biao and the Gang of Four is not at all clear. In fact, there is some evidence to suggest that, despite a transient alliance on some issues during the first years of the Cultural Revolution (1966–69), more divided Lin and the Gang than united them in terms of long-range political interests.

There is a close parallel between the issues raised in the critiques of ultra-Leftism in the post-Lin (1971–73) and post-Gang (1977–81) periods, which we shall discuss in chapter 7. However, this does not necessarily imply the existence of a real political link between Lin and the Gang—especially if, as argued above, Lin, as an individual, was secondary, perhaps even incidental, to the struggle over the critique of ultra-Leftism in the early 1970's. In fact, we can infer from several sources that by 1968 or 1969 Lin and the Gang were at odds with one another and were locked in a political struggle of their own. A post-Mao analysis characterized the changing relationship between Lin and the Gang as follows:

In the early period of the Great Cultural Revolution the "Gang of Four," not yet firmly established, were like fungi growing on rotten wood and had to rely on the "big tree" of Lin Biao for support. At the same time, Lin Biao wanted to recruit followers in order to look more powerful. During that period their relations were highly harmonious, but as the situation of class struggle developed, their relative positions and powers changed correspondingly, and contradictions began to grow between them.[83]

What were some of the possible sources of conflict between these former allies in the Cultural Revolution? First of all, the Gang of Four were likely dismayed by the virulence with which the army under Lin's command had suppressed the Red Guard movement and restored order in urban areas, schools, and industrial units in 1967–68. Also, Lin's resistance to turning over authority to the newly established Revolutionary Committees on the provincial, municipal, and work-unit levels must have irritated those who advocated mass organizations as a leading force in reconstituting a post–Cultural Revolution order. Such intervention by the military could well have been perceived by Mao and the radicals as a prelude to military dominance of the political system. Thus, the Gang of Four might well have considered such actions as tantamount to vitiating whatever type of alliance they had had with Lin in the earlier phases of the Cultural Revolution.[84]

Second, Lin seems to have supported, in part, the efforts in 1967–68 of the "May 16th Group" to carry the Cultural Revolution purge into the high military ranks.[85] The campaign to "drag out the small handful of capitalist roaders in the army" eventually ran into opposition from Mao as he came to realize the disastrous consequences that resistance to the movement by entrenched provincial commanders would have in undermining one of the last bastions of nationwide authority. When Jiang Qing and Yao Wenyuan rallied to Mao's side in condemning the "May 16 Group," they may well have found themselves in conflict with Lin Biao on yet another score.

Third, the Gang of Four may have split with Lin in 1970–71 over the issue of the latter's advocacy of certain rural policies that even the Gang found excessivly radical. Thus, the Gang could have decided to join an "anti-Lin coalition" with Zhou Enlai and others in order to preserve their own positions at the Center and to protect other Cultural Revolution programs about which they felt more strongly.[86]

Fourth, one source has suggested that Jiang Qing and her associates were more closely allied with Chen Boda than with Lin Biao and that Chen's purge in 1970 was Lin's doing, as part of his struggle with his rivals within the radical ranks.[87] On the other hand, another analysis has stated that the Gang of Four was also pleased to get rid of Chen since his ouster allowed them to move in as Mao's closest associates.[88] A logical inference of this line of argument would be that the Gang was also jealous of Lin's official designation as the Chairman's "close comrade-in-arms and successor" and would stand to gain much from his political demise.

Just as the nature of the actual link between Lin and the Gang is uncertain, so, too, is the Lin-Chen relationship. Central Committee documents on the Lin case either do not mention or are extremely superficial in describing the alleged "Lin Biao–Chen Boda Anti-Party Clique." The real link between Lin and Chen may have been mostly a reflection of the fact that both lost out in a political struggle at the Center after which the "victors" found it convenient to manufacture a history of collusion between those over whom they had prevailed in the effort to keep the official history of inner-Party conflict within the bounds of the struggle between the two lines.

Fifth, Lin's "Project 571" hardly treated certain members of the Gang of Four as allies; in fact, other than Mao, the real target of the coup plan appears to have been Zhang Chunqiao. The coup plan stated that one priority was to seize power in Shanghai and that "Zhang Chunqiao must be captured. Then immediately bring into play all the instruments of public opinion to publicize his traitorous crimes."[89] In its catalogue of complaints about the political situation in China that served as the rationalization for the coup, the "Project" made a reference to the "social fascism" of "the Trotsky-ist clique wielding the pen" and singled out their "theory of contin-uous revolution" and their "false revolutionary rhetoric" for criti-cism. It does not take too great a leap of the imagination to assume that this refers to the Gang of Four.[90]

In addition, Li Weixin, one of the alleged principal co-conspir-ators who was arrested after Lin's death, stated in his confession as appended to the Central Committee document containing the ex-posé of "Project 571" that the arrest of Zhang Chunqiao and Yao Wenyuan (and Mao's personal bodyguard, Wang Dongxing) was to be a key part of the coup. Li also claimed that Lin and his allies considered placing the blame for an assassination attempt against Mao on Zhang and Wang "in collusion with Wang [Li], Guan [Feng], Qi [Benyu]" (who had already been denounced as leaders of the ultra-Left "May 16 Group").[91] Having thus aroused public opinion, Lin and the army could seize power in the name of national security against an ultra-Left conspiracy.

It is certainly possible that the "Outline of 'Project 571'"—or some parts of it—were forged to justify the purge of Lin from the leadership. In that case, the claim that Zhang Chunqiao and other radicals were among the coup's primary targets could have been inserted by certain "interested parties" to establish some distance between Lin and the Cultural Revolutionaries to avoid guilt by association. This explanation would detract from the hypothesis that there was more conflict than unity in the relationship between Lin and the Gang, but it would not diminish the contention that the radicals had a vested interest in dissociating the criticism of Lin Biao from a critique of ultra-Leftism. It should be noted that the "Ad Hoc Investigation Committee" in charge of compiling materials and reporting on the Lin Biao affair was dominated by persons associated in one way or another with the Cultural Revolutionaries. The Committee members were: Zhang Chunqiao, Wang Dongxing, Ji Denggui, Li Desheng, Chen Xilian, and Ye Jianying. Only Ye can be considered as part of the Veteran Revolutionaries' camp; all the others have since been linked with the ultra-Left trend.[92]

In fact, the Gang went to great lengths to paint themselves as "anti-Lin heroes" and to portray their opposition to Lin as long-standing. A 1978 analysis of this ploy depicted it as a protective reaction by the Gang to Mao's growing disenchantment with Lin after the 1970 Lushan Plenum and as an example of the Gang's skill at "trimming their sails to the wind."[93] The radicals' strategic position in ideological and security apparatuses would also have given them an advantage in "trimming" the official version of the "Outline of 'Project 571'" to suit their own political purposes.

Finally, in her talks with Roxane Witke in mid-1972, Jiang Qing briefly described her conflict with Lin Biao. Her assertion that Lin's henchmen tried repeatedly to kill her and Mao with bombs and poison supports the hypothesis that whatever link may have existed at one time between the Gang and Lin had dissolved completely in the heat of the political conflicts of 1969–71.[94]

We may conclude by restating the major hypotheses that are suggested by the preceding analysis of the political struggle surrounding the campaign to criticize the "Swindlers like Liu Shaoqi" in 1971–73. First, the nature of the relationship between Lin Biao and the Gang of Four—both of whom have been accused by the post-Mao leadership of pursuing an ultra-Left line—is so questionable that one may fairly say that after 1969 it was characterized by political conflict rather than by ideological unity. Furthermore, the evidence indicates that the real bone of contention between Lin Biao and the Veteran Revolutionaries in the Party leadership was Lin's factional activities aimed at consolidating his personal political power rather than his advocacy of a consistent ultra-Left line in the form of a defense of the "fruits" of the Cultural Revolution.

Nevertheless, the similarities of the issues raised in the post-Lin and the post-Gang critiques of ultra-Leftism are unmistakable. Therefore, it seems likely that the real target of the critique of ultra-Leftism as carried out under the rubric of the campaign against the "Swindlers like Liu Shaoqi" was the Cultural Revolutionaries still in power. Recognizing the intentions of the Veteran Revolutionaries to utilize this campaign as an assault on their political legitimacy and ideological preferences, the radicals launched a successful effort in 1972–73 to curb the growing critique of ultra-Leftism as a destructive trend in China's socialist development. Their "victory" in this struggle enabled the Cultural Revolutionaries to survive at the Center with their political power and influence sufficiently secure to permit another offensive in pursuit of their objectives in 1975–76. From the point of view of the Veteran Revolutionaries, the aborted critique of ultra-Leftism meant that the excesses of the Cultural Revolution were not subjected to thorough criticism or rectification. Consequently, the Party leadership in 1973 remained sharply divided by differing perceptions of the legacy of the Cultural Revolution and divergent prescriptions for the road ahead. These unresolved contradictions at the Center became the fuel for another round of intense political struggle within the highest levels of leadership. Thus, in a very real sense, the struggle over the critique of ultra-Leftism during the campaign against the "Swindlers like Liu Shaoqi" was a dress rehearsal for the ultimate showdown between the Veteran Revolutionaries and their radical adversaries following the death of Mao Zedong in 1976.

6

From Ultra-Right to Ultra-Left:
The Campaign against the Gang of Four

> In our Party it has always been difficult to correct "Left-
> ist" errors and comparatively easy to correct Rightist mis-
> takes. Whenever something "Leftist" comes up, it always
> prevails over everything, and many people dare not speak
> out.   Peng Dehuai (1959)

The post-Mao Chinese leadership has, at various times, described
the case of the Gang of Four as one of the most important and complex political struggles in the history of the Chinese Communist
movement. At the Second National Congress on Learning from
Dazhai in Agriculture held in December 1976, Hua Guofeng referred to the showdown with the Gang as "a fierce, momentous
struggle," "a battle of particular gravity," and as reflecting "a grave
situation [that] had never risen since the founding of our People's
Republic and was rarely seen in the history of our Party."[1] At the
Eleventh National Congress of the Chinese Communist Party, Hua
declared that the struggle with the Gang was one of great significance because "on its outcome hinge[d] the future and the destiny
of our Party and our country."[2] A provincial radio broadcast summarized the general evaluation of the seriousness of the case of the
Gang of Four: "The crimes committed by the Gang were more serious, more damaging, and of a more lasting nature than any other
erroneous line in the history of our Party."[3]

The underlying assumption of this evaluation was that had the
Gang retained its power within the Party, their line would have
brought ruin to China's political and economic system. The situation was all the more important and complex, it was argued, because it took place in the context of the growing incapacitation and
eventual deaths of Zhou Enlai and Mao Zedong and therefore became a struggle to determine the succession to the two most important figures in the Chinese Revolution.

152   *From Ultra-Right to Ultra-Left*

But the case of the Gang of Four is also of great importance in the history of the Chinese Communist Party for reasons that go beyond those made explicit in official pronunciations; these reasons were implicit in the way in which the campaign of criticism against the Gang evolved following their purge in October 1976. The analysis of the Gang's "erroneous line" and the rectification of the concrete damage alleged to have been caused by that line led to a comprehensive critique of ultra-Leftism as a problem in China's socialist development. This critique not only involved the most thorough analysis so far of the issue of Left deviations in socialist revolution and construction but also gave rise to fundamental redefinitions of such key ideological concepts as "class struggle," "revisionism," "capitalist restoration," and "Rightism," which had fueled Chinese politics for more than twenty years. These redefinitions incorporated new perspectives on such vital issues as the interpretation of the entire history of the Party, the rationale of the Great Proletarian Cultural Revolution, and the evaluation of the leadership of Mao Zedong in much of the post-Liberation era. In sum, the critique of ultra-Leftism that evolved after the downfall of the Gang of Four effected a far-reaching adjustment of the ideological structure of Chinese communism; this readjustment, in turn, had an enormous influence on the immediate post-Mao political environment in China. The case of the campaign against the Gang of Four is important, therefore, not only for what it reveals about the overall issue of the critique of ultra-Leftism in Chinese politics, but also because of the part it played in shaping the structure and legitimacy of China's development programs for the last decades of the twentieth century.

Before discussing the content of the criticism of the Gang of Four's ultra-Left line (a subject we shall take up in the next chapter), we must dissect the rather curious chronology of the anti-Gang campaign as it unfolded following their purge in October 1976, for in the amazing history of this campaign we can detect the influence of previous incomplete critiques on the ability of the post-Mao leadership to come to grips with the legacy of ultra-Leftism in Chinese politics. The factional struggle over the direction of the criticism of the Gang also reflects the enduring political sensitivity of the critique of ultra-Leftism even after the downfall of the most powerful and visible advocates of the radical line.

Phase One: The Gang as Ultra-Rightists

The Gang of Four was arrested on October 6, 1976, about a month after the death of Mao Zedong and in the midst of the campaign to criticize Deng Xiaoping (*Pi Deng*).[4] Deng had been purged once again from the leadership the previous spring as a result of the escalating confrontation between the Veteran Revolutionaries and the Cultural Revolutionaries.[5] This struggle had revived in 1975 as both sides jockeyed for position to control the impeding succession crisis. The Gang of Four was later accused of having launched both the campaign against Deng and its antecedent, the campaign "to repudiate the Right deviationist attempt to reverse the correct verdicts [of the Cultural Revolution]," for the purpose of furthering their own political ambitions and blunting Deng's efforts to turn China's energies toward a full-scale modernization drive stressing pragmatic economic policies that the radicals found ideologically unacceptable. The rhetoric of the anti-Deng campaign continued unabated in the immediate aftermath of the purge of the Gang, especially as it emphasized the twin necessities of taking class struggle as the "key link" in the formulation of all Party policies and opposing "capitalist roaders" in positions of authority.[6]

The first official account of the arrest of the Gang of Four came in a Xinhua (New China News Agency) report on October 21—two weeks after the arrest, and after the news had been made known to the public by way of big character posters and mass demonstrations in several Chinese cities.[7] The Xinhua report established the themes that would dominate the campaign against the Gang for the next several months. It highlighted the Gang's conspiratorial activities and stressed the Rightist nature of their political line; they were described as "typical representatives of the bourgeoisie inside the Party" who sought to "usurp Party and state power, subvert the dictatorship of the proletariat, and restore capitalism."[8]

The "conspiracy" theme of the early criticism of the Gang was sounded even before the formal announcement of their arrest by the repeated invocation in the media of Chairman Mao's "three basic principles": "Practice Marxism, not revisionism; unite and don't split; be open and aboveboard, don't intrigue and conspire." These principles had been formulated initially as a warning to Lin Biao in 1971 and were revived in October 1976 as a prelude to the direct criticism of the Gang of Four.[9] The Rightist nature of the Gang's line was at first hammered home by explicitly linking criticism of them with the still-continuing campaign against Deng Xiaoping. For instance, in his speech to the mass rally held on October 24 to celebrate the "smashing" of the Gang, Peking mayor Wu De (himself later purged for his mishandling of several incidents in the months preceding the arrest of the Gang) stated: "We must thoroughly expose and criticize the anti-Party clique of Wang Hongwen, Jiang Qing, Zhang Chunqiao, and Yao Wenyuan, continue to criticize Deng Xiaoping, and repulse the Right deviationist attempt to reverse correct verdicts, consolidate and develop the victories of the Great Proletarian Cultural Revolution. . . . We must take class struggle as the key link."[10] This theme was repeated in a joint editorial of the three major central propaganda organs on October 25, which hailed "A Great Historic Victory" over the Gang. This editorial contained the important embellishment that the Gang "pursued a counterrevolutionary revisionist line, *an ultra-Right line.*"[11]

By late October, the designation of the Gang's political line as "an ultra-Right counterrevolutionary revisionist line" had become the core of the mounting criticism campaign. However, there was a simultaneous acknowledgment that the Gang had adopted a "revolutionary" disguise in order to push a counterrevolutionary line. Even before the joint editorial of October 25 hung the label of ultra-Rightism on them, a Shanghai newspaper had described the Gang as "unrepentant capitalist roaders" who were also "cunning and treacherous swindlers of sham Marxism" and "sham revolutionaries and capitulationists who sneaked into the rank and file of the workers . . . maggots who *disguised themselves as Leftists* and climbed to higher positions."[12]

Once again, the example of Wang Ming was invoked, but with emphasis on the Rightist nature of his "second" erroneous line, which was said to demonstrate the insincerity of his original ultra-Leftism. Citing the necessity of stripping the Gang of their pseudo-revolutionary masks in order to bare their ultra-Right essence, *Renmin ribao* said:

Red caps have never been able to hide black hearts . . . In the past, how red did Wang Ming tint his cap with the "100% Bolshevik" color, but was not his black heart quickly exposed? . . . Although the caps of Wang Hongwen, Jiang Qing, Zhang Chunqiao, and Yao Wenyuan are tinted very red with the color of "representatives of the correct line," their black hearts . . . have been exposed by the revolutionary people.[13]

At the same time, considerable effort was expended in denying that the Gang was really Leftist and reinforcing the judgment that, despite appearances, the main target of criticism must be their ultra-Rightism. The Gang's factionalism and conspiracies were particularly emphasized as being the key in any analysis of their exact political line. The logic of the argument was that although the Gang engaged in certain political and ideological maneuvers that seemed to be revolutionary, their real inclinations were evident in their factional machinations around the issue of succession to Zhou and Mao; since these machinations were aimed at usurping power and overthrowing Chairman Mao's revolutionary line, the Four were obviously counterrevolutionaries and revisionists. In other words, in the ideological framework that had prevailed since the Cultural Revolution, all counterrevolutionaries and revisionists were necessarily Rightists; but the Gang's crimes were so extreme—being aimed directly at Premier Zhou and Chairman Mao—that they made the Gang *ultra*-Rightists.

Beyond this "logical" inference that equated counterrevolutionary conspiracy and factionalism with an ultra-Right political line, more specific charges were levied against the Gang as a way of proving that the anti-Rightist orientation of the criticism was justified. In an article entitled, "The Gang of Four Is a Group of Out-and-Out Bourgeois Rightists," *Wenhui bao* listed a number of what it called Rightist errors: sabotaging the Cultural Revolution, attacking revolutionary cadres, trying to turn the Chinese Communist Party into a fascist organization and the dictatorship of the proletariat into a fascist dictatorship, worshiping foreigners and foreign things in private (despite their public stance of hardline xenophobia), and representing the interests of the overthrown landlords and bourgeoisie in seeking a restoration of capitalism.[14]

Beginning in early November 1976 the campaign took another curious turn. The criticism of the Gang's line on various policies, particularly in regard to production and economic development, began to focus on what were obviously Left errors, but these errors were given an interpretation that sought to reinforce the claim that the Gang was really Rightist. For example, the Gang was accused of distorting the proper dialectical relationship between economic work and political work by stressing class struggle to the neglect of production. They were also castigated for wielding the "big stick" of the "theory of productive forces" as a weapon against their political opponents, scientists, technicians, managers, and others who favored giving priority to economic development over continuous revolutionary change.[15]

However, this seemingly ultra-Left approach to the relationship between revolution and production was subordinated to an imputation of *subjective motive* and *projected result* as the key factors for analyzing the true nature of the Gang's political line. Primary importance was attached to the allegation that the Gang had deliberately sought to undermine the socialist economy to facilitate their seizure of power (subjective motive), which led in turn to conditions favorable to the restoration of capitalism (projected result). It was these "facts" that were said to determine the ultra-Right essence of the Gang's line, not the ultra-Left tactics that they employed to promote their Rightist ends.

This interpretation of the nature of the Gang's line was reflected in a long article on their efforts to undermine China's modernization that appeared in the December 1976 issue of *Hongqi*. After detailing a catalogue of what, on the surface, appeared to be Leftist deviations in dealing with questions of production, the article concluded:

In attempting to usurp Party and state power, the Gang of Four used disruption of production as a major means of undermining the revolution. . . . [They sought] to throw the normal socialist production order into confusion so they could benefit from confusion, usurp power amid chaos and turn the dictatorship of the proletariat into a dictatorship of the bourgeoisie . . . [and] the socialist economy into a capitalist economy. . . . They are the chief culprits in undermining the socialist revolution and construction, typical representatives of the bourgeoisie inside the Party and capitalist roaders still traveling on the capitalist road. . . . We must completely tear off their masks and expose their anti-Party, anti-socialist, and anti-people ultra-Rightist features to bright daylight.[16]

A similar interpretive line was used when analyzing the Gang's impact on education policy. For example, Zhang Chunqiao was criticized for causing serious harm to the quality of China's education system by his call for "exercising all-round dictatorship"[17] over "bourgeois academic authorities" and by his advocacy of carrying Cultural Revolution reforms in education to extremes. Such errors would appear to fall into the realm of ultra-Leftism; but just the opposite case was made:

Zhang Chunqiao blustered that he would rather have a "laborer without culture" [than an "intellectual aristocrat with culture"]. He was openly peddling the cancellation of intellectual development and advocating the theory that "reading books is useless." The essence of his fallacy is ultra-Right . . . [because] he refused to allow proletarian revolutionary successors to learn necessary cultural and scientific knowledge of socialism. How can they [then] overthrow the bourgeoisie in the superstructure? Thus we can see that his glib talk about exercising "all-round dictatorship" over the bourgeoisie was only an ulterior motive.[18]

Charges of this sort went to great lengths to prove that ultra-Left was really ultra-Right and reflect the fact that the first phase of the criticism of the Gang of Four was carried out within the Cultural Revolution framework of the two-line struggle between the proletariat and the bourgeoisie. Within this framework, there could be struggle between revolutionary Left and counterrevolutionary Right but never any serious threat to the socialist revolution from an ultra-Leftist line.

The effort to cast the Gang as Rightists was intensified in late 1976 by a campaign of character assassination. This attack took two forms: vivid exposés of the Gang's decadent and debauched mode of living, and detailed revelations of their long histories of counterrevolutionary activities and bad class backgrounds. As proof of the Gang's decadence, the criticism described Jiang Qing's passion for imported fashions, Wang Hongwen's insistence on air-freighting fresh lobsters from Hainan Island to satisfy his gourmet palate, private showings of foreign and pornographic films by the Gang, and their squandering of state funds for their own enjoyment and comfort.[19]

The second line of personal vilification was more substantive and more integral to bolstering the contention that the Gang was really ultra-Rightist in essence. Revelation of the Gang's past activities began in November 1976 with numerous highly critical recountings of the political history of Zhang Chunqiao. The main charge against Zhang was that he advocated capitulation (a Rightist error) to both the Japanese and the Guomindang in the 1930's. Various references to Zhang's suspect views at the time were offered, among them a 1936 criticism by Lu Xun of Zhang for allegedly downplaying resistance to Japan when Zhang was a young Party propagandist writing under the pen name Di Ke.[20] An article written by Zhang in 1938 was described as urging capitulation to the Guomindang because it advocated a "united command" against the Japanese at a time when Chiang Kai-shek was more intent on crushing the Communists than on building a coordinated national defense. "Reading this [1938] article," *Renmin ribao* declared, "will give us a clearer vision to see through the sham Marxist and political swindler Zhang Chunqiao, who is used to pretending to be a 'Leftist' and is skilled at using his tongue to build up his reputation and deceive the people. This shows that Zhang Chunqiao is an old, out-and-out Rightist."[21]

In the course of the next several months, articles appeared detailing Jiang Qing's collaboration with the Guomindang, Yao Wenyuan's landlord class background and his links to a group of "anti-Party" cultural workers in the 1950's, and Wang Hongwen's personal and political degeneration.[22] These accusations laid the basis for what became the stock analysis that the Rightist nature of the Gang's political line was determined by the fact that it was perpetrated by a "Guomindang secret agent" (Zhang), a "renegade and traitor" (Jiang), an "alien class element" (Yao), and a "new bourgeois element" (Wang).

A summary judgment on the nature of the Gang's line was provided by Hua Guofeng in his speech at the Second National Conference on Learning from Dazhai in Agriculture in late December 1976. His remarks are particularly interesting in retrospect since the formulation he offered was criticized in 1979 as an example of the obfuscation that had diverted the course of the opening phase of the campaign against the Gang. In his speech, Hua described the Gang in the bluntest of terms:

The Wang-Jiang-Zhang-Yao anti-Party clique is a bunch of ultra-Rightists and their counterrevolutionary revisionist line is an ultra-Right line. They are ultra-Rightists because they practice revisionism, create splits, and engage in intrigues and conspiracies under the cloak of Marxism, trying by hook or by crook to usurp supreme leadership in the Party and the state, subvert the dictatorship of the proletariat, and restore capitalism.[23]

After acknowledging that the Gang had camouflaged themselves as Leftists and revolutionaries in order to deceive people and facilitate the realization of their counterrevolutionary objectives, Hua listed twelve reasons why the Four were, in fact, ultra-Rightists (later widely publicized as the "Twelve Whys") and then emphatically added: "They are ultra-Rightists, out-and-out capitalist roaders, and the most ferocious counterrevolutionaries. What 'Leftists'! What 'radicals'! *They could not have pursued a line farther to the Right!*"[24]

The "Twelve Whys" and the formulation "They could not have pursued a line farther to the Right!" quickly became important guidelines for the campaign against the Gang.[25] A joint editorial of the three major propaganda organs cited Hua's whole speech as one of the key documents for establishing the official direction in the anti-Gang campaign.[26]

On February 6, 1977, *Renmin ribao* ran an article entitled "Sham Left Faction, Real Right Faction" (*Jiazuopai, zhenyoupai*), which singled out the Gang's factional and conspiratorial activities as the most important ingredient of their political line.[27] After noting with approval Hua's statement that the Gang's line "could not have been farther to the Right," the article commented: "This scientific conclusion drawn from an analysis based on Marxism exposes the reactionary nature of the members of the Gang of Four, strips off their masks, and exposes the true features of this gang of ultra-Rightists."[28] And then, as if addressing "some comrades" who still might be inclined to believe that the Four were true Leftists or who might be pressing for a critique of their errors from the standpoint of the problem of ultra-Leftism, the article asked rhetorically: "Are there any Leftists who have tried to restore capitalism as this gang did? Are there any radicals who have tried to subvert the dictatorship of the proletariat as this gang did?"[29]

A short time later, anarchism was brought up in criticisms of the Gang. A breakdown of worker and student discipline was pointed to as an obvious effect of the political line that was dominant when the Gang was said to have held sway within the leadership, and the Gang was attacked for turning the Cultural Revolution reform of irrational rules and regulations into an all-out assault on any limits to the behavior of workers and students. The Gang was declared to have promoted an anarchist trend in industrial enterprises and schools under the slogan of rebellion against "bourgeois control, check, and suppression." Rather than manifesting ultra-Left attitudes toward authority, this trend was said to be part of a broad scheme to usurp power. One commentator said:

... did the Gang of Four really want anarchism? No, their anarchism aimed at doing away with the government of the proletariat while keeping the government of the bourgeoisie. . . . The Gang of Four's opposition to the so-called "bourgeois control, check, and suppression" was aimed at fanning up anarchism. Their promotion of anarchism was aimed at seizing power in the [midst of] confusion, overthrowing the dictatorship of the proletariat and establishing a fascist dictatorship of the bourgeoisie. This was the ultra-Rightist essence hidden behind the Gang's slogan.[30]

The effort to cast the Gang's anarchism into an ultra-Right mold even went so far as to make the case that Marx's old nemesis, Bakunin, had been an ultra-Rightist just like the Gang of Four! Bakunin, this line of argument claimed, came from a bad class background, had betrayed fellow revolutionaries when arrested, had weaseled his way into the proletarian ranks to carry out his counterrevolutionary schemes, and had organized a clique to seize power in the Communist International; he had also attempted to cover up his ultra-Right nature by adopting the cloak of anarchism to make himself appear very revolutionary.[31] All this applied equally to the Gang of Four: "By comparing the behavior of the counterrevolutionary conspirator's clique assembled by the careerist Bakunin in the First International with that of the Wang-Jiang-Zhang-Yao Gang of Four, one can get a clearer understanding of the ultra-Rightist essence of the Gang's counterrevolutionary revisionist line."[32] In other words, Bakunin, the Gang of Four, and other seemingly ultra-Leftist leaders in the socialist movement were really ultra-Rightists who only used anarchist slogans and extreme revolutionary stances to create conditions that would make it possible for them to seize power from the true vanguard of the proletariat. Repudiation of their sinister deeds had to focus on exposing their Rightist essence and not get sidetracked by the secondary phenomenon of their ultra-Left tactics. The legacies of the anti-Rightist movements of 1957–58, the 1959 Lushan Plenum, the protracted witch-hunt for "capitalist-roaders" in the Party that had begun in the mid-1960's, the outcome of the campaign against the "Swindlers like Liu Shaoqi," and the virulent criticism of Deng Xiaoping's sabotage of the "correct verdicts" of the Cultural Revolution had so constrained the ideological limits of the times that the possibility of giving serious consideration to the problem of deviations to the Left within the leadership was effectively precluded.

In July 1977, as part of the prelude to the reinstatement of Deng Xiaoping, the media began a refutation of the Gang of Four's attack on the series of reports and proposals concerning China's modernization that had been drawn up under Deng's guidance in 1975–76.[33] The Gang had labeled these documents the "three big poisonous weeds" (*san da ducao*) and had used them as evidence for their assault on Deng as an "unrepentant capitalist roader still on the capitalist road."[34] The refutation of this charge upheld the validity of Deng's vision of China's socialist modernization against the imputation of revisionism. It was claimed that what really irked the Gang about Deng's "poisonous weeds" was not simply the recommendations for speeding up China's economic development but the fact that these recommendations contained a pungent criticism of radical policies, policies that Deng and his supporters believed had greatly hampered China's modernization efforts since the Tenth Party Congress in August 1973. This criticism was said to have "offended the Gang of Four, reopened their old wounds, and touched their sore spot."[35]

The term "ultra-Left" was not used at this stage in referring to the erroneous trend that prevailed under the Gang's influence; rather, the emphasis was on refuting the various "fallacies" (*miulun*) spread by the Gang in pushing their own line and in attacking Deng's proposals. Still, a critique of ultra-Leftism was clearly implied in the specific errors mentioned as contrasted to Deng's "correct" line. A repudiation of anarchism, for example, was coupled with support for rules, regulations, and effective enterprise management to ensure labor discipline and productivity; opposition to an exaggeration of the principle of self-reliance in national development was linked to a reaffirmation of the necessity of importing foreign technology; and a rejection of egalitarianism in distribution and wage policies was combined with a call for increased use of material incentives and stricter observation of the principle of distribution according to labor.[36]

The obvious inconsistency in exposing the Gang's attack on Deng's modernization proposals at the same time a case was being made that the Gang were ultra-Rightists apparently did not seem bothersome. Supposedly, the Gang viewed Deng's plans as a blueprint for capitalist restoration in China, but it was not explained why, if the Four were themselves ultra-Rightists intent on subverting socialism and restoring capitalism, they would condemn a program that, according to their criticism, was designed to achieve just such an objective!

At the Eleventh Party Congress that met in August 1977 Hua Guofeng made a detailed report on the case of the Gang of Four.[37] In this report he officially labeled the struggle against the Gang as "the eleventh major struggle between the two lines in our Party's history," and he hailed the "smashing" of the Gang as "the triumphant conclusion of the first Great Proletarian Cultural Revolution."[38] Again and again, Hua drove home the point of the Gang's

ultra-Rightism, and emphasized their questionable backgrounds as
the key in analyzing the essential nature of their line:

> The causes that led the Gang of Four to plot the usurpation of supreme
> power in the Party and the state in the hope of reversing the course of his-
> tory and restoring capitalism in China are deep-rooted in their class origin
> and past records. . . . The Gang of Four are a sinister clique of old and new
> counterrevolutionaries who sneaked into our Party. They are typical repre-
> sentatives in our Party of landlords, rich peasants, counterrevolutionaries,
> and bad elements, as well as of the old and new bourgeoisie. . . . *Their re-*
> *actionary class nature determines the ultra-Right essence of their counter-*
> *revolutionary revisionist line and underlies all their criminal activities.*[39]

Hua also issued a call for "vigorously waging a people's war
to thoroughly expose and criticize the ultra-Right essence of the
Gang's counterrevolutionary revisionist line in all its manifestations."[40] Less than two months later, in a major media editorial on
the first anniversary of the Gang's arrest, this call was formally
launched as the "third campaign" to expose and criticize the Gang.[41]
The first campaign had focused on criticizing the Gang's conspiracy
to seize power; the second had concentrated on exposing their
"criminal counterrevolutionary histories."[42] Although the "third
campaign" had an explicit mandate to reveal the Gang's ultra-Right
essence, the slight shift in emphasis was, in fact, the beginning of a
gradual evolution toward the more direct confrontation with the
problem of ultra-Leftism that began in mid-October 1977.

Phase Two: Stripping Off the Leftist Camouflage

One of the main points of emphasis in Hua's Political Report to
the Eleventh Party Congress and the joint editorial that followed
was the need for eliminating the "pernicious influence" (*liudu he*
yingxiang) of the Gang of Four in "economic, political, ideological,
cultural, military, and Party affairs"[43]—a "pernicious influence"
that was identified as the "manifestation" of the Gang's ultra-Right
line in various fields. From the way in which the term was used in
succeeding months, it is clear that "pernicious influence" really
meant "ultra-Left influence." This was not the first time that the
term "pernicious influence" had been applied to the Gang, and the
fact that its use can be traced back to the earliest part of the campaign may indicate that the issue of ultra-Leftism was at least lurk-
ing in the background from the very start.[44] However, the attention

paid to eliminating the Gang's "pernicious influence" was greatly intensified in the last quarter of 1977 and became the major focus of criticism by early 1978, while exposure of their ultra-Rightism gradually receded into the background.

An article in *Renmin ribao* on October 14, 1977, clearly showed a shift in emphasis. This article, entitled "Thoroughly Strip Off the Sham Leftist Camouflages of the Gang of Four," maintained that although the Gang was still to be considered "reactionary moribund ultra-Rightists," it was imperative to "pay attention to their sham Leftist camouflage."[45] It recalled Mao's long-standing warning to be on guard against Left deviations:

> Chairman Mao had on many occasions said that in order to adhere to materialist dialectics and the correct line we must struggle on two fronts— both opposing the Right and the "Left." In the many political movements following the founding of the People's Republic of China and in the course of the struggle to oppose and criticize Right deviationist opportunism, Chairman Mao also frequently opposed the error of "Left" deviation and criticized the view that "Left" is better than Right.[46]

The "sham Left" manifestations of the Gang were still secondary to their Rightist nature as determined by their class origins and the subjective motives and projected results of their political line, but, the article pointed out, one of the major problems in the case of the Gang of Four had been their ability to take advantage of ultra-Leftist tendencies that existed in the Party and in society as a result of the lingering influence of petty bourgeois thinking. It was therefore necessary to "isolate and expose the handful of Rightists who vainly attempt to use the 'Left' sentiments among part of the masses to mobilize the masses" and to see clearly "certain connections between the 'Left' deviations [in society at large] and the Gang of Four's sham Leftism."[47] The article went on to say that "sham Leftism" led people to believe that the Gang's exaggerations of various revolutionary slogans and their extreme interpretation of Cultural Revolution policies were the correct expression of "Chairman Mao's revolutionary line," and that that sort of extremism in turn led to widespread sectarianism and factionalism as masses and cadres came to believe "such ideas as 'Only I am the Leftist' and 'Only I am the revolutionary,'" and violently attacked their political and ideological opponents as enemies of socialism.[48]

Another significant point made in the October 14 article had to do with the question of why the Gang had blocked the criticism of Lin Biao's "sham Leftism" in the period 1971–73. The article squarely accused the Gang of perpetrating a concerted campaign of "forbiddance of guarding against the 'Left'" in order to protect their own sinister schemes:

The Gang of Four took over Lin Biao's sham Leftist old mask and disguised themselves more tactfully than he did. . . . They exceeded Lin Biao in fabricating all sorts of absurdities and rendered their sham Leftist camouflage as somewhat "theoretical." They forbade the exposure and criticism of Lin Biao for *pursuing an ultra-Right line by means of the sham Left method.* Anyone who criticized Lin Biao as a sham Leftist would be vilified as negating the ultra-Rightist nature of Lin Biao's line.[49]

On December 12, following up this first hint that official attention was shifting from the Gang's ultra-Right conspiracies to their Leftist deviations, *Renmin ribao* ran another article on the Gang of Four in which it applied the label "sham Left, real Right" as the authoritative designation of the Gang's line.[50] Though the Four were still to be considered ultra-Rightists so far as their ultimate political objectives and class backgrounds were concerned, the article said, analysis of their actual impact on China's political life and economic development had to focus on revealing their "sham Leftism." The first phase of the criticism had also made reference to the Leftist smoke screen put up by the Gang to obscure their counter-revolutionary activities, but it had more or less dismissed the Gang's Leftist tactics as a key point in understanding their erroneous line. In the phase that began in late 1977 the priority was reversed: now it was permissible to expose the "fake Left" aspect of the Gang's activities. For the first time since the Gang's downfall, their ultra-Leftism was to be attacked directly.

In this *Renmin ribao* analysis, it was argued that the Gang had pursued a "Left revisionist" line in their attitude toward the role of class struggle in socialist society. Class struggle is the foundation of Marxism, and the essence of revisionism is determined by the way in which it alters that foundation. Right revisionists like Liu Shaoqi tamper with Marxism by advocating the "theory of the dying out of class struggle," but "Left revisionists" like the Gang take a different tack: "The Gang of Four so craftily practised their form of revisionism that they found no need to deny the existence of class struggle throughout the period of socialism. They first plucked the term class struggle out of the comprehensive framework of Marxism and then adopted it as a slogan and overemphasized its existence from their 'Leftist' point of view."[51] But this attack from the Left really had a Rightist impact on China's socialist development: the Gang had used the exaggeration of class struggle to undermine production and disrupt political unity, a consequence that ultimately strengthened the bourgeoisie and weakened the proletariat.

Though this kind of contorted logic that redefined ultra-Leftism as ultra-Rightism continued, after December 1977 the predominant theme of the criticism campaign was analysis of the Gang's Leftist errors. Rightist class origins, conspiratorial activities, and restorationist objectives were still mentioned during the year or so when the Four were being attacked within this framework, but never as a major point in the criticism. Criticism of the Gang's Rightist nature was now called "abstract and intangible" unless it was linked with the reality of its Leftist manifestations. Thus, it was argued, the analysis of the Gang must shift gears:

Disregarding the existence of false images is tantamount to abandoning the orientation of the essence of knowledge. To truly criticize the ultra-Rightist essence of [the Gang's] line, it is necessary to link the criticism of its false Leftist appearance with the criticism of its ultra-Rightist essence, thereby recognizing reality by unmasking it. The more thoroughly we unmask its Leftist disguise, the more fully we reveal its ultra-Rightist essence.[52]

Although this type of argument still bent over backward to maintain the interpretation of the ultra-Right *essence* of the Gang's political line, it nonetheless signified a very important step in rationalizing a focus on criticizing the *phenomenon* of ultra-Leftism. Thenceforth, and ever increasingly, the campaign against the Gang concentrated on the need to eliminate their "pernicious influence," which was now explicitly equated with the "sham Left" quality of their line:

With regard to those counterrevolutionary conspiratorial activities which [the Gang] carried out behind the "revolutionary" phrases and "Leftist" camouflage, we should of course conduct penetrating exposure and thorough criticism. With regard to those phrases and that camouflage, we shouldn't take them lightly either, but should conduct the same penetrating exposure and thorough criticism. The reason for doing so is that they were what the Gang of Four all along vigorously propagated as Marxism–Leninism–Mao Zedong Thought; what duped many of our comrades who regarded them as the correct line; and *primarily comprised the things which created the deepest pernicious influence*, the more extensive effects, the greatest damage, and the strongest fetters among the people.[53]

The schizophrenic character of the transition period in the criticism of the Gang is demonstrated by the fact that attacks on

the Gang's "pernicious influence" in rural policy—such as egalitarianism in distribution and overrestriction of sideline production[54]—expanded alongside a "One Criticism, Two Blows" campaign against "spontaneous capitalist forces" in the countryside.[55]
Throughout this period, there was a marked inconsistency in the
labeling of the Gang's political line. Though the most common formula by the spring of 1978 was the designation "fake Left, real
Right counterrevolutionary revisionist line,"[56] many reports continued to refer to the Gang's "ultra-Right counterrevolutionary
revisionist line,"[57] while others dropped the Left-Right label altogether and simply criticized the Gang's "counterrevolutionary revisionist line."[58] In this rather ambiguous phase of the campaign,
evidently, the essential nature of the Gang's erroneous line was still
deserving of analysis in terms of ultra-Rightism even though the
principal target of criticism was to be their ultra-Left "pernicious
influence."

Ultra-Leftism was still considered a tactical problem, however.
One commentator, for example, was able to assert that "nothing
could have been more 'Left' than the *tricks* [the Gang] resorted
to,"[59] notwithstanding Hua Guofeng's statement (of August 1977)
that the Gang "could not have pursued a line farther to the Right."
Another article declared: "The Gang of Four's 'Leftism' was extra-
ordinary. It was so surprisingly, dreadfully, despicably, and hatefully
'Left' that only the word 'ultra' can describe it."[60] But then, after
describing in considerable detail the specific content of the Gang's
ultra-Leftism, the same article concluded that such maneuvers were
really means to an ultra-Right end:

Their evil aim was to topple the proletarian revolutionaries of the older
generation and the masses of veteran cadres, destroy our Party, our dictatorship of the proletariat, our army, discredit our socialist system, confuse our thinking, policies, and ranks, and drain our material base and pool
of talent for the Four Modernizations. Their ultimate goal was to usurp
Party and state power, bring about a change of dynasty, and restore capitalism in China.[61]

An article on the Gang's "pernicious influence" in education described their goal as seeking "to keep the proletariat and the working people in a permanent state of ignorance so that [they] could
unobstructively usurp Party and state power and restore capitalism."[62] Because the Gang's "Leftism" was considered to be "sham"
or "pseudo-Leftism," each analysis of their line in a particular pol-

icy area had to conclude with some statement about their ultimate objective of capitalist restoration as determining their ultra-Right essence.

Several analyses between late 1977 and mid-1978 went to great lengths to demonstrate that there were three types of ultra-Leftism and that the Gang was guilty of the worst sort: "pseudo-Leftism." There was an ultra-Leftism that was a reflection of petty-bourgeois individualism and impetuosity to achieve quick results in "making revolution"; ultra-Leftism of this type resulted in "going beyond the stage of development of the revolution in thinking, mak[ing] reckless advances in general and specific policies, and in action; [and] carrying things too far on the question of struggle."[63] Ultra-Leftists of this sort "subjectively still wanted to make revolution although they had [objectively] harmed the revolution."[64] It was also pointed out that ultra-Leftism of this broad type could take two forms: "Left deviations," which involved only "a few errors in work-style,"[65] or "Left opportunism," which involved much more serious contradictions and resulted when Left deviations went unchecked and congealed into a coherent political line involving "system, policy, [and] program."[66] Although both "Left deviations" and "Left opportunism" were committed by people who "subjectively still want to make revolution," the former was a reflection of an "erroneous trend within the revolutionary ranks"[67] whereas the latter had escalated to the level of line struggle.[68]

"Pseudo-Leftism," too, involved struggle between correct and erroneous lines, but unlike the "Left opportunists," the "pseudo-Leftists" did not even subjectively want revolution; rather, they —and that meant the Gang of Four—were motivated by the most sinister conspiratorial and restorationist aims:

The Gang of Four are reactionaries representing the landlord and bourgeois class in vainly turning back the wheels of history so that the bright reality of socialism will revert back to the dark abyss of capitalism. Their "Leftism" is neither petty-bourgeois fanaticism and an infantile disorder nor "Leftist" opportunism. It is a counterrevolutionary "Leftist" camouflage and a vicious conspiratorial trick.[69]

The Gang's line aimed at "wasting the wealth of socialism and . . . making the entire nation illiterate."[70] Their ultra-Leftism was judged to be only "a manifestation of their ultra-Rightist line and a tactical measure for attaining their ultra-Rightist goal."[71] Therefore, their "pseudo-Leftism" must not be equated with more benign types of ultra-Leftism: "Their problem was not one of making reckless advances, but of turning back the wheel of history and making China slip back into the old semi-colonial and semi-feudal society."[72]

Although the entire notion of "pseudo-Leftism" would later be repudiated as a hindrance to a thorough critique of the Gang's ultra-Leftism, the distinction between different types of ultra-Leftism that was made in 1977–78 reflected the deepening sophistication with which the Party leadership was analyzing the Gang's erroneous line.

The analytical differentiation between types of ultra-Leftism also contained a notion of *degeneration*, in which milder manifestations of ultra-Leftism could become more virulent. Minor "Left deviations," if not rectified at an early stage, could degenerate into a "Left opportunist" line; "Left opportunism" might lead to "pseudo-Leftism" if the "Left opportunists" let their political ambitions outweigh their subjective desire for revolution. *Jiefang ribao* provided the following prescription for just such a process of degeneration:

. . . the great majority of people who have committed "Leftist" errors can mend their ways if they thoroughly realize, through education, the reasons and circumstances which caused them to make such errors and the ways to correct such errors. However, we must also realize that there are some people who at the beginning commit some errors under the influence of ultra-"Leftist" ideas. Later under the pernicious influence of petty bourgeois individualism they went farther and farther down the revisionist road and finally took the path of setting themselves against the people.[73]

The effort to distinguish different types of ultra-Leftism and the introduction of the idea of degeneration provided the basis for the more systematic analysis of the problem of Leftist deviations in Chinese socialism that began in 1979. However, it is important to note that one of the original intentions of this differentiation was to legitimize "fake Left, real Right" (or pseudo-Leftism) as a category for criticism of the political line of the Gang of Four.

Phase Three: The Frontal Attack on Ultra-Leftism

The next phase of the campaign against the Gang of Four rejected the whole concept of "pseudo-Leftism" as an appropriate mode of analysis of a political line and insisted that criticism of the Gang's ultra-Left line be separated from exposure of their personal histories, conspiratorial activities, and political ambitions. This important distinction was set in motion by the Third Plenum of the Eleventh Central Committee, which was held in December 1978.[74] Although the communiqué issued by the Plenum did not affix a label to the political line that underlay the "sabotage" of Lin Biao and the Gang of Four (linked together as objects of criticism since early 1978), it strongly reaffirmed the slogans "Seek truth from facts" (*Shishi qiushi*) and "Practice is the sole criterion of truth" (*Shijian shi jianyan zhenlide weiyi biaozhun*) as symbolizing the basic political orientation of the times.[75] These slogans became the nucleus of the reevaluation of the legacy of Mao Zedong and the increasingly pragmatic economic policies of the post-Mao leadership, and they were invoked as the rationale for reopening the whole question of the true nature of the political line of Lin Biao and the Gang of Four.

Ironically, the new phase in the critique of ultra-Leftism was immediately preceded by a call (restated by the Third Plenum) to bring to an end "the mass movement to expose and criticize Lin Biao and the Gang of Four."[76] Several explanations of the apparent contradiction between the call to halt the mass criticism of Lin and the Gang and the subsequent deepening critique of their ultra-Left line are possible.

On the one hand, it is clear that there was some dispute within the Party leadership over whether to undertake a more thorough analysis and rectification of ultra-Left trends in China's recent history. Evidence concerning the existence of conflict between a "Whatever" faction ("We are determined to support whatever policy decisions were made by Chairman Mao") and a "Practice" faction ("Practice is the sole criterion of truth") suggests that the critique of ultra-Leftism could well have been an issue of dispute at the Plenary session. Both factions were aware that such a critique would inevitably have an important effect on their respective political positions. The Third Plenum was a crucial juncture in the struggle between these two groups; the time lapse between the call to end the mass criticism of Lin and the Gang and the vigorous critique of ultra-Leftism that began in early 1979 reflects the uncertain period when the general ascendency of the "Practice" faction within the Party leadership was being extended to a consolidation of their authority over propaganda organs and ideological affairs.[77]

It is also possible that the call to end the mass phase of the campaign against Lin and the Gang was a conscious preliminary step in the subsequent blunt attack on ultra-Leftism. From its inception, an important emphasis of the campaign had been on investigating and ferreting out co-conspirators, supporters, and fellow-travelers of the radicals at various levels; this was particularly the case with the nationwide mass criticism rallies that became part of the campaign in the first year following the downfall of the Gang. By calling an end to the mass movement phase of that campaign, the leadership may have been seeking to defuse this personally vengeful and antagonistic avenue of attack and replace it with a more analytical and potentially constructive critique of ultra-Leftism. Thus, while proclaiming a "victorious conclusion" of the "mass movement to criticize the Gang of Four" in late 1978–early 1979, the media also stated that dealing with the "counterrevolutionary revisionist line and the reactionary ideological system of Lin Biao and the Gang of Four is a long-term, arduous task."[78] Another report welcomed the end of the mass campaign, but asserted the continuing necessity of combatting the "pernicious influence" and "mental shackles" imposed by the Gang and declared that "Future criticism and exposure should be carried out in close connection with the Party's central tasks and the ideological realities of the people in the New Long March."[79] In this light, the reorientation of the criticism of the Gang was consistent with the dictum of the Third Plenum that "large scale turbulent class struggles of a mass character have, in the main, come to an end" and that the emphasis of the nation's work had shifted to "socialist modernization."[80]

The whole notion of "pseudo-Leftism" as a definitive analysis of the nature of an erroneous political trend was called into question in late January 1979 when *Guangming ribao* declared that "'fake Left' is not a scientific summation of the opportunist line of Lin Biao and the Gang of Four."[81] In the course of the following months, the nature of the political line propounded by Lin and the Gang was redefined through a process that evolved into the most thorough analysis of ultra-Leftism since the founding of the Chinese Communist Party.

Despite some permutations in the specific label applied to the line of Lin and the Gang, the most important features of the critique of ultra-Leftism that emerged after late January 1979 remained quite consistent. This critique included an acknowledgment that the discussion of "pseudo-Leftism" that lasted from December 1977 to

December 1978 was a breakthrough in the criticism of Lin and the Gang because "it was really something new and in criticizing revisionism, it helped lift the taboo that permitted people to criticize the Right and not the 'Left.'" [82] At the same time, it was argued that the use of the term "fake Left, real Right" had become an obstacle to a full "scientific" repudiation of the "Left opportunist" line because it had obscured the most important ramifications of the specific political program espoused by Lin and the Gang. That term had incorrectly implied that the havoc wreaked by their erroneous line was due more to the line's "real Right" essence than to its "fake Left" manifestations:

In determining the line of Lin Biao and the "Gang of Four" the term "fake Left" gives the impression that, first, the line of Lin Biao and the Gang of Four was devoid of [actual] "Left" opportunism; second, [that] there was a very revolutionary and correct "real Leftist" opportunist line; third, [that] their line was bad not because it was "Leftist," but because it was "fake"; and fourth, [that] there is no "Leftist" but only Rightist deviation in the socialist period. [83]

Another weakness of the "pseudo-Leftist" label, it was pointed out, was its implication that Left errors in line were not of serious consequence to socialist development because those who committed such errors were "sincere" in their subjective desire to "make revolution." The new critique of ultra-Leftism was based on the assertion that individual subjective motivation (benevolent or malevolent) was not a reliable criterion for the classification and analysis of a political line.

One of the distinctions made previously to differentiate "Left opportunists" from "pseudo-Leftists" was that the former were said to have "still wanted to make revolution" whereas the latter really sought to undermine the socialist revolution despite their ultra-Left appearance. Although subjective motives might be important in criticizing and rectifying individual errors, it was now argued, this must not be allowed to obscure the fact that people with very different motives can and do push similar political lines. The nature of that line and its effects do not change regardless of the motives of the individuals involved. As one commentary put it, "When a warehouse is on fire, it is still a fire whether it was set by a bad man or by a comrade." [84]

Furthermore, the description of the line of Lin Biao and the Gang of Four as "fake Left, real Right" had been based on the allegation that ultra-Rightist restorationist aims and conspiratorial political activities lay beneath their "Leftist" appearance. Now it was suggested that even though they may have had Rightist motives and engaged in Rightist activities, their *line* was not necessarily ultra-Rightist:

> There is no natural link between the subjective motives of the formulators of an erroneous line and the carrying out or the characteristics of a line, whether it is correct or incorrect, "Left" or Right. In order to carry out counterrevolutionary goals, an enemy element who has infiltrated the Party may push an erroneous line. . . . So may a real revolutionary, because a real revolutionary motive cannot guarantee the correctness of a line. A counterrevolutionary may push a Right or a "Left" deviationist line. . . . Furthermore . . . we cannot confuse an erroneous line with counterrevolutionary conspiratorial activities.[85]

Just as the subjective desire for revolution or counterrevolution did not justify a distinction between "Left opportunism" and "pseudo-Leftism," neither could the existence of ultra-Right objectives or "counterrevolutionary conspiratorial activities" impart a Rightist essence to Leftist errors. As one analysis pithily summarized this idea, "If a line is 'Left' it is 'Left'; if a line is Right, it is Right."[86]

Another important ingredient in the earlier case that the line of Lin and the Gang was really Rightist in nature was the point that their "pseudo-Leftist" policies so severely undermined the socialist economy and the dictatorship of the proletariat as to create conditions conducive to the resurrection of the bourgeoisie and the restoration of capitalism. Thus, the *projected results* of the particular variant of ultra-Leftism pushed by Lin and the Gang were said to make the essence of their line equivalent to an ultra-Right line.[87] This type of reasoning was explicitly rejected in early 1979:

> Is it not possible to regard "Left" as essentially Right by assuming that a "Leftist" opportunist line is also aimed at wrecking the revolution? *This will confuse the line itself with the adverse results caused by the line*. In fact, the revolution can be ruined either from the Right or from the "Left," in the same way a village can be wiped out by fire or by mountain torrents.[88]

To continue to labor under such false reasoning would only give credence to the fallacy that Left errors were somehow less serious than Right errors and would prevent a thorough rectification of the ultra-Left trend of recent years:

Just as people do not attribute to a flood the destruction of a village by fire, so the adverse consequences of the "Leftist" line should not be attributed to the Rightist line. The view that "Leftist" errors in ruining the revolution should also be considered Rightist ones is illogical. . . . This is no different than urging people to protect villages against mountain torrents but not against fires or to combat the Right in line struggle rather than the "Left." Practical experience has shown that this will facilitate the emergence of a "Leftist" opportunist line.[89]

In sum, the repudiation of the formulations "fake Left, real Right" and "pseudo-Leftism" as modes of ideological criticism involved a denial of both *subjective motivation* and *projected result* as valid criteria for differentiating Left versus Right deviations. Rather, the only standard of analysis was said to be the *objective content* of the line as expressed in "slogans, principles, [and] systems which guide people's actions."[90] Left and Right erroneous lines must not be analytically mixed up because they were diametrically different in "political program, demands, methods, and tactics."[91] This shift to objective content as the key determinant in line analysis was linked to the new emphasis on practice as the touchstone of theory and policy:

What should we base ourselves on when we classify the line of Lin Biao and the "Gang of Four"? Practice is the sole criterion for testing truth. We must base ourselves on the things which Lin Biao and the Gang of Four did and which adversely affected the revolutionary cause. We must see whether the line they actually pursued "outstripped" [a Left error] or "failed to advance" with [a Right error] objective reality.[92]

In rejecting the classification of the line of Lin and the Gang as ultra-Right, one article implicitly criticized Hua Guofeng when it bemoaned the degree to which the "pernicious influence" of the last decade had precluded an earlier direct critique of ultra-Leftism. Without mentioning Hua by name, the article pointedly denounced previous characterizations of the Gang's line that had been popularized following Hua's use of them in his speech at the Second Dazhai Conference: "Because we were mentally shackled for a long time, we were unable to emancipate our minds overnight. This is why we still used such formulations as 'the ultra-Right line,' 'they could not have been farther to the Right,' and the 'ultra-Right essence of the counterrevolutionary revisionist line' in criticizing the Gang of Four."[93]

Following the criterion of objective content, the political line of Lin and the Gang was at first (January 1979) dubbed a "thick and long Left opportunist line."[94] Only a few days later, the label "Left opportunist" was joined by the seemingly more damning rubric "ultra-Left counterrevolutionary revisionist line."[95] This formulation was then shortened (in February) to simply "ultra-Left political line," and the phrase "counterrevolutionary revisionist" was simultaneously rejected as an inappropriate appellation for describing a line struggle within the Party.[96] These terminological changes may have seemed minor, but in retrospect it is clear that they provided the theoretical foundation for a far-reaching reinterpretation of the relationship between line struggle and class struggle in socialist society, which was one of the most significant consequences of the critique of ultra-Leftism as it evolved in 1979–80.

A letter to *Guangming ribao* in early February 1979 commenting on the previous trend in the criticism of the Gang stated that it was "unscientific" to call their line a "counterrevolutionary revisionist line" because such usage "will only confuse, in a political sense, correct and erroneous lines with revolution and counterrevolution and thus aggravate class struggle."[97] This distinction was elevated to official status a short time later. Counterrevolution, it was argued, was a manifestation of class struggle between the proletariat and the bourgeoisie (or between "the enemy and the people") and must be resolved through the coercive instrumentality of the dictatorship of the proletariat. Line struggle within the Party, however, was "a question of distinguishing between right and wrong. This kind of question should be solved according to the method of struggle within the Party, namely the method of criticism and self-criticism. It must not be solved by the methods reserved for the enemy and counterrevolutionaries."[98] Largely because of the ultra-Left influence of Lin and the Gang, questions of line struggle and class struggle had "from the Cultural Revolution up to now . . . been mixed together," resulting in great "harm and confusion."[99]

Further confusion on this issue was said to have been caused by the fact that, in the case of Lin Biao and the Gang of Four, "the questions of line and counterrevolution were closely related."[100] Lin and the Gang were indeed counterrevolutionaries who pushed an ultra-Left line; nonetheless, these two aspects of their political character must be kept analytically distinct when criticizing their various mistakes:

Our struggles with Lin Biao and the Gang of Four were two line struggles. Lin Biao and the Gang of Four did openly push a fairly comprehensive "Left" opportunist line within the Party. Nevertheless, our struggles with them were not limited to the question of political line. The struggle had the nature of those between revolutionaries and counterrevolutionaries. Because of their dual nature, these struggles were extremely acute and complex. Despite this nature, these two kinds of struggle can and must be distinguished.[101]

In this context, the formulation "fake Left, real Right" was sanctioned as an appropriate description of Lin Biao and the Gang as a political *faction*, but not as a characterization of their political *line*. In labeling a political faction, it was deemed proper to take into account the subjective motives and conspiratorial activities of the individuals involved. Thus, in delineating the scope within which the label "fake Left, real Right" could legitimately be applied, *Renmin ribao* argued:

. . . it can be reasonably and scientifically applicable only to the nature of the reactionary political faction of Lin Biao and the Gang of Four. This is because they are through and through reactionaries, counterrevolutionaries, and Rightists. In order to cover themselves up and deceive others . . . they appeared to be "Leftists," but were Rightists, or sham Leftists, but real Rightists. That is to say, it is appropriate to use the term "sham Left, real Right" to generalize about their political features. It is entirely irrational to use this term to describe anything beyond this scope, especially when referring to the line of Lin Biao and the Gang of Four.[102]

This bifurcation between line and faction implied that line struggle within the Party involved nonantagonistic contradictions to be resolved through the process of criticism and self-criticism with the aim of rectification and unity; factional struggle, on the other hand, reflected antagonistic contradictions between "the people and the enemy" that could only be resolved through class struggle and the dictatorship of the proletariat. Therefore, the sincere followers of a mistaken political line should be treated differently from the members of a counterrevolutionary faction who simply made cynical political use of that line. In advocating relatively lenient treatment for those "comrades" influenced by the Gang's ultra-Leftism, *Renmin ribao* commented that there were many people "who are obsessed with the [ultra-Left] line and who are still following it." However, it pointed out, "these people definitely are not renegades, enemy agents, or counterrevolutionaries. They only made mistakes in their political line. . . . One can say that they followed a line that could be easily used by counterrevolutionaries, but one cannot say that by following that line they were opposing the revolution." [103]

Although the ultra-Left line of Lin and the Gang was said to have been the source of the greatest harm to China's socialist development for more than two decades, it was strongly implied that what really brought about the cataclysmic showdown of October 1976 was their factional political activities around the issue of succession to Zhou and Mao, not their ultra-Leftism per se. The dichotomy drawn between line and faction suggested an extension of the notion of *degeneration*, which was an important part of the "fake Left, real Right" analysis of Lin and the Gang. In that context, degeneration occurred when proponents of an ultra-Left line allowed political ambition to overshadow their enthusiasm for revolution. The interpretation of the cases of Lin Biao and the Gang of Four as it developed in 1979–80 suggested an intertwining of line struggle and factional struggle in a process of *amalgamation* that permanently escalated the level of the contradictions involved. The amalgamation could result from degeneration in either of two directions. For example, the struggle with Lin Biao went through a "process of development" that began as only "a question of line within the Party." Although Lin pursued an ultra-Left line from an early point in his political and military career, he "used that seemingly revolutionary line to serve his anti-Party ambition and *gradually* became a counterrevolutionary." [104] After he became a counterrevolutionary, the issue of his ultra-Left line was only a secondary aspect of the contradiction between Lin, on the one hand, and the Party and the people, on the other. As *Renmin ribao* commented,

. . . if we still consider [Lin's] question as one of line and go on to discuss whether his "Outline of 'Project 571'" and his attempt to assassinate Chairman Mao was a "Left" or a Right line after Lin Biao's counterrevolutionary features had been exposed and after he had become an out-and-out heinous counterrevolutionary, then we are deliberately trying to confuse the matter or [are] stupid fools. [105]

The Gang of Four pushed the same ultra-Left line as Lin, but "their individual problems were not the same." They were "traitors, enemy agents, and class aliens who had wormed their way into the Party. . . . [A]s soon as they began pushing their [ultra-Left] political line, they acted from counterrevolutionary motives of endangering the Party and usurping Party power." [106] The Gang's counterrevolutionary features were said to have been deeper in origin, and also better hidden than Lin's because their ultra-Leftism was even more extreme and systematic. Still, in analyzing the Gang and in dealing with their "pernicious influence," their Rightist counterrevolutionary features must not be equated with their ultra-Left political line: "If we consider their line as simply a question of counterrevolution, then we are oversimplifying and, in fact, covering up their extremely harmful line. . . . [A]nd if we consider their question of counterrevolution as simply a question of line, then we are beautifying them."[107]

The process of amalgamation of line and faction in the case of Lin Biao thus evolved *from* ultra-Leftism *to* counterrevolution, whereas in the Gang's case the process was just the reverse. This pointed distinction was meant to imply that, so far as the consequences were concerned, there was no objective difference in the two cases involving the amalgamation of an ultra-Left political line and counterrevolutionary activities. But the *potential* for resolution of the original contradiction in the two cases in the early stages of development was fundamentally different: in the Lin-type case the contradiction originated in principled differences in line within the Party, whereas in the Gang-type case the question of revolution versus counterrevolution dictated a much more antagonistic character to the struggle from the very start. In other words, from this point of view, Lin Biao began as a "sincere" ultra-Leftist and only later got carried away by his lust for power, whereas the Gang were, from the beginning, dyed-in-the-wool reactionaries with bad class backgrounds and dubious political histories, and they callously made use of the ultra-Left trend in Chinese political life to serve their own political ends.

The more trenchant critique of the ultra-Left line that developed in 1979–80 did not involve a denial that ultra-Rightism as manifest in the form of factionalism and conspiracy was a decisive aspect of the struggle with Lin and the Gang. The call to "expose and criticize their way of using their ultra-Left line to carry out their conspiracies"[108] did not appear, on the surface, to contradict earlier formulations such as "The more thoroughly we unmask . . . the 'Leftist' disguise [of the political line of Lin and the Gang], the more we fully reveal its ultra-Right essence,"[109] or "Strip off . . . their pseudo-revolutionary masks to thoroughly criticize their reactionary nature."[110] However, the post-1979 rendition of how to balance the Leftist and Rightist aspects of the cases of Lin and the

Gang clearly elevated the problem of the ultra-Left line from the level of being an associated phenomenon (a "mask" or a "disguise") to that of a very serious political and ideological matter that must be dealt with on its own terms.

Lin Biao and the Gang of Four were both still considered to represent "fake Left, real Right" political factions who pushed an ultra-Left line. The goal of their factions, it was argued, was to turn China into a "feudal fascist dictatorship."[111] They sought to achieve this goal by espousing a line built on what was dubbed a theory of "sham socialism"[112] (as opposed to "scientific socialism"), which derived its ultra-Left character from its underemphasis on the material factors in historical development and its overemphasis on the scope of the proletarian dictatorship and class struggle in socialist society. One of the most detrimental legacies of the Lin-Gang era was said to be that many people "took 'sham socialism' for genuine socialism." Such people were either still wedded to an ultra-Left viewpoint in evaluating socialist development or had come to equate socialism with lack of material progress and had concluded that "socialism is not as good as capitalism."[113]

TABLE I

The Gang of Four: Ultra-Left Political Line, Ultra-Right Political Faction

Category	Gang of Four's political *line*	Gang of Four as a political *faction*
Nature (and essence)	Ultra-Left (Left opportunist)	Ultra-Right (fake Left, real Right)
Nature determined by	Objective content (slogans, principles, policies, systems)	1. Subjective motivation (restore capitalism) 2. Political behavior (conspiracy) 3. Class origins and political history (landlord, Guomindang, etc.)
Key issued involved	Correct vs. incorrect policies to build socialism	Revolution vs. counterrevolution
Type of contradiction	Inner-Party/ nonantagonistic	People vs. enemy/antagonistic
Method of resolution	Criticism–self-criticism	Class struggle/dictatorship of the proletariat
Result if unchecked	Sham socialism	Feudal fascism

The practical impact of the analytical distinction between the Gang's ultra-Left political line and their counterrevolutionary faction (see Table 1) on politics in post-Mao China will be discussed in more detail in the concluding chapter. Here it is only important to note that this distinction was immediately regarded as a matter with important implications beyond the realms of theory and criticism. It was argued that the implementation of policies to correct the Leftist trend of the past would be severely impeded if preoccupation with the Gang's conspiratorial activities precluded a thorough critique of ultra-Leftism. Obscuring the difference between line and faction would also lead people to follow the Gang's example in treating nonantagonistic political errors as instances of class struggle.[114] Such shortcomings in the critique of the Gang of Four would be "a theoretical mistake detrimental to our practice" and would leave the possibility of a resurgence of ultra-Leftism in the future.[115]

Explaining the Anti-Gang Critique

Why did the post-Gang critique of ultra-Leftism evolve in the way it did? Why did the criticism of the Gang begin with an extensive effort to label their line as ultra-Rightist, then shift to an attack on them as "fake Left, real Right," and only take up a direct critique of ultra-Leftism in January 1979—more than two years after the Gang's fall from power?

One explanation lies in the fact that, as in the campaign against the "Swindlers like Liu Shaoqi," the critique of ultra-Leftism also became a bone of political contention between leadership groups after the purge of the Gang—though it never reached the level of intensity or acrimony of the confrontation between the Veteran Revolutionaries and the Cultural Revolutionaries in 1971–73. The more muted nature of the later struggle over the critique of ultra-Leftism suggests some measure of consensus within Party ruling circles over the targets to be criticized; it also reflects the fact that the forces within the leadership who would have gained from a curtailment of the critique of ultra-Leftism were politically fragmented and ideologically immobilized to an important degree after the ouster of the Gang and were therefore unable to offer sustained resistance to the expanding anti-Leftist campaign.

Nevertheless, the circumlocutious development of the campaign against the Gang must be at least partly attributed to a factional struggle that emerged in the Party following the death of Mao Zedong in September 1976.[116] On the one hand, a group called the "Practice" faction (*shijianpai*) had everything to gain by an all-out assault on ultra-Leftism. This group, led by Deng Xiaoping and the resurrected Veteran Revolutionaries, derived its name from the slogan "Practice is the sole criterion of truth," which it disingenuously appropriated from a saying by Mao as a catch-all rubric for discarding the radical policies of the preceding decade and debunking the Maoist precepts that had provided the ideological rationale for the Cultural Revolution. Claiming to have been the unjust victims of the Gang of Four's persecution of veteran cadres and making the case that an ultra-Left line had brought China to the brink of ruin, the "Practice" faction used the critique of ultra-Leftism as a potent instrument to legitimize both their political power and their pragmatic modernization program.

On the other hand, another leadership group had sound reasons for resisting a thorough investigation and repudiation of the ultra-Left trend, especially as such efforts involved a reexamination of the legacy of Mao Zedong. This group was pejoratively designated by their opponents as the "Whatever" faction (*fanshipai*) because of their alleged adherence to a pledge made in a major media editorial in February 1977 "to support *whatever* policy decisions were made by Chairman Mao and . . . unswervingly follow *whatever* instructions were given by Chairman Mao."[117] Wang Dongxing, Mao's long-time bodyguard who rose quickly in the Party hierarchy after the Chairman's death, and Hua Guofeng, who had become both premier and Party chairman through Mao's personal endorsement, have been identified as key figures of the "Whatever" faction.[118] As Lucien Pye has pointed out, members of this faction had played a vital role in the arrest of the Gang of Four and "certainly did not want to abandon the Four Modernizations and revive the policies of the Cultural Revolution."[119] Despite some similarity of interests between the "Practice" and the "Whatever" factions, a comprehensive critique of ultra-Leftism did threaten the legitimacy of the latter's rise to power in the final stages of the Cultural Revolution and during the succession crises of 1976; furthermore, such a critique would raise embarrassing questions concerning the role of the "Whatevers" in the campaign to criticize Deng Xiaoping in 1975–76 and in the suppression of the "Tian An Men Incident," which had erupted from a spontaneous anti-Gang rally in the center of Peking in April 1976. A critique of ultra-Leftism also contradicted the "Whatevers'" relatively strict interpretation of Maoist principles and policies.

The dogged effort to pin the label of ultra-Rightism on the Gang of Four between October 1976 and early 1979 can partly be explained by the attempt of the "Whatever" faction to keep the anti-Gang campaign from turning into a full-scale critique of ultra-Leftism. The influence of the "Whatevers" over the media and in ideological affairs gave them an advantageous position from which to shape the contours of the criticism of the Gang of Four. However, following the formal reinstatement of Deng Xiaoping in August 1977, the "Practice" faction was gradually able to undercut the "Whatevers" and neutralize their opposition to the critique of ultra-Leftism. The Third Plenum of the Eleventh Central Committee in December 1978 was, according to the 1981 Resolution on Party History, "a crucial turning point" in the criticism of the Gang of Four; the Plenum "put an end to the situation in which the Party had been advancing haltingly in its work since October 1976 and began to correct conscientiously and comprehensively the 'Left' errors of the 'cultural revolution' and earlier." [120] During the following year, the "Whatever" faction was further isolated within the leadership, and in February 1980 several key members of the faction (Wang Dongxing, Ji Dengkui, Wu De, and Chen Xilian) fell victim to the rectification campaign that accompanied the deepening critique of ultra-Leftism and were removed from their state and Party positions. [121] The political eclipse of Hua Guofeng, who also was caught up in the anti-Leftist rectification movement, was more protracted: he was replaced as premier in September 1980 and as Party chairman in June 1981, giving way in both cases to protégés of Deng Xiaoping. Among the charges leveled at Hua to justify his demotion was the allegation that "he promoted the erroneous 'two-whatevers' policy . . . and he took a long time to rectify the error." [122]

The degree to which the "Whatever" faction and Hua Guofeng truly fit into the category of ultra-Leftists is open to question; [123] nevertheless, the close timing of the demise of the "Whatever" Faction and the expanded critique of ultra-Leftism in 1979–80 looks to be more than coincidental. Yet factionalism within the Party leadership was not the only factor contributing to the rather curious pattern of the anti-Gang campaign.

Another explanation lies in the complexity of unraveling the problem of ultra-Leftism as it was seen to have affected China's development since 1949. Any leader, whatever his personal stakes or factional affiliation, must have taken some pause at what could have come of launching a thorough critique of ultra-Leftism—which could open a Pandora's box of political and ideological questions that could threaten the foundations of the Party's legitimacy. Such a critique would inevitably call into question such milestones of the Chinese road to socialism as the Great Leap Forward and the Great Proletarian Cultural Revolution, and, therefore, the leadership and ideology of Mao Zedong; and certainly Mao's legacy could not be tarnished without affecting the public image of the Party as a whole. Furthermore, unlike the well-established framework for analyzing and rectifying Rightist errors that had been Mao's preoccupation for at least twenty years, there was little precedent in either theory or practice for engaging in a thorough critique of ultra-Leftism. The post-Mao leadership therefore had some reason to move carefully toward such a critique, for it represented a step into unknown and possibly dangerous territory.

The initial effort to focus the criticism of the Gang of Four on their ultra-Rightist activities provided a convenient camouflage for the near-total obliteration of the concrete program of the Cultural Revolution without precipitously negating the "revolutionary tradition" of which it was an integral part.[124] The dismantling of the Cultural Revolution model of development proceeded in almost uninterrupted fashion after the fall of the Gang regardless of whether their line was being labeled as ultra-Right, "fake Left, real Right," or ultra-Left. Thus, the various stages in the criticism of the Gang may have been part of the new leadership's effort to undertake a gradual critique of ultra-Leftism while providing a buffer against too rapid a turnabout in the official ideology. The sequencing of the campaign we have described may have been, in part, the product of a conscious decision to discredit the Gang politically by first exposing their ultra-Right conspiracies and personal histories before tackling the more thorny problem of their ultra-Left line.

In sum, the evolution of the post-Gang critique of ultra-Leftism reflected the fact that late 1976 through 1980 was a transitional period in which a challenge to the legitimacy of much of China's recent past became an issue of factional struggle. The critique was also a matter of such enormous potential impact on the Chinese political system that it demanded cautious handling by all those concerned.

7
The Ultra-Leftism of Lin Biao
and the Gang of Four

> A bourgeoisie is . . . as necessary a precondition of the
> socialist revolution as the proletariat itself. A person who
> says that this revolution can be carried out easier in a
> country which has no proletariat or bourgeoisie proves by
> his statement that he still has to learn the ABC's of
> socialism.
>
> Engels (1875)

Despite its aborted result, the critique of ultra-Leftism during the
campaign against the "Swindlers like Liu Shaoqi" in 1971–73 did
raise a number of important issues. As we saw in chapter 5, the
radicals in the Party leadership were able to forestall an all-out assault on the Cultural Revolution following the death of Lin Biao;
nevertheless, for a brief time, Lin's demise and the "Swindlers"
campaign provided the critics of the ultra-Left with a vehicle for
challenging the prevailing direction of Chinese politics. On a variety of fronts, the Veteran Revolutionaries questioned the legacy of
the Cultural Revolution, hoping to foster major policy readjustments that would turn attention away from the violent class
struggles of the previous decade and toward what they saw as the
pressing tasks of modernization. Some concrete changes were effected in the early 1970's,[1] but most efforts at policy reform were
short-circuited by the radicals' political offensive between 1973 and
1975, which heralded a revival of many of the themes of the Cultural Revolution.[2]

I have described the confrontation between the Veteran Revolutionaries and the Cultural Revolutionaries over the critique of ultra-
Leftism in 1971–73 as a "dress rehearsal" for the 1976 political
showdown over the succession to Zhou Enlai and Mao Zedong.
The connection between these two periods is further demonstrated
by the striking parallel in the issues raised during the anti-Leftist
phase of the "Swindlers" campaign and in the criticism of the Gang
of Four.[3] Not only is the content of both installments of the critique
of ultra-Leftism similar, but even the verbal presentations assailing

various Leftist deviations are often virtually identical. These parallels illustrate the protractedness of the ideological conflict in the Chinese Communist Party and confirm our earlier point that the real aim of the first part of the "Swindlers" campaign was a discrediting of the remaining Cultural Revolutionaries in the leadership and not an ex post facto excoriation of Lin Biao.

Even though the links between the anti-Lin and the anti-Gang campaigns may seem obvious in retrospect, it was not until early 1978 that the criticism of the Gang of Four was officially connected with criticism of Lin Biao. Up to that time, the two cases were treated separately, except that they were both considered to be examples of serious line struggles (the tenth and eleventh, respectively, in the Party's history) that had been waged against "unrepentant capitalist roaders." [4] Later on, when the focus of the campaign against the Gang had shifted from their ultra-Rightism to their "fake Left, real Right" political line, Lin and the Four came to be described in phrases like "jackals of the same lair," "badgers of the same hole," and "tweedledum and tweedledee in respect to line, ideology, and theory." [5] This lumping together was part of the effort of Deng Xiaoping and his followers in the "Practice" faction to broaden the attack on the Cultural Revolution and solidify the ideological basis of the Four Modernizations, and it was apparently resisted by those in the leadership (the "Whatever" faction) who preferred to see the campaign keep its narrow focus on the Gang's conspiratorial activities rather than expand into a comprehensive critique of ultra-Leftism.[6] With the political collapse of the "Whatever" faction following the Third Plenum in December 1978, the media consistently linked the criticism of Lin Biao and the Gang of Four and thereafter treated them as proponents of a similar ultra-Left line.[7]

The first part of this chapter will highlight some of the thematic parallels between the post-Lin and post-Gang critiques of ultra-Leftism. We shall then turn to a discussion of the more substantive analysis of the ultra-Left line of Lin Biao and the Gang of Four that developed after 1976.

Thematic Links between the Two Critiques

The issues raised in the critique of ultra-Leftism in 1971–73 never congealed into a systematic dissection of the origins or impact of Leftist deviations in socialist society. Rather, what emerged

in that period was a haphazard critique that offered a random catalogue of complaints about Leftist trends in specific policy areas
along with a few morsels of alleged ideological errors. This dis-
jointed character was due in part to the contention that the whole
question of the critique had aroused in the Party, and it also reflected the Party's unpreparedness to undertake a trenchant analysis
of ultra-Leftism in a political environment still under the influence
of the virulent anti-Rightist ideology of the Cultural Revolution.
Although the death of Mao and the purge of the Gang of Four in
1976 and the dissipation of the "Whatever" faction in 1978–80
had made possible a more penetrating criticism of ultra-Leftism,
the expanded critique was colored by carryovers from the earlier
fragmented critique, particularly in the analysis of Leftist errors in
rural development, policies toward industry, science, and technology, the treatment of veteran cadres and intellectuals, the relationship between the goals of revolution and production, and the proper
evaluation of Mao Zedong Thought in the changing conditions of
socialism in China.

Rural Development

Jürgen Domes has argued that Lin Biao spearheaded an attempt
to revive many of the radical policies of the Great Leap Forward
under the rallying banner of a vigorous campaign in 1970–71 to
"Learn from Dazhai"—the model brigade in Shanxi Province that
epitomized the Cultural Revolution call to put "politics in command" of agricultural development.[8] Lin is alleged to have pushed
rural policies that reflected a resurgence of egalitarianism and other
ultra-Leftist trends that had been criticized during the Great Leap.
An equally obvious parallel, however, is between the post-Lin critique of Leftist errors in rural development and similar themes in
the criticism of the Gang of Four.

The "Swindlers" were criticized for implementing policies that
enhanced the power of the production brigade and the commune at
the expense of the authority of the production team. These policies
may have been intended to elevate the level of socialization in the
countryside, but they actually resulted, it was charged, in mismanagement, bureaucratization, and commandism, and had a con-
sequent negative effect on production. Contravention of "the policy
of 'ownership at three levels with the production team as the basis'
. . . [was] interference from the Left sabotaging Chairman Mao's
revolutionary line."[9]

Violation of the authority of the production team was said to affect four areas of rural policy.

  1. *Planning.* The higher levels reserved for themselves too much power and responsibility for the planning of agricultural production instead of encouraging more input of the unit most directly involved in the actual work, the production team. One commune described the problem this way:

> Some comrades of the production brigade and the commune did not take care to consult with the production team cadres and masses, and when making plans for production activities, they invariably insisted on unanimity of action. When making arrangements for the planting areas of crops and popularizing fine seed strains from outside, they likewise paid no attention to actual conditions, but laid stress on uniformity.[10]

This sort of "blind direction" of production was said to be the result of "commandism" by brigade and commune cadres who considered the team to be a retrogressive level of ownership with latent capitalist tendencies that could only be constrained by aggressively restricting the scope of team authority in economic management. In the post-Gang period, there has also been a strong reassertion of the rights of the team to plan their own production on the basis of their knowledge of local conditions; there has also been sustained criticism of the ultra-Left fallacy that the Chinese countryside was either materially or ideologically prepared for more centralized planning in local agricultural affairs.[11]

  2. *Distribution.* In December 1971, the Central Committee issued a "Directive Concerning the Question of Distribution in the Rural People's Communes." This Directive, very similar in tone and content to resolutions issued as part of the Great Leap readjustments, addressed a series of problems in rural distribution that had appeared in the midst of the 1970–71 "Learn from Dazhai" campaign.[12] One observation, for example, was:

> Some communes "partition all and eat all"; others increased production collectively, but commune members' income did not increase; and some others have many households that overdraw, making normal distribution impossible. Still others, having criticized "work points take command," exercised egalitarianism in paying for labor. All these impaired the thorough implementation of Chairman Mao's revolutionary line.[13]

The policy of distribution based on labor was strongly reaffirmed and the ultra-Left trend in remuneration repudiated with the claim, "In the current stage, attention must be paid to overcoming egalitarianism."[14]

Similar criticisms of the Gang of Four's influence on rural distribution were raised by a media campaign excoriating the deleterious impact of egalitarianism on rural development and extolling the virtues of "getting rich" as an incentive for hard work.[15] Furthermore, the commune "Regulations" of 1962 on which the 1971 Directive on distribution was based were revived in 1979 as the basic guideline for all aspects of management in the people's communes.[16]

3. *Accounting.* The question of which unit should be in charge of financial accounting has been closely related to the issue of distribution in the critique of ultra-Leftism in rural affairs. One of the features of the Dazhai model was that it took the brigade as the unit of accounting and distribution; this procedure was copied elsewhere in 1970–71 but without much regard for the objective situation or the desires of the masses. This pattern of accounting was judged to be "premature implementation today of a policy which was designed for the future" and was said to have dampened the peasants' enthusiasm for labor because it weakened the link between individual effort and reward.[17] In the brigade-level accounting system, the share of collective output earmarked for personal income distribution was based on the labor contributed by a much larger pool of households than in the case of team accounting, and there was little personal relationship among the peasants joined together in the distribution process. Peasants began to feel that they were working for the benefit of "strangers" rather than for just themselves and their families and close neighbors. Though the wider range of inputs in the brigade-based distribution pool (including labor power, machinery, and natural endowments) may have raised the average output of the constituent units, richer teams resented the results as "leveling" and felt that they were contributing much and getting too little in return. This ultra-Left trend in rural accounting was said to have led to a significant decline in agricultural productivity because of its disincentive effect on many individual peasants. In the post-Gang era, the spread of inappropriate brigade-level accounting also became one of the principal fallacies attributed to the repudiated Dazhai model in agriculture.[18]

4. *Uncompensated requisition of labor and property.* The 1971 Central Committee Directive on Distribution also cautioned higher levels (county, commune, brigade) against diverting funds or utilizing labor power from the teams without consultation or adequate compensation.[19] On several occasions in 1972, cadres were criticized for violating the policy of "exchange at equal value" when

requisitioning team labor to engage in brigade or commune projects such as road building or irrigation construction. Uncompensated labor may have boosted the collective economy in the short
run, it was argued, but it lowered the team's (and therefore the individual's) income, and led in turn to a decline in labor enthusiasm
and agricultural productivity.[20] Similar themes were raised in the
1977–78 campaign to "lighten the production team's burden." An
important aspect of this campaign was to protect team income by
proscribing the "arbitrary transfer of manpower, material, and financial resources" by the higher levels.[21]

In their effort to "cut off the tail of capitalism in the countryside," the "Swindlers" were accused of carrying out wholesale suppression of legitimate sideline production by peasants and restricting the operation of rural trade fairs where output from these
endeavors could be sold or bartered. This curtailed an important
source of supplemental income for many rural households and also
led to a severe shortage of many commodities ranging from pork to
woven bamboo ware that could not be adequately supplied by the
collective economy. According to the critique of this ultra-Left
trend, "The crux is not whether side-occupation is carried out or
not, but lies in what line is followed and what policy is carried out
in doing side-occupations."[22] One of the major themes of post-Mao
agricultural policy has been the revitalization of the private sector
in the rural economy. Not only is the Gang of Four's line in this
regard attacked as ultra-Left, but family plots, sideline activities,
and rural markets have been lauded as "progressive" in aiding the
expansion of overall production, raising household incomes, and,
thereby, contributing to the strength of the socialist system.[23]

The "Swindlers" were also criticized for going to extremes in the
implementation of the policy of "taking grain as the key link,"
which was designed to maximize grain production to achieve local
and national self-reliance and provide a secure basis for state taxa-
tion and surplus purchases. The Left deviation in the carrying out
of this policy was "grasping only grain production, but not multiple
undertakings"; the Rightist error would have been "grasping multiple undertakings to make money and seeking one-sidedly to increase cash income and raise the value of work points."[24] Whereas
the Rightist approach undermined the collective rural economy by
fostering capitalist tendencies, the ultra-Left trend hurt the material
basis of socialism in the countryside by severely limiting the diversity of the rural economy in its policy of reducing the production of

"economic crops" like tea, tobacco, peanuts, and ginger that would yield higher profits. The indiscriminate application of the policy of "taking grain as the key link" also led to the giving over to grain of unsuitable land or land that would be much more efficiently used for other crops.[25] A similar distortion in agriculture policy was attributed to the Gang of Four. Beginning in 1979 an increasingly large amount of land was turned over to the production of "economic crops" in order to enhance the income potential of the rural sector; there was also a marked emphasis on putting "animal husbandry first" in suitable areas in order to transform the composition of China's overwhelmingly grain-based diet.[26]

As mentioned above, many of the policies that were criticized in 1971–73 as manifestations of ultra-Leftism in rural affairs were carried out under the banner of a revived "Learn from Dazhai" campaign. With the repudiation of the "Swindlers'" line in agriculture came a mild rebuke of the way in which the Dazhai model had been popularized. For example, the 1971 Directive on Distribution contained a note of caution about the overzealous adoption of the Dazhai model: "To learn from Dazhai's labor administration methods, we must start from the actual situation and discuss the matter with the masses, but not adopt the methods wholly without consideration."[27] At no time did the criticism of the Dazhai model in 1971–72 approach the level of the later campaign of 1979–80, nor did it directly repudiate the *essence* of the model itself (as opposed to criticism of the *misapplication* of the model). Nearly every aspect of the Dazhai experience has now been judged irrelevant to the program for agricultural modernization, and both Dazhai and Xiyang County, of which it is a part, have been accused of falsifying production records and misrepresenting the degree of self-reliance in their development.[28] Even though it is argued that "Dazhai was held up as the ultimate model during the Cultural Revolution because many of its practices conformed to the ultra-Left line pushed by Lin Biao and the Gang of Four,"[29] a strong case was made during the early phases of the criticism of the Gang that Jiang Qing had a vehement hatred of Dazhai because of its economic success which, to her mind, reflected a neglect of politics.[30]

Industry, Science, and Technology

The breakdown of industrial discipline as a result of the spread of anarchist ideas during the Cultural Revolution was one of the earliest and most persistent charges against the "Swindlers." In summing up the struggle against ultra-Left tendencies in one factory, *Renmin ribao* reported:

To give the broad masses a correct understanding of regulations and systems, the Party committee and revolutionary committee of the factory led the masses in vigorously criticizing renegade, hidden traitor, and scab Liu Shaoqi's counterrevolutionary revisionist line and the idea of the ultra-"Left" who call for a break with all regulations and systems. A sharper line is drawn between socialist regulations and systems and revisionist measures designed for the control, strangling, and suppression of workers. Everyone's consciousness of observance of revolutionary discipline and execution of regulations and systems is raised. Development of production is insured.[31]

Likewise, the Gang of Four has been criticized for labeling any efforts to enforce labor discipline as "controlling, checking, and suppressing the workers." On these grounds, they are said to have "wildly opposed the establishment of rational rules and regulations and encouraged anarchism for the sole purpose of usurping Party and state power."[32]

The roles of technicians and managers in China's industry had been greatly circumscribed by the "anti-elitist" emphasis of the Cultural Revolution and the introduction of revolutionary committees and "three-in-one" technical innovation groups providing for worker participation in enterprise affairs that had formerly been considered the province of experts.[33] The 1971–73 criticism of the ultra-Left line suggested that some of the Party leaders thought this trend had gone much too far and was compromising China's ability to modernize by depriving a critical sector of the economy of much needed expertise and leadership. For example, the critique argued that although experts should, indeed, engage in some productive labor from time to time in order to remain in touch with ordinary workers and the "basic situation" in production, they should be assigned the major responsibility for technical work in the factories. Rather than being vilified as "bourgeois elements" because of their specialized skills, they should be encouraged to "study technique for the revolution."[34] An effort was also made to bolster the role of enterprise managers and "to prevent the tendency of laying emphasis on *mass* management while neglecting *special* management."[35] In other words, there were limits to worker participation in technical innovation and the direction of production and to management participation in labor.

Like the "Swindlers," the Gang of Four has been charged with undermining industrial development because their political line "described the strengthening of the production command system as 'making the Party exist in name [only],' vilified efforts made for technical innovation . . . as 'putting technique in command,' smeared those who devoted themselves to technical research as 'taking the road of becoming specialists without socialist consciousness,' and slandered the strengthening of proletarian discipline as following the 'theory of docile tools.'"[36] The restoration of the role of management specialists and technical experts has also been an important theme of post-Mao changes in industrial organization, symbolized by the abolition of the revolutionary committees in 1978 and their replacement with direct management structures.[37]

The ultra-Left line of the "Swindlers" was said to have interfered with the development of science and technology as contributing factors in China's socialist construction. Implying that Leftist errors in science and technology policy were at that time more serious than Rightist errors, one newspaper stated: "The counterrevolutionary aim of the fallacy of 'technique first' advocated by Liu Shaoqi and other political swindlers like him and the 'theory that technology is useless'—*another form of this fallacy in the new current situation*—is to undermine socialist construction and disintegrate the socialist economy."[38] This article enunciated the goals "to build our country into a modernized powerful socialist country in not too long an historical period" and "to catch up with and surpass the world's advanced [scientific] level"—goals strikingly similar to the rallying cry of the post-Gang modernization program. It then went on to repudiate the ultra-Left distortion of the relationship between politics and technology: "Technology itself has nothing to do with politics. But when it is mastered and used by different classes, it shows its clear-cut political character. . . . Putting politics in command does not mean exclusively grasping politics without grasping technique."[39] Deng Xiaoping's assertion in a 1978 speech that "science is part of the productive forces" of society rather than an element of the superstructure reflecting class relationships was indicative of a similar effort to depoliticize science and technology. The post-Mao leadership has sought to dispel the "confusion" caused by the ultra-Left notion that scientific work should be judged by ideological standards apart from its contribution to the material development of socialism.[40]

The Treatment of Intellectuals and Veteran Cadres

The criticism of the "Swindlers'" treatment of technicians and scientists carried over into a general critique of ultra-Leftist policies toward intellectuals in all fields. The ultra-Left was said to have "put emphasis on the remolding of intellectuals without paying attention to using them" in the service of building socialism in China.[41] To counter the assumption of the "Swindlers" that all intellectuals were suffused with "bourgeois" ideology because their labor was mental rather than physical, the argument was put forth in 1972 that the only criterion for determining the political orientation of intellectuals should be whether they were willing to utilize their skills in the interests of socialism.[42] This argument anticipated the criticism of the Gang of Four's alleged "estimate" that most intellectuals were "class enemies of socialism" because of the nature of their work and should for that reason be regarded as "targets" of the dictatorship of the proletariat rather than as allies in the building of socialism.[43] It also foreshadowed the point of view expressed by Deng Xiaoping at the 1978 Science Conference:

The basic question about the world outlook [of intellectuals] is whom to serve. If a person loves our socialist motherland and is serving socialism and the workers, peasants, and soldiers of his own free will and accord, it should be said that he has initially acquired a proletarian world outlook and, in terms of political standards, cannot be considered white [i.e., bourgeois] but should be called red.[44]

This argument was extended to the claim that, far from being enemies of the proletariat, the vast majority of intellectuals should be considered as "part of the working class" with as vital a role to play in socialist society as those engaged in manual labor.[45]

In 1972 there was a good deal of criticism of those who were opposed to the reinstatement of veteran cadres who had been purged during the Cultural Revolution. The issue here was whether veteran cadres who had been criticized were sufficiently rectified to be entrusted again with positions of responsibility and authority, or whether they were untrustworthy simply because they were veteran cadres. For example, the Shenyang No. 3 Machine Tool Plant described the resistance of "some comrades" to the decision to reinstate several old cadres:

. . . the Party committee and the revolutionary committee . . . made preparations gradually for some cadres, including those who had made mistakes, to assume leadership work, so as to further carry out the Party's cadre policy. But being influenced by the ultra-Left ideas spread by Liu Shaoqi and other swindlers like him, some cadres were not confident in letting the old cadres take the leading posts again, and they were afraid that the old cadres would return to the old road.[46]

This type of criticism still carried the notion that the veteran cadres were truly guilty of "mistakes" that merited their overthrow in the Cultural Revolution. When the same theme was raised in the post-Gang critique of ultra-Leftism, any political or ideological malfeasance on the part of veteran cadres prior to the Cultural Revolution was vigorously denied; instead, the dominant issue in the critique of the Gang's line on this matter has been the miscarriage of justice perpetrated by the ultra-Left as part of their general persecution of veteran cadres who did not live up to the standards of "redness" established by the Cultural Revolution or who stood in the way of the political ambitions of the Cultural Revolutionaries at the Center and their followers.[47]

Revolution and Production

Lin Biao and the Gang of Four have together been accused of replacing proper dialectical analysis of various problems in socialist society with a series of what might be called "malcontradictions." This resulted from the dogmatic tendency of the ultra-Leftists to inject a high degree of irreconcilability into the handling of competing priorities in socialist development, to the point where overwhelmingly positive value was attached to one priority while nearly total negative value was ascribed to its opposite, or dialectical complement. The correct approach, the critics have argued, is to understand and act upon the interrelation between differing aspects of a contradiction rather than posing them against one another in an antagonistic fashion. The way in which the "Swindlers" and the Gang allegedly valued only "redness" (high ideological consciousness) and devalued "expertise" in judging the individual merit of cadres and intellectuals is one example of such a "malcontradiction."[48]

On the level of economic units such as factories and communes, the ultra-Leftists have been charged with fostering a "malcontradiction" between the goals of revolution and production. In a sense, this error lies at the heart of the critique of ultra-Leftism: by their one-sided approach to political and ideological questions, Lin Biao and the Gang of Four are said to have disrupted the economy to the

point of undermining the material basis of socialism and impover-
ishing the Chinese people.

In 1971–73, the "Swindlers" were castigated for seeking to "split
politics from economics, and revolution from production." Their
voluntarist theory that "spirit is omnipotent" led to much "empty
talk" and many political meetings, which diverted attention away
from production. They "dealt blows" at cadres and workers who
dared to "grasp production for the sake of revolution," and "whoever failed to heed their treacherous words would be branded as
'putting production above everything else' and 'putting vocational
work in command'" rather than politics. Finally, the ultra-Leftists
were criticized for their belief that politics "would suffice" to stimulate productivity.[49]

An almost identical barrage of charges was unleashed against the
Gang of Four after their downfall in 1976. They were attacked for
sabotaging the economy with their "three poisonous arrows" aimed
at turning the relationship between revolution and production into
an antagonistic contradiction. These "three poisonous arrows"
were their attitudes that "production is a matter of little importance" in comparison with politics; that "production will increase
as a matter of course if revolution is carried out properly"; and that
"those who grasp production are bound to be revisionists."[50] The
post-Gang line refuted the ultra-Leftist notion that revolutionary
politics would automatically unleash an upsurge in production; it
also proclaimed the unity rather than the antagonism between politics and economics and declared that "where production is in a
mess, there must be a problem in revolution."[51] Similarly the new
leadership in China has revived and expanded a theme first broached
during the "Swindlers" campaign that accused the ultra-Left of deni-
grating the importance of sound fiscal management in industrial enterprises. Profits and politics are not incompatible, the new line has
asserted, and the accumulation of capital is a noble revolutionary
task when it is carried out in the service of socialist modernization
and the people's livelihood.[52]

The Evaluation of Mao Zedong Thought

Since Lin Biao was so intimately identified with the cult of personality built up around Mao Zedong during the Cultural Revolution, it was inevitable that a campaign of criticism aimed, at least in
part, at discrediting Lin would entail some repudiation of the Mao

cult. This repudiation mainly took the form of denouncing the "theory of genius" and the "theory that heroes make history," which Lin supposedly used for his own cynical political purposes.[53] Neither of these "theories" has a specifically ultra-Left content: as a matter of fact, it could be argued that an ultra-Left position would scorn such elitist characterizations as "genius" and "heroes," while extolling the virtues of the masses, and indeed the "Swindlers" *were* criticized at one point for propagating "the fallacy that any mass movement is 'naturally rational' . . . a variation of the 'theory of spontaneity' which Marxism refuted long ago."[54]

Nevertheless, since those who promoted what was later denounced as an ultra-Left line gained substantial legitimacy for their policies and their power by being closely associated with Mao, it could also be argued that they would have an understandable political motive for supporting the development of a personality cult around the Chairman. One article in *Renmin ribao* suggested as much when it charged: "Swindlers of the Liu Shaoqi type elevate Mao Zedong Thought in appearance, but in reality debase and denigrate it. Outwardly they establish Chairman Mao's absolute authority, but actually they establish their own authority."[55]

The accusation that Lin Biao promoted a "theory of genius" as a vehicle for his own political ambition persisted as an important theme of criticism even after Lin had been clearly labeled an ultra-Rightist in 1973. But during the anti-Leftist phase of the "Swindlers" campaign several other themes emerged that anticipated, in a milder form, the much more penetrating reevaluation of Mao Zedong Thought that occurred following the downfall of the Gang of Four. Anyone familiar with the rhetoric of the post-Gang era will hear the clear echo of the reevaluation of Mao and his ideology that unfolded in the late 1970's in the following examples drawn from the campaign against the "Swindlers like Liu Shaoqi."

The "Swindlers" were criticized for espousing a dogmatic approach to the interpretation and application of Mao Zedong Thought. They were said to have rigidly applied specific "instructions" of the Chairman without regard either to the situation or historical context. As *Renmin ribao* put it:

Swindlers of the Liu Shaoqi type ceaselessly vary their tactics in opposing Marxism–Leninism–Mao Zedong Thought. At first they made Marxism-Leninism absolute and denied that Mao Zedong Thought was a development of Marxism-Leninism. After this tactic failed, they turned around and made Mao Zedong Thought absolute, denying that Mao Zedong Thought would continue to develop. . . . To make Mao Zedong Thought absolute and solidified is in itself contrary to Mao Zedong Thought.

Marxism–Leninism–Mao Zedong Thought has not put a conclusion to truth, but ceaselessly opens a way to knowing truth in practice.[56]

In other words, Mao Zedong Thought should be regarded not as inflexible dogma but as an ideology that must be adapted or modified to fit changing circumstances.

A correlative criticism held that the "Swindlers" had taken Mao Zedong Thought as an "absolute truth" that could solve all problems and was universally and eternally valid. This approach to ideology was supposedly based on the assumption that since Mao was infallible as a revolutionary leader, his revolutionary teachings, too, must be infallible. This assumption was debunked by several media commentaries, such as one that asked:

What is absolute truth? Chairman Mao has a simple definition for it: absolute truth is "the sum total of innumerable relative truths." Since they are innumerable, they naturally cannot be all counted or all known. Therefore no single individual can know all of the absolute truth exhaustively or enjoy absolute authority in science. . . . The so-called "genius" who "cannot make any mistake" and the "superman" who has exhausted the absolute truth are . . . non-existent.[57]

The implication was obvious enough: even Chairman Mao was a human being who was apt to make human mistakes or omissions, and therefore it was only natural that his Thought would reflect his fallibility.

Another article, after criticizing the "Swindlers" for their insistence on the absoluteness of certain theories allegedly derived from Mao Zedong Thought, sternly warned its readers: "Chairman Mao teaches us 'The criterion for truth can only be social practice.' Whether it is true or false Marxism, the correct or wrong line, it must be subjected to the test of practice." [58]

Remarks like this all had the same point: all theories—even Mao Zedong Thought—had to be continually judged and evaluated against reality and be corrected or rejected when found in conflict with the lessons of social practice. The error of "apriorism," or placing theory above social practice, was one of the key epistemological fallacies of the ultra-Left attacked in the criticism of the "Swindlers" in 1971–73.

The "Swindlers" were also said to have "plagiarized individual

Marxist terms and phrases in an attempt to tamper with and emas-
culate fundamental Marxist principles."[59] Their goal in doing this
was said to have been to manipulate the ideology to serve their own
political ends by conveying the image that their political line was in
keeping with the letter and spirit of Marxism–Leninism–Mao
Zedong Thought. The implication was that they wrapped their line
in the mantle of revolution while portraying their adversaries as
counterrevolutionaries whose actions and policies were in violation
of the true interests of socialism in China.

　　Although none of these themes concerning the nature of Mao
Zedong Thought was very fully developed during the campaign
against the "Swindlers like Liu Shaoqi," this sort of questioning of
the prevailing ideology seems to have been the part of the attack on
ultra-Leftism as it emerged after the death of Lin Biao that most
alarmed the Cultural Revolutionaries—alarmed them enough, at
any rate, to make them take steps to stop the critique. Quite obviously, a penetrating critical appraisal of Mao Zedong Thought
would also challenge the validity of their own attitudes toward socialist revolution in China, and would, moreover, compromise the
legitimacy of their claim to rule as the true bearers of Chairman
Mao's revolutionary line. Following the death of Mao, the purge of
the Gang of Four, and the gradual disappearance of the influence of
the Cultural Revolutionaries at the Center, the themes of the fallibility and relativity of Mao Zedong Thought and the correctness of
a pragmatic approach to the application of revolutionary ideology
to solving concrete problems of socialist development were revived
and extensively elaborated. By 1978–79 these themes had become
a major component of the critique of ultra-Leftism.[60]

The Core Content of the Ultra-Left Line

　　A major breakthrough in the criticism of the Gang of Four and of
ultra-Leftism in general was signified by the shift in early 1979 to an
emphasis on objective content as the key determinant in the analysis of deviations in a political line. Heretofore, the campaign had
concentrated on exposing the Gang's Rightist essence, showing
their counterrevolutionary motives to usurp power and demon-
strating how the restoration of capitalism was their real aim; the
Gang's Leftist errors were, in this analysis, tactical maneuvers, of
only minor concern as compared with the baseness of their broad

goals. The emergence of an unprecedented comprehensive critique of ultra-Leftism became possible only after the consolidation of power in the Party leadership by those who favored such a critique and the acknowledgment that ultra-Leftism constituted a distinct ideological malignancy that was analytically distinct from Rightism in terms of the content of its attendant political line.

We now turn to a discussion of the major characteristics of the line attributed to Lin Biao and the Gang of Four, which is said to have been the culmination of an ultra-Left trend that dominated the Party and adversely affected China's socialist development "for an entire historical period" of more than twenty years.[61] The approach here is different from that of the preceding section, which highlighted the similarities in some of the issues raised in the aborted critique of ultra-Leftism in 1971–73 and in the campaign against the Gang of Four after 1976. That discussion focused on the more concrete policy manifestations of ultra-Leftism, which drew the attention of the critics of the Cultural Revolution. Our main concern here is with the components that form the underlying theoretical framework of what has been described as the "complete system" (*wanzhengde tixi*) of the ultra-Left line of Lin Biao and the Gang of Four.[62] This systemization through theory is said to be a major reason why the ultra-Left line had such enormous influence between 1966 and 1976; though the deviations described are attributed to both Lin and the Gang, it is the latter who are credited with having carried out the most systematic formulation of the ultra-Left line.[63] Our analysis will consider, in turn, the economic, political, and philosophical aspects of the ultra-Left line of Lin Biao and the Gang of Four, with emphasis on one or two central precepts of each of these aspects that have been identified as the theoretical core of the errant ideology.

Economic Content

A summary judgment on the economic aspects of the Gang of Four's ultra-Left line was contained in the criticism that they advocated a "transition in poverty" (*qiongguodu*) from socialism to communism.[64] That is to say, their economic policies were framed on the premise that the period of socialist construction that is also a period of transition to communism could proceed apace in spite of a relatively weak material base. To put it in a more positive vein, the radicals did not see China's level of economic development as a hindrance to continuous revolutionary change in the superstructure and the relations of production. On the contrary, they believed that such change was the most important priority in socialist development, following the theory that politically induced change motivated by a high degree of ideological consciousness could compensate for China's material underdevelopment in building a more purely socialist society. This approach has been criticized as placing too much emphasis on human subjective will ("voluntarism") as a motive force in historical development to the neglect of objective economic factors.[65]

Though by no means completely ignoring economic matters, Lin and the Gang are said to have followed the logic that production was best promoted by "grasping revolution"[66] and that "when the revolution is handled well, production will automatically go up."[67] According to this line of critique,

Lin Biao and the Gang of Four lauded "transition in poverty" as something very Left and very revolutionary. While concocting the "theory of the superstructure as the decisive factor," they also dished up the "theory of the relations of production as the decisive factor," believing that in a socialist society it is the relations of production, not the productive forces, that decide production. They seemed to think that the faster the relations advance, the faster the forces of production will develop.[68]

The obverse of this "theory" of the decisiveness of the superstructure and the relations of production was the "theory of productive forces," which was the catch-all label that the radicals used to describe the approach to socialist development of those who they felt put too much stress on economic matters and neglected politics and ideology.[69]

In the initial phases of the criticism of the Gang (October 1976–December 1978), the exaggeration of the role of the superstructure and the relations of production and the correlative minimization of the role of the forces of production were interpreted in such a way as to bolster the then prevalent contention that their line should be analyzed as ultra-Right, or "fake Left, real Right" in essence. The argument here was that the Gang sought to undermine socialist construction by creating chaos in the superstructure (e.g., in education, politics, culture) and the relations of production (e.g., in factory management, commune administration and organization) in order to sabotage production, which would ultimately advance their goal of usurping power and restoring capitalism.[70] There was never a denial that turning the revolution/production dialectic into a "malcontradiction" favoring its political aspect reflected a revision of Marxism from the Left; however, this manifestation of the Gang's line was subordinated to the attribution of subjective motivation (usurping power) and projected result (capitalist restoration) in determining that the principal focus of criticism should be on their ultra-Rightist essence, rather than their Leftist disguise. When the content criterion of line analysis was adopted in early 1979, the Gang's "theory" of the decisiveness of the superstructure and the relations of production as motive factors in socialist development was singled out as the theoretical core of the Gang's "sham socialism." This "sham socialism" itself was described as "an ultra-Left theory [that] advocates universal poverty to hoodwink the people." [71]

The "transition in poverty" aspect of the Gang's line has been evaluated as ultra-Left in nature because it posited that the "socialist newborn things"—such as egalitarian educational policies, maximum worker participation in enterprise management, elevation of the level of ownership or accounting from production team to production brigade in the countryside—could grow and develop independently of a modernized material base. It equated such advanced relations of production and elements of a revolutionary superstructure with the essence of the transition to communism, whereas the post-Gang judgment is that "it is preposterous to pursue 'progressive' relations of production without considering the productive forces' level of development." [72] Advocating inherently revolutionary ideas and policies at a time when conditions do not favor their realization epitomizes the ultra-Left errors of letting subjective factors outrun objective conditions and confusing the socialist and communist stages of historical development—errors that were also at the heart of the critique of ultra-Leftism in the aftermath of the Great Leap Forward. [73]

Part of the original argument implicit in the charge that the Gang's line was ultra-Right was based on a particular interpretation of a key principle of the Marxist theory of historical materialism. [74] Marx stated that the motive force of social revolution was the class struggle generated when the superstructure and relations of production of a given era were out of phase with changes in the material base of society:

At a certain stage of their development, the material productive forces of society come into conflict with the existing relations of production or—

what is the legal expression of the same thing—with the property relations within which they have been at work hitherto. From forms of development of the productive forces, these relations turn into their fetters. Then begins the epoch of social revolution.[75]

This thesis was the foundation of Marx's idea of the development of history as a series of stages from slave society to communism. In each stage, revolution ensues when the prevailing relations of production come into contradiction with the expansive potential of the forces of production embodied in the rise of a new "progressive" class that challenges and eventually overthrows the old order. In the era of feudalism, for example, the relations of production typified by the organization of the manorial economy acted as a restraint on the development of capitalism; it was the task of the emergent bourgeoisie to lead the revolution against the "fetters" of feudalism and in so doing pave the way for a new mode of production characterized by mercantilism and industrialization. Accordingly, the socialist revolution would occur when capitalism had run its course and had, in its turn, become a hindrance to the further development of the forces of production; at that point, the proletariat, created and impoverished by the capitalists, would rise from the factory floor and violently displace the moribund bourgeoisie, thus ushering in an era that would eventually culminate in the blossom of full communism.

Since it was believed that the type of changes that the line of the Gang of Four had brought about in the superstructure and the relations of production had, indeed, become "fetters" on the further development of the forces of production, it was not too great an extension of Marxist logic to contend that the essence of the Gang's line must be counterrevolutionary. A joint editorial of the three main propaganda organs put it this way in making its case that the Gang's line must be judged as Rightist in nature: "Why do we say that the theory, line, policy and ideology of the Gang of Four, the media under their control, and the bourgeois factional setup constitute an ultra-reactionary and rotten-to-the-core superstructure? In the end, it is because this superstructure stands opposed to the dictatorship of the proletariat, undermines the socialist economic base, and obstructs the development of the productive forces."[76]

What was later criticized about this line of reasoning was not the observation concerning the effect of the Gang's line on the economy, but the implicit conclusion of the editorial—indeed, of the whole criticism campaign against the Gang as it unfolded in the two years following their downfall—that any deviation that hinders socialist development must be Rightist in essence. When the direct critique of ultra-Leftism emerged in early 1979, it was argued that it was not just the fact that a deviant line interferes with the development of the economic base that determines its nature; rather, the specific content of the line must be analyzed in order to ascertain whether it reflects a Rightist error, in which the relations of production *lag behind* the forces of production, or an ultra-Left error, in which the relations of production *exceed* the level of material development. "Left deviation," according to this differentiation, "is the basic content and characteristic of the opportunist line of Lin Biao and the Gang of Four"[77] because its various theories and policies "exceeded the possibilities of the present era [and] overstepped the limitations of reality."[78]

The Party may at the outset have been reluctant to analyze the economic content of the Gang's line as a manifestation of ultra-Leftism because of its close ideological kinship to one of the basic tenets of Mao Zedong Thought. Mao said in his essay, "On Contradiction" (1937): "In certain conditions, such aspects as the relations of production, theory, and the superstructure in turn manifest themselves in the principal and decisive role. . . . When the superstructure (politics, culture, etc.) obstructs the development of the economic base, political and cultural changes become principal and decisive."[79] Tang Tsou has called this thesis a key element of the "reformulation of historical materialism" by which Mao adapted Marxism to the circumstances of the Chinese revolution.[80] The Gang's notion that continuing revolutionary change in class structure, social institutions, modes of distribution, and patterns of authority and hierarchy rather than economic development constituted the major contradiction of the socialist period was based on a logical, if somewhat exaggerated, derivation of this Maoist "reformulation." The post-Mao leadership would certainly have been wary of any obvious questioning of the ideological implications of the so-called "transition in poverty." It was easier to deal with the Gang's errors in the established context of past line struggles that linked all major inner-Party deviations to counterrevolution from the Right rather than tackle the much more formidable task of a direct assault on ultra-Leftism, and—inevitably—Maoism itself.

Another of the distinctive contributions of Mao Zedong Thought to Marxist theory is the insight that socialism can degenerate into revisionism, which, in turn, can foster a restoration of capitalism.[81] This allowance for a *mutant* pattern of development was an important embellishment of the orthodox Marxist view of the more or less inevitable progressive march of history. But even this Maoist innovation hardened into an orthodoxy of its own through the process of the dogmatization of theory that was part of the Cultural Revolution. This new dogma dictated that revisionism could only come from the Right ("the capitalist road") while denying that Leftist deviations constituted a fundamental threat to socialist construction. This rigidity in conceptualizing and responding to line struggles within the Party explains, in part, the contorted nature of the evolution of the critique of the Gang of Four after their fall in 1976. It was not until after the "taboo" against criticizing the Left was broken more than two years after the death of Mao and the purge of the Gang that the possibility that ultra-Leftism could be a source of major contradictions in the development of socialism was subjected to anything approaching a rigorous analysis. Such an analysis portends an elaboration of the Marxist theory of historical development as fundamental as Mao's ruminations on the problem of "capitalist restoration."

A heuristic summary of orthodox and mutant patterns of historical materialist development is given in Table 2. It is presented here as an extension of the logic underlying the critique of the economic content of the ultra-Left line. This elaboration admittedly goes well beyond the explicit content of the criticism of Lin Biao and the Gang of Four in attempting to probe one implication of the critique of ultra-Leftism in the context of the Marxist theory of historical materialism. Nevertheless, it demonstrates that the critique of ultra-Leftism as it has evolved in the post-Mao era is based on a consistent and sophisticated interpretation of socialist doctrine and is not just an ex post facto rationalization by the victors in a power struggle.

The orthodox patterns of historical materialist development listed in Table 2 need little explanation. They are derived from Marx's analysis of the course of the transitions from feudalism to capitalism, capitalism to socialism, and socialism to communism. In each of these stages of development, growth in the forces of production presages and induces changes in the prevailing relations of production; these changes, in turn, herald the emergence of a new mode of

TABLE 2

Orthodox and Mutant Patterns of Historical Materialist Development

Historical era[a]	(A) Relations of production	(B) Forces of production	Balance[b] between (A) and (B)	Mode of production
Orthodox patterns				
1. Late feudalism	feudal	advanced	correct	capitalism
2. Late capitalism	bourgeois	advanced	correct	socialism
3. Late socialism	socialist	advanced	correct	communism
Mutant patterns				
4. Socialism	bourgeois	advanced	"Right"	revisionism/ capitalism
5. Early socialism	communist	backward	"Left"	"sham socialism"
6. Socialism	feudal	backward	"Right"	"feudal fascism"
7. Early capitalism	socialist	backward	"Left"	"proto-socialism"

[a] "Historical era" refers to the stage of development in a particular society, not on a world-wide scale.

[b] "Correct" refers to the situation when, according to Marxist theory, the contradiction between the "backward" relations of production and the "advanced" forces of production is ripe enough to generate revolutionary change. Mutant patterns occur when this essential contradiction is not fully developed (in "balance"): i.e., when the relations of production "lag behind" the development of the forces of production, the result is a Rightist deviation; when the forces of production are not suitably advanced to sustain and support "revolutionary" changes in the relations of production and the superstructure, the result is a Leftist deviation.

production that defines the fundamental character of a particular historical era. The transition from socialism to communism (3) is *evolutionary* in nature because the contradictions that induce the historical change are nonantagonistic; that is, the ruling class of the socialist era (the proletariat) does not stand opposed to the progressive alteration of the relations of production and the superstructure made possible by further material development. In contrast, the transitions of earlier phases (1 and 2) are, by definition, *revolutionary* because of the efforts of the feudal and bourgeois ruling classes to forestall any challenge to their power and privilege.

The mutant patterns of historical development, however, require some elaboration. These patterns are examples of possible aberrations in the process of socialist revolution and construction. Such aberrations occur when the relationship (or "balance") between the relations and the forces of production is not suited to the type of change being sought. Either the relations of production have been insufficiently transformed to sustain the transition to a higher stage of development (4 and 6); or the level of the productive forces is insufficient to support the desired degree of revolutionary change in the relations of production (5 and 7).

The first mutant pattern (4) is illustrated by Mao's analysis of the danger of revisionism and the possibility of capitalist restoration in socialist society. The Cultural Revolution was predicated, in large part, on the assumption that China in the early 1960's was succumbing to just such a case of mutated development; Mao's analysis (based partly on his evaluation of the contradictions in Soviet society)[82] was that the incomplete revolution in the relations of production and the superstructure had allowed the "representatives" of the bourgeoisie to seize a sizable portion of Party and state power; the only hope for correcting this mutation and returning China to the socialist road was to overthrow the usurpers by means of a mass movement and to create, in the broadest sense, a truly proletarian culture. The refutation of this estimate of the danger of revisionism in China's socialist society has been one of the most important ingredients of the post-Mao critique of ultra-Leftism.

Mutant pattern 5 reflects a situation in which revolutionary social change outpaces economic development. This variant typifies the criticism of those erstwhile revolutionaries who neglect the limits on social change dictated by material reality and overestimate the readiness of society for radical transformation. This is the pattern that is at the heart of the critique of ultra-Leftism as described in this study. If allowed to hold sway in the Party and gain influence among the people, such a Leftist mutation of historical materialism results in a highly unstable situation—"sham socialism" as it has been called in the criticism of the Gang of Four—a situation where "progressive" relations of production are imposed on an insufficiently developed material base. "Sham socialism" hinders the ultimate realization of communism by undermining the economic development of socialist society. The post-Mao critique of the Gang's insistence on harshly restricting all vestiges of "bourgeois right" in China and on implementing a variety of "socialist newborn things" prior to the necessary development of the productive forces reflects criticism of two aspects of this pattern of mutated socialist development, as did the critique of the "communist wind" and "the sprouts of communism" in the Great Leap Forward.

The next mutant pattern (6) is closely related to the previous case. The Gang of Four is charged with attempting to use the vehicle of "sham socialism" to establish a "feudal fascist dictatorship" conducive to their sinister ends. By weakening the material basis of socialist society, the Gang allegedly prepared the groundwork for seizing power. This pattern thus embodies the aspect of the analysis of the Gang that has continued to focus on their ultra-Rightist activities as a political faction, as distinct from their ultra-Left political line. This mutant pattern is possible only in a society that still suffers from strong feudal influences despite having adopted certain socialist forms; such an apparent contradiction in the stages of historical development is possible when the transformation of the backward, small-scale productive forces of a feudal or semifeudal society is incomplete and, therefore, unable to support the eradication of traditional relations of production.

In the case of China, this pattern reflects the problems engendered for socialist construction by the legacy of that country's bureaucratic and autocratic traditions, the persistence of feudal attitudes toward authority, the absence of even rudimentary experience with bourgeois democracy, and a whole complex of other social relationships that still bear the imprint of China's long feudal history as well as of its truncated capitalist development. In fact, the critique of Lin Biao and the Gang of Four has blossomed into a sustained and rigorous investigation into the pervasive influence that feudal ideas still have in many aspects of social and political life in China.[83] The assumption of the critique is that it was the persistence of these feudal ideas that provided the necessary fertile ground for the troubles of the two decades between 1957 and 1976. What this analysis suggests is that the political and ideological struggles of the socialist transition in China should have been directed at the deep-rooted remnants of feudalism, not at the superficial "tails of capitalism."

The final mutant pattern (7) suggests the argument that a socialist revolution cannot occur—or can occur only in an aberrant form—in societies that have not gone through the full process of capitalist economic and bourgeois political development; otherwise neither the forces nor the relations of production are sufficiently transformed to sustain a truly socialist mode of production. When socialism is proclaimed in a state of underdevelopment, the inevitable result, this perspective claims, is degeneration into some combination of "sham socialism" and "feudal fascism." From this view, the whole of the Chinese revolution has been an ultra-Left deviation from the "scientific" pattern of historical materialist development because China was and is materially unprepared for socialism. In fact, all self-proclaimed socialist countries can at best be said to reflect a kind of "state capitalism" or "proto-socialism" characterized by heavy-handed bureaucratic rule, relatively low levels of productivity, and a very unequal social division of labor.[84]

The last three mutant patterns of socialist revolution amplify important aspects of the criticism of the Gang of Four's ultra-Leftism. They also relate to the aspect of the generic critique of ultra-Leftism in Marxism–Leninism–Mao Zedong Thought that concerns the contradiction that arises when impatient revolutionaries seek to accelerate the process of change by telescoping the separate stages of historical development.

The line that has emerged since the fall of the Gang of Four has been emphatic about "the main and decisive role [that] the productive forces and the economic base generally play in the development of history as a whole."[85] The drive for the Four Modernizations has been justified by the claim that "revolution means the liberation of the productive forces."[86] The 1979 reinvocation of the September 1956 "Resolution of the Eighth Party Congress on the Political Report of the Central Committee" emphasized the importance now attached to the task of developing socialist production. According to the 1956 Resolution, after the period of consolidation and transformation in the early 1950's, the major contradiction facing the Party was

that between the people's demand that an advanced industrial country be built and the realities of a backward agricultural country, between the people's need for rapid economic and cultural development and the inability of our present economy and culture to meet that need. Since a socialist system has already been established in our country, this contradiction is essentially between the advanced socialist system and the backward productive forces of society.[87]

Commenting on the relevance of this Resolution to the situation in 1979, *Guangming ribao* said, "The overall spirit of this Resolution is correct and conforms with the objective needs of our society's development. . . . The Resolution unequivocally told us: henceforth, the emphasis of the work of our Party and country should be in promoting the development of the productive forces."[88]

During the Cultural Revolution, the Resolution of the Eighth Party Congress was frequently attacked as summing up the ideology that was allegedly leading China down the "capitalist road." Its resurrection in the post-Mao era symbolizes the repudiation of the approach to the relationship between economic development and socialist revolution, which has been criticized as the embodiment of the ultra-Leftist theory of the "transition in poverty."

Political Content

"Broadening [the scope] of class struggle" (*dagao jieji dousheng kuodahua*) and "reversing the relationship between the enemy and ourselves" (*diandao diwo guanxi*) have been held up as the essence of the political content of the ultra-Left line.[89] Like the "theory" propounding the decisiveness of the superstructure and the relations of production, the ultra-Left view of the role of class struggle in socialist society evolved from an exaggerated, but logical, extension of another of Mao Zedong's distinctive contributions to Marxist theory: the thesis that class relations persist even after the socialization of the means of production and that the struggle against the inequality inherent in those relationships is a vital ingredient in propelling a socialist society forward toward communism. Lin Biao and the Gang of Four have been accused of misinterpreting Mao's instruction to take "class struggle as the key link" as meaning "class struggle ousting everything else" and as conflicting with rather than mutually supporting the other "key links" of the struggle for scientific experiment and the struggle for production.[90] The ultra-Leftists are said to have expanded the legitimate role of class struggle in socialist society "to the point where [class struggle] was everywhere, seeing an enemy behind every bush and tree. It was in the Party and outside the Party; it was in society and in the family. They hoisted such evil banners as 'There's no place without [class struggle]'; 'Every place is a battlefield of class struggle'; and even 'all-round civil war.'"[91]

The ultra-Left line was built on the premise that certain persistent patterns of political, social, and economic inequality in socialist society reflected *antagonistic* class relationships, which if unresolved would result in a resurgence of the bourgeoisie and a restoration of capitalism.[92] Practices and policies that appealed to individual material interest to motivate productivity were judged to be vestiges of "bourgeois right" left over from capitalist society, which must be actively and aggressively restricted (even eliminated) during the socialist transition. Such matters as peasant private plots, rural trade fairs, differential wage scales and incentive schemes in industry, and the whole question of the implementation of the socialist principle of distribution according to labor became focal points for acrimonious political and ideological struggle.[93]

Furthermore, in the political and social spheres, new class relationships were seen as likely to emerge from any group that derived power, prestige, or privilege from their occupations or positions of responsibility.[94] The bureaucracy and academic institutions were considered the most fertile breeding grounds for a "new bourgeoisie," although factories and communes could spawn class enemies as well, among cadres, peasants, and workers whose skills, experience, or economic self-interest contaminated their ideological purity. Like "bourgeois right," this "new bourgeoisie" had to be opposed in the never ending battle with creeping revisionism. In the course of carrying out this struggle, the ultra-Leftists are said to have labeled indiscriminately as class enemies persons who should have been considered well within the ranks of the "people": "[The Gang of Four] confused the two types of contradictions calling veteran cadres 'capitalist roaders' and 'targets for opposition'; calling veteran workers 'the privileged ones' and 'targets of the revolution'; and calling intellectuals 'the stinking ninth category' and 'targets of the dictatorship'; and calling peasants 'small producers' and 'targets of struggle.'"[95]

A welter of consequences are attributed to this escalation of class struggle. The economy is said to have been severely disrupted between 1966 and 1976 as workers were urged to place participation in political activities above concern for production; as peasant incentive for labor was sapped by overrestriction on various avenues for increasing personal income; as enterprise administration was thrown into chaos through unrelenting attacks on managers coupled with counterproductive experiments in factory democracy; as anarchy and slackness undermined labor discipline owing to the indiscriminate abolition of factory rules and regulations governing work procedures. Politically, exaggerated class struggle severely damaged democratic life in society and in the Party as participation was constrained by the high costs of making a political "mistake" and as debate was replaced with ritualism and dogma; similarly, legality was undermined as objective standards and procedures for the administering of law gave way to an informal and subjective (and therefore often arbitrary) system of class justice.[96] The pervasive influence of class struggle in the ranks of Party and state cadres is also said to have undermined the functioning of administrative organs at all levels of the system. Veteran cadres were persecuted, demoted, or dismissed because of "suspect" backgrounds or lack of sufficient revolutionary enthusiasm; they were replaced by inexperienced but politically zealous cadres (referred to pejoratively in the critique of ultra-Leftism as "helicopters" because of their rapid rise to positions of authority during the Cultural Revolution). The result was a combination of organizational paralysis and incompetence that affected the whole polity and economy.

The Gang of Four's advocacy of intensive and extensive class struggle in socialist society was at first interpreted as part of their ultra-Right plot to seize power through destabilization and sabotage. But when the issue of a deviant political line was shown to be separate from the problem of factional and conspiratorial politics, it was gradually acknowledged that the Gang's approach to class struggle had to be criticized as a key manifestation of ultra-Leftism. Several specific characteristics of the Gang's line on class struggle have been identified as giving it an ultra-Left nature.

1. The Gang "plucked the term 'class struggle' out of the comprehensive framework of Marxism . . . and overemphasized its existence." A Rightist line on the same issue would have advocated "the theory of the dying out of class struggle," which was one of the most important ideological sins attributed to Liu Shaoqi and his fellow "capitalist roaders" during the Cultural Revolution.[97]

2. The ultra-Left line unjustly expanded the scope of the dictatorship of the proletariat by indiscriminately broadening the category of the "enemy" and narrowing the category of the people; the result was a misapplication of the instruments of coercion and suppression in the resolution of nonantagonistic contradictions and the illegitimate constriction of participation and dissent in socialist society. The Rightist approach would have been to dilute the effectiveness of the dictatorship of the proletariat by narrowing the definition of the "enemy" and broadening the definition of the "people" to include those elements and individuals who rightly should be suppressed.[98]

3. The Gang of Four imposed unrealistic standards of purity in their class analysis of occupational groups, cultural works, academic debates, and individual ideological orientations; this had the effect of imparting a high level of political antagonism into the whole range of social relations. The Right deviation, on the other

hand, would have been to abandon class analysis altogether and adopt a "supra-class" perspective on the evaluation of various aspects of human and social development.[99]

4. The objective of the Gang's emphasis on restricting "bourgeois right" through class struggle was to "block the capitalist road" in China's economy; in doing so, they are said to have committed the ultra-Left error of overestimating China's material and ideological preparedness to adopt purer socialist forms of organization and distribution and underestimating the necessity of retaining certain quasi-capitalist practices during the early transition period. An ultra-Right line would have erased the distinction between socialism and capitalism by allowing persisting elements of "bourgeois right" in socialist society to develop into entrenched patterns of inequality derived from exploitation.[100]

5. Anarchy was often a direct result of the influence of the Gang's ultra-Left position on class struggle. Workers were urged to overthrow rules and regulations used to "suppress" them; students were sanctioned to rebel against "bourgeois academic authorities"; citizens were prompted to hunt down and expose all varieties of "capitalist roaders"; and peasants were mobilized to "cut off the tail of capitalism" in the countryside. In consequence, economic, social, and political discipline often broke down. Such an anarchic situation was manifest in either spontaneous disruptions such as strikes, prolonged struggle campaigns, and unresponsiveness toward any type of authority, or in apathy and cynicism regarding the value of political participation or labor. In the framework of Marxism-Leninism, anarchism is generally considered a manifestation of ultra-Leftism in that it is based on the assumption of rebellion against all authority and the maximization of freedom and mass participation regardless of the social or political outcome.[101] A Rightist error on the question of authority would have emphasized strict economic and political obedience, while minimizing opportunities for effective citizen participation and input into government.[102]

In sum, the Gang of Four is said to have regarded class struggle as "the only motive force propelling socialist society forward."[103] Most of the policies and programs emanating from their ultra-Left line therefore took the heightening of class struggle as the starting point and the standard of evaluation. This approach was consistent with their theory of historical development, which stressed continuous revolutionary change in the superstructure and relations of production. In other words, since class struggle was, in the ultra-Left view, the essence of the relations of production and the relations of production were the essential locus of historical change, it logically followed that class struggle should be touted as the most important factor in ensuring progress toward communism during the transition period. It is just such internal consistency, the post-Mao Chinese leadership has claimed, that gave the ultra-Left line its strength as a relatively complete system of theory.

Although the deleterious effect on China's economy of the ultra-Left line's emphasis on class struggle became a clear and constant theme of the criticism of the Gang of Four almost from the start,[104] along with the renewed emphasis on production and modernization by the post-Mao leadership, the new line on class struggle emerged rather tentatively, perhaps reflecting the relatively greater difficulty in disentangling the impact and import of what had become the "motive force" of the last decade of China's development. The persecution of veteran cadres and intellectuals under the guise of promoting class struggle was also an important ingredient of the early criticism of the Gang.[105] But this only jelled into an alternative line on the role of class struggle in socialist society through a series of cautious steps.

The criticism began, soon after the Gang's downfall, with a repudiation of the Gang's one-sided emphasis on class struggle and their neglect of economic matters. The message was rather mixed, however, and the ideological imprint of the new drive for rapid modernization was somewhat obfuscated by the call "to develop socialist production . . . by persisting in taking class struggle as the key link."[106] About a year later, this point of view began to be clarified with such statements as the one that claimed that the "ultimate aim" of class struggle was to "free the productive forces" rather than the pursuit of ideological purity in socialist society.[107]

A third increment in the redefinition of class struggle was introduced in the assertion that "class struggle in the socialist period must succumb to the needs of developing the productive forces."[108] This view was further refined by the argument that economic modernization itself should be viewed as a form of class struggle because politics is the "concentrated expression" of economics; therefore, those who devoted themselves to the tasks of modernization were, in fact, living up to the true meaning of Mao's dicta to put "politics in command" and to uphold the principle of class struggle.[109] An epitaph for the central political component of the ultra-Left line was issued in the summary judgment of the 1979 meeting of the National People's Congress that "class struggle is no longer the principal contradiction in our society."[110] In other words, the concept of class struggle as the motive force of socialist development has been replaced by a stress on the contrary values of unity and stability as the operative principles of post-Mao politics. This new orthodoxy is embodied in the revival of the idea of the "revolutionary united front," which calls for "uniting with all the forces that can be united with and mobilizing all positive factors to serve the socialist cause."[111]

Philosophical Content

The issues to be examined in this section fall into the category of what in Chinese is referred to as *zai sixiangshang*.[112] Although this phrase is most accurately translated as "ideological," I shall use the word "philosophical" here to avoid confusion with the term "ideology," which is generally used to denote the whole system of the ultra-Left line of Lin Biao and the Gang of Four, including the political and economic content discussed above as well as the more theoretical points.

The matter of demarcating the philosophical aspects of the ultra-Left line from its more concrete characteristics is further complicated by the fact that the criticism of Lin and the Gang has involved repudiation of a plethora of so-called "theories" as embodying various parts of their line. Nearly every specific evil attributed to the ultra-Leftists has been linked with one or another sinister "theory," such as the "theory of the decisiveness of the relations of production," the "theory that class struggle ousts everything else," the "theory of the transition in poverty," the "theory that study is useless," and the "theory that the political line decides everything." No doubt the exact rendering of such "theories" is more the result of the ex post facto critique than a precise representation of the explicit formulations used by Lin and the Gang to express their political program, but they do nonetheless capture the post-Mao leadership's perception of the impact of the ultra-Left line, and the use of the term "theory" (however pejorative) accurately conveys the systematic nature of that line.

The focus in this section is on two abstract questions (although with serious practical ramifications) that can be said to have formed the philosophical framework of the ultra-Left line. The first is a question of epistemology, or more specifically, the relationship between theory and practice in the accumulation and advancement of human knowledge and the formulation of policy. The second concerns the nature of contradiction as a principle of universal existence and an agent of social change.

The spiral development of human knowledge through a dialectical process in which theory and practice unceasingly transform each other is another important pillar of Mao Zedong Thought.[113] Although Mao stressed the fundamental importance of practice— some would say the "primacy" of practice[114]—in the correct analysis of human affairs, the essence of his epistemology is the dialectical unity of theory and practice.

There are two ways in which the ultra-Left line is said to have turned this dialectical relationship into a "malcontradiction" that counterposed theory to practice. First, Lin and the Gang have been accused of "reversing the relationship between theory and practice [and] going in for dogmatism in a big way" (*diandao lilun he shijiande guanxi, dagao jiaotiaozhuyi*) through their particular interpretation and application of Marxism-Leninism-Mao Zedong Thought.[115] They are accused of violating the systematic nature of the ideology by taking bits and pieces of the theories of the "revolutionary teachers" out of context and elevating them to the level of "timeless, supra-historical absolute truth" (*chaoshikong, chaolishide jueduizhenli*) in order to provide ideological legitimacy for their political line.[116] In doing so, they violated the precept that all theory—even theory espoused by the "revolutionary teachers"— must stand the test of practice and that all truth is, therefore, relative and timebound.[117]

Dogmatism can reflect either a Rightist or a Leftist error. The dogmatism of Lin and the Gang is labeled Left dogmatism because of what they took out of context and what they chose to exaggerate. Their distortion of the theory of the decisiveness of the relations of production and their exacerbation of the role of class struggle in socialist society have been analyzed as Left errors in line. Their alleged mutilation of Marxism–Leninism–Mao Zedong Thought, in turn, consisted of isolating and exaggerating the elements of the ideology that supported key aspects of their line through a dogmatic exegesis of some of the more ambiguous fragments. As *Hongqi* put it, "the dogmatism of Lin Biao and the Gang of Four distorts the words and the theories of the revolutionary teachers from the 'Left,' pushes them to extremes and turns truth into falsehood." [118] By that sort of manipulation, the Gang set revolutionary theory apart from revolutionary practice. From the standpoint of the discussion of the philosophical content of the ultra-Left line, this overemphasis on theory to the neglect of practice is the most important point to be noted. Besides giving an ideological legitimacy to their line, this "malcontradiction" took a concrete political form as part of the Gang's belittling of the skill and experience of veteran cadres as a source of political authority and their simultaneous insistence on loyalty to their version of Marxism–Leninism–Mao Zedong Thought as the most important measure of revolutionary commitment. [119]

However, the ultra-Left line also reflected the theory/practice "malcontradiction" in the form of an overemphasis on practice to the neglect of theory. In the context of their radical program, Lin and the Gang are alleged to have debased the role of theory and to have placed overwhelming importance on practical experience. This was most clearly shown in the Cultural Revolution education system, where great emphasis was put on policies like "open-door schooling" (*kaimen banxue*) in which teachers and students devoted much of their time to manual labor unrelated to their studies, the idea being that classroom teaching and the learning of theoretical knowledge were secondary concerns in the revolutionary school curriculum. [120] This same distrust of theory also applied in the ultra-Leftist policies for science and technology, where the emphasis on practical science led to a serious curtailment of pure research, [121] and in the policies for economic administration, which scorned theories of "scientific management" as inherently "capitalist" and had managerial and technical personnel spending time on the production line as ordinary workers. [122] The Gang's emphasis on practice and minimization of theory is considered to be an ultra-Left abberation that betrays their class analysis of the contradictions in socialist society as discussed above. And it reflects the point of view that theory can be the "capital" of bourgeois intellectuals, which can be parlayed into power and profit, and that the pursuit of such theory is inherently corrupting of true revolutionary values.

Thus it seems that in the realm of ideology the ultra-Leftists are criticized for putting too much emphasis on theory, whereas in more concrete policy matters they are condemned for elevating the role of practice to an extreme. In both instances, this "malcontra-diction" has been judged to be an important part of the ultra-Left line in which theory and practice were juxtaposed in a conflicting relationship that destroyed their proper dialectical unity.

So far as the interpretation and application of Marxism–Lenin-ism–Mao Zedong Thought are concerned, the current orthodoxy is that "practice is the sole criterion of truth" and that the theories of the "revolutionary teachers" should be evaluated in the historical context in which they were devised and then adapted according to accumulated experience and changing circumstances.[123] This would appear to suggest a gradual lessening of reliance on the specific con-tent of the writings of Marx, Lenin, and Mao and a greater empha-sis on their critical and analytical methods as the standard by which to measure adherence to or contravention of the formal ideology. In matters relating to education, science and technology, and economic administration, the post-Gang view is that theoretical knowledge has a vital role to play in fostering socialist development and that classroom learning, pure research, and "scientific management" are all revolutionary endeavors if pursued in the interests of the Four Modernizations.[124]

The second component of the philosophical content of the ultra-Left line concerns the nature of contradiction as a factor in univer-sal existence and social development. The theory of contradiction is the essence of the Marxian dialectical method, and it is an espe-cially important element in Mao's political thought.[125] In brief, this theory holds that change (natural and social) takes place as a result of the interaction between the positive and negative forces inherent in all matter and being. These contradictions have two aspects, unity and struggle; unity gives matter and being the stability that is necessary for identity and existence, while struggle imparts to all things the quality of unceasing flux and change that provides the motive force for development. The task of the revolutionary is to be aware of these social contradictions and manipulate them for po-litical ends. To accomplish this within the dictates of dialectical ma-terialism, the revolutionary must recognize the limits imposed on human action by material circumstances and make allowances for both the unity and the struggle aspects of contradictions in society in order to avoid the Rightist error of promoting "unprincipled peace" with class enemies as well as the Leftist error of "dealing ruthless blows" against unwarranted targets.

The expansion of class conflict attributed to Lin Biao and the Gang of Four is a concrete manifestation of what is deemed the ultra-Left degradation of the theory of contradiction through the exaggeration of the role of struggle and the denial of the importance of unity in socialist society. On the more philosophical plane that concerns us here, the ultra-Leftist approach to the problem of resolving persisting social contradictions is said to be symbolized by the misuse of the slogan "one divides into two" (*yi fen wei er*). This slogan had become the focus of an intense philosophical debate in 1964 that is now regarded as an augury of the ideological conflict that soon thereafter burst forth in the storm of the Cultural Revolution.[126] At that time, Yang Xianzhen, the director of the Higher Party School which was charged with the ideological training of upper-level cadres, became the target of an attack in the media for his thesis that "two unites into one" (*he er er yi*) rather than "one divides into two" was the principal method for dealing with contradictions in socialist society. Yang's view was criticized for reflecting a desire for compromise with bourgeois and revisionist ideology and challenging Mao's insistence on "continuing the revolution under the dictatorship of the proletariat."

The way in which this philosophical debate over the relationship between unity and struggle in resolving social contradictions was turned into a bitter political conflict has been blamed on the influence of the ultra-Left line. Lin and the Gang have been criticized for "obscuring the demarcation line between academic disputes and the struggle between the enemy and ourselves."[127] They are condemned for imposing unwarranted class analysis on a scholastic issue and for invoking dogmatic ideological criteria to decide questions that ought to have been "resolved by conducting extensive and deep-going academic research and discussion"; the proper method for handling such matters, it is argued, would have been to encourage the "exchange of views" and to "allow people to air differing opinions, even wrong ones."[128]

More importantly, the one-sided emphasis on "one divides into two" has been identified as one of the key philosophical expressions of the ultra-Left line. Lin Biao and the Gang, it has been charged, "succeeded in setting the identity and struggle of contradictions as absolute opposites, changing the materialist dialectical law of the unity of opposites into the law of 'the struggle of opposites' and distorting the relationship between the two aspects of a contradiction as merely one of 'struggle' and 'division.'"[129] It has also been charged that the elevation of "one divides into two" to the status of official ideology helped legitimize class struggle as the principal contradiction in socialist society and impeded the process of "mobilizing all positive forces" necessary for China's modernization. The question has been asked: "Are the philosophy of 'struggle' and the ultra-Leftist line of 'overthrowing all' . . . not closely related [to] the theoretical confusion created by the criticism of 'combining two into one?' This metaphysics . . . seriously shackled the mind, so that for a considerably long time people dared not mention the words 'unity,' 'getting united,' and 'combine.'"[130]

The post-Gang interpretation of the nature of social contradiction is that it is wrong to neglect either struggle or unity (and particularly the latter). The ideas that "two unites into one" and "two opposite aspects are inseparably connected" are now said to reflect "a much expounded viewpoint of the revolutionary teachers."[131] This philosophical perspective is consistent with the post-Mao emphasis on such notions as "revolutionary united front," the "unity of mental and manual labor," and "the unity of red and expert," which are contrasted to the undialectical preoccupation with struggle and confrontation characteristic of the ultra-Left line.

Summary

The enormous appeal and widespread influence of the ultra-Left line that grew out of the Cultural Revolution can be explained in part by two factors that have been implicit themes of the analysis in this chapter. First, the ultra-Leftism of Lin Biao and the Gang of Four reflected a logically consistent worldview that imparted to their line a highly systematic character.[132] This system may be judged to have been "metaphysical" and to have had a disastrous effect on China's socialist development, as the post-Mao leadership has contended in their labeling of it as ultra-Left; or, as its advocates would argue, it may be evaluated as reflecting the correct application of Mao Zedong's distinctive contributions to the theory and practice of socialist revolution.[133] But regardless of one's summary judgment concerning its nature and its impact, the line pursued by Lin Biao and the Gang of Four did undeniably embody, in its own terms, a rational and highly persuasive model of development.[134]

The influence of the ultra-Left line can also be attributed to the fact that its core components and its composite worldview were directly derived from Mao Zedong Thought. All the economic, political, and philosophical cornerstones of the ultra-Left line—the decisiveness of the relations of production in socialist development, class struggle as the "key link" in socialist politics, the contradiction between theory and practice and the emphasis on "one divides into two" as major principles of socialist epistemology and philosophy—are closely related to what are generally identified as some of the distinguishing features of Maoism. Whether this relationship reflects "exaggeration" or "correct application" is a matter of debate; but no thorough analysis of the rise and spread of the ultra-Left line is possible without noting that it gained much legitimacy through its logical derivation from Mao's ideology.[135]

8

The Critique of Ultra-Leftism and China's Socialist Revolution

> A political party's attitude towards its own mistakes is one of the most important and sure ways of judging how earnest the party is and how it fulfills in practice its obligations towards its class and the working people. Frankly acknowledging a mistake, ascertaining the reasons for it, analyzing the conditions that have led up to it, and thrashing out the means of its rectification—that is the hallmark of a serious party.
>
> Lenin (1920)

The cases presented in this study contain important continuities and contrasts that illuminate the evolution and function of the critique of ultra-Leftism in Chinese politics. Rather than being distinct and separate events that lend themselves to grand theorizing, these cases are episodes in a process that is itself a part—an important part—in the development of the theory and practice of socialism in China. We now turn to a consideration of some of the implications of that process, as seen both in retrospect, in terms of the way in which the critique of ultra-Leftism unfolded after 1958, and for the future, so far as we can judge from the effects the last episode of the critique has had on the political environment of post-Mao China.

The Critique in Retrospect

Political Contention and Incomplete Critiques

We have examined in some detail the pattern of political dynamics involved in the three main cases of the critique of ultra-Leftism since Liberation. Here we shall look at some of the connections between these cases to see how the critique as a whole developed.

In each of the periods we have examined, the critique of ultra-Leftism became a matter of serious political contention between opposing leadership groups in the Chinese Communist Party. Each of these groups had different reasons for supporting or suppressing a concerted campaign of criticism and rectification of alleged Leftist deviations. In the cases discussed, three clear adversarial pairs were evident: Peng Dehuai versus Mao Zedong in the midst of the Great Leap Forward; the Veteran Revolutionaries versus the Cultural Revolutionaries following the death of Lin Biao; and the "Practice" faction versus the "Whatever" faction in the aftermath of the purge of the Gang of Four. The contention between these groups greatly affected the way in which the critique of ultra-Leftism evolved in each period.

The character and the outcome of the first incident of such political contention—the sequence of action and reaction around Peng Dehuai's criticism of the Great Leap Forward in mid-1959—set a momentous precedent for the handling of inner-Party policy disputes, a precedent that profoundly influenced the way in which the critique of ultra-Leftism developed over the next twenty years. The upshot of Mao's successful maneuverings at the Lushan Plenum was to escalate the conditions and consequences of elite conflict in China.[1] The way in which this occurred established the idea that Left deviations (such as those that were widely acknowledged to be responsible for the obvious malfunctions of the Great Leap strategy) were much less a threat to China's socialist development than were the sins of "Right opportunism" (such as those attributed to Peng Dehuai and other critics of the Leap). The attitude that Left errors in political line were relatively benign in both origin and impact lent ideological justification to the fact that a comprehensive critique of ultra-Leftism was not undertaken as part of the general retreat from the Leap in the early 1960's. The notion that "Left is better than Right" also helped to reduce Party sanctions as well as public opprobrium against Left deviations—at the very time when Mao's long-simmering preoccupation with the dangers of revisionism was gradually being translated into the widespread political paranoia that made the Cultural Revolution possible. Thus, after Lushan, ultra-Leftism was severely diminished as a focus of legitimate concern or criticism in Chinese Communist politics and ideology.

Although Mao recognized the need for modifying some of the most glaring excesses of the Leap (as in the utopian predictions concerning the pace of the ultimate transition to communism), he followed his "victory" at Lushan with a renewed effort to induce rapid economic development and expand some of the "sprouts of communism" (like the rural mess halls and the urban communes). When this "Second Leap Forward" floundered in mid-1960 in the wake of peasant resistance and natural disasters, policies were implemented to salvage the economy and establish a footing for future development based on a less visionary strategy. But in the anti-Rightist political environment created by the outcome of the showdown at Lushan, it was not possible to carry out a thorough critique of the line that had been responsible for the design and implementation of the Great Leap. This meant that there was only an *incomplete critique*, in which a rectification of many of the policy errors of the Leap proceeded apace without a corresponding criticism and analysis of the general problem of ultra-Leftism. Thus Lushan made a comprehensive critique of ultra-Leftism politically impossible as well as ideologically "unnecessary." The very fact that the most fundamental questions arising from the Great Leap experience were left unresolved greatly affected the course of the subsequent critiques described in this study.

Intra-elite political contention resulting in an incomplete critique (rectification without criticism) of an ultra-Left line was also characteristic of the post–Lin Biao and post–Gang of Four cases. In the former, what began as a comprehensive critique of ultra-Leftism in the guise of the campaign against the "Swindlers like Liu Shaoqi" was aborted by mid-1973 primarily owing to pressures of the struggle between the Veteran Revolutionaries—the leadership group centered around Zhou Enlai and Deng Xiaoping—and the Cultural Revolutionaries—whose core consisted of those radical Party leaders now dubbed the Gang of Four. The Cultural Revolutionaries succeeded in diverting critical propaganda from Lin's ultra-Left errors to his ultra-Right essence in order to forestall any link between the attack on Lin and themselves. Nevertheless, the Veteran Revolutionaries were able to sponsor the implementation of some important correctives to what they perceived as the policy excesses of the Cultural Revolution (particularly in such areas as education and cadre rectification). Therefore, like the Great Leap Forward episode, the development of the campaign was from a comprehensive critique to an incomplete critique in which rectification of Leftist policies continued to be implemented despite the absence of a thoroughgoing criticism of ultra-Leftism itself.

In the post-Gang period, the unfolding of the critique occurred in a reverse sequence. For more than two years after the Gang fell from power, criticism was focused on their ultra-Right nature as determined by their conspiratorial activities and alleged objective to restore capitalism in China. Yet, even while the Gang was being excoriated for their ultra-Rightism, a significant policy rectification of the obviously Left errors of their line was going on. Thus, in the first phases of the criticism of the Gang we once again observe the incongruous situation of policy rectification aimed at ultra-Left deviations being carried out without a corresponding critical analysis of the deeper origins and implications of the ultra-Left line. In the case of the post-Gang period, however, this incomplete critique preceded a comprehensive critique, which only began to emerge in late 1978 and early 1979. In the Great Leap and "Swindlers" episodes the incomplete critique was an aftereffect of an abortive attempt at a more comprehensive effort.

One can offer several explanations for this different sequence in the case of the Gang of Four. First, the initial stage of the post-Gang critique was bound up in the campaign to criticize Deng Xiaoping and other manifestations of the radicals' last effort to control the succession to Zhou and Mao. Therefore it took some time before the criticism of the Gang could be disentangled from the anti-Rightist barrage of the preceding months. Second, the shifting of gears to a more direct criticism of ultra-Leftism was further impeded by the lingering influence of a leadership group (the "Whatever" faction) with a political interest in curtailing a massive assault on the legitimacy of the Cultural Revolution. But a more important explanation for the reverse order and circuitous development of the critique of the Gang's line lies in the enormously complex and sensitive nature of the process, since it was bound to involve a painful reevaluation of two decades of China's recent history and the perhaps ambiguous role of Mao Zedong in that history. It was also a reflection of the extent to which the incomplete critiques of 1958–60 and 1971–73 had made the Party incapable of dealing analytically or politically with ultra-Leftism as a problem in post-Liberation development.

Mao Zedong and the Critique of Ultra-Leftism

Mao's role in the critique of ultra-Leftism was both ideological and political, partly indirect and partly direct. The core concepts of the ultra-Left line were all based directly on ideas that have been identified as cornerstones of Mao Zedong Thought, and the widespread influence that the ultra-Left line secured was certainly due in part to its apparent fidelity to some of the basic tenets of Maoism. Indeed, this legitimacy gave the ultra-Left line an important degree of immunity from criticism since the distinction between what was ultra-Left and what was truly "Maoist" was not always a very sharp one. Furthermore, the ambiguous and sometimes contradictory form in which the Chairman's Thoughts were often expressed made them susceptible to manipulation by competing factions.[2]

Mao's preoccupation in the last twenty years of his life with the dangers of revisionism also greatly affected the development of the critique of ultra-Leftism. His concern with Right deviations exerted such a potent influence on Chinese Communist ideology from 1956 on that it would not be unfair to characterize the prevailing values of Chinese political culture as highly myopic when it came to critical judgments concerning errors in political line. At best, ultra-Leftism was only a peripheral ideological concern for a revolutionary party. At worst, criticizing ultra-Leftism became a risky business for Chinese politicians; even to broach the subject was to invite the danger of invoking the Chairman's ire and being strung up on the ideological cross of Rightism. Despite Mao's injunction that a true revolutionary is one who dares to stand "against the tide," there were few comrades at any level of the system who had either the power or the nerve to challenge the decisive turns to the Left sponsored by Mao and his close associates. Ultra-Leftism was relegated to the category of aberrant and incidental phenomena that resulted from a well-intended but overzealous pursuit of a correct line. Manifestations of ultra-Leftism such as the "five winds" of the Great Leap Forward and the anarchy of the Red Guards in the early phases of the Cultural Revolution were looked upon as serious deviations, but not worthy of critical evaluation—like revisionism from the Right—as deviations representing a clear and conscious political line. This critical myopia in Chinese Communist ideology must be largely explained as an extension of the particular biases in the post-Liberation development of Mao Zedong Thought.

The political relationship between Mao and the critique of ultra-Leftism can be examined from several angles. The first and most obvious are the close personal ties between the Chairman and the major protagonists of the ultra-Left line of the Cultural Revolution era. Jiang Qing not only was Mao's wife, but like Lin Biao, Zhang

Chunqiao, Yao Wenyuan, and Wang Hongwen, she owed her political fortunes to Mao's patronage. Whether these alleged ultra-Leftists were acting with Mao's confidence and support or were betraying their patron in committing the Left errors of which they have been accused is a moot point. Certainly they were perceived as Mao's most loyal lieutenants and the faithful purveyors of his revolutionary line. Thanks to that reputation, they were more or less politically invulnerable, and until Mao himself turned on them (as in the case of Lin Biao) or was no longer on the scene (which was a necessary condition for the arrest of the Gang of Four), they were safe—for reasons of deference to or fear of Mao—from a frontal assault by their critics.

Second, Mao was politically responsible for launching the two major campaigns that allowed the ultra-Left line to gain full expression: the Great Leap and the Cultural Revolution. It was very hard to criticize or control various policy excesses that derived from these radical political initiatives since, like the ideological core of the ultra-Left line, they appeared to bear the stamp of the Chairman's approval.

Third, Mao must also be held responsible for the change in the style of inner-Party struggle, which greatly escalated the stakes for the losers in policy conflicts. This change, which Frederick Teiwes has described as a process of decline from persuasive to coercive modes of elite rectification,[3] began at Lushan and culminated in the Cultural Revolution. This intensified conflict was justified by Mao as the reflection inside the Party of the life-and-death struggle between the proletariat and the bourgeoisie. Post-Mao Chinese analysis argues that this change in the long-established norms for handling policy differences within the Party leadership was itself a prime manifestation of the ultra-Left view of the expanded scope of class struggle in socialist society. However, it is more significant for our investigation to note that the brunt of the increasingly coercive sanctions imposed for line errors fell on those political actors at all levels of the system who might otherwise have served as critics of an ultra-Left trend. We shall return to the relationship between the critique of ultra-Leftism and changing Party norms when we discuss the implications of the critique in the post-Mao period; here, it is only necessary to point out that the decline of Party norms altered the political environment in such a way as to make any development of a comprehensive critique of ultra-Leftism nearly impossible. And it was Mao's political actions and ideological authority that precipitated the decline.

The final point to be made here is that in the various episodes we have discussed, Mao never sanctioned the critique of ultra-Leftism. His evaluation of the problems of the Great Leap Forward (including his self-criticism) were more grudging concessions to reality than an invitation to a thorough critique of ultra-Leftism as an erroneous political line. When Peng Dehuai dared utter what might have been the opening chord in such a critique, Mao came down so hard on Peng's "Right opportunism" that he not only stifled the criticism of the Leap but also left a chill that was obviously unfavorable to any future criticisms of Leftist errors.

The Chairman's role in the post-Lin critique of the "Swindlers like Liu Shaoqi" is less clear. As suggested in chapter 5, Mao may have intervened to enforce a compromise between the factions that were squabbling over whether a criticism and rectification should be carried out following Lin Biao's death in September 1971. If he did so, then Mao contributed to the incomplete critique of that period, which left the pot of elite antagonisms seething just below the boiling point and established the context for the cataclysmic showdown of October 1976.

There is little question, however, from the available documents, that Mao's major complaint against Lin in the period leading up to the crisis had more to do with Lin's conspiracies and personal ambitions than with any substantive ideological or policy issues related to Left deviations. One can infer from this that Mao was hardly inclined to support the efforts of the Veteran Revolutionaries to launch a comprehensive critique of ultra-Leftism in 1971–73, and probably considered such a critique irrelevant to solving the major contradictions posed by the Lin Biao affair.

Likewise, Mao's numerous warnings to the Gang of Four in the few years before he died dealt almost exclusively with the problem of factionalism.[4] Although according to Marxism–Leninism–Mao Zedong Thought sectarianism is a political trait particularly characteristic of comrades who are afflicted with ultra-Left thinking and work style, it is, at most, a secondary phenomenon, and hardly an essential component of an erroneous line. Here, too, Mao's perception of the Gang's "problem" suggests that he was not interested in undertaking a criticism and rectification of an ultra-Left line. How much Mao's attitude had to do with the thwarting of Deng Xiaoping's attempt to incorporate a critique of ultra-Leftism into his 1974–75 draft programs for China's modernization is a matter of speculation. But it is perhaps significant that Mao did nothing to stop the Gang of Four's campaign to "repulse the Right deviationist wind of reversing the correct verdicts" of the Cultural Revolution, which was launched partly to abort Deng's attack against the radicals.

Even after Mao died, his ghost hovered over the critique of ultra-Leftism as it first developed following the fall of the Gang of Four. One of the important reasons for the rather tortuous evolution of the anti-Gang campaign was the post-Mao leadership's realization that a truly comprehensive analysis of the origins and impact of the ultra-Left line could not but cast a deep shadow on the Chairman's later years. For some time the new leaders avoided making an explicit link between Mao and the disasters of the ultra-Left line. For example, in 1979 *Renmin ribao* declared: "It is now very clear that Comrade Peng Dehuai's proposals at the Lushan meeting in 1959 were correct . . . [and that] opposition to him . . . was wrong";[5] and in 1980 a Plenum of the Central Committee called the purge of Liu Shaoqi "the biggest frame-up our Party has ever known in its history."[6] But, initially, nothing was said about what role Mao Zedong might have had in what were now found to be two of the grossest injustices perpetrated by the ultra-Left.

In 1979–80, the person of Mao was drawn more directly into the critique of ultra-Leftism.[7] Although efforts continued to separate the Chairman from the most perfidious political machinations of Lin Biao and the Gang of Four, he was judged culpable of serious ideological errors that provided the rationale and motive force for the ultra-Left line. Despite such errors, the overall assessment of Mao's legacy has concluded that his contributions to the Chinese revolution far outweighed his shortcomings. As the 1981 Resolution on Party history claimed, "Chief responsibility for the grave 'Left' error of the 'cultural revolution,' an error comprehensive in magnitude and protracted in duration, does indeed lie with Comrade Mao Zedong. But after all it was the error of a great proletarian revolutionary."[8]

In sum, Mao Zedong had an enormous impact on the development of the critique of ultra-Leftism in post-Liberation Chinese politics, but in a negative rather than a positive way. The influence of his political actions and his ideology had the cumulative effect of both undermining vigilance against Left errors as a concern in Chinese political culture and confounding the efforts of those leading comrades in the Party who sought to stem the Leftist tide.

Recurring Themes in the Critique of Ultra-Leftism

In many respects, the content of the critiques of the Great Leap, the "Swindlers like Liu Shaoqi," and the Gang of Four was so similar as to be literally interchangeable. Though each case had its particular emphases, the targets of criticism were always nearly the same specific policy questions. For example, all three critiques raised such issues as the nature of income distribution policies in the socialist economy, particularly as they related to the use of material incentives; the treatment, transformation, and utilization of intellectuals, managers, technicians, and veteran cadres in socialist development (the red vs. expert dilemma); the relationship between various levels of ownership in the countryside (especially as they affect the authority of the production team vis-à-vis higher levels); and the role of class struggle in socialist society.

Boiled down into a single ideological error from which all other alleged deviations derived, all these errors have to do with a fundamental misunderstanding of the *transitional* nature of the historical stage of socialism. The ultra-Leftists, because of their supposedly subjective world view and dogmatic approach to the concrete problems of revolution, seriously misjudged the political methods and policy priorities appropriate to the task of building a socialist society. Their error can be regarded as the manifestation of two ideological fallacies that reflect a faulty comprehension of the relationship between capitalism and socialism, on the one hand, and between socialism and communism, on the other, as separate, yet interrelated stages in the materialist conception of development.

The first fallacy draws too sharp a distinction between the interconnected stages of historical change associated with the transition to socialism. It does not take adequate account of the objective constraints imposed on the development of socialist society by the capitalist society out of which it inevitably grows; the ultra-Left mistakenly analyzes certain remnants of capitalism ("bourgeois right") as precursors to a restoration of capitalism, rather than as "natural" and necessary elements of a long-term transitional process. This fallacy is expressed concretely in the form of what we can call *negative* ultra-Leftism, which emphasizes unremitting struggle against the corrosive influence of capitalist practices and bourgeois ideas.

The second ultra-Left fallacy that undermines the materialist approach to revolutionary change does not draw a sharp enough distinction between the stages of historical development. This fallacy is based on ideas that are too "advanced" for society's objective level of economic and ideological development—that is, it uses the standards of a future communist society with its material abundance and its manifest consciousness to determine what priorities are suitable for a transitional society that is, in reality, far less perfect. The result is *positive* ultra-Leftism, which focuses on the advocacy and implementation of policies designed to hasten the transition to communism through the building of more highly socialized and egalitarian institutions, the development of less hierarchical processes of decision making, and the popular inculcation of more communitarian values.

Put another way, the twin fallacies of the ultra-Left, according to its critics, are to *underestimate* constraints imposed upon the evolution of socialist society as a transition from capitalism and to *overestimate* the immediacy of the potential of socialism as a transition to communism.[9] Both variants of ultra-Leftism were targets in each of the cases we have discussed. Although the dominant themes of the critique of the Great Leap Forward were the debunking of claims concerning the imminent realization of the communist utopia and the exposing of the futility of inducing a rapid maturation of the "sprouts of communism," the retreat from the Leap also incorporated an important element of rectifying negative ultra-Left errors such as the devaluation of the roles of scientists, technicians, and other intellectuals in socialist development because of their inherent "bourgeois" nature. The critique of the Cultural Revolution, as reflected in the campaigns against the "Swindlers like Liu Shaoqi" and the Gang of Four, was principally aimed at the ultra-Left's overzealous restriction of the vestiges of "bourgeois right," their use of repressive measures to eliminate corrupting influences in the arts, their persecution of "bourgeois academic authorities," and their witch-hunt for "capitalist roaders" among veteran cadres; yet that critique also involved a thorough repudiation of the "socialist newborn things" (like the more egalitarian worker-peasant-soldier enrollment system for higher education), which were touted by the ultra-Left line as essential to the continuation of the revolution under the dictatorship of the proletariat.

Although all three episodes contain important elements of critiques of both types of ultra-Leftism, it is fair to characterize the Great Leap critique as having focused on the positive aspect while the "Swindlers" and the Gang cases dwelt much more on the negative. It was this heavily negative content that provided the bridge between line errors and counterrevolution that imparted to the latter two cases their particularly complicated and virulent nature.[10]

To summarize, the following points seem most salient in assessing the function and impact of the critique of ultra-Leftism in Chinese politics between the Great Leap Forward and the first years of the post-Mao era. First, it is clear that ultra-Leftism has not merely been a residual label of excoriation imposed for narrow political purposes by one faction on their adversaries in a power struggle. Factional maneuverings did play a vital role in shaping the evolution of the campaigns, but the critique of ultra-Leftism is better understood as symptomatic of the profound disagreement over the very meaning of socialism that permeated the Chinese leadership for more than two decades. The critique has embodied the constant perspective of certain leading cadres that the ideological and policy preferences of some of their comrades were disastrously misguided and had brought great harm to the revolution. In fact, ultra-Leftism as a label of disapproval in the Chinese Communist Party has been used much more rigorously and consistently than the more ideologically flacid and politically abused labels of revisionism and Rightism.[11]

Second, the line now condemned as ultra-Leftist was not simply the fantastical manufacture of political opportunists. Though some cynics used the banner of radicalism as a vehicle for their personal ambitions, there is no denying that the so-called ultra-Left line reflected ideas and sprouted programs that attracted many honest adherents to its purer vision of socialism and its unremitting antagonism toward the perceived enemies of the revolution.

Third, the power and appeal of the ultra-Left line was immeasurably enhanced by its close association with the person and the philosophy of Mao Zedong. The central ideas and principles of that line were derived from core precepts of Mao Zedong Thought, and its advocates appeared to be backed by the Chairman's formidable authority. Any attempts to challenge the ultra-Left line were severely proscribed by the ideological and political legitimacy it gained from the mantle of the Great Helmsman.

Finally, from 1957 on, the values of Chinese political culture became increasingly skewed to the Left. The cumulative effect of the anti-Rightist campaign, the Great Leap Forward, the Lushan Plenum, the ascendancy of Lin Biao and the Gang of Four, and, more importantly, Mao's twenty-year battle against revisionism was to induce an ideological paralysis in the Chinese political system that effectively stifled those who might have spoken out against the spread of the ultra-Left trend. In these circumstances, it is no wonder that the critique of ultra-Leftism was a difficult and problematic venture. It is also not surprising that the more comprehensive critique of ultra-Leftism could emerge only after Mao had left the scene.

The Critique of Ultra-Leftism and the Post-Mao Political Environment

So far in this chapter we have looked at the incompleteness and underdevelopment of the critique of ultra-Leftism in the years prior to the death of Mao—the ways in which a comprehensive criticism and rectification of Left errors in political line were stymied by elite conflict and ideological delegitimization, and the numbing effect that an earlier period of incomplete critique had on subsequent efforts for a more systematic campaign. Now we shift our focus from an analysis in retrospect of the incomplete critique to an analysis of the later, more comprehensive critique of ultra-Leftism (after the fall of the Gang of Four) and how it has affected the post-Mao political environment in China.

Inner-Party Struggle, Line Errors, and Counterrevolution

The major implication that the deepening critique of ultra-Leftism seems to hold for the future concerns the elaboration of the important distinction between errors in political line and counterrevolutionary activities. The making of this distinction was a crucial step in the development of the criticism of the Gang of Four and the whole generic problem of ultra-Leftism. Differentiating between the nonantagonistic contradictions posed by line errors in the Party and antagonistic contradictions of counterrevolution versus revolution made it possible to divide the campaign against the Gang of Four into two channels: a critical analysis of their ultra-Left political line and an exposé of their factional machinations, for which they are still labeled "Right in essence." The campaign has also made a further distinction between inner-Party struggle, line struggle, and class struggle. The analysis of these three types of struggle in socialist society has had important ramifications for the way in which Party history has been reinterpreted and for the conduct of Chinese Communist politics.

Inner-Party struggle has been defined as reflecting contradictions within the Party "between the correct and the erroneous, between the advanced and the backward, and between proletarian and non-proletarian ideologies." [12] Line struggle is of a more serious nature and constitutes "principled differences in relatively comprehensive theory, program, and action that arise within the Central Committee over important questions affecting the whole situation for achieving a certain goal in revolution or construction in a certain period such as assessing the basic situation, adopting strategy and tactics, and drawing up major principles and policies." [13] Inner-Party struggle results from contradictions that "are present everywhere," the resolution of which is part of the "Party's normal democratic life." Line struggle, on the other hand, "usually occurs at a turning point of the revolution and does not occur regularly." [14] But both types of conflict are only variants of struggles *within* the Party that reflect contradictions among comrades to be resolved through the nonantagonistic methods of criticism and self-criticism.

Juxtaposed to these inner-Party struggles are contradictions between the proletariat and the bourgeoisie (or between the people and their enemies). These contradictions take the form of "a conflict between antagonistic classes over fundamental differences." [15] The Party's instrument for such class struggle is the coercive mechanism of the dictatorship of the proletariat.

Current doctrine stresses that infrequent major line struggles must be separated from the more normal and frequent inner-Party struggle. Similarly, line struggles that are conflicts "between right and wrong within the vanguard force of the proletariat and . . . a contradiction or struggle between comrades" must be distinguished from the "life and death" class struggle. [16] The critical point of distinction between inner-Party struggle and line struggle, on the one hand, and class struggle, on the other, has to do with the "principled differences" involved in the former and the "fundamental differences" inherent in the latter.

The three types of struggle are seen as interrelated because they all reflect the persistence of contradictions in a transitional society and because the less serious forms of struggle may escalate into a graver variant if allowed to go unchecked. Post-Mao doctrine holds that the different types of struggle must not be confused analytically or politically (as the Gang of Four is accused of having done in their relentless pursuit of "capitalist roaders" in Party and society). As *Hongqi* rather mildly concluded, one result of the Gang's exaggeration of the prevalence of class struggle in the socialist period was that "for a considerably long period since the founding of new China, some anomalies have appeared in inner-Party struggles."[17]

The effort to straighten out these "anomalies" in the post-Mao era by making a clear distinction between the various types of ideological struggle has had a profound effect on the interpretation of Party history. After the Lushan Plenum, Party history was written largely in terms of a series of cataclysmic two-line struggles between "Chairman Mao's revolutionary line" and the "bourgeois revisionist line."[18] Even the conflict with the Gang of Four was portrayed in this framework by being labeled as "the eleventh major struggle between the two lines in our Party's history." Some of these two-line struggles have now been explicitly defined out of existence by the posthumous rehabilitation of the chief "villain" involved; such is the case with Peng Dehuai and Liu Shaoqi, the one-time antagonists in the eighth and ninth line struggles, who were rehabilitated in December 1978 and February 1980, respectively.[19]

But even the interpretations of somewhat more distant confrontations that are still considered as true line struggles have been given a new gloss. *Hongqi* offered the following explanation:

A two-line struggle is a matter of major importance in which the correct line must triumph, but it has never been a matter of life and death between the classes. . . . Inside our Party, when some people have charted and advocated a wrong line which leads the revolutionary cause to failure, the whole Party has strong reasons to terminate its wrong leadership and relentlessly struggle against its wrong line. . . . But this kind of struggle does not mean dealing a fatal blow at the comrades who once followed a wrong line.[20]

This line of reasoning has been extended to conclude that the pre-Liberation line struggles involving Chen Duxiu, Wang Ming, and Zhang Guotao should never have been labeled and treated as class struggles. In their initial manifestations, these line struggles merely reflected principled debates within the Party over the direction of the Chinese revolution. They were not interpreted as fundamental class struggles until the post-Liberation recounting of Party history when the ultra-Left began to distort the historical record for their own political purposes. It is acknowledged that the errors of Chen, Wang, and Zhang did eventually turn into contradictions between the people and the enemies of the people (i.e., class struggles); but the reason for this degeneration had nothing to do with "principled differences" in line. Rather it was due to the "fundamental differences" injected into the struggles when the perpetrators of the wrong lines ultimately betrayed the Party by engaging in various sorts of counterrevolutionary activities, including treason.[21]

Li Lisan has similarly been reevaluated, but with the significant difference that he has been completely exonerated of charges that he ever committed counterrevolutionary acts. Though it is acknowledged that Li "initiated the erroneous 'Left' deviationist line" in 1930 involving the ill-fated urban strategy for revolution in China, he is credited with having quickly become aware of his mistakes and accepting the Party's criticism. The casting of this nonantagonistic line struggle as an antagonistic manifestation of class struggle and the accompanying "cruel persecution" of Li during the Cultural Revolution has been attributed to the handiwork of Lin Biao and the Gang of Four.[22]

As noted in chapter 1, when the Gang of Four and the surviving co-conspirators in the Lin Biao affair were brought to trial in late 1980 the indictment against them dealt exclusively with their alleged counterrevolutionary crimes. They were charged specifically with

attempting to overthrow the government and split the state, . . . attempting to engineer an armed rebellion, . . . having people injured or murdered for counterrevolutionary ends, . . . framing and persecuting people for counterrevolutionary ends, . . . organizing and leading counterrevolutionary cliques, . . . conducting demogogical propaganda for counterrevolutionary ends, . . . extorting confessions by torture, . . . and illegally detaining people.[23]

The indictment did not mention the word "ultra-Leftism," nor were the defendants formally charged with committing errors in political line. To have put them on trial under a charge of ultra-Leftism would have violated the prevailing analysis that distinguished between line errors and counterrevolution; it would also have run counter to the notion that line struggles, however serious, must be handled as nonantagonistic contradictions within the Party instead of being resolved through the legal instruments of the dictatorship of the proletariat. Similarly, though Mao has been posthumously criticized for serious Leftist deviations in his work style, he has been exonerated of committing any criminally culpable acts. As one commentary on the trial put it, "there is a difference in principle between Mao's mistakes and the crimes of Lin Biao, Jiang Qing, and their cohorts."[24] This judgment further exemplifies the concrete application of the distinction between line errors and counterrevolution, which has been one of the major ideological offshoots of the critique of ultra-Leftism.

In addition to contributing to the reinterpretation of the past, the distinction made between the three types of struggle has had an impact on the nature of elite politics in post-Mao China. For the most part, the post-Liberation history of the Chinese Communist Party shows a gradual but unmistakable broadening of the scope and intensification of the methods of ideological struggle within the upper echelons of the leadership and in the political system as a whole.[25] Prior to the anti-Rightist campaign of 1957, inner-Party rectification had relied largely on persuasive methods of control and re-education of errant cadres, following an implicit understanding that, in the Party framework of criticism and self-criticism, differences over policy questions were not to be treated as targets for rectification but were to be handled through democratic centralism. But after the dismissal of Peng Dehuai led to a campaign to purge and rectify critics of the Great Leap Forward, the "traditional" norms guiding inner-Party conflict were put aside for increasingly coercive methods. The result was that "the winners and losers of policy debates were much more likely to have their political careers directly affected by the outcome of such disputes."[26]

The Cultural Revolution signified a major escalation in the use of verbally and often physically violent means of "mass criticism" to deal with ideological deviance within the Party.[27] Because Mao preferred to use the campaign against Liu Shaoqi primarily for the purpose of educating the people about the dangers of revisionism, the criticism process emphasized mobilization over rectification; the original objective of rectification to achieve "political redemption and renewed unity" gave way to "non-redemptive purges and rampant factionalism" based on notions of class struggle.[28] In other words, between the late 1950's and the arrest of the Gang of Four, the distinction between the three types of struggle (inner-Party, line, and class) broke down. The resulting indiscriminate mixing of these different modes of ideological conflict injected a high degree of bitterness and instability into the Chinese political system.

The comprehensive critique of ultra-Leftism as it developed after 1979 may portend a reversal of the process of the decline in the norms of elite conflict. Not only has the critique roundly condemned the intrusion of class struggle into Party politics, but it has explicitly incorporated a redifferentiation of the three types of struggle as a key ingredient of the deepening analysis of Lin Biao and the Gang of Four. This suggests a probable revival of the informal guidelines for inner-Party struggle that were in force prior to Lushan and the Cultural Revolution. Consequently, we may witness a significant mitigation of the costs to the "losers" in elite conflicts over policy.

A case in point is the fate of the members of the "Whatever" faction following a series of political defeats at Party meetings beginning with the Third Plenum of the Eleventh Central Committee in December 1978 and culminating with the Fifth Plenum in February 1980. When their reservations about some of the specific policies of the Four Modernizations and their less than enthusiastic positions on such issues as the reevaluation of Mao and, indeed, the scope of the critique of ultra-Leftism were repudiated by a majority of the Central Committee under the influence of Deng Xiaoping and his allies in the "Practice" faction, the individual "Whatevers" were first demoted from strategic positions and then "gently" purged from their leading Party and state posts. Their removal was, in fact, couched in terms of a decision by the Central Committee "to approve the requests to resign of *Comrades* Wang Dongxing, Ji Dengkui, Wu De, and Chen Xilian."[29] Furthermore, their ouster was not accompanied by public invective concerning their political and ideological shortcomings. The manner of Hua Guofeng's demotion between 1980 and 1982 is another example of the deescalation of the costs of inner-Party struggle. Hua was removed from his leading posts as Party chairman, premier of the State Council, and member of the Politburo and was subjected to public censure for various Leftist errors ranging from suppression of the "practice is the sole criterion of truth" campaign to fostering a self-serving personality cult; however, he retained his seat on the Central Committee and was commended for his role in overthrowing the Gang of Four and for his "useful work after that." [30]

Besides providing a justification for moderating the stakes involved in elite conflict, the separation of inner-Party struggle and line struggle from class struggle could foreshadow a gradual movement toward greater tolerance of political diversity within the leadership and the eventual evolution of something akin to a "loyal opposition" within the one-party system. [31] The emergence of such institutionalized opposition—which can be said to have characterized the "balance of power" that existed in the Party hierarchy prior to Lushan—would depend on a lessening of extreme ideological polarization within the Party leadership (which has been partially accomplished by the removal of the Gang of Four and the "Whatevers") and also on a regularization of procedures for handling policy disputes.

What might be the leadership's motive for promoting a relative pacification in the internal dynamics of Party politics? Clearly, such steps fit in with the new emphasis on unity and stability, which are seen as essential for mobilizing support for and participation in the modernization effort. Some assurance that the pattern of antagonistic mass campaigns and violent purges of the past will not be repeated is necessary to convince oft-burned bureaucrats and intellectuals to commit themselves and their skills to the new order. Furthermore, the post-Mao regime desperately needs to restore the legitimacy of the Party. That legitimacy was compromised by the political demolition of a succession of leading figures who were turned from the touted objects of Mao's trust and public confidence into targets of mass calumny through the sharp line struggles that rent the Chinese leadership between the Lushan Plenum and the end of the Cultural Revolution. A period of protracted inner-Party peace would go a long way toward refurbishing faith in the system, whereas renewed ideological conflict would only exacerbate the legitimacy crisis that is one of the main legacies of those many years of unremitting strife and turmoil. [32]

The "Twenty-Year Estimate"

Another interesting effect of the critique of ultra-Leftism on the political environment of early post-Mao China has been the heightened awareness of the problems of Left deviations in socialist development. This observation may seem a bit tautological on the surface; but given the earlier peripheralization of the critique of ultra-Leftism in Chinese Communist ideology and political culture, the increased urgency of the danger posed by Left line errors reflects a shift of no small magnitude. Like the differentiation between the three kinds of struggle, this new sensitivity to ultra-Leftism has had an impact both on the interpretation of the past and on the conduct of current politics.

First, the view that ultra-Leftism has been of much greater over-all harm to China's socialist development in the thirty-plus years since Liberation than has revisionism from the Right was gradually but unmistakably articulated beginning in 1979–80. A letter to *Guangming ribao* published in February 1979 and obviously selected to express emerging official opinion stated: "A review of the history of the past three decades since the founding of the new China shows that we really have suffered more from the 'Left' than from the Right." [33] Another letter asked rhetorically: "Why is it that our country—a big one practicing the superior socialist system and having 800 million highly conscious people—remains poor and backward after conducting socialist revolution and construction for nearly thirty years? . . . The root cause was the Left deviationist line pushed by Lin Biao and the Gang of Four." [34]

The widespread influence of the ultra-Left line during these years has been attributed, in part, to the fact that its content was attractive to many people who would normally fall well within the revolutionary ranks. In addition, some people were hesitant to criticize Left errors because previous rectification campaigns gave the impression that Left deviations were just "slight diseases" whereas the intense critical fire was to be aimed at Rightist deviations, which were diagnosed as "dangerous cases." [35] The combined result of the tendencies to underestimate the threat from the Left and to overestimate the threat from the Right was that the ultra-Left line was allowed to run amok to the point where it brought serious harm to China's development. As one article put it: "To the Chinese people, Right opportunism is a wolf with a villainous face while 'Left' opportunism is a tiger with a smiling face. We have been bitten so badly by this smiling tiger that our bodies are all covered by wounds and we have almost lost our lives." [36]

From this overall evaluation of the damage caused by Left errors since Liberation has emerged what might be called the "Twenty-Year Estimate," which suggests that the principal source of troubles in China's socialist development between 1957 and 1976 was ultra-

Leftism. This is an ironic contrast to the Gang of Four's much-heralded "Seventeen-Year Estimate," which postulated that the revisionist line held sway in the Party between 1949 and 1966.[37] It is now claimed that the ultra-Left line "dominated the Party for an entire historical period."[38] The time span of this "historical period" was made implicit in a discussion of the pattern of rural development in Anhui province since 1949. After lauding "the stable and vigorous situation in our country's rural areas from 1954 [to] 1957," this report went on to state:

However, over the past two decades, there have been great and small movements one after another and there have been struggles of this kind and that. As a result of these struggles, people have lost their enthusiasm, leading bodies have become paralyzed, and our ranks have been in chaos. . . . As far as Anhui is concerned, ever since the start of the movement to oppose Right deviationist ideas during the agricultural cooperative movement [1955] the majority of rural policies have been ultra-Left.[39]

The anti-Rightist campaign of 1957 is clearly indicated as the beginning of the ascendancy of the ultra-Left trend. As a whole, the objectives of the campaign to repel the "wild attack" of the Rightists against the Party and the socialist system are still judged to have been "entirely correct and necessary," but it is nonetheless acknowledged that "the scope of this struggle was made far too broad" and had far-reaching "unfortunate consequences."[40] Furthermore, one of the implications of the reversal of wrong verdicts from that period and the removal of all labels of Rightism even from those cases considered to have been correctly handled at the time[41] is that the campaign created the conditions conducive to the spawning of the ultra-Left line by so deeply ingraining in Chinese political life the notion that the greatest threat to the revolution came from the Right.

This "Twenty-Year Estimate" has encompassed a thorough reinterpretation of the Great Leap Forward and the Cultural Revolution. Both movements have been cast into the realm of manifestations of the ultra-Left line. In lauding the superiority of the socialist system, the years 1953–57 and 1962–66 have been singled out as periods that "show that socialism did work."[42] The implication is that the periods not mentioned—that is, 1958–61 (the Great Leap Forward) and 1966–76 (the Cultural Revolution)—were periods when socialism did *not* work because the ultra-Left line prevailed. Furthermore, by bestowing the label "socialist" on the period 1962–

66, the whole raison d'être of the Cultural Revolution is negated by implication, since, according to the Cultural Revolution view, the early 1960's were the years when the position of the revisionist line and the "capitalist roaders" inside the Party was consolidated and achieved dominance.

For a while an effort was made to salvage—at least officially—a semblance of legitimacy for the *idea* of the Cultural Revolution and to attribute its acknowledged disasters to the "sabotage and interference" of Lin Biao and the Gang of Four. During the "fake Left, real Right" phase of the campaign against the Gang of Four (December 1977–December 1978) it was denied that criticizing them was tantamount to a negation of the Cultural Revolution; rather, criticism of the Gang's line was portrayed as an indispensable step in "affirming the Great Cultural Revolution" and as part of the effort "to safeguard the fruits of victory of the Great Cultural Revolution."[43] When the criticism of the Gang's line shifted to include a direct attack on ultra-Leftism, a blunter appraisal of the period 1966–76 appeared, as expressed in a letter to *Guangming ribao* that asked: "Why was the Great Cultural Revolution such a disaster for the Chinese people? The root cause was the 'Left' deviationist line pushed by Lin Biao and the Gang of Four."[44] Still, by blaming the problems of the Cultural Revolution on the ultra-Leftism of Lin and the Gang, this formulation implied that the original intention (or line) of the movement was correct.

But the critical evaluation of the Cultural Revolution as part of the "Twenty-Year Estimate" was taken one step further by Ye Jianying in his speech in October 1979 commemorating the thirtieth anniversary of the founding of the People's Republic. Ye, speaking in his capacity as vice-chairman of the Central Committee of the Party and chairman of the Standing Committee of the National People's Congress, offered this analysis:

The Cultural Revolution was launched with the aim of preventing and combatting revisionism. For a proletarian party in power, it is of course necessary to be constantly on guard against going down the revisionist road. . . . But the point is that, at the time when the Cultural Revolution was launched, the estimate made of the situation within the Party and the country ran counter to reality, no accurate definition was given of revisionism, and an erroneous policy and method of struggle were adopted.[45]

Ye's depiction of the Cultural Revolution barely maintained the legitimacy of the motivating idea of the movement but repudiated its practice from start to finish. The posthumous rehabilitation of

Liu Shaoqi in February 1980 was another step toward the total obliteration of the legacy of the Cultural Revolution. This process was symbolically concluded by the "authoritative assessment" of the 1981 Resolution on Party History. "The 'cultural revolution,'" the Resolution declared, "was responsible for the most severe setback and the heaviest losses suffered by the Party, the state, and people since the founding of the People's Republic," and "the principal theses for initiating this revolution conformed neither to Marxism-Leninism nor to Chinese reality." [46]

At the same time that the critique of ultra-Leftism has stripped certain periods of past history of their legitimacy, it has also played a vital legitimization function for the post-Mao leadership. Simply in terms of the leadership's own political power, the increased sensitivity to Left errors and the "Twenty-Year Estimate" have provided a justification for both the reaccession to authority of cadres purged, criticized, or pushed aside during the Cultural Revolution and the demotion or removal from office of those whose careers flourished under the program of what is now denounced as part of the ultra-Left line. Thus the critique has negated the charges of line deviation or counterrevolution levied against the victims of the Cultural Revolution and, as well, glorified their political and personal persecution as a kind of revolutionary martyrdom.

More important in the long run is the role of the critique of ultra-Leftism in creating ideological legitimacy for Deng Xiaoping's emphasis on economic development as the principal task of the socialist period. The "Twenty-Year Estimate" recasts the history of the People's Republic in such a way as to both repudiate the specific content of the ultra-Left line and destigmatize the overall development priorities and concrete policies once labeled "revisionist" but now resurrected to serve China's modernization drive.

A clear example of this is reflected in the situation in education in post-Mao China. On the one hand, the Cultural Revolution reforms in education have been condemned for their overemphasis on practice to the neglect of theoretical training; for egalitarianism in admissions policies, which filled universities with underprepared students; for encouraging lack of student discipline and seriousness toward study under the guise of rebelling against the "bourgeois academic authorities"; and for wrecking curriculum and school administration in the name of putting "politics in command." At the same time, in the period since the fall of the Gang of Four, new educational measures have brought a tracked system with stress on rigorous academic standards of admission and advancement, a reassertion of professional administration and teacher authority, and a strong emphasis on imparting scientific and technical skills deemed relevant to the Four Modernizations. These new measures not only are a complete negation of the Cultural Revolution model but, indeed, are nearly a carbon copy of the education system of the early 1960's (and pre-Leap 1950's), which was so fiercely reviled by the ultra-Left line.[47] The "Twenty-Year Estimate" has been essential to making such a policy about-face ideologically palatable.

The new leadership has considered it necessary to delegitimize the specific policies of the Cultural Revolution through the critique of ultra-Leftism in order to eradicate the remnants of the "pernicious influence" of the line of Lin Biao and the Gang of Four. Lingering traces of Leftism have been said to make some cadres dubious about the content and direction of the prevailing line. In a lengthy criticism of such cadres, *Renmin ribao* gave the following examples:

> For instance, when the policy towards intellectuals is being carried out and conditions are being created for their work and study, some people have said that this means we are being overly lenient with them. When cases in which people have been wronged, misjudged, or framed are redressed and cases left over from history are solved, some people say that this means negating what was done in the past. When the wrong designation of Rightists is corrected and the labels are removed from landlords and rich peasants who have been successfully remolded, some people doubt whether the class line is correct. When democracy is promoted, some people interpret it as bourgeois "freedom." When practice is upheld as the only criterion for testing the truth, some people regard this as holding the revolutionary teachers in contempt. . . . These attitudes are the result of looking at problems from the ultra-Leftist viewpoint.[48]

The "Twenty-Year Estimate" is designed, in part, to obviate the source of doubts of this kind, which are considered to be a serious impediment to China's modernization program.

The continuing campaign against ultra-Leftism could induce a new skewing of Chinese political values. This skewing would take the form of making people so fearful of being labeled "ultra-Leftist" that they refrain from criticizing what they perceive as Rightist tendencies in current policies or lean a bit further to the Right in their political orientation than they might otherwise do in order to prove that they have overcome the "pernicious influence" of the ultra-Left line. To some degree, the possiblity of a renewed ideological orthodoxy of the Right conflicts with the suggestion made above that the critique of ultra-Leftism may contribute to a more open political life within the Party and society as a whole because of the critique's emphasis on deescalating the stakes associated with debate and dissent. It is conceivable, in particular, that in the quest for power, vengeance, and modernization, the post-Mao leadership might severely repress any potential challenge from the Left and strictly control the development of oppositional politics in China. It seems more likely, however, that there will be an ambiguous combination of orthodoxy and openness. Ambiguity of this sort may be compatible with creating a relatively more stable political order, but it will do little to mitigate the pervasive cynicism about political participation, which is one of the deepest legacies of the Cultural Revolution.

Several factors reinforce the probability of an ideological skewing to the Right. For one thing, there has been steady propaganda that policies condemned in the past as Rightist were, in fact, correct in terms of the principal tasks of building socialism in China. The people have been asked "to overcome the fear of being labeled a Rightist" in order to rectify the excesses of the ultra-Left line.[49] Most especially, ultra-Leftism has been settled on as the scapegoat for all problems, past and present, in China's post-Liberation development.[50] Out of all this may come a new dogma that is inclined toward intolerance of any sort of feedback or dissent that might be interpreted as reflecting even the slightest shading of Leftist sentiment. In that kind of atmosphere, ambitious cadres and cautious citizens could come to believe that "Right is better than Left"—in an ironic reversal of the notion that "Left is better than Right" which emerged in the aftermath of the anti-Rightist campaign of 1957 and ultimately was pushed to the point of frenzy during the Cultural Revolution.[51]

If this this new form of shortsighted ideological criticism were to take hold, it would certainly have a far-reaching impact on politics in post-Mao China. Besides its obvious effect on policy debates, it could also obscure the real source of problems that were not so much a result of the ultra-Left line as they were a cause of the abuses of political power that contributed to the ascendancy of those pushing that line. Certainly it is one thing to blame the ultra-Leftists for undermining democracy and the legal system and quite another to act upon the realization that Lin Biao and the Gang of Four (and Mao) were able to do what they did because of the weakness of China's political institutions. As one source put it:

We have paid a high price, but learned what we didn't know before. We have come to understand: the Gang of Four's emergence in the land of China had deep social and political roots and was a product of history. The incompleteness of our laws, the imperfection of our legal system, and the absence of reliable organizations and systems to safeguard socialist democracy gave Lin Biao and the Gang of Four opportunities to exploit. . . . This is an extremely deep, painful lesson which history taught us. The revolutionary people cannot help but remember this lesson and seize the weapons of democracy and the legal system.[52]

The post-Mao period has witnessed a flood of propaganda heralding a new era of "socialist democracy and legality," and important steps have been taken toward broadening political participation and instituting judicial procedures to protect civil liberties.[53] Yet the scope and meaning of these reforms are seriously called into question by acts like the elimination in 1980 from the state constitution of the so-called "Four Big Freedoms" (*sida*)—to "speak out freely, air views fully, hold great debates, and write big character posters"—under the pretext that these freedoms had been abused by the ultra-Left and had "never played a positive role in safeguarding the people's democratic rights."[54] Moves such as this reflect the inclination of the Party to treat an important aspect of ultra-Leftism as a cause rather than a symptom of continuing contradictions in China's political development.

In many ways, the critique of ultra-Leftism as it developed after the fall of the Gang of Four was part of an ideological catharsis in contemporary Chinese political culture. The shift from the Cultural Revolution to the Four Modernizations implies a profound reorientation of China's development strategy.[55] The post-Mao leadership has employed the critique of ultra-Leftism as one instrument for establishing the legitimacy of the new order by discrediting the values that guided China for more than twenty years. But enduring stability cannot be built only on a negative assessment of the past. China's future will be determined by how successful its leaders are in promoting healthy change in both the political and the economic life of the nation. To fail in this endeavor will do more than bring additional strife and hardship to the Chinese people; it will also most assuredly provoke another round in the "looking glass war" of Left against Right, which for so long engulfed Chinese politics in the conflagration of bitter struggle between competing visions of the road to socialism.

Reference Matter

Notes

The following abbreviations are used in the Notes. Complete authors' names, titles, and publication data for the works cited in short form are given in the Bibliography, pp. 293–303.

AAS	Anarchism and Anarcho-Syndicalism
CB	Current Background
CLG	Chinese Law and Government
ECMM	Extracts from China Mainland Magazines
GMRB	Guangming ribao (Bright Daily, Peking)
FBIS-CHI	Foreign Broadcast Information Service, Daily Report: China
HQ	Hongqi (Red Flag, Peking)
JFJB	Jiefangjun bao (Liberation Army Daily, Peking)
JFRB	Jiefang ribao (Liberation Daily, Shanghai)
JPRS	Joint Publications Research Service
MMTTT	Miscellany of Mao Tse-tung Thought
NFRB	Nanfang ribao (Southern Daily, Canton)
PDA	Communist China: Policy Documents with Analysis
RMRB	Renmin ribao (People's Daily, Peking)
SCMM	Survey of China Mainland Magazines
SCMP	Survey of China Mainland Press
SR	Selected Readings from the Works of Mao Tse-tung
SW	Selected Works of Mao Tse-tung
WHB	Wenhui bao (Wenhui Daily, Shanghai)
ZGQN	Zhongquo qingnian (China Youth, Peking)

Chapter One

1. According to the perspective of the post-Mao leadership, the Great Proletarian Cultural Revolution lasted for the ten years 1966–76. They officially divide the Cultural Revolution into three stages: (1) from the launching of the movement "on a full scale" at the Enlarged Politburo meeting in May 1966 and the Eleventh Plenum of the Eighth Central Committee in August of that year to the Ninth Party Congress in April 1969, which "legitimized the erroneous theories and practices of the 'cultural revolution'" and formally sanctioned the ascendency of Lin Biao as Mao's closest "comrade-in-arms" and chosen successor; (2) from the Ninth to the

Tenth Party Congress in August 1973, during which time Lin Biao died after an attempted coup against Mao and the Gang of Four consolidated their position within the leadership; and (3) from the Tenth Congress to the "smashing" of the Gang of Four in October 1976, a period of intense political conflict between radicals and moderates over the impending succession to Zhou Enlai and Mao Zedong. See *Resolution on Certain Questions*, pp. 36–41.

I shall use this ten-year span delimiting the Cultural Revolution throughout this study even though most Western analysts of Chinese politics still consider the movement to have run its course between 1966 and 1969, when it gave way to a brief period of consolidation before lapsing into another round of struggle over the succession. See, e.g., Maurice Meisner, *Mao's China*, chap. 18.

2. *Beijing Review*, 1981, no. 5, p. 14.

3. *Ibid.*, p. 16.

4. Beijing Domestic Service, Sept. 27, 1980, in *FBIS-CHI*, Sept. 28, 1980, p. L2.

5. For a compilation of the most important documents from the proceedings see *A Great Trial in Chinese History*.

6. See Mark R. Amstutz, *An Introduction to Political Science: Management of Conflict* (Glenview, Ill.: Scott, Foresman, 1982).

7. Tilly, "Revolutions and Collective Violence," p. 512. See also Tilly, *From Mobilization to Revolution*, chap. 7; Trotsky, chap. 9; and Amann, pp. 59–60.

8. See Kramnick, "Reflections on Revolution"; Hopper, p. 237; Gunneman, *The Moral Meaning of Revolution*.

9. For more on this see Johnson, *Revolutionary Change*; Arendt, *On Revolution*; and Hagopian, *The Phenomenon of Revolution*.

10. This is not to suggest that such conflicts have not also shaped the course of "lesser" revolutions. Note, for example, the struggles between Zapata and the Constitutionalists in Mexico or between adherents of the Sierra (mountain) and Llano (plains) strategies of revolution in Cuba. On the former, see John Womack, Jr., *Zapata and the Mexican Revolution* (New York: Vintage Books, 1968); on the latter, see Che Guevara, *Reminiscences of the Cuban Revolutionary War* (New York: Monthly Review Press, 1968).

11. For a comprehensive study of these divergent perspectives see Gray, "The Two Roads."

12. For a discussion of the origins of these terms see Caute, pp. 26–32.

13. See Soboul, pp. 56–85.   14. Caute, p. 9.

15. See Waller, pp. 62–66.   16. *Ibid.*, pp. 63–67.

17. In the course of the criticism of the Gang of Four, the Chinese Communist Party has debated the relationship between minor Leftist deviations and an ultra-Left line, coming to the conclusion that the difference between them is only one of degree. They claim that to draw too sharp a distinction between them merely complicates efforts to correct such errors. At the same time, the Party has vacillated on the use of quotation marks to distin-

guish Leftist deviations from true Leftism. In current usage, they tend to omit the quotation marks when referring to ultra-Leftism (rather than ultra-"Leftism"), but retain them when using the word "Left" alone in a pejorative sense. See, e.g., *GMRB*, Feb. 6, 1979, in *FBIS-CHI*, Feb. 16, 1979, pp. E7–E9, for a call to remove the quotation marks from all designations of Leftist errors; also, *Beijing Review*, 1982, no. 27, p. 3.

18. See, e.g., Kristov, ed., *Maoism through the Eyes of Communism*. For a comprehensive discussion of the Soviet appraisal of the Chinese Revolution between the mid-1950's and the Cultural Revolution see Peck, "Revolution versus Modernization and Revisionism."

19. Mao, *SR*, pp. 79–80.

20. *Ibid.*, p. 80.

21. "Things Are Beginning to Change," May 15, 1957, in Mao, *SW* 5: 441.

22. Waller, p. 64.

23. *Ibid.*, pp. 37–39.

24. Lewis, *Leadership in Communist China*, pp. 87–97.

25. *Ibid.*, p. 94.

26. Waller, pp. 42–43.

27. Lewis, ed., *Major Doctrines of Communist China*, p. 5.

28. Waller, p. 41; see also Tilly, *From Mobilization to Revolution*, pp. 218–19 and Petee, p. 55.

29. See, e.g., Drachkovitch, ed., *The Revolutionary Internationals*; Borkenau, *World Communism*; Claudin, *The Communist Movement*.

30. Dittmer, "'Line Struggle' in Theory and Practice," p. 680.

31. The most exhaustive study of the critique of Rightism is Dittmer, *Liu Shao-ch'i and the Chinese Cultural Revolution*. See also any number of the other works on the origin and impact of the Cultural Revolution, e.g., Daubier, *A History of the Chinese Cultural Revolution*; Bettelheim, *Cultural Revolution and Industrial Organization in China*; Hinton, *Turning Point in China*; and the several essays in Schram, ed., *Authority, Participation, and Cultural Change in China*.

32. See, e.g., White, "Politics and Social Status in China."

33. See, e.g., Bettelheim, "The Great Leap Backward."

34. For a comprehensive view of policy developments in the early post-Mao era see Baum, ed., *China's Four Modernizations*.

35. See Starr, *Ideology and Culture*, pp. 8–13.

36. Nathan, "Policy Oscillations," pp. 728, 732.

37. For a discussion of such conflict in communist movements in comparative perspective see Lowenthal, "Development vs. Utopia in Communist Policy."

38. See, e.g., Gardner and Idema, "China's Educational Revolution"; Riskin, "Maoism and Motivation"; Lampton, *Health, Conflict, and the Chinese Political System*.

39. *Ideology and Organization in Communist China*, pp. 22–24.

40. *Ibid.*, Prologue; see also Starr, *Ideology and Culture*, p. 10.

41. The notion of "political decay" and the cited elements of its op-

posite, political development, are taken from Huntington, *Political Order in Changing Societies*, pp. 1–3.

42. On the use and misuse of political labels in Chinese politics see Bennett, "Political Labels and Popular Tension."

43. Nathan, "Policy Oscillations," p. 732.

44. See Harding, "China after Mao"; Oksenberg and Goldstein, "The Chinese Political Spectrum"; and Lieberthal, "Strategies of Conflict."

45. See Mao, "Correct the 'Left' Errors in Land Reform Propaganda," Feb. 11, 1948, in *SW* 4: 197–99.

46. For Mao's comments that this campaign had "serious defects" because it eroded "the enthusiasm of the cadres and the masses" see "Talk Opposing Right Deviation and Conservatism," Dec. 6, 1955, in *MMTTT*, *JPRS* 61269–2, pp. 467–69.

47. On the case of the "Shengwulian" Red Guards (the "Hunan Provincial Proletarian Revolutionary Great Alliance Committee"), who clamored for the establishment of a People's Commune of China in 1967–68, see Mehnert, *Peking and the New Left*. On a similar ultra-Left rebellion in Shanghai see Walder, *Chang Ch'un-ch'iao and Shanghai's January Revolution*, and Nee, "Revolution and Bureaucracy." On the anarchy in Peking's universities during the early phases of the Cultural Revolution see Hinton, *Hundred Day War*. For Mao's views on these developments see "Dialogues with Responsible Persons of (the) Capital Red Guards Congress," July 28, 1968, in *MMTTT*, pp. 469–97.

48. See Burton, "The Cultural Revolution's Ultra-Left Conspiracy," and Gurtov, "The Foreign Ministry and Foreign Affairs."

49. See Nathan, "A Factionalism Model of CCP Politics"; Tsou's reply to Nathan's model, "Prolegomenon to the Study of Informal Groups in CCP Politics"; and Pye, *The Dynamics of Chinese Politics*.

50. Dittmer, *Liu Shao-ch'i*, pp. 214–93.

51. For a rudimentary attempt at such a meta-critique of the critique of ultra-Leftism see Evans, *China after Mao*.

52. The brief review in chapter 2 of the struggles of Marx, Engels, and Lenin against a Left opposition in the Communist International and the Russian revolutionary movement is illustrative of this problem in contexts other than China. For a polemical critique of Leftist deviations within the U.S. communist movement in the 1970's see 2, 3, *Many Parties of a New Type*.

53. See, e.g., Lewis, "Leader, Commissar, and Bureaucrat."

54. See, e.g., Gray, "The Two Roads."

55. See, e.g., Schwartz, pp. 3–19, and Lewis, "Political Aspects of Mobility in China's Urban Development."

56. The use of the terms "revolution" and "modernization" to describe the conflicting lines should only be taken as reflections of relative emphases within each line. The advocates of the revolution line thought they were promoting the basis for China's socialist modernization; the proponents of the modernization line thought they were pursuing socialist revolution.

57. The phrase is from John LeCarré's *The Looking Glass War* (New York: Bantam Books, 1975).

Chapter Two

1. A very helpful compilation of commentaries by Marx, Engels, and Lenin on issues related to ultra-Leftism can be found in *Anarchism and Anarcho-Syndicalism: Selected Writings by Marx, Engels, Lenin* (hereafter *AAS*).

2. The political struggles and writings of Joseph Stalin might also have been included in this survey as they both deal explicitly with the question of ultra-Leftism and are sometimes cited by the Chinese as an authoritative source on the subject. Stalin's comments, however, add little of substance to the critique of ultra-Leftism beyond the application of Lenin's ideas to new circumstances (such as collectivization). For a representative sampling of Stalin's views on ultra-Leftism see "The Fight against Right and 'Ultra-Left' Deviations," Jan. 22, 1926, in Stalin's *Collected Works*, 8: 1–10; "Dizzy with Success," Mar. 2, 1930, 12: 197–205; and "Reply to Collective-Farm Comrades," Apr. 3, 1930, 12: 207–34.

3. The principal Marxist critiques of utopian socialism can be found in Marx and Engels, *The Communist Manifesto*, pp. 39–42, and in Engels, pp. 31–44. For an interesting debate as to whether Marx's early references to "crude communism" constitute a critique of utopian socialism or a prediction as to the nature of the early stage of a future communist society see Resnick, "Crude Communism and Revolution," and Shlomo Avineri, "Reply to David Resnick," and Resnick's reply, in *American Political Science Review*, 70, no. 4 (1976): 1136–55.

4. "Utopian Socialist Themes," p. 216. Much of this discussion on utopian socialism is based on this excellent essay.

5. *Communist Manifesto*, pp. 40–41.

6. *Ibid.*, p. 40.

7. For a comprehensive discussion of the Proudhonist anarchists and the whole history of anarchism from its earliest origins to the Bolshevik Revolution see Nomad, "The Anarchist Tradition"; see also Ulam, *The Unfinished Revolution*, pp. 95–118, and Thomas, chap. 2.

8. Nomad, p. 61. The term "peaceful anarchists" is from R. Palme Dutt, p. 48.

9. *Communist Manifesto*, pp. 38–39.

10. See, e.g., correspondence between Marx and Engels, c. 1851, in *AAS*, pp. 30–40.

11. See Tucker, *The Marxian Revolutionary Idea*, chap. 2.

12. From the Draft Program of the German Social Democratic Party (the "Gotha Program"), 1875, cited in *ibid.*, p. 40.

13. "Critique of the Gotha Program," in Tucker, ed., *Marx-Engels Reader*, pp. 382–98.

14. Nomad, pp. 62–69. For a thorough study of the life and philosophy of Bakunin see Masters, *Bakunin: The Father of Anarchism*.

15. Nomad, pp. 69–90, and Thomas, chap. 5. The major Marxist critiques of anarchism are the following: Engels, "On Authority" (1873); Marx and Engels, "The Alliance of Socialist Democracy and the International Workingman's Association" (1873), Engels, "The Bakuninists at Work: An Account of the Spanish Revolt in the Summer of 1873" (1873);

and Marx, "The Conspectus of Bakunin's Book, *State and Anarchy*" (1874–75). Excerpts from each may be found in *AAS*, pp. 100–104, 105–22, 128–46, and 147–52.

16. See Maurice Meisner, "Utopian Socialist Themes," pp. 223–28. See also Maurice Meisner, "Leninism and Maoism," and Ulam, *In the Name of the People.*

17. Maurice Meisner, "Utopian Socialist Themes," p. 227. Lenin's many critiques of populism can be found in the first three volumes of his *Collected Works*; see especially the following essays cited by Meisner (p. 229): "The Economic Content of Narodism," 1894, 1: 340–508; "A Characterization of Economic Romanticism," 1897, 2: 129–266; and "The Heritage We Renounce," 1897, 2: 491–534.

18. See, e.g., "On the Provisional Revolutionary Government," 1905, and "The Faction of Supporters of Otzovism and God-Building," 1907, in *AAS*, pp. 189–96 and 235–41.

19. See, e.g., "The Youth International," 1916, in *AAS*, pp. 259–60.

20. A good summary of this conflict can be found in Bettelheim, *Class Struggles in the USSR.*

21. *Ibid.*, pp. 372–74.

22. See, e.g., "The Immediate Task of the Soviet Government," 1918, in *AAS*, pp. 287–91.

23. See, e.g., "Preliminary Draft Resolution of the Tenth Congress of the R.C.P. on the Syndicalist and Anarchist Deviation in Our Party," 1923, in *AAS*, pp. 326–29; also Bettelheim, *Class Struggles*, pp. 150–52, 383–84.

24. See Bettelheim, *Class Struggles*, pp. 374–79.

25. In *Collected Works*, 27: 323–54.

26. Tucker, ed., *Lenin Anthology*, p. 550. The full text of the essay is on pp. 550–618.

27. See Rue, *Mao Tse-tung in Opposition, 1927–1935*. For the prelude to this period see Brandt, *Stalin's Failure in China, 1924–1927*.

28. One of the most comprehensive Chinese sources on the struggles of this period is the "Resolution on Certain Questions in the History of Our Party," adopted on April 20, 1945, by the Enlarged Seventh Plenary Session of the Sixth Central Committee of the Chinese Communist Party (hereafter "Resolution," 1945). This "Resolution" was appended to the essay "Our Study and the Current Situation" (Apr. 12, 1944) in vol. 3 (pp. 177–225) in the early editions of the *Selected Works of Mao Tsetung* (Peking: Foreign Languages Press, 1965). Mao had delivered the speech "Our Study" as part of a continuing discussion during 1943–44 aimed at bringing cadres to "a thorough understanding of the character of the erroneous lines of the past" (p. 164n.) An introductory note to the speech states that the 1945 "Resolution" reflected the "detailed conclusion arrived at by the Central Committee on the errors of the 'Left' opportunist line that was pursued from the beginning of 1931 to the end of 1934." Since the "Resolution" appeared in the *Selected Works* it can be assumed that it was probably written by Mao himself or at least under his close supervision, even though it was issued in the name of the Central Committee. In any case, it certainly reflects Mao's

thinking circa 1945 on the causes and effects of the Left lines in the Party's history, and it is therefore taken to be an important ingredient in the contribution of Maoism to the critique of ultra-Leftism.

The "Resolution" was deleted from the 1967 edition of the *Selected Works*. The reasons have not been explained, but one Hong Kong writer has suggested that the omission was a conscious political decision (by Mao? Lin Biao? the Gang of Four?) that was part of the burgeoning Left trend of the Cultural Revolution; see Qi Xin's article, "Wenge 'zuo' qingde jidu fazhan," p. 78.

For a post-Mao analysis of the historical importance and the continuing relevance of the 1945 Resolution see *Beijing ribao* (Peking Daily), June 29, 1981, in *FBIS-CHI*, July 6, 1981, pp. K5–K8.

29. Rue, pp. 118–36.

30. See Onate, *Chairman Mao and the Chinese Communist Party*, p. 142, for a table showing the essential points of conflict between Mao, on the one hand, and Li Lisan and the Comintern, on the other. For more on the Li Lisan line see Guillermaz, pp. 195–206, and Harrison, pp. 166–68.

31. "Resolution," 1945, p. 187.

32. Harrison, p. 235.

33. "Resolution," 1945, p. 193.

34. On the Zunyi Conference see Harrison, pp. 245–50, and Guillermaz, pp. 253–57.

35. In the introductory note to his 1937 essay "On Practice," Mao says that he wrote the essay "to expose the subjectivist errors of dogmatism and empiricism—*especially the error of dogmatism*." *SR*, p. 66; emphasis added.

36. See "Rectify the Party's Style of Work," Feb. 1, 1942, and "Oppose Stereotyped Party Writing," Feb. 8, 1942, in *SR*, pp. 209–29 and 230–49. For a comprehensive selection of materials from this period see Compton, ed., *Mao's China: Party Reform Documents, 1942–1944*. For details on the rectification campaign see Onate, *Chairman Mao*, pp. 213–21; Guillermaz, pp. 363–68; and Harrison, pp. 323–47.

37. See, e.g., "Correct the Left Errors in Land Reform Propaganda," Feb. 11, 1948, and "Essential Points in Land Reform in the New Liberated Areas," Feb. 15, 1948, in *SW* 4: 197–99 and 201–22. For a vivid description of the "poor peasant line" in action and Party efforts to rectify it see Hinton, *Fanshen*.

38. See, e.g., "Request for Opinions on the Tactics for Dealing with Rich Peasants," Mar. 12, 1950, in *SW* 5: 24–25; and "Talks Opposing Right Deviation and Conservatism," Dec. 6, 1955, in *MMTTT*, pp. 27–29.

39. "The Debate on the Cooperative Transformation of Agriculture and the Current Class Struggle," Oct. 11, 1955, in *SW* 5: 221. See also "Refute Right Deviationist Views That Depart from the General Line," June 15, 1953, and "Concluding Speech at the National Conference of the Communist Party of China," Mar. 31, 1955, in *SW* 5: 93–94 and 167.

40. "On the Question of Agricultural Cooperation," July 31, 1955, in *SR*, p. 390.

41. On the unfolding and implications of this all-important struggle see

MacFarquhar, *Origins of the Cultural Revolution*, pp. 99–168. For relevant speeches and directives see *Communist China, 1955–1959: Policy Documents with Analysis*, pp. 164–255. For Mao's response to the Resolution of the Eighth Party Congress that proclaimed production to be the major task facing the Chinese Communist Party see "Talk at the Third Plenum of the Eighth Central Committee," Oct. 7, 1957, in *MMTTT*, pp. 72–76.

42. "Speech at the Chinese Communist Party's National Conference on Propaganda Work," Mar. 12, 1957, in *SW* 5: 435.

43. See, e.g., "Talks at the Nanning Conference," Jan. 11–12, 1958, in *MMTTT*, pp. 77–84.

44. See, e.g., "Speech at the Sixth Plenum of the Eighth Central Committee," Dec. 19, 1958, and "Speech at a Conference of Provincial and Municipal Committee Secretaries," Feb. 1959, in *MMTTT*, pp. 140–48 and 151–58.

45. See, e.g., "Speech at the Tenth Plenum of the Eighth Central Committee," Sept. 24, 1962, in Schram, ed., *Chairman Mao Talks to the People*, pp. 188–96.

46. On the anarchism of the Red Guards during the high tide of the Cultural Revolution see "Dialogues with Responsible Persons of Capital Red Guards Congress," July 28, 1968, in *MMTTT*, pp. 469–97. On the purge and criticism of the "May 16th Group" see Burton, "The Cultural Revolution's Ultra-Left Conspiracy."

47. "Indifference to Politics." Jan. 1873, in *AAS*, p. 95.

48. "Left-Wing Communism: An Infantile Disorder," 1920, in Tucker, ed., *Lenin Anthology*, p. 564.

49. "Rectify the Party's Style of Work," Feb. 1942, in *SR*, pp. 218–19. See also "On Contradiction," Aug. 1937, in *SR*, p. 99.

50. "Rectify the Party's Style of Work," Feb. 1942, in *SR*, p. 213; "The Role of the Chinese Communist Party in the National War," Oct. 1938, in *SR*, p. 155.

51. Letter to P. Lafargue in Madrid, Dec. 30, 1871, in *AAS*, p. 59.

52. "Resolution," 1945, p. 212. See also "Reform Our Study," May 1941, in *SR*, pp. 200–205.

53. Letter to T. Cuno in Milan, Jan. 24, 1872, in *AAS*, p. 70.

54. "Left-Wing Childishness and the Petty-Bourgeois Mentality," 1918, in Lenin, *Collected Works*, 27: 331.

55. "Left-Wing Communism," 1920, pp. 590, 606, 610.

56. "Indifference to Politics," Jan. 1873, in *AAS*, p. 96.

57. "The Faction of Supporters of Otzovism and God-Building," 1909, in *AAS*, pp. 238, 235. See also Lenin, "A Caricature of Bolshevism," 1909, in *AAS*, pp. 224–28.

58. "Left-Wing Communism," 1920, p. 602; see also Lenin's letter to Sylvia Pankhurst, Aug. 28, 1919, in *AAS*, pp. 297–98. In "Left-Wing Communism," pp. 574–75, Lenin makes a similar argument about participation by the revolutionary proletariat in nonrevolutionary trade unions.

59. Letter to C. Terazaghi in Turin, Jan. 14–15, 1872, in *AAS*, p. 68.

60. "On Authority," December 1873, in *AAS*, p. 103. See also Engels' letter to P. Lafargue in Madrid, Dec. 30, 1871, in *AAS*, pp. 58–59.

61. "Left-Wing Communism," 1920, p. 569. For Mao's comments on the problem of ultrademocracy and lack of Party discipline see "On Correcting Mistaken Ideas in the Party," Dec. 1929, in *SW* 1: 108–10.

62. See Lenin, "The Immediate Tasks of the Soviet Government," April 1918, in *AAS*, pp. 287–91. For Engels' view that the state must continue to function after the revolution see "On the Occasion of Karl Marx's Death," May 12, 1883, in *AAS*, p. 172. Mao invoked a similar argument in his criticism of the Shanghai Commune that was set up in 1967 during the Cultural Revolution. In replying to the demand of the rebels that a non-hierarchical system of government be established, Mao wrote: "The slogan of 'Doubt everything and overthrow everything' is reactionary. The Shanghai People's Commune . . . [wants to] do away with all heads . . . in reality, there will still always be 'heads.' . . . Communes are too weak when it comes to suppressing counterrevolution." See "Talks at Three Meetings with Comrades Chang Ch'un-ch'iao and Yao Wen-yuan," Feb. 1967, in Schram, ed., *Chairman Mao Talks to the People*, pp. 277–78. For a slightly different version see "Directive on Great Cultural Revolution in Shanghai," Feb. 12, 1967, in *MMTTT*, pp. 451–55.

63. See, e.g., "The Party Crisis," 1921, and "Preliminary Draft Resolution of the Tenth Congress of the R.C.P. on the Syndicalist and Anarchist Deviation in Our Party," 1923, in *AAS*, pp. 319 and 326–29.

64. See "Left-Wing Childishness," 1918, pp. 323–54.

65. *Ibid.*, p. 334.

66. *Ibid.*, p. 341.

67. See, e.g., "Report to the Seventh Central Committee of the Communist Party of China," Mar. 5, 1949, in *SW* 4: 361–75.

68. "Resolution," 1945, p. 199.

69. See, e.g., "On Policy," Dec. 25, 1940, in *SW* 2: 441–49.

70. See, e.g., "On Some Important Problems of the Party's Present Policy," Jan. 18, 1948, "Essential Points in Land Reform in the New Liberated Areas," Feb. 15, 1948, and "A Circular on the Situation," Mar. 20, 1948, in *SW* 4: 181–89, 201–202, and 219–26. For an early comment by Mao on problems of egalitarianism in the Red Army see "On Correcting Mistaken Ideas in the Party," Dec. 1929, in *SW* 1: 110–11.

71. "Correct the 'Left' Errors in Land Reform Propaganda," Feb. 11, 1948, in *SW* 4: 197.

72. See "Resolution," 1945, p. 196.

73. *Ibid.*, pp. 215–16.

74. *Ibid.*, p. 199; emphasis added. In this same essay Mao used a similar rationale to argue against the "new" dogmatism that insisted on maintaining the rural character of the Chinese revolution instead of recognizing that objective circumstances made it urgent "to shift the center of gravity of our work to [the] cities in the mid-1940's."

75. "On Practice," July 1937, in *SR*, p. 80. In another essay, Mao remarked that "there are two kinds of subjectivism in our Party, dogmatism

and empiricism." It is clear from the context of this statement that dogmatism was considered a Left deviation, whereas empiricism was a Right deviation. Empiricism is, in a sense, the opposite of dogmatism in that it interprets doctrine *too* loosely and emphasizes social investigation to the neglect of revolutionary theory. See "Rectify the Party's Work-Style," Feb. 1942, in *SR*, pp. 217–18. Elsewhere, Mao commented that those he considered dogmatists had once labeled *him* as an "empiricist" for his contention based on various "rural surveys" that the peasantry would be the leading force in China's social revolution. See "Preface to *Rural Surveys*," Mar. 17, 1941, in *SR*, p. 196.

76. "Programme of the Blanquist Communards," 1874, cited in Lenin, "Left-Wing Communism," p. 587. See also "The Bakuninists at Work: An Account of the Spanish Rebellion in the Summer of 1873," Oct. 1873, in *AAS*, p. 128.

77. "Two Tactics of Social Democracy in the Democratic Revolution," 1905, in *AAS*, pp. 198–99.

78. "Resolution," 1945, p. 197; emphasis added. See also "On New Democracy," Jan. 1940, in *SW* 2: 358–60.

79. "Critique of the Gotha Programme," 1875, in Tucker, ed., *Marx-Engels Reader*, pp. 386–87.

80. Lenin, "Two Tactics of Social Democracy," 1905, in *AAS*, p. 198.

81. "Left-Wing Communism," 1920, p. 574.

82. "Speech at the Chengchow [Zhengzhou] Conference," Mar. 5, 1959, in *CLG*, 9 (1976–77), no. 4: 32. See also speech of Feb. 27, 1959, in *ibid.*, p. 32.

83. "The Faction of Supporters of Otzovism," 1909, in *AAS*, p. 236.

84. "Left-Wing Communism," 1920, pp. 584, 579, 580.

85. "Left-Wing Childishness," 1918, p. 334.

86. "The Conspectus of Bakunin's *State and Anarchy*," 1874–75, in *AAS*, pp. 148–49; first emphasis in original, second added.

87. See Wakeman, *History and Will*, and Starr, *Continuing the Revolution*, pp. 32–35.

88. "Left-Wing Communism," 1920, p. 585.

89. "Reform Our Study," May 1941, in *SR*, p. 203.

90. "Speech at the Chengchow Conference," Feb. 27, 1959, in *CLG*, 9 (1976–77), no. 4: 15, 18. See also "Speech at a Conference of Provincial and Municipal Committee Secretaries," Feb. 1959, in *MMTTT*, p. 157.

91. See, e.g., Lenin, "The Teachings of Karl Marx," 1914, in Burns, ed., pp. 566–67.

92. Letter to P. Lafargue in Paris, Apr. 19, 1870, in *AAS*, pp. 45–46.

93. "Left-Wing Communism," 1920, p. 581.

94. "The United Front in Cultural Work," Oct. 30, 1945, in *SW* 3: 236–37. See also "Correct the 'Left' Errors in Land Reform Propaganda," Feb. 11, 1948, in *SW* 4: 197–99.

95. Speech at the Chengchow Conference, Feb. 27, 1959, in *CLG* 9 (1976–77), no. 4: 16. See also speech of Feb. 28, 1959, in *ibid.*, pp. 47–48. Mao made similar points concerning the excessive speed with

which cooperatives were formed in some places in 1955; but neither the "adventurism" nor the subsequent criticism or rectification of the ultra-Left trend within the cooperativization movement was as extensive as in the Great Leap. For Mao's warnings in this context "not to advance anything before the overwhelming majority of the people are satisfied with the advance" see "Talk on the Question of Intellectuals at a Meeting Convened by the Central Committee," Jan. 20, 1956, in *Issues and Studies*, 10 (1974), no. 8: 96—97.

96. See, e.g., "On the Question of Agricultural Cooperation," July 31, 1955, in *SR*, pp. 389—90.

97. "Speech at a Conference in Shansi-Suiyuan Liberated Area," Apr. 1948, in *SW* 4: 232. See also "Correct the 'Left' Error in Land Reform Propaganda," Feb. 11, 1948, in *SW* 4: 197—99.

98. "Debate on the Cooperative Transformation of Agriculture and the Current Class Struggle," Oct. 11, 1955, in *SW* 5: 230.

99. "The Alliance of Socialist Democracy and the International Workingman's Association," Aug. 1973, in *AAS*, p. 121.

100. *State and Revolution*, 1918, in *AAS*, p. 285.

101. Engels, "Address of the General Council to All Members of the International Workingman's Association," Aug. 4—6, 1872, in *AAS*, p. 81.

102. "The Alliance of Socialist Democracy and the International Workingman's Association," Aug. 1873, in *AAS*, p. 106.

103. Letter to C. Cafiero in Barletta, July 1—3, 1871, in *AAS*, p. 49. For Lenin's views on the "divisive influence" of the anarchists on the "broad fighting alliance" of the revolutionary movement see "Socialism and Anarchism," 1905, in *AAS*, pp. 202—6.

104. "Resolution," 1945, p. 209. Lenin chided the "Lefts" for their tendency to "fence themselves off from [the masses] with artificial and childishly 'Left' slogans" and their sectarian refusal to sully their principles by working in labor unions that they considered to be dominated by a "labor aristocracy"; the result of this sectarianism was that these revolutionaries cut themselves off from the very constituency that they should have been mobilizing for the cause of socialism. "Left-Wing Communism," 1920, p. 578.

105. "The Role of the Chinese Communist Party in the National War," Oct. 1935, in *SR*, pp. 151—53. For Mao's views on early sectarianism toward intellectuals see "Recruit Large Numbers of Intellectuals," Dec. 1, 1939, in *SW* 2: 301—3.

106. "Oppose Stereotyped Party Writing," Feb. 8, 1942, in *SR*, p. 236.

107. "On the Correct Handling of Contradictions among the People," Feb. 27, 1957, in *SR*, p. 447.

108. "The Alliance of Socialist Democracy," Aug. 1873, in *AAS*, p. 117. p. 117.

109. See Engels, letter to C. Cafiero in Barletta, July 1—3, 1871, in *AAS*, p. 48.

110. "Resolution," 1945, p. 209.

111. *Ibid.*, pp. 209—10.

112. *Ibid.*
113. "Strengthen Party Unity and Carry Forward Party Traditions," Aug. 30, 1956, in *SW* 5: 319–20.
114. "Differences in the European Labour Movement," 1919, in *AAS*, p. 243.
115. See, e.g., Lenin, "The Liquidation of Liquidationism," July 1909, in Lenin, *Against Liquidationism* (Moscow: Progress Publishers, 1973), pp. 39–46.
116. "Left-Wing Communism," 1920, p. 559. See also Mao, "Resolution," 1945, p. 216.
117. "Resolution," 1945, p. 216.
118. *Ibid.*, p. 214.
119. Marx, "The Conspectus of Bakunin's *State and Anarchy*," 1874–75, in *AAS*, p. 151; Engels, "The Bakuninists at Work," Oct. 1873, in *AAS*, p. 128.
120. "Left-Wing Communism," 1920, p. 560.
121. "Resolution," 1945, p. 181.
122. *Ibid.*, p. 185.
123. "Our Study and the Current Situation," Apr. 12, 1944, in *SW* 3: 164.
124. See "Resolution," 1945, p. 216; "A Circular on the Situation," Mar. 20, 1948, in *SW* 4: 219; "On Policy," Dec. 25, 1940, in *SW* 2: 444; "On Some Important Problems of the Party's Present Policy," Jan. 18, 1948, in *SW* 4: 181–82.
125. See Engels, letter to C. Cafiero in Barletta, July 1–3, 1871, in *AAS*, p. 48.
126. "Bellicose Militarism and the Anti-Militarist Tactics of Social Democracy," 1908, in *AAS*, p. 223.
127. Letter to Sylvia Pankhurst, Aug. 28, 1919, in *AAS*, pp. 294–95.
128. "Left-Wing Communism," 1920, p. 598.
129. *Ibid.*
130. "Our Study and the Current Situation," Apr. 12, 1944, in *SW* 3: 164. See also "Resolution," 1945, pp. 196, 213.
131. May 15, 1957, in *SW* 5: 440.
132. *Ibid.*, pp. 440–41; emphasis added.
133. "Speech at the Chengchow Conference," Feb. 28, 1959, p. 53.
134. "Speech at the Lushan Conference," July 23, 1959, in Schram, ed., *Chairman Mao Talks to the People*, p. 133. See also "Speech at the Sixth Plenum of the Eighth Central Committee," Dec. 19, 1958, in *MMTTT*, p. 142.
135. "Dialogues with Responsible Persons of Capital Red Guards Congress," July 28, 1968, in *MMTTT*, pp. 469–97.
136. *Ibid.*, p. 493.
137. Letter to F. Bolte in New York, Nov. 23, 1871, in *AAS*, p. 56.
138. "The Alliance of Socialist Democracy," Aug. 1873, in *AAS*, p. 114. See also "The Bakuninists at Work," Oct. 1873, in *AAS*, p. 128.
139. Letter to C. Cafiero in Barletta, July 1–3, 1871, in *AAS*, p. 49.
140. Mao said that Chen Duxiu had been expelled from the Party in

1929 because he and his supporters had formed a faction within the Party, not because "they had refused to accept the Party's advice" (i.e., followed the wrong line). "Resolution," 1945, p. 181.

141. "Things Are Beginning to Change," May 15, 1957, in *SW* 5: 441. But Mao was also of the opinion that Rightism was, in some ways, more dangerous than ultra-Leftism to the cause of socialist construction because conservatism "discouraged 600 million people" whereas the policy of "bold advances" could "preserve enthusiasm, encourage hard work, and the spirit of surging ahead." "Talks at the Nanning Conference," Jan. 11–12, 1958, in *MMTTT*, pp. 78, 83.

142. "Left-Wing Communism," 1920, p. 617.

143. "The Bakuninists at Work," Oct. 1873, in *AAS*, p. 140.

144. "Speech at the Sixth Plenary (Enlarged) Session of the Seventh Central Committee of the Chinese Communist Party," Oct. 11, 1955, in *MMTTT*, p. 25. For a similar but milder (edited) version of the same point see *SW* 5: 231.

145. Letter to C. Cafiero in Barletta, July 1–3, 1871, in *AAS*, p. 48.

146. "Address of the General Council to All Members of the International Workingman's Association," Aug. 4–6, 1872, in *AAS*, p. 82.

147. "Left-Wing Communism," 1920, p. 569.

148. Mao, "Resolution," 1945, p. 209. See also Engels, letter to C. Cafiero in Naples, June 14, 1872, in *AAS*, p. 78.

149. "The Alliance for Socialist Democracy," Aug. 1873, in *AAS*, p. 113. See Resnick, p. 1139.

150. "On Authority," Dec. 1873, in *AAS*, p. 102.

151. "The Youth International," Dec. 1916, in *AAS*, p. 259.

152. "The Bakuninists at Work," Oct. 1873, in *AAS*, p. 146.

153. "Left-Wing Communism," 1920, p. 584.

Chapter Three

1. There had certainly been other efforts to criticize and rectify Leftist errors in policy implementation since the founding of the People's Republic. But the Great Leap Forward was the first time that the critique of ultra-Leftism was an important aspect of a major split within the Party leadership.

2. For example, ideological polarization and political alienation within the top Party leadership were still relatively muted throughout the Great Leap and the subsequent retreat. This meant that the critique of ultra-Leftism and its consequences during this period were less acerbic than the critiques that followed the Cultural Revolution when leadership divisions were deep and irreconcilable.

3. Among the sources that have been particularly useful in constructing the context of this case are: Ahn, *Chinese Politics and the Cultural Revolution*, chaps. 2–4; Chang, *Power and Policy in China*, chaps. 3–5; Teiwes, *Politics and Purges in China*, chaps. 8–10; Solomon, *Mao's Revolution*, chap. 18; Maurice Meisner, *Mao's China*, chaps. 12–14; Lippet, "The Great Leap Forward Reconsidered"; and Kataoka, "Political Theory of the Great Leap Forward."

4. See *PDA*, Introduction, pp. 17–18.

5. See Harding, *Organizing China*, pp. 169–77.

6. Liu Shaoqi, "The Present Situation, the Party's General Line for Socialist Construction and Its Future Tasks," May 5, 1958, in *PDA*, p. 427.

7. *Ibid.*, p. 433.

8. In Marxist theory, the historical era after the proletarian revolution is generally divided into two stages: socialism (the "lower" stage) and communism (the "higher" stage). In every sense, the former is a transition to the latter, and it is only in the latter stage that the material and ideological bases exist for the realization of the program of "full communism." The era of socialism is still characterized by "the birthmarks of the old society [capitalism] from whose womb it emerges" (Marx, "Critique of the Gotha Program," 1875, in Tucker, ed., *The Marx-Engels Reader*, pp. 386–87), and these "birthmarks" (inequality, division of labor, distribution according to work, and state political power, for example) can only be eliminated and replaced by truly just economic life, social institutions, and human relationships over a relatively long period of time. See Ollman, "Marx's Vision of Communism."

9. "Resolution of the Central Committee of the Chinese Communist Party on the Establishment of the People's Communes in the Rural Areas," (hereafter cited as Beidaihe Resolution), in *PDA*, p. 456. Actually, the transition to communism first became a theme of the Great Leap prior to the Beidaihe Conference; see *PDA*, Introduction, pp. 22–23.

10. For instance, the people's communes first emerged in the spring of 1958 as a result of the spontaneous amalgamation of collectives following a particularly good harvest in Henan, Hebei, and parts of the Northeast; they received formal sanction only after a series of inspection tours by high-ranking Party leaders including Mao. See Maurice Meisner, *Mao's China*, pp. 230–32, and "Tentative Regulations (Draft) of the Weixing People's Commune," one of the earliest communes, in *PDA*, pp. 463–70. Mao commented at Lushan that the rural mess halls were "not invented by us, but created by the masses," in *The Case of P'eng Teh-huai*, p. 23.

11. Much of this summary is based on Chang, *Power and Policy*, pp. 96–110.

12. See, e.g., *RMRB*, Sept. 3, 1958, in *PDA*, pp. 459–63.

13. *Jiefang* (Liberation), 1958, no. 6, in *CB* 537: 1–4; see also Harding, *Organizing China*, pp. 190–93. For a brief description of Zhang's political background see Walder, pp. 5–8.

14. See "The Confession of Wu Leng-hsi," *Hongse xinhua* (Red New China), no. 43, May 1968, in *CLG*, 2 (1969–70), no. 4: 63–86. Much of this section is based on pp. 74–75 of this "Confession."

15. *RMRB*, Oct. 13, 1958, in *CB* 537: 1.

16. "Confession," p. 75; *Anhui ribao* (Anhui Daily), Sept. 29, 1958, cited in Chang, *Power and Policy*, p. 99.

17. For a compilation of articles from this debate see *CB* 537: 5–37.

18. For an interesting reference to Deng's assertion that the wage system "has not systematized the bourgeois hierarchy of inequality" and his criticism of the supply system, see *RMRB*, Oct. 17, 1958, in *CB* 537: 9.

19. In 1960, Mao forcefully reiterated his continuing support for the introduction of a supply system as part of the transition to communism: "In handling the free supply system, the Marxist style and the bourgeois style of work stand opposed in communist life. In my view, the rural work style and guerilla attitude are still good; in 22 years of war these were victorious. . . . Why is building communism [now] unacceptable? Why must we grasp a wage system? . . . In the very beginning, the collective lived an egalitarian life. In work, everyone was industrious and in warfare all were courageous. There was absolutely no reliance on material incentives, but rather a reliance on the drumbeat of revolutionary spirit." "On the Free Supply System," in *MMTTT*, p. 233.

20. "Resolution on Some Questions Concerning the People's Communes" (hereafter cited as Wuhan Resolution), Dec. 10, 1958, in *PDA*, pp. 488–503.

21. *Ibid.*, p. 502.

22. *Ibid.*, pp. 492, 494.

23. *Ibid.*, p. 492.

24. See Teiwes, *Politics*, pp. 335–36, and Chang, *Power and Policy*, pp. 101–5. For an analysis of strains within the Leadership during the early phases of the Great Leap Forward see MacFarquhar, "Communist China's Intra-Party Dispute."

25. The epigraph to this chapter is the poem of despair written by Peng Dehuai after his inspection tour of the communes in the Northwest and central China, cited in Ahn, p. 39.

26. These speeches are collected in *CLG*, vol. 9 (1976–77), no. 4.

27. See Mao's speech of Feb. 27, 1959, in *ibid.*, pp. 22–23.

28. *Ibid.*, p. 16.

29. See speech of Mar. 5, 1959, in *ibid.*, p. 75; and speech in March 1959, in *ibid.*, p. 91.

30. "Speech at a Conference of Provincial and Municipal Committee Secretaries," Feb. 2, 1959, in *MMTTT*, p. 157.

31. Speech of Feb. 27, 1959 (p.m.), in *CLG* 9 (1976–77), no. 4: 29.

32. Speech of Feb. 28, 1959, in *ibid.*, p. 53; emphasis added.

33. Speech of Feb. 27, 1959, in *ibid.*, pp. 31, 43.

34. *Ibid.*, p. 43.

35. Speech of Mar. 5, 1959, in *ibid.*, p. 77.

36. Speech of Feb. 27, 1959 (p.m.), in *ibid.*, p. 30.

37. *Ibid.*, p. 34.

38. The term "ultra-Left" was seldom if ever used during this period by the critics of the Leap—undoubtedly a lingering effect of the anti-Rightist campaign, which had made criticism of the Left a risky business in Chinese politics.

39. See Teiwes, *Politics*, pp. 398–406.

40. Ahn, p. 37; Chang, *Power and Policy*, p. 108.

41. See Teiwes, *Politics*, chap. 9.

42. For a general account of the events at Lushan see *ibid.* and Charles, "The Dismissal of Marshal P'eng Teh-huai."

43. See Chang, *Power and Policy*, pp. 110–14, and Gittings, chap. 11.

44. Teiwes, *Politics*, pp. 406–7; Ahn, p. 40.

45. See speech by Mao at Lushan, in *CLG* 1 (1968–69), no. 4: 27–43, cited in Teiwes, *Politics*, p. 406.

46. These documents can be found in *The Case of Peng Teh-huai*.

47. "Letter of Opinion," in *ibid.*, p. 10–12.

48. *Ibid.*, p. 12.

49. Teiwes, *Politics*, p. 405.

50. Speech of Aug. 2, 1959, in *The Case of Peng Teh-huai*, p. 30.

51. *Ibid.* The translation of "Gua gongchanfeng meiyoule, yi ping, er diao, san tikuan meiyoule, fukua meiyoule" is slightly altered here for accuracy. For the Chinese text see *ibid.*, p. 415.

52. Speech of July 23, 1959, in *ibid.*, p. 21; see also Ahn, pp. 40–41.

53. Teiwes, *Politics*, pp. 420–23.

54. For the resolution see *The Case of Peng Teh-huai*, pp. 39–44; for the communiqué see *PDA*, pp. 533–35.

55. Ahn, p. 43.

56. Vogel calls this period "The Revival of the Leap" in *Canton under Communism*, p. 262; Teiwes refers to it as "a new high tide . . . in the leap forward," *Politics*, p. 435.

57. Ahn, p. 43.

58. Teiwes, *Politics*, pp. 428–36; see also Joffe, *Between Two Plenums*.

59. Communiqué of the Ninth Plenum of the Eighth Party Congress, Jan. 20, 1961, cited in Teiwes, *Politics*, pp. 448–49.

60. Ahn, pp. 44–45; and Teiwes, *Politics*, pp. 435–36, 448–457.

61. Teiwes, *Politics*, pp. 458–59.

62. *Ibid.*, pp. 444–45; Ahn, pp. 46–47, 54–58.

63. Teiwes, *Politics*, pp. 471–76.

64. Ahn, p. 86.

65. For instance, Deng Xiaoping and Peng Zhen allegedly directed the Party Secretariat to draft the Sixty Articles in early 1961 without consulting Mao. This prompted the Chairman to criticize such a method of policy formulation by asking in a speech at a Party Work Conference in Canton, "Which Emperor decided this? Without investigation no one has the right to speak." (Cited in Ahn, p. 54, and in Chang, *Power and Policy*, p. 131.) Furthermore, Mao complained in 1966 that Deng had treated him like a "dead ancestor" at Party meetings and had never sought his advice on any important policy matters for over six years; see Schram, ed., *Chairman Mao Talks to the People*, pp. 266–67.

66. "Decision Approving Comrade Mao Tse-tung's Proposal That He Will Not Stand as Candidate for Chairman of the People's Republic of China for the Next Term of Office," Dec. 10, 1958, in *PDA*, pp. 487–88. For the origins of this proposal see "Sixty Points on Working Methods—A Draft Resolution from the Office of the Center of the CCP," Feb. 19, 1958, in Ch'en, ed., p. 75.

67. Teiwes, *Politics*, pp. 491–92.

68. *Ibid.*, pp. 405–6.

Chapter Four

1. For a brief discussion of many of the issues taken up in this chapter see Qi Xin, "Gongshehua he dayuejinde 'zuo' qing."

2. Overall economic success since 1949 may have contributed to the confident attitude of the Chinese leadership on the eve of the Great Leap Forward, but it is also true that the search for a new strategy of development was motivated by serious problems resulting from the adoption of the Soviet model in China. For instance, declining growth rates in agriculture, severe sectoral imbalances, and increasing urban underemployment all indicated that there were sound material reasons for China to attempt some new economic measures. See Lippet, "The Great Leap Forward Reconsidered," pp. 93–104, and Harding, *Organizing China*, pp. 165–67.

3. For a discussion of the different positions of various leaders and the debate on the launching of the Great Leap see Ahn, chap. 2, and MacFarquhar, "Communist China's Intra-Party Dispute."

4. "The Present Situation, the Party's General Line for Socialist Construction and Its Future," in *PDA*, p. 428; emphasis added.

5. *Ibid.*, pp. 429, 438.

6. *PDA*, p. 453; see also Introduction, p. 22.

7. *Ibid.*, p. 456.

8. *RMRB*, Aug. 6, 1958, in *PDA*, p. 23.

9. For example, the Wuhan Resolution (December 1958), which signified the first round of readjustment in the communes, still forecast that the modernization of China that was an essential precondition for a communist society could be completed in 15–20 years (see *PDA*, p. 492). At the Zhengzhou Conference in February 1959 Mao, while warning against undue haste, expressed similar confidence that "in fifteen or twenty years or a bit longer, the socialist commune will develop into the communist commune." Speech of Feb. 27, 1959, in *CLG* 11 (1976–77), no. 4: 36. Still, by mid-1959, there was no longer any mention of the Great Leap as the opening of the door for an imminent entry into the communist society. Even during the "Second Leap Forward" following the Lushan Plenum, propaganda was limited to support for the goal of accelerating the pace of socialist construction with only incidental mention of the transition to communism.

10. *HQ*, 1958, no. 12, in *ECMM* 156: 2–3.

11. *Lilun zhanxian* (Theoretical Front), 1959, no. 3, in *ECMM* 169: 27.

12. *Xin jianshe* (New Construction), 1959, no. 2, in *ECMM* 167: 5.

13. *ZGQN*, 1959, no. 1, in *ECMM* 160: 15–21. For an earlier claim that the transition to communism was "objectively possible" see *Jilin ribao* (Kirin Daily), Nov. 22, 1958, in *SCMP* 1947: 7.

14. See, e.g., *Xin jianshe*, 1959, no. 8, in *SCMM* 184: 6–17.

15. See, e.g., *Xin jianshe*, 1959, no. 2, in *ECMM* 167: 1–6.

16. See Maurice Meisner, *Mao's China*, pp. 206–15; Peck, "Revolution versus Modernization and Revisionism," esp. pp. 96–122; Starr, *Continuing the Revolution*, esp. pp. 301–8; Young, "From Contradictions among

the People to Class Struggle"; Schram, "Mao Tse-tung and the Theory of the Permanent Revolution."

17. "Speech to the Supreme State Conference," Jan. 28, 1958, in Schram, ed., *Chairman Mao Talks to the People*, p. 94.

18. *RMRB*, Jan. 22, 1959, in *SCMP* 1947: 12.

19. *RMRB*, Jan. 31, 1959, in *SCMP* 1955: 10.

20. *ZGQN*, 1959, no. 1, in *ECMM*, 160: 15.

21. For a concise statement of the meaning and use of these concepts in Marxism see Gurley, pp. 8–16.

22. See, e.g., *Dagong bao* (Peking), Oct. 25, 1958, in *CB* 537: 29–33.

23. See Maurice Meisner, *Mao's China*, pp. 146–61; MacFarquhar, *Origins*, pp. 15–19.

24. *Lilun zhanxian*, 1959, no. 3, in *ECMM* 169: 21–22. See also *Xin jianshe*, 1959, no. 1, in *ECMM* 161: 22–29; this article was written by Xue Muqiao, an economist who became one of the chief planners of post-Mao economic policy.

25. See Sklar, "Relations of Production, Productive Forces, and the Mass Line in the Formation of the People's Communes in China."

26. The most comprehensive treatment of Chinese Communist leadership techniques and theory remains Lewis's *Leadership in Communist China*.

27. *Ibid.*, p. 70. For more on the mass line see *ibid.*, chap. 3; Mitch Meisner, "Dazhai: The Mass Line in Practice"; Young, "On the Mass Line."

28. Lewis, *Leadership*, p. 72.

29. *Ibid.*, pp. 83–86.

30. See Teiwes, "Origins of Rectification."

31. *HQ*, 1959, no. 3, in *ECMM* 160: 31.

32. *ZGQN*, Nov. 16, 1958, in *ECMM* 154: 23–24.

33. *Ibid.*, p. 24; emphasis added.

34. On the various anti-Rightist campaigns see Teiwes, *Politics*, pp. 275–332, 336–66, 428–36.

35. In *PDA*, p. 456.

36. See speech of Feb. 27, 1959, in *CLG* 9 (1976–77), no. 4: 36, 43.

37. See Harding, *Organizing China*, pp. 163–77.

38. See Vogel, pp. 224–25; Chang, *Power and Policy*, chap. 2; Lippet, "The Commune in Chinese Development"; Riskin, "Small Industry and the Chinese Model of Development."

39. Lewis, *Leadership*, pp. 220–32; Lee, "The Hsia-Fang System."

40. Vogel, p. 227.

41. See *Union Research Service*, Aug. 10, 1962, pp. 198–200; Teiwes, *Politics*, pp. 450–57; Ahn, pp. 44–45.

42. *ZGQN*, 1959, no. 11, in *ECMM* 177: 30.

43. *Ibid.*, p. 29.

44. *HQ*, 1958, no. 3, in *ECMM* 158: 7.

45. Speech of Feb. 27, 1959, in *CLG*, 9 (1976–77), no. 4: 24.

46. Speech of Feb. 28, 1959, in *ibid.*, pp. 47–48. In this passage, Mao's use of the term "communist style" has a positive connotation in reference

to the eagerness of the peasantry to support the Great Leap; in this sense it is distinct from the "communist wind" as a work-style deviation.

47. *Lilun zhanxian*, 1959, no. 3, in *ECMM* 169: 27.

48. Commandism can be either a Left or a Right error in work style depending on the literal content of the command given. Because the commandism that was criticized during the Great Leap usually involved coercing peasants to participate in policies that theoretically were consistent with the ultimate goals of socialism and communism though practically inappropriate to China's level of development (e.g., the mess halls), we are justified in treating it as an example of an ultra-Left deviation in leadership. See article 34 in "Rules and Regulations for the Operation of the Rural People's Communes (Draft)," March 1961, in *Union Research Service*, Aug. 10, 1962, p. 205, for a reassertion of the principle of voluntary participation in the mess halls.

49. *HQ*, 1959, no. 3, in *ECMM* 154: 27.

50. See Lewis, *Leadership*, p. 78.

51. Speech at the Sixth Plenum of the Eighth CCP Central Committee, December 1958, in *MMTTT*, pp. 144–45.

52. *NFRB*, Nov. 3, 1960, in *SCMP* 240: 6–8.

53. *HQ*, 1959, no. 11, in *ECMM* 175: 1.

54. *Ibid.*, pp. 2–3.

55. See Qi Xin, "Gongshehua he dayuejinde 'zuo' qing," pp. 33–34; Prybyla, pp. 275–82. For Peng Dehuai's criticism of the mass campaign to produce steel see *The Case of Peng Teh-huai*, p. 9.

56. *Qunzhong* (The Masses), 1959, no. 2, in *SCMP* 165: 33, 36. For an early (February 1958) statement by Mao that may have legitimized the use of "high targets" as a stimulus to production see "Sixty Points on Working Methods," in Ch'en, p. 60.

57. See, e.g., *ZGQN*, 1961, no. 7, in *SCMP* 259: 9–12.

58. See, e.g., *HQ*, 1959, no. 12, in *ECMM* 177: 25–27.

59. *Ibid.*, pp. 26–27.

60. *ZGQN*, 1959, no. 11, in *ECMM* 175: 8.

61. See, e.g., Teiwes, *Politics*, p. 122; Solinger, *Regional Government and Political Integration*.

62. Deng Xiaoping, "Report on the Revision of the Constitution" at the Eighth Congress of the Communist Party of China, cited in Lewis, *Leadership*, p. 192.

63. See Harding, *Organizing China*, pp. 185–86.

64. *HQ*, 1959, no. 4, in *ECMM* 165: 41.

65. See, e.g., *RMRB*, May 25, 1959, in *SCMP* 2038: 1–5.

66. *ZGQN*, 1959, no. 11, in *ECMM* 175: 7.

67. See, e.g., *HQ*, 1959, no. 16, in *SCMP* 226: 12–31.

68. Speech of Feb. 28, 1959, in *CLG*, 9 (1976–77), no. 4: 53.

69. See, e.g., *Zhongguo qingnian bao* (China Youth Daily), May 19, 1959, in *SCMP* 2025: 2–4, for the detailed account of one young cadre who was criticized for serious errors of commandism and blind direction of production, yet was judged to be "devoted to rural socialist construction."

70. *RMRB*, Sept. 12, 1959, in *SCMP* 2105: 6.

71. *The Case of Peng Teh-huai*, p. 3. This perspective on the commune movement is shared by the post-Mao leadership. For a cautious criticism of the errors of the Great Leap in this respect see the article with the ironic title, "Renzhen xuexi Maozhuxi guanyu renmin gongshede lilun" (Seriously Study Chairman Mao's Theory of the People's Commune), *HQ*, 1978, no. 8, pp. 70–78.

72. On the rural mess halls see "Dalu nongcun gonggong shitangde fazhan" (The Development of the Rural Public Mess Halls in the Mainland), in *Zuguo* (Motherland, Hong Kong), 33, no. 13 (n.d.): 300–303. On the urban communes see Salaff, "The Urban Communes and Anti-City Experiment." On the backyard steel campaign see note 55 above.

73. See Lewis, "The Leadership Doctrine of the Chinese Communist Party," and Skinner, "Marketing and Social Structure in Rural China, Part III." Much of this discussion of the size of the people's communes is derived from these two articles.

74. In *PDA*, pp. 454–55.

75. Skinner, pp. 383–84.

76. Lewis points out that the scale of the commune caused problems because it violated "a fundamental maxim of traditional and mass line politics: power comes from face-to-face relationships rather than from large impersonal organizations." ("Leadership Doctrine," p. 463.) Skinner, too, emphasizes the "artificial" nature of the new units, which were three times as large as the traditional marketing community, as the key to why the communes were unworkable in their original design. Both authors agree that the commune as initially designed was destined to fall prey to intervillage antagonisms that would undermine efforts at cooperation and coordination.

77. According to Skinner (pp. 396–97), the adjusted communes were coequal to the "natural marketing community."

78. See Ahn, pp. 273–304, for a comprehensive comparison of the 1958 and 1962 commune structures; see also Gargi Dutt, *Rural Communes of China*. These comments about the pervasive modification of the original commune model are not meant to imply that the institution of the people's commune during the Great Leap had no lasting effect on rural life in China. As the agricultural economy recovered from the combination of man-made and natural disasters of 1958–61, the commune gradually came to play a significant role in administrative, capital construction, communications, and welfare functions in the countryside. Even the size of the average commune increased over time as reflected in the fact that by 1979–80 there were approximately 55,000 communes in China as compared with the 74,000 in 1962–63; in other words, there were a smaller number of larger communes covering rural China. In a sense, this pattern of gradual expansion of the size of the communes supports the argument of some of the critics of ultra-Leftism that it was not the *idea* of the communes that was wrong in 1958–59 but the assumption that such an idea could be implemented in its maximum form at the time. For more on the people's communes see Lippet, "The Commune in Chinese Development";

Crook, "The Commune System in the People's Republic of China, 1963–1974"; Bennett, *Huadong.*

The structure of the people's communes was further modified in the early post-Mao era. In the first wave of reform, greater responsibility for production planning and execution devolved to the teams and households through a system of contracts and quotas. In 1982, the communes were divested of all political functions while retaining important, if diminished, economic authority over large-scale undertakings; the township (*xiang*) was revived as the new unit of political power in the countryside. On these changes see Domes, "New Policies in the Communes"; Tsou et al., "The Responsibility System in Agriculture"; *Beijing Review*, 1982, no. 29, pp. 15–17.

79. Skinner, p. 392.

80. *Ibid.*, pp. 384–86.

81. See "Regulations on the Work in the Rural People's Communes (Revised Draft)" (also known as the "New Sixty Articles"), September 1962, in *Issues and Studies*, 15 (1979), no. 10: 93–111 (Part 1), and no. 12: 106–15 (Part 2). Article 4 of these regulations includes the following comment on the size question: "The size of the people's communes is based on a town[ship], either large or small. The size of each commune will remain unchanged for a long period once it is decided." Part 1, p. 94.

82. For a discussion of this and other aspects of the Chinese Communist perspective on distribution issues see Hoffman, "The Basis of Communist China's Incentive Policy." For an interesting attempt to trace the failure of the Taiping and other peasant rebellions to the error of egalitarianism see "Lun pingjunzhuyide gongguo yu nongmin zhanzhengde changbai" (The Merits and Faults of Egalitarianism in the Success and Failure of Peasant Wars), *Lishi yanjiu* (Historical Studies), January 1980, pp. 12–20. This article reflects the pervasive effect of the critique of ultra-Leftism in post-Mao China as manifest in analyses of traditional history.

83. See, e.g., *RMRB*, Oct. 1, 1958, in *SCMP*, 1887: 13.

84. Marx, "Critique of the Gotha Program," in Tucker, ed., *Marx-Engels Reader*, p. 388.

85. See, e.g., *Xin jianshe*, 1959, no. 1, in *ECMM* 162: 20–24.

86. For more on these two types of ownership in socialist society see "Public Ownership of the Means of Production in China," *Peking Review*, 1972, no. 51, pp. 5–7.

87. See, e.g., the Wuhan Resolution, in *PDA*, p. 493.

88. See, e.g., *Caijing yanjiu* (Financial and Economic Research), 1959, no. 1, in *ECMM* 162: 25–29.

89. *Xin jianshe*, 1959, no. 1, in *ECMM* 162: 24.

90. On the brigade as the basic unit see, e.g., *NFRB*, Nov. 3, 1960, in *SCMP* 2415: 1–5. On the delineation of the revived powers of the team, which effectively protected that level from expropriation and exploitation from above, see "Regulations on the Work in the Rural People's Communes (Revised Draft)," Part 1, pp. 101–11.

91. The problems of "leveling" and appropriation without compensation were referred to as "yi ping, er diao" ("one, equalization; two, trans-

fer"). Sometimes a third category of deviation was added: "san shoukuan" ("three, recall of loans"), which described the precipitous demand by the commune for repayment of loans made to lower levels in order to finance capital construction projects undertaken by higher authorities during the Great Leap. See, e.g., Mao's speech at Zhengzhou, Feb. 27, 1959 (p.m.), in *CLG*, 9 (1976–77), no. 4: 33.

92. See, e.g., "Rules and Regulations for the Operation of the Rural People's Communes (Draft)," March 1961, articles 5, 20, 31, and 33, pp. 201–6. For a discussion of how such "leveling" affected one brigade in Guangdong see *NFRB*, Nov. 17, 1960, in *SCMP* 2045: 2–4.

93. Speech of Feb. 28, 1959, in *CLG*, 9 (1976–77), no. 4: 49.

94. Speech of Mar. 5, 1959, in *ibid.*, pp. 71–72, 74.

95. Speech of Feb. 27, 1959, in *ibid.*, p. 16.

96. Speech of Mar. 5, 1959, in *ibid.*, p. 77.

97. For an account of the evolution of the supply system see *PDA*, Introduction, pp. 27–29.

98. In *PDA*, p. 456.

99. *Zhengzhi xuexi* (Political Study), Oct. 13, 1958, in *ECMM*, vol. 151, cited in Chang, *Power and Policy*, pp. 99–100.

100. See, e.g., *Dagong bao*, Oct. 25, 1958, in *CB* 537: 29–33.

101. *HQ*, 1958, no. 10, in *ECMM* 155: 26.

102. See *PDA*, p. 29.

103. In *PDA*, p. 494.

104. *Ibid.*

105. See, e.g., *RMRB*, Jan. 20, 1959, in *SCMP* 1947: 1–5.

106. See, e.g., *HQ*, 1959, no. 6, in *ECMM* 166: 28–30.

107. Even though fixed wages were eliminated from the agricultural sector entirely in the early 1960's, the supply system—though denounced as an ultra-Left error in its high-tide extreme—did have a lasting impact on the Chinese countryside. Since the Great Leap, a small portion of peasant income has been made up of "basic food grain" (*jiben kouliang*), in which some amount of rice, sorghum, wheat, etc. has been distributed on a straightforward per capita basis independent of labor performed; thus, peasants are guaranteed at least a bare subsistence living. See Ahn, pp. 294–99. It is possible that this rather weak "communist sprout" in the Chinese countryside will be uprooted in the revamped commune structure of the post-Mao era.

108. See, e.g., *Gongren ribao* (Worker's Daily), Oct. 18, 1958, in *CB* 537: 17–18.

109. *RMRB*, Oct. 16, 1958, in *CB* 537: 7.

110. See, e.g., *ZGQN*, 1959, no. 10, in *ECMM* 178: 6–10.

111. *RMRB*, Oct. 13, 1958, in *CB* 537: 3.

112. For Zhang's later views on this subject see his "On Exercising All-Round Dictatorship over the Bourgeoisie," *Peking Review*, 1975, no. 14: 5–11. This article was a major document in the Gang of Four's struggle against their old nemesis, Deng Xiaoping, following his first political rehabilitation.

113. See, e.g., *RMRB*, Oct. 18, 1958, in *CB* 537: 15–17.

114. *RMRB*, Oct. 17, 1958, in *CB* 537: 8–9.
115. *Ibid.*, p. 9; see also *ibid.*, pp. 11–12.
116. *RMRB*, Feb. 3, 1959, in *SCMP* 1957: 5–9. See also *RMRB*, Jan. 3, 1959, in *SCMP* 1957: 1–4.
117. *RMRB*, Feb. 3, 1959, in *SCMP* 1957: 7.
118. For a comprehensive account of these matters see Walker, pp. 71–87. On tne question of the restriction of rural trade see Skinner, pp. 366–82.
119. See, e.g., *Zhengzhi xuexi*, 1959, no. 14, in *ECMM* 184: 42–43.
120. See "Rules and Regulations for the Operation of the Rural People's Communes (Draft)," articles 36 and 38; and "Regulations on the Work in the Rural People's Communes (Revised Draft)," Part 2, pp. 106–8; and Walker, pp. 86–98.
121. See Ahn, pp. 85–86.

Chapter Five

1. Maurice Meisner, *Mao's China*, part 4; Brinton, chap. 8.
2. Maurice Meisner, *Mao's China*, p. 267.
3. See *ibid.*, chaps. 15–16; Wheelwright and McFarlane, chap. 3.
4. See Maurice Meisner, *Mao's China*, pp. 298–99, 309–17.
5. On Lin's background and his rise and fall from power see Kau, ed., *The Lin Piao Affair*; van Ginnekan, *The Rise and Fall of Lin Piao*; and Bridgham, "The Fall of Lin Piao."
6. See Maurice Meisner, *Mao's China*, pp. 364–70; and Gottlieb, *Chinese Foreign Policy Factionalism*.
7. See "Communiqué of the Central Committee of the Chinese Communist Party Concerning Lin [Biao's] 'September 12' Anti-Party Incident," in Kau, pp. 69–70.
8. See Kau, pp. 202–21, for Zhou's speech and the first public denunciation of Lin by name. Lin had been mentioned by name earlier in brief allusions to his attempted coup and death in Mao Zedong's interviews with Ceylon's Prime Minister Sirimavo Bandaranaike (June 28, 1972) and France's Foreign Minister Maurice Schumann (July 10, 1972); see *Issues and Studies*, 8 (1972) no. 12: 8, and Agence France Presse Report, July 27, 1972. Lin was also mentioned directly in Zhou's interview with American newspaper editors in October 1972; see *New York Times*, Oct. 12, 1972. However, the Tenth Party Congress signaled the onset of the overt and sustained criticism of Lin by name in the Chinese media.
9. *China News Analysis*, no. 851 (1971), p. 2.
10. For a study of Chen Boda's relationship with Mao see Wylie, *The Emergence of Maoism*.
11. See Bridgham, pp. 428–38.
12. See Burton, "The Cultural Revolution's Ultra-Left Conspiracy," and van Ginnekan, pp. 226–28.
13. Mao called this warning a tactic of "throwing stones" at Lin and his military associates. See "Summary of Chairman Mao's Talks to Responsible Local Comrades during his Tour of Inspection," mid-August to Sept.

12, 1971, in Kau, p. 62. Chen surfaced again as one of the co-defendants in the 1980–81 trial of the "Lin Biao–Jiang Qing counterrevolutionary cliques." He was found guilty of attempting to overthrow the government and of "framing and persecuting" various veteran cadres during the Cultural Revolution. He was sentenced to eighteen years in prison and "deprivation of political rights for five years." See *Beijing Review*, 1981, no. 5, pp. 24–28.

14. See Domes, *China after the Cultural Revolution*, pp. 77–90, for a chronological account of the campaign against Chen Boda in 1970–71.

15. See *RMRB*, Aug. 15 and 29, 1971, in *SCMP* 4966: 22 and 4973: 19.

16. See *HQ*, 1971, no. 4, p. 8, cited in *China News Analysis*, no. 851 (1971), p. 6; and *RMRB*, July 23, 1971, in *SCMP* 4951: 133.

17. See Hinton, *Hundred Day War*, pp. 275–86; van Ginnekan, pp. 232–33. Kuai and his closest Red Guard associates, such as Nie Yuanzi, disappeared from the center stage of politics after being repudiated during the anti–ultra-Left phase of the "Swindlers" campaign, but they returned to active involvement in university politics under the patronage of Jiang Qing et al. after a period of reeducation, and after the criticism of the "Swindlers" was diverted from its purposes as a critique of ultra-Leftism. These Red Guard leaders were arrested again in 1978 and subjected to a mass-struggle session in December of that year as part of the campaign against the Gang of Four. Information on Kuai's and Nie's first fall from grace in 1971 is based partly on my interviews at Peking University in April 1972; for their later history see Beijing Domestic Service, Dec. 28, 1978, in *FBIS-CHI*, Jan. 8, 1979, pp. K2–K4.

18. See, e.g., *GMRB* Oct. 26, 1971, in *SCMP* 5010: 55.

19. See, e.g., *ibid.* and *RMRB*, Oct. 29, 1971, in *SCMP* 5011: 103.

20. *GMRB*, Oct. 18, 1971, in *SCMP* 5010: 60.

21. *GMRB*, Oct. 6, 1971, in *SCMP* 4999: 186.

22. *RMRB*, Oct. 30, 1971, in *SCMP* 5012: 178–82.

23. *GMRB*, Dec. 13, 1971, in *SCMP* 5045: 5.

24. See, e.g., *GMRB*, Dec. 4, 1971, in *FBIS-CHI*, Dec. 29, 1971, p. B1; and Peking Domestic Service, Nov. 28, 1971, in *FBIS-CHI*, Dec. 1, 1971, p. C4.

25. See Domes, *China after the Cultural Revolution*, pp. 153–66.

26. *RMRB*, Mar. 23, 1978, in *FBIS-CHI*, Mar. 28, 1978, p. E17.

27. *Ibid.*

28. See, e.g., numerous articles in *RMRB* in late August 1972, in *FBIS-CHI*, Aug. 23–25, 1978, sect. E; see also Domes, *China after the Cultural Revolution*, pp. 157–59.

29. See, e.g., Heilongjiang Provincial Service, Aug. 31, 1972, in *FBIS-CHI*, Sept. 7, 1972, p. G2.

30. Sichuan Provincial Service, Sept. 8, 1972, in *FBIS-CHI*, Sept. 11, 1972, p. G1; see also Shenyang Radio, Sept. 1, 1972, in *FBIS-CHI*, Sept. 7, 1972, p. G2.

31. See, e.g., Kirin Provincial Service, Sept. 9, 1972, in *FBIS-CHI*, Sept. 12, 1972, p. G5.

32. *Issues and Studies*, 9 (1973), no. 3: 92; also in Kau, p. 98.

33. See *RMRB*, Mar. 23, 1978, in *FBIS-CHI*, Mar. 28, 1978, p. E17, for the reference to Zhou's instructions to the Party newspaper to step up the criticism of ultra-Leftism.

34. *RMRB*, Oct. 14, 1972, in *SCMP* 5241: 58.

35. *Ibid.*

36. *Ibid.*, p. 60.

37. See, e.g., *RMRB*, Oct. 17, 18, and 23, 1972, in *SCMP* 5246: 92; 5247: 152; and 5249: 1.

38. See, e.g., *RMRB*, Oct. 24 and 25, 1972, in *SCMP* 5251: 105, 113; and *GMRB*, Nov. 14, 1972, in *SCMP* 5262: 166.

39. See, e.g., *GMRB*, Oct. 20 and Nov. 5, 1972, in *SCMP* 5247: 159 and 5256: 102; *RMRB*, Oct. 29 and Nov. 13, 1972, in *SCMP* 5254: 1 and 5262: 159.

40. *GMRB*, Oct. 21, 1972, in *SCMP* 5249: 10; emphasis added.

41. *RMRB*, Mar. 23, 1978, in *FBIS-CHI* Mar. 28, 1978, pp. E17–E21.

42. *Wenhui bao*, a newspaper clearly under the strong influence of the Gang of Four, had run a series of articles in late October 1972 emphasizing the necessity for continuing to focus on criticizing the revisionism of the "Swindlers" at the same time that much of the other national media was in the midst of a high tide of criticism of the ultra-Left trend and anarchism; see *SCMP Supplement* 309: 17–22.

43. *RMRB*, Mar. 23, 1978, in *FBIS-CHI*, Mar. 28, 1978, pp. E18–E19.

44. *RMRB*, May 18, 1978, in *FBIS-CHI*, May 24, 1978, p. E10.

45. *HQ*, 1972, no. 12, in *SCMM* 743–44: 8; emphasis added. The author of this article used the pen name Gao Ge, the characters for which are a homophone for a phrase meaning "Make Revolution."

46. *Ibid.*, p. 9.

47. *RMRB, JFJB, HQ,* Jan. 1, 1973, in *SCMP* 5294: 1.

48. See Domes, *China after the Cultural Revolution*, pp. 174–75.

49. Sichuan Provincial Service, Jan. 30, 1973, in *FBIS-CHI*, Jan. 31, 1973, pp. E3–E4; emphasis added.

50. *Hunan Daily*, Feb. 2, 1973, in *FBIS-CHI*, Feb. 8, 1973, p. D1; see also *Xinjiang Daily*, Feb. 12, 1973, in *FBIS-CHI*, Feb. 14, 1973, p. H5; and *Tibet Daily*, Feb. 19, 1973, in *FBIS-CHI*, Feb. 20, 1973, p. E7.

51. Hunan Provincial Service, May 8, 1973, in *FBIS-CHI*, May 9, 1973, p. D2; see also Sichuan Provincial Service, Mar. 2, 1973, in *FBIS-CHI*, Mar. 23, 1973, p. E1.

52. See, e.g., Hubei Provincial Service, Feb. 20, 1973, in *FBIS-CHI*, Feb. 21, 1973, p. D3.

53. *Ibid.*, p. D4.

54. *Tibet Daily*, Feb. 13, 1973, in *FBIS-CHI*, Feb. 20, 1973, p. E8.

55. Yunnan Provincial Service, Feb. 16, 1973, in *FBIS-CHI*, Feb. 22, 1973, p. E1.

56. *HQ*, 1973, no. 3, in *FBIS-CHI*, Mar. 13, 1973, p. B2; see also Sichuan Provincial Service, Jan. 30, 1973, in *FBIS-CHI*, Jan. 31, 1973, p. E3.

57. Henan Provincial Service, Mar. 21, 1973, in *FBIS-CHI*, Mar. 23, 1973, p. D3; see also Domes, *China after the Cultural Revolution*, p. 175.

58. See, e.g., Liaoning Provincial Service, Feb. 20, 1973, in *FBIS-CHI*, Feb. 21, 1983, p. G3.

59. The case of Zhang Tiesheng occurred in Liaoning Province, which was under the influence of Mao Yuanxin, Mao Zedong's nephew and a close associate of the Gang of Four. After the fall of the Gang, Zhang was denounced as a "counterrevolutionary clown" and was depicted as symbolic of the ludicrousness of the ultra-Left line in education. On the extolling of Zhang as a "hero" who "dares to go against the tide" see *RMRB* Aug. 10, 1973; for a post-Mao exposé of the case see *Beijing Review*, 1977, no. 8, pp. 14–16.

60. Xinhua Domestic Service, July 22, 1973, in *FBIS-CHI*, Aug. 7, 1973, p. C16.

61. Domes, *China after the Cultural Revolution*, p. 178.

62. See Xinhua Domestic Service, Mar. 16, 1973, for a report on the criticism of the "Swindlers" in a Liaoning PLA unit, in *FBIS-CHI*, Mar. 22, 1973, p. G7; and Hunan Provincial Service, May 8, 1973, for a report on the exposure of the "Swindlers" and their ultra-Right line in the Hunan Rubber Works, in *FBIS-CHI*, May 9, 1973, p. D2.

63. "Report to the Tenth National Congress of the Communist Party of China," Aug. 24, 1973, in Kau, pp. 202–21.

64. *Ibid.*, p. 203.   65. *Ibid.*, p. 207.

66. *Ibid.*   67. *Ibid.*

68. *Ibid.*, p. 209; emphasis added.

69. *Ibid.*, p. 211.

70. *HQ*, 1973, no. 9, pp. 59–78.

71. See *NFRB*, Sept. 16, 1973, for the article launching the campaign, in *FBIS-CHI*, Sept. 19, 1973, p. D1; see also Goldman, "China's Anti-Confucian Campaign."

72. For a report on how the Gang of Four allegedly used the *Pi Lin, Pi Kong* campaign to oppose Zhou Enlai see *Beijing Review*, 1977, no. 16, pp. 27–29.

73. See, e.g., Peking Domestic Service, Sept. 19, 1973, in *FBIS-CHI*, Sept. 20, 1973, P. B5; Shanghai City Service, Sept. 17, 1973, in *FBIS-CHI*, Sept. 19, 1973, p. C8; Xinhua Report, Sept. 19, 1973, in *FBIS-CHI*, Sept. 29, 1973, p. B4.

74. See Pepper, pp. 867–70.

75. The Resolution on Party History adopted by the Sixth Plenum of the Eleventh Central Committee in June 1981 commented: "During the criticism and repudiation of Lin Biao in 1972, [Zhou Enlai] correctly proposed criticism of the ultra-Left trend of thought. . . . Comrade Mao Zedong, however, erroneously held that the task was still to oppose the "ultra-Right." *Resolution on Certain Questions*, p. 38.

76. "Summary of Chairman Mao's Talks to Responsible Local Comrades during his Tour of Inspection," mid-August to Sept. 12, 1971, in Kau, pp. 55–66.

77. "Struggle to Smash the Lin-Chen Anti-Party Clique's Counter-revolutionary Coup (Part II)," document of the Central Committee of the CCP, *Zhongfa*, 1972, no. 4, in Kau, pp. 78–95.

78. For these documents see Kau, pp. 71–73, 96–105, 110–17.

79. *RMRB*, Mar. 23, 1978, in *FBIS-CHI*, Mar. 28, 1978, pp. E16–E22.

80. See, e.g., Domes, *China after the Cultural Revolution*; Maurice Meisner, *Mao's China*, pp. 360–71.

81. For a sampling of almost all the charges leveled against Lin Biao in 1971–73 see *Wenhui Daily* (Hong Kong) articles of November 1973, in Kau, pp. 222–44.

82. See Goldman, "Teng Hsiao-ping," p. 48.

83. *RMRB*, May 18, 1978, in *FBIS-CHI*, May 24, 1978, p. E10.

84. See Meisner, *Mao's China*, pp. 324–38; and Joffe, "The Chinese Army after the Cultural Revolution."

85. See Burton, pp. 1045–46.

86. See Domes, *China after the Cultural Revolution*, pp. 88–89.

87. *Issues and Studies*, 8 (1972), no. 10: 94.

88. *China News Analysis*, no. 851 (1971), p. 7.

89. In Kau, p. 88.

90. *Ibid.*, p. 83.

91. *Ibid.*, pp. 92–93; romanization altered by author.

92. *Ibid.*, p. 74. However, Ye Jianying was later identified by some foreign analysts as one of the opponents of the de-Maoization campaign that accompanied the critique of ultra-Leftism after the purge of the Gang of Four; see, e.g., Pye, p. 34.

93. *RMRB*, May 18, 1978, in *FBIS-CHI*, May 24, 1978, p. E10.

94. Witke, p. 366.

Chapter Six

1. *Peking Review*, 1977, no. 1, pp. 33–34.

2. Hua Guofeng, "Political Report to the Eleventh National Congress of the Communist Party of China," Aug. 12, 1977, in *Peking Review*, 1977, no. 35, pp. 25, 37–38.

3. Heilongjiang Provincial Service, Nov. 5, 1977, in *FBIS-CHI*, Nov. 10, 1977, p. L2.

4. See Onate, "Hua Kuo-feng and the Arrest of the 'Gang of Four.'"

5. See Rice, "The Second Rise and Fall of Teng Hsiao-p'ing." On one specific aspect of the "Pi Deng" campaign see Fenwick, "Chinese Foreign Trade Policy and the Campaign against Deng Xiaoping."

6. See, e.g., *RMRB*, Oct. 13, 1976, in *SCMP* 6206: 1.

7. For the Xinhua report of Oct. 21, 1976, see *SCMP* 6210: 22–25; for foreign press reports on the wall posters and demonstrations see, e.g., *FBIS-CHI*, Oct. 15, 1976, p. E3, and Oct. 21, 1976, pp. E2–E5.

8. *SCMP* 6210: 24.

9. For the original usage of the "3 Basic Principles"—also called the "3 Do's and 3 Don'ts"—see Kau, p. 57; for use of the "3 Basic Principles" in reference to the Gang of Four see, e.g., Shanghai City Service, Oct. 16, 1976, in *FBIS-CHI*, Oct. 20, 1976, p. G9.

10. Xinhua, Oct. 24, 1976, in *FBIS-CHI*, Oct. 26, 1976, p. E7.

11. *RMRB, JFJB, HQ*, Joint Editorial, in *FBIS-CHI*, Oct. 26, 1976, p. E21; emphasis added.

12. *WHB*, Oct. 22, 1976, in *FBIS-CHI*, Oct. 27, 1976, p. G3; emphasis added.

13. *RMRB*, Oct. 24, 1976, in *SCMP* 6211: 61.

14. See *WHB*, Nov. 1, 1976, in *FBIS-CHI*, Nov. 5, 1976, p. G4.

15. See, e.g., *RMRB*, Nov. 14, 1976, in *FBIS-CHI*, Nov. 15, 1976, pp. E9–E13.

16. *HQ*, 1976, no. 12, in *FBIS-CHI*, Dec. 14, 1976, p. E20; see also *RMRB*, Nov. 28, 1976, in *FBIS-CHI*, Nov. 29, 1976, pp. E1–E4.

17. See Zhang Chunqiao, "On Exercising All-round Dictatorship over the Bourgeoisie," in *Peking Review*, 1975, no. 14, pp. 5–11.

18. *GMRB*, Nov. 23, 1976, in *FBIS-CHI*, Nov. 30, 1976, p. E8.

19. Charges like these were usually levied through the unofficial, but effective mediums of big character posters, cartoon art, and "lane news" (i.e., gossip). See, e.g., Agence France Presse report on big character posters at Peking University attacking Jiang Qing for her extravagant "taste for fine clothes," in *FBIS-CHI*, Oct. 29, 1976, p. E9; also the compilation of cartoons and commentaries caricaturing the Gang's various misdeeds, entitled, "*Sirenbang" Yanxinglu*.

20. *RMRB*, Oct. 21, 1976, in *FBIS-CHI*, Oct. 28, 1976, pp. E11–E13; Xinhua, Nov. 10, 1976, in *FBIS-CHI*, Nov. 10, 1976, pp. E1–E3.

21. *RMRB*, Nov. 13, 1976, in *FBIS-CHI*, Nov. 15, 1976, p. E16. Here, Zhang is accused of following Wang Ming's "*Right* capitulationist" line of the late 1930's rather than his earlier "Left opportunist" line; later on, when the Gang's line was being criticized as ultra-Left in nature, the earlier line was emphasized.

22. Xinhua, Nov. 21, 1976, in *FBIS-CHI*, Nov. 22, 1976, pp. E17–E19; Jiangxi Provincial Service, Jan. 22, 1977, in *FBIS-CHI*, Jan. 24, 1977, pp. G6–G10; *RMRB*, June 3, 1977, in *FBIS-CHI*, June 6, 1977, pp. E15–E17.

23. Hua Guofeng, "Speech at the Second National Conference on Learning from Dazhai in Agriculture," Dec. 25, 1976, in *Peking Review*, 1977, no. 1, p. 34.

24. *Ibid.*, p. 36; emphasis added.

25. See, e.g., Beijing Domestic Service, Feb. 14, 1977, in *FBIS-CHI*, Mar. 4, 1977, pp. E9–E22.

26. *RMRB*, *JFJB*, *HQ*, Joint Editorial, Feb. 7, 1977, in *FBIS-CHI*, Feb. 7, 1977, pp. E1–E3.

27. *RMRB*, Feb. 6, 1977, in *FBIS-CHI*, Feb. 8, 1977, pp. E2–E3.

28. *Ibid.*, p. E2.

29. *Ibid.*, p. E3; see also Xinhua, May 17, 1977, in *FBIS-CHI*, May 18, 1977, pp. E9–E12.

30. *RMRB*, Feb. 17, 1977, in *FBIS-CHI*, Feb. 23, 1977, pp. E10–E11; see also *RMRB*, Feb. 17, 1977, in *FBIS-CHI*, Feb. 18, 1977, pp. E15–E16.

31. Xinhua, Apr. 18, 1977, in *FBIS-CHI*, Apr. 28, 1977, pp. E4–E5.

32. *Ibid.*, p. E4.

33. See, e.g., Xinhua, July 22, 1977, in *FBIS-CHI*, July 22, 1977, pp. E13–E18.

34. For a translation of the full texts of the "three big poisonous weeds"

see Qi Xin, *The Case of the Gang of Four* (Hong Kong: Cosmos Books, 1977), pp. 201–95. See also Goldman, "Teng Hsiao-p'ing, pp. 46–69.

35. *RMRB*, July 16, 1977, in *FBIS-CHI*, July 18, 1977, p. E1. This particular article is a refutation of the Gang's attack on one of Deng's "poisonous weeds," "Some Problems in Accelerating Industrial Development" ("The 20 Points").

36. *Ibid.*, pp. E2–E5.

37. Hua Guofeng, "Political Report," in *Peking Review*, 1977, no. 35, pp. 25–39.

38. *Ibid.*, pp. 25, 39. In his speech at the Second Dazhai Conference, Hua had referred to the conflict with the Gang as "another major struggle between the two lines in the annals of our Party" (*Peking Review*, 1977, no. 1, p. 34). But the Eleventh Party Congress was the first time a number was attached to that line struggle.

39. Hua, "Political Report," p. 30; emphasis added. Following his removal as Party chairman in mid-1981, Hua was criticized for various Leftist errors during his tenure. Among his mistakes was his role in the Eleventh Party Congress, which "reaffirmed the erroneous theories, policies, and slogans of the 'cultural revolution' instead of correcting them." *Resolution on Certain Questions*, p. 49.

40. Hua, "Political Report," p. 44. In December 1976, at the Second Dazhai Conference, Hua had called for waging "a people's war to expose and criticize the Gang of Four thoroughly and intensively in the political, ideological, and organizational spheres." See *Peking Review*, 1977, no. 1, p. 137.

41. *RMRB, JFJB, HQ*, Joint Editorial, Oct. 6, 1977, in *FBIS-CHI*, Oct. 6, 1977, pp. E1–E5.

42. *Ibid.*, p. E2. Again, it is interesting to note how a later formulation of the staging of the three "campaigns" reflected the shifting focus of the criticism of the Gang. In launching the "third campaign," Hua explicitly called for exposing the ultra-Right essence of the Gang's line. In early 1979, when the mass phase of the criticism of the Gang was declared to have ended, the "third campaign" was characterized as having "centered on the theoretical criticism of the Gang's line which opposed Marxism–Leninism–Mao Zedong Thought." (*Beijing Review*, 1979, no. 3, p. 4.) The absence of any mention of an ultra-Right *or* an ultra-Left essence of the Gang's line illustrates the transitional stage of the political line at that juncture.

43. *FBIS-CHI*, Oct. 6, 1977, p. E3; Hua, "Political Report," p. 44.

44. At the Second Dazhai Conference, Hua said, "Through exposure and criticism we must eradicate the pernicious influence of the Gang of Four on all fronts." See *Peking Review*, 1977, no. 1, p. 38.

45. See *FBIS-CHI*, Oct. 17, 1977, pp. E1–E4.

46. *Ibid.*, p. E1.

47. *Ibid.*, pp. E2, E4.

48. *Ibid.*, p. E3.

49. *Ibid.*, p. E1; emphasis added.

50. See *FBIS-CHI*, Dec. 15, 1977, pp. E2–E7.

51. *Ibid.*, p. E3.

52. *JFRB*, Jan. 19, 1978, in *FBIS-CHI*, Jan. 20, 1978, p. E4.

53. *Ibid.*, p. E7; emphasis added. See *JFRB*, June 9, 1978, for the start of a series of articles collectively entitled, "Case Studies on the Fake-Left Pernicious Influence of Lin Biao and the Gang of Four," in *FBIS-CHI*, June 12, 1978, pp. E10–E11; see *Peking Review*, 1978, nos. 37 and 38, for excerpts from those articles.

54. See, e.g., Guangxi Regional Service, Mar. 12, 1978, in *FBIS-CHI*, Mar. 14, 1978, pp. H8–H9; *RMRB*, Apr. 20, 1978, in *FBIS-CHI*, Apr. 28, 1978, p. E10.

55. See, e.g., *RMRB*, Jan. 12, 1978, in *FBIS-CHI*, Jan. 13, 1978, pp. E5–E7; Anhui Provincial Service, June 9, 1978, in *FBIS-CHI*, June 14, 1978, pp. G1–G3. This campaign consisted of "criticism" of the Gang of Four and striking "blows" at class enemies and capitalist forces in the countryside.

56. See, e.g., *RMRB*, Mar. 24, 1978, in *FBIS-CHI*, Mar. 31, 1978, p. E17, for one of the earliest usages of this formulation.

57. See, e.g., *RMRB*, May 18, 1978, in *FBIS-CHI*, May 24, 1978, p. E9.

58. See, e.g., Hua Guofeng's Speech at the All Army Political Work Conference, May 29, 1978, in *FBIS-CHI*, June 5, 1978, p. E7.

59. *RMRB*, Jan. 26, 1978, in *FBIS-CHI*, Feb. 1, 1978, p. E13; emphasis added.

60. *RMRB*, June 28, 1978, in *FBIS-CHI*, July 5, 1978, p. E8.

61. *Ibid.*, p. E10.

62. Xinhua, Mar. 16, 1978, in *FBIS-CHI*, Mar. 20, 1978, p. E20.

63. *RMRB*, June 28, 1978, in *FBIS-CHI*, July 5, 1978, p. E11.

64. *Ibid.*

65. *RMRB*, Dec. 12, 1977, in *FBIS-CHI*, Dec. 15, 1977, p. E6.

66. *JFRB*, Feb. 23, 1978, in *FBIS-CHI*, Feb. 24, 1978, p. E9.

67. *Ibid.*

68. *RMRB*, Jan. 26, 1978, in *FBIS-CHI*, Feb. 1, 1978, p. E13.

69. *Ibid.*

70. *RMRB*, June 28, 1978, in *FBIS-CHI*, July 5, 1978, p. E11.

71. *Ibid.*

72. *Ibid.*, p. E12.

73. *JFRB*, Feb. 23, 1978, in *FBIS-CHI*, Feb. 24, 1978, p. E9.

74. For a detailed description of the unfolding of the criticism of ultra-Leftism following the Third Plenum see Chiang Hsin-li, "The Anti–Ultra-Leftist Struggle and the De-Maoization Movement."

75. Communiqué of the Third Plenary Session of the Eleventh Central Committee of the Communist Party of China, Dec. 22, 1978, in *Peking Review*, 1978, no. 52, pp. 6–16.

76. For the call to bring to a conclusion the mass movement phase of the criticism of Lin and the Gang see, e.g., *JFRB*, Dec. 12, 1978, in *FBIS-CHI*, Dec. 13, 1978, pp. E1–E3; *RMRB*, Jan. 5, 1979, in *FBIS-CHI*, Jan. 8, 1979, pp. E12–E15.

77. For speculation about the showdown between the "Whatever" and the "Practice" factions at the Third Plenum and related personnel changes in key Party propaganda organs see the following Hong Kong sources: *Jing Bao*, 1979, no. 18, in *FBIS-CHI*, Jan. 10, 1979, pp. N1–N5; *Dong Xiang*, 1979, no. 4, in *FBIS-CHI*, Jan. 23, 1979, pp. N1–N6; *Zheng Ming*, 1979, no. 16, in *FBIS-CHI*, Jan. 30, 1979, pp. N3–N7. As Brantly Womack (p. 774) has aptly put it, the factional struggle over the critique of ultra-Leftism during 1978 was "a time of confrontation between those who wanted to start a new paragraph in China's post-Liberation history and those who wanted to start a new book."

78. Xinhua, Jan. 3, 1979, in *FBIS-CHI*, Jan. 4, 1979, p. G3.

79. *RMRB*, Jan. 5, 1979, in *FBIS-CHI*, Jan. 8, 1979, p. E15.

80. Communiqué of the Third Plenum, p. 11.

81. *GMRB*, Jan. 23, 1979, in *FBIS-CHI*, Feb. 2, 1979, p. E9.

82. *Ibid.*, p. E10.

83. *Ibid.*, p. E9. Another report that rejected the label "fake Left, real Right" also acknowledged that the first appearance of the formulation in relation to the analysis of the Gang's line had been something of a breakthrough into the "forbidden zone" of criticizing the "Left" and commented that it had "helped to eliminate the mistaken idea that Lin Biao and the Gang of Four were 'radicals' or 'Leftists' as maintained abroad by some muddle-headed people with good intentions as well as clear-minded persons with evil intentions." *RMRB*, Feb. 28, 1979, in *FBIS-CHI*, Mar. 1, 1979, p. E8.

84. *GMRB*, Jan. 23, 1979, p. E9.

85. *RMRB*, Feb. 28, 1979, in *FBIS-CHI*, Mar. 1, 1979, p. E9.

86. *Ibid.*

87. See Tsou, "Mao Tse-tung Thought," esp. pp. 525–26, for an explanation of this line of argument. Tsou cites the fact that the Gang of Four "were using ultra-Rightist political methods" and "adopting an ultra-Rightist style of life" as additional explanations of why they were being labeled as ultra-Rightists at the time he wrote the article. He also suggests that by calling the Gang's obviously ultra-Left line ultra-Right, the post-Mao leadership was allowing itself room to preserve some aspects of that program—a process that would have been made more difficult had they undertaken a wholesale assault on the ultra-Left trend. The thoroughness of both the dismantling of the ultra-Left political program and the critique of ultra-Leftism since January 1979 vitiates much of Tsou's argument on this point. Nevertheless, his article is still one of the best descriptions of the ultra-Left content of the Gang of Four's political line.

88. *RMRB*, Jan. 23, 1979, in *FBIS-CHI*, Feb. 2, 1979, p. E8; emphasis added.

89. *Ibid.*, p. E9.

90. *RMRB*, Feb. 28, 1979, in *FBIS-CHI*, Mar. 1, 1979, p. E9.

91. *RMRB*, Feb. 16, 1979, in *FBIS-CHI*, Feb. 22, 1979, p. E10.

92. *GMRB*, Jan. 23, 1979, in *FBIS-CHI*, Feb. 2, 1979, p. E5. These criteria for distinction between Left and Right errors are drawn from Mao's essay "On Practice," *SR*, pp. 79–80.

93. *RMRB*, Feb. 28, 1979, in *FBIS-CHI*, Mar. 1, 1979, pp. E7–E8.
94. *GMRB*, Jan. 23, 1979, in *FBIS-CHI*, Feb. 2, 1979, p. E5. Up to this point, it had been standard practice to use quotation marks to offset the designation "Left" when referring to "Left" deviations, "Left" opportunism, etc., in order to differentiate between true, revolutionary Left and ultra-"Left" errors of various sorts. In February 1979 *GMRB* called for an end to the use of quotation marks in reference to ultra-Leftism. It said, "A Left or Right line is erroneous and deviates from what is correct. So there is no difference between a 'Left' opportunist line and a Left opportunist line." Therefore, the quotation marks should be removed in order to clarify the target by "destroying a hiding place for Left opportunism" that was maintained along with the "unscientific" analysis of the Gang's line as "fake Left, real Right." *GMRB*, Feb. 17, 1979, in *FBIS-CHI*, Mar. 1, 1979, p. E11. See also *GMRB*, Feb. 6, 1979, in *FBIS-CHI*, Feb. 16, 1979, p. E9, for a letter to the editor on the same subject. The Chinese media has not been uniform or consistent in the adoption of this suggestion and still generally uses quotation marks to offset references to various ultra-Left errors.
95. See, e.g., *RMRB*, Jan. 26, 1979, in *FBIS-CHI*, Jan. 31, 1979, p. E19.
96. See, e.g., *RMRB*, Feb. 16, 1979, in *FBIS-CHI*, Feb. 22, 1979, p. E8.
97. *GMRB*, Feb. 6, 1979, in *FBIS-CHI*, Feb. 16, 1979, p. E7.
98. *RMRB*, Feb. 16, 1979, in *FBIS-CHI*, Feb. 22, 1979, p. E8. See also *HQ*, 1979, no. 3, for a long article that draws a further distinction between inner-party struggle, two-line struggle, and class struggle, in *FBIS-CHI*, Apr. 10, 1979, pp. L1–L9.
99. *RMRB*, Feb. 16, 1979, in *FBIS-CHI*, Feb. 22, 1979, p. E8.
100. *Ibid.*
101. *RMRB*, Feb. 28, 1979, in *FBIS-CHI*, Mar. 1, 1979, p. E10.
102. *Ibid.*, p. E9; see also *GMRB*, Jan. 23, 1979, in *FBIS-CHI*, Feb. 2, 1979, p. E10. In criticizing past misuse of the term, "fake Left, real Right," the *RMRB* article listed ten ways in which the phrase had been utilized in the media in the period between December 1977 and January 1979: (1) as a clique or faction (*paibie*); (2) as a line (*luxian*); (3) as a theory or viewpoint (*lilun guandian*); (4) as an ideological system (*sixiang tixi*); (5) as "Left" revisionism ("*zuo*" *de xiuzheng zhuyi*); (6) as policy (*zhengce*); (7) as a means or tactics (*shoufa*); (8) as a slogan (*kouhao*); (9) as the sum total of the theory and practice of Lin Biao and the Gang of Four (*Lin Biao he Sirengang sixiang he xingdong de quanbu zonghe*); (10) as the link between Lin Biao, the Gang of Four, and all sorts of other problems (*yu Lin Biao, Sirenbang youguande yi qie de wenti*). Only the first usage was judged to be "scientific." This listing is not translated in the *FBIS* version of the article. See page 4 of the original *RMRB* for media references and explicit examples of each of the above misapplications of "fake Left, real Right."
103. *RMRB*, Feb. 16, 1979, in *FBIS-CHI*, Feb. 22, 1979, p. E9.
104. *Ibid.*, p. E12; emphasis added.
105. *Ibid.* See also *RMRB*, Feb. 28, 1979, in *FBIS-CHI*, Mar. 1, 1979, p. E10, which stated that a mistaken line appears overtly in the Party and

cannot be covert. "Project 571" (Lin's coup plans) was said to "absolutely not belong to the category of struggles between the two lines. That was a counterrevolutionary action by a class enemy."
106. *RMRB*, Feb. 16, 1979, in *FBIS-CHI*, Feb. 22, p. E12. This passage refers specifically to Jiang Qing, Zhang Chunqiao, and Yao Wenyuan as the "ringleaders" of the Gang of Four, omitting any mention of Wang Hongwen. This omission was perhaps intended to suggest that Wang's case was more akin to Lin Biao's—i.e., he degenerated from an ultra-Leftist to a counterrevolutionary, rather than beginning with counterrevolutionary intentions as the other members of the Gang are said to have done.
107. *Ibid.*, p. E8. The Gang were said to have been much more sophisticated in masking their counterrevolutionary schemes than was Lin. Lin's "wild ambitions" were "naked" (e.g., "Project 571") whereas the Gang's evil intentions were shrouded by "a heavy fog of [ultra-Left] theory." *RMRB*, May 8, 1979, in *FBIS-CHI*, May 19, 1979, p. E8.
108. *RMRB*, Feb. 16, 1979, in *FBIS-CHI*, Feb. 22, 1979, p. E8.
109. *JFRB*, Jan. 19, 1979, in *FBIS-CHI*, Jan. 20, 1979, p. E4.
110. Heilongjiang Provincial Service, Nov. 18, 1976, in *FBIS-CHI*, Nov. 23, 1976, p. L1.
111. See, e.g., Shandong Provincial Radio, Apr. 28, 1979, in *FBIS-CHI*, May 3, 1979, pp. O3–O5; *GMRB*, Apr. 28, 1979, in *FBIS-CHI*, May 9, 1979, pp. L8–L9.
112. *RMRB*, May 9, 1979, in *FBIS-CHI*, May 11, 1979, pp. L16–L19.
113. *JFRB*, May 7, 1979, in *FBIS-CHI*, May 7, 1979, p. O4.
114. See *RMRB*, Feb. 28, 1979, in *FBIS-CHI*, Mar. 1, 1979, p. E9.
115. *Ibid.*, p. E10; see also *GMRB*, Jan. 23, 1979, in *FBIS-CHI*, Feb. 2, 1979, p. E9.
116. See note 77 above.
117. *RMRB*, *JFJB*, *HQ*, Feb. 7, 1977, cited in *Zheng Ming* (Hong Kong), 1979, no. 16, in *FBIS-CHI*, Jan. 30, 1979, p. N4; emphasis added. The original Chinese text reads, " . . . fanshi Mao Zhuxi zuochude juece, women dou jianjue weihu, fanshi Mao zhuxi zhishi, women dou shizhong buyude zunxun." (*HQ*, 1977, no. 3, p. 18.) The official translation in *Peking Review*, 1977, no. 8, p. 17, is as follows: "Let us . . . resolutely defend all [Chairman Mao's] policies, [and] steadfastly abide by all his instructions." The name "Whatever" faction is appropriately derived from the use of the term "fanshi" ("whatever") in the original Chinese.
118. See Chang, "The Rise of Wang Tung-hsing."
119. Pye, p. 164.
120. *Resolution on Certain Questions*, pp. 49–50.
121. See Communiqué of the Fifth Plenary Session of the Eleventh Central Committee of the Communist Party of China, Feb. 29, 1980, in *Beijing Review*, 1980, no. 10, p. 10.
122. *Resolution on Certain Questions*, pp. 48–49.
123. Pye, p. 23.
124. For an alternative explanation see Tsou, p. 526.

Chapter Seven

1. See Domes, "New Course in Chinese Domestic Politics."
2. See Harding, *Organizing China*, pp. 309–17.
3. For a brief comment on the parallels between the two critiques see John Bryan Starr's review of Domes's *China after the Cultural Revolution*, in *China Quarterly*, no. 77 (1979): 126–29.
4. See, e.g., Hua Guofeng, "Political Report to the Eleventh National Congress of the Chinese Communist Party," in *Peking Review*, 1977, no. 35, pp. 33–34.
5. *RMRB*, May 18, 1978, in *FBIS-CHI*, May 24, 1978, pp. E2, E7; *RMRB*, Oct. 4, 1978, in *Peking Review*, 1978, no. 42, p. 18.
6. Womack, pp. 775–76.
7. See, e.g., *RMRB*, Feb. 15, 1979, in *Beijing Review*, 1979, no. 15, pp. 13–16.
8. Domes, *China after the Cultural Revolution*, chaps. 4 and 7. On Dazhai (Tachai) see Maxwell, "Learning from Tachai," and Mitch Meisner, "In Agriculture, Learn from Tachai."
9. *RMRB*, Aug. 24, 1972, in *SCMP* 5209: 58–59.
10. *Ibid.*, p. 54.
11. See, e.g., *RMRB*, Feb. 16, 1978, in *FBIS-CHI*, Feb. 17, 1978, pp. E14–E17.
12. For the 1971 Directive (*Zhongfa*, no. 82, 1971), see *Issues and Studies*, 9, no. 2 (1972): 92–95. The Great Leap documents referred to are "Rules and Regulations for the Operation of the Rural People's Communes (Draft)," March 1961, and "Regulations on the Work in the Rural People's Communes (Revised Draft)," September 1962. See chapter 4, notes 48 and 81 above.
13. *Zhongfa*, no. 82 (1971), p. 93. For the response of a single district in Yunnan to the directive see "Document of the Simao District CCP Committee" (*Sidangfa*, no. 22, 1972), in *Issues and Studies*, 9, no. 6 (1972): 91–97, cited in Domes, *China after the Cultural Revolution*, p. 158.
14. *Zhongfa*, no. 82 (1971), p. 94. See also *RMRB*, Aug. 5 and Oct. 17, 1972, in *FBIS-CHI*, Aug. 23, 1972, p. B4, and *SCMP* 5246: 92.
15. See, e.g., Guizhou Provincial Service, Mar. 11, 1978, in *FBIS-CHI*, Mar. 11, 1978, p. J1; and Sichuan Provincial Service, Jan. 4, 1980, in *FBIS-CHI*, Jan. 8, 1980, pp. Q2–Q3.
16. See *Beijing Review*, 1979, no. 16, p. 16.
17. *RMRB*, Aug. 7, 1972, in *FBIS-CHI*, Aug. 24, 1972, p. B8; see also *RMRB*, Oct. 18 and 22, 1972, in *SCMP* 5253: 207 and *SCMP* 5248: 188.
18. For the reaffirmation of the team as the basic accounting unit in Chinese agriculture see "CCP Central Committee Decision on Agricultural Development," article II.5, Xinhua, Oct. 5, 1979, in *FBIS-CHI*, Oct. 25, 1979 (supplement), p. 6.
19. *Zhongfa*, no. 82 (1971), pp. 93–95.
20. See *RMRB*, Mar. 18, 1972, in *SCMP* 5104: 134. For a specific example of the deleterious effects of uncompensated expropriation for communal use of private manure stocks see *RMRB*, Aug. 4, 1972, in *FBIS-*

CHI, Aug. 23, 1972, p. B5; on the illegitimate collectivization of fruit trees see *RMRB*, Oct. 23, 1972, in *SCMP* 5249: 1.

21. Guangdong Provincial Service, Mar. 17, 1978, in *FBIS-CHI*, Mar. 20, 1978, pp. H4-H5. Efforts to reestablish the authority of the production teams in agricultural affairs in both the post-Lin and post-Gang periods led to a division of the teams into smaller work units. In 1972, some areas experimented with the introduction of sub-team units called "work groups" (*zuoyezu*), which were supposed to increase productivity by giving peasants greater control over the planning, production, and distribution of crops. In 1979, there was a somewhat more spontaneous trend toward the dissolution of production teams as peasants in certain areas interpreted too literally the instructions of higher authorities to loosen the centralization of rural policy. In both periods, these trends were quickly curtailed as inimical to the collective economy and as an overreaction to former ultra-Leftist agricultural policies; however, the production responsibility system that was introduced in the rural areas in the early 1980's tacitly sanctioned a major retrenchment in the level of collectivization in the Chinese countryside by vesting important economic authority in peasant households. On the 1972 experimentation with "work groups" see Radio Anhui, Jan. 26, 1972, cited in Domes, *China after the Cultural Revolution*, p. 156; on the unsanctioned dissolution of the teams in 1978 see Hebei Provincial Service, Mar. 14, 1979, in *FBIS-CHI*, Mar. 16, 1979, pp. H4-H5; on the responsibility system see chapter 4, note 78, above.

22. *RMRB*, Oct. 18, 1972, in *SCMP* 5247: 153; see also *RMRB*, Oct. 22, 1972, in *SCMP* 5248: 190.

23. See, e.g., *RMRB*, Jan. 31, 1978, in *FBIS-CHI*, Feb. 15, 1978, pp. E16-E18; and *RMRB*, Nov. 30, 1978, in *FBIS-CHI*, Dec. 7, 1978, p. E13.

24. Fujian Radio, June 5, 1972, in *Union Research Service*, 67, no. 22 (1972): 304.

25. See *Zhongfa*, no. 82 (1971), p. 95, and *Sidangfa*, no. 22 (1972), p. 96.

26. *Beijing Review*, 1980, no. 4, pp. 23-24.

27. *Zhongfa*, no. 82 (1971), p. 94; see also *Sidangfa*, no. 22 (1972), p. 92. For a flavor of the political tug-of-war that was going on over the critique of ultra-Leftism in 1971-72 see Hunan Provincial Service, June 8, 1972, in *BBC Summary of World Broadcasts: Far East*, June 15, 1972, section BII, pp. 1-11, which gives a ringing defense of the Dazhai model and everything it stood for in rural policy.

28. See, e.g., *RMRB*, Oct. 3, 1979, in *FBIS-CHI*, Oct. 10, 1979, pp. L16-L20.

29. *Beijing Review*, 1980, no. 32, p. 5.

30. *Peking Review*, 1976, no. 46, pp. 6-9.

31. *RMRB*, Oct. 29, 1971, in *SCMP* 5011: 104; see also *RMRB*, Jan. 24, 1972, in *SCMP* 5072: 86-88.

32. *RMRB*, Feb. 1, 1977, in *FBIS-CHI*, Feb. 3, 1977, p. E10. Although there was some criticism during the "Swindlers" campaign of ultra-Left trends in industrial wage policy, this does not appear to have gone as far as

the similar effort in rural distribution. The "Swindlers" were blamed for enforcing a freeze on industrial wages in the late 1960's, and a 10 percent wage increase scheduled for 1972 did not go into effect (see Howe, p. 251). It is reasonable to assume that the Cultural Revolutionaries were instrumental in forestalling the wage increase as part of their attempt to restrict the "bourgeois right" inherent in any distribution system based on labor. There was also some effort in 1971–73 to lessen the importance of political criteria as a factor in the determination of industrial wages (see Howe, p. 252), which can be seen as a precursor to the revival of bonus and piecework schemes in the post-Mao era; see, e.g., *Beijing Review*, 1980, no. 19, pp. 16–23.

33. See Andors, chaps. 7 and 8.

34. *GMRB*, Oct. 15, 1972, in *SCMP* 5244: 13; see also *RMRB*, Oct. 7, 1972, in *SCMP* 5239: 171.

35. *RMRB*, Oct. 24, 1972, in *SCMP* 5251: 115; emphasis added.

36. *RMRB*, Feb. 12, 1977, in *FBIS-CHI*, Feb. 14, 1977, p. E7.

37. See, e.g., *Peking Review*, 1978, no. 42, pp. 12–15.

38. *GMRB*, Oct. 6, 1971, in *SCMP* 4999: 187; emphasis added.

39. *Ibid.*, p. 189.

40. "Speech at the Opening Ceremony of the National Science Conference," Mar. 18, 1978, in *Peking Review*, 1978, no. 12, p. 10.

41. *GMRB*, Jan. 20, 1972, in *SCMP* 5066: 62.

42. See, e.g., *GMRB*, Oct. 28, 1972, in *SCMP* 5253: 213.

43. See, e.g., *GMRB*, May 18, 1977, in *FBIS-CHI*, June 2, 1977, pp. E7–E8.

44. "Speech at the Opening Ceremony of the National Science Conference," pp. 13–14.

45. *Ibid.*, p. 11; see also *Beijing Review*, 1980, no. 13, pp. 23–25. There were also important parallels in the post-Lin and post-Gang critiques of ultra-Leftism in the realm of general policies toward education. In both periods, the ultra-Left was criticized for overemphasizing ideology, politics, and class struggle and neglecting academic standards in the schools; the breakdown of classroom discipline and the denigration of the authority and prestige of teachers were also parallel themes in both critiques. On the ultra-Left trend in education in the early 1970's see *GMRB*, Nov. 25, 1972, in *SCMP* 5271: 145; *RMRB* Oct. 15 and 29, 1972, in *SCMP* 5244: 4 and *SCMP* 5254: 3, respectively. On the post-Gang critique of ultra-Leftism in relation to education see *GMRB*, Mar. 28, 1977, in *FBIS-CHI*, Apr. 8, 1977, p. E5; and Deng Xiaoping, "Speech at the National Educational Work Conference," Apr. 22, 1978, in *Peking Review*, 1978, no. 18, pp. 6–12.

46. *GMRB*, Jan. 24, 1972, in *SCMP* 5069: 182, see also *GMRB*, Oct. 26, 1971, and Jan. 21, 1972, in *SCMP* 5010: 55 and *SCMP* 5068: 144, respectively.

47. See, e.g., *Peking Review*, 1977, no. 14, pp. 6–12.

48. See, e.g., *GMRB* Oct. 24, 1972, in *SCMP* 5249: 13; and Deng Xiaoping, "Speech at the Opening Ceremony of the National Science Conference," p. 13.

49. Zhejiang Provincial Service, Dec. 4, 1972, in *FBIS-CHI*, Dec. 8, 1972, pp. C7–C8.

50. *GMRB*, Dec. 6, 1976, in *FBIS-CHI*, Dec. 16, 1976, pp. E6–E7.

51. *HQ*, 1976, no. 12, in *FBIS-CHI*, Dec. 14, 1976, p. E18.

52. See, e.g., *RMRB*, Nov. 6, 1972, in *SCMP* 5256: 158; *HQ*, 1977, no. 8, in *FBIS-CHI*, Aug. 31, 1977, p. E1; and *Beijing Review*, 1980, no. 3, pp. 24–26.

53. Kau, pp. xxxv–xxxvi and 160–74.

54. *Peking Review*, 1972, no. 29, cited in Kau, p. 170.

55. *RMRB*, Jan. 28, 1972, in *SCMP* 5071: 50.

56. *Ibid.*

57. *Ibid.*

58. *GMRB*, Jan. 25, 1972, in *SCMP* 5071: 56. The phrase "Practice is the sole criterion of truth" or some variation on the same theme was used by the critics of the ultra-Left line as well as by the defenders of the Cultural Revolution line, though for different reasons. The former seem to have invoked the sanctity of practice to support their position on questions of economic policy and ideology, whereas the latter made the most use of the practice criterion in defense of their policy preferences in matters relating to education and science and technology; for an example of this latter usage see *HQ*, 1972, no. 12, in *SCMM* 743–44: 9.

59. *GMRB*, Jan. 25, 1972, in *SCMP* 5071: 55.

60. See, e.g., *Beijing Review*, 1979, no. 47, pp. 9–14; and *Resolution on Certain Questions*, pp. 56–73.

61. *RMRB*, Feb. 16, 1979, in *FBIS-CHI*, Feb. 22, 1979, p. E10.

62. *HQ*, 1979, no. 4, p. 26.

63. *RMRB*, May 8, 1979, in *FBIS-CHI*, May 19, 1979, p. E8.

64. See, e.g., *JFRB*, Dec. 5, 1978, in *FBIS-CHI*, Dec. 7, 1978, pp. E9–E12.

65. For a brief comment on how the Gang of Four "exaggerated" the role of "revolutionary spirit" see *RMRB*, Feb. 16, 1979, in *FBIS-CHI*, Feb. 22, 1979, p. E11; see also Lewis, "The Social Limits on Politically-Induced Change."

66. See, e.g., *RMRB*, Mar. 9, 1979, in *FBIS-CHI*, Mar. 13, 1979, pp. E1–E2, for a criticism of the key Cultural Revolution slogan "Grasp Revolution, Promote Production" (*zhuageming, cushengchan*).

67. For an ex post facto criticism of this alleged formulation of the Gang see *GMRB*, Nov. 30 and Dec. 6, 1976, in *FBIS-CHI*, Dec. 16, 1976, pp. E6–E7. For the use of a similar concept, "Revolution continues to propel production forward," in its original context in an article expressing the line of the Gang of Four, see *Peking Review*, 1974, no. 39, p. 25.

68. *JFRB*, Dec. 5, 1978, in *FBIS-CHI*, Dec. 7, 1978, p. E12.

69. See Tsou, "Mao Tse-tung Thought," pp. 510–12.

70. See, e.g., *GMRB*, Jan. 17, 1978, in *FBIS-CHI*, Feb. 28, 1978, pp. E8–E10.

71. *RMRB*, May 9, 1979, in *FBIS-CHI*, May 31, 1979, p. L7.

72. *JFRB*, Dec. 5, 1978, in *FBIS-CHI*, Dec. 7, 1978, p. E12.

73. For specific criticisms of how the error of confusing subjective and

objective factors in revolutionary development applies to the line of the Gang see, e.g., *RMRB*, Jan. 26, 1978, in *FBIS-CHI*, Feb. 1, 1978, p. E13; and *RMRB*, Jan. 22, 1979, in *FBIS-CHI*, Feb. 2, 1979, p. E5.

74. See Cornforth, *Historical Materialism.*

75. Karl Marx, "Preface to the Critique of Political Economy," in Tucker, ed., *Marx-Engels Reader*, pp. 4–5.

76. *RMRB, JFJB, HQ*, Jan. 1, 1979, in *FBIS-CHI*, Jan. 3, 1979, p. E5.

77. *GMRB*, Jan. 23, 1978, in *FBIS-CHI*, Feb. 2, 1978, p. E5.

78. *RMRB*, Feb. 16, 1979, in *FBIS-CHI* Feb. 22, 1979, p. E11.

79. *SW*, 1: 336.

80. Tsou, "Mao Tse-tung Thought," pp. 498–501.

81. See Esherick, "On the 'Restoration of Capitalism.'"

82. See Mao Tse-tung, *A Critique of Soviet Economics*, and Wei Chi, *The Soviet Union under the New Tsars.*

83. See, e.g., *Beijing ribao*, Aug. 15, 1980, in *FBIS-CHI*, Sept. 5, 1980, pp. R1–R2; and *Beijing Review*, 1980, no. 45, pp. 15–19.

84. For variations on this argument see Maurice Meisner, *Mao's China*, Conclusion, and Harris, *The Mandate of Heaven*. For an application of this type of analysis to Soviet political history see Ticktin, "Towards a Political Economy of the Soviet Union." See also Sweezy (p. 24) for a brief and undeveloped comment on the implications for Marxist theory of the possibility that "a proletarian revolution can give rise to a non-socialist society."

85. Beijing Domestic Service, Nov. 14, 1976, in *FBIS-CHI*, Nov. 15, 1976, p. E18.

86. *HQ*, 1976, no. 12, in *FBIS-CHI*, Dec. 14, 1976, p. E18.

87. Cited in *GMRB*, Feb. 17, 1979, in *FBIS-CHI*, Feb. 28, 1979, p. E23; for Liu Shaoqi's Political Report to the Eighth Party Congress on which the Resolution was largely based see *PDA*, pp. 164–203.

88. *GMRB*, Feb. 17, 1979, in *FBIS-CHI*, Feb. 28, 1979, p. E23.

89. *HQ*, 1979, no. 4, p. 21. Tsou ("Mao Tse-tung Thought," p. 506) calls the issue of class struggle in socialist society "the central theoretical problem which the Gang of Four and their followers tried to solve."

90. *RMRB*, Dec. 12, 1977, in *FBIS-CHI*, Dec. 15, 1977, p. E3.

91. *HQ*, 1979, no. 4, p. 21.

92. See Tsou, "Mao Tse-tung Thought," pp. 506–9.

93. See, e.g., *Peking Review*, 1978, no. 6, pp. 11–14.

94. See Schurmann, "On Revolutionary Conflict," p. 49, for a discussion of how power differentials in society become a "latently revolutionary situation."

95. *HQ*, 1979, no. 4, p. 21.

96. For discussion of the Gang's influence on socialist democracy and legality see, e.g., *Beijing Review*, 1979, no. 2, pp. 25–30, and *Peking Review*, 1978, no. 4, pp. 21–22.

97. *RMRB*, Dec. 12, 1977, in *FBIS-CHI*, Dec. 15, 1977, p. E3.

98. On the Gang's extension of the applicability of the dictatorship of the proletariat see, e.g., *Peking Review*, 1978, no. 3, pp. 10–13.

99. For a foreign observer's polemical but effective description of the Gang's "cultural despotism" see Leys, *Chinese Shadows*. For a discussion

of the struggle over what standards of "purity" should be used when determining the class status of individuals see White, *The Politics of Class and Class Origin.*

100. The Gang of Four's argument was that any type of inequality was a manifestation of "bourgeois right" that must be restricted. The broader definition of "bourgeois right" considers that it involves the twin elements of inequality and exploitation; under the transitional conditions of early socialist development, it is particularly the exploitative element that must be actively restricted, whereas inequality as expressed in differential income and status has, in fact, a positive role to play in spurring productivity.

101. According to the Chinese analysis, in some circumstances anarchism can also result from Rightist errors. In the rectification campaign following the Hundred Flowers movement of 1956–57, for example, the "bourgeois" intellectuals who had severely criticized Party leadership were accused of fomenting anarchist trends. Such anarchism from the Right was an unintended result of the intellectuals' criticism, however, not an explicit component of their ideological makeup. They were not advocating rebellion against all authority as a value in itself, but merely challenging the scope of Party authority as then constituted. The Gang of Four, on the other hand, is accused of inducing a more thorough type of anarchism as an important component of their ultra-Left line. For a discussion of the Party's fears that the Hundred Flowers movement would incite anarchy and disorder (or *luan*) see Solomon, pp. 278–85.

102. The Gang of Four are said to have used the ultra-Left idea of anarchism in a selective fashion, fomenting disorder in places where they hoped to create enough confusion to allow their supporters to seize power. In places where they already held power, they are said to have practiced the most repressive type of dictatorship in order to suppress their opponents, e.g., in their Shanghai "base area." This dual approach to authority has been called "a superb application of anarchism" to further the Gang's counterrevolutionary ends. *RMRB,* May 9, 1978, in *FBIS-CHI,* May 15, 1978, p. E8.

103. *HQ,* 1979, no. 4, p. 22.

104. See, e.g., *RMRB,* Nov. 14, 1976, in *FBIS-CHI,* Nov. 15, 1976, pp. E9–E13.

105. See, e.g., *JFRB,* Nov. 15, 1976, in *FBIS-CHI,* Nov. 23, 1976, pp. E3–E7.

106. *WHB,* Nov. 4, 1976, in *FBIS-CHI,* Nov. 5, 1976, p. G16.

107. *RMRB,* Dec. 12, 1977, in *FBIS-CHI,* Dec. 15, 1977, p. E3.

108. *GMRB,* Feb. 17, 1979, in *FBIS-CHI,* Feb. 28, 1979, p. E24.

109. *RMRB,* Apr. 11, 1979, in *Beijing Review,* 1979, no. 17, pp. 10–13; see also the Communiqué of the Third Plenum of the Eleventh Central Committee, December 1978, in *Peking Review,* 1978, no. 52, pp. 6–16.

110. Hua Guofeng, "Report on the Work of the Government" at the Second Session of the Fifth National People's Congress, June 18, 1979, in *Beijing Review,* 1979, no. 27, p. 10.

111. Hua Guofeng, "Report to the First Session of the Fifth National People's Congress," Feb. 26, 1978, in *Peking Review,* 1978, no. 10, p. 34.

112. This phrase is extracted from the following context: ". . . Lin Biao, 'sirenbang' de 'zuo' xiang jihuizhuyi luxian . . . you liangge xianzhu tezheng: yi shi zai zhengzhishang diandao diwo guanxi, dagao jiejidouzheng kuodahua; er shi *zai sixiangshang* diandao lilun he shijiande guanxi, dagao jiaotiaozhuyi." (. . . the "Left" opportunist line of Lin Biao and the "Gang of Four" . . . has two outstanding characteristics: the first is political, reversing the relationship between the enemy and ourselves and going in for the expansion of class struggle in a big way; the second is *ideological,* reversing the relationship between theory and practice [and] going in for dogmatism in a big way.) *HQ,* 1979, no. 4, p. 21: emphasis added.

113. Tsou, "Mao Tse-tung Thought," pp. 501–3. For a substantive discussion of Mao's epistemology and its relation to political action see Lewis, *Leadership in Communist China,* pp. 70–76.

114. Tsou, "Mao Tse-tung Thought," p. 502.

115. *HQ,* 1979, no. 4, p. 21.

116. *Ibid.*

117. See, e.g., *RMRB,* May 8, 1978, in *FBIS-CHI,* May 19, 1978, pp. E7–E8.

118. *HQ,* 1979, no. 4, p. 22.

119. On the Gang's opposition to "empiricism" see, e.g., *JFRB,* Nov. 15, 1976, in *FBIS-CHI,* Nov. 23, 1976, pp. E3–E7. The Gang's discounting of the importance of practice in the evaluation of revolutionary theory is traceable, in part, to the influence of Mao's essay "Where Do Correct Ideas Come From?" (1963). In this work, Mao departed briefly from his earlier insistence that all theory must be firmly rooted and continuously tested in social practice; instead he argued that some correct ideas may meet with failure or suffer defeat when first put into practice, but should, nevertheless, be retained as they "are bound to triumph, sooner or later." See *SR,* pp. 502–4. I am indebted to Harry Harding, then at Stanford University and now at the Brookings Institution, for pointing out the connection between Mao's essay and this aspect of the ultra-Left line.

120. See, e.g., *GMRB, RMRB,* Sept. 24, 1978, in *FBIS-CHI,* Sept. 26, 1978, pp. E5–E8.

121. See Goldman, "Teng Hsiao-ping and the Debate over Science and Technology."

122. See, e.g., *RMRB,* Feb. 12, 1977, in *FBIS-CHI,* Feb. 14, 1977, pp. E3–E8. This ultra-Left preoccupation with participation in labor by intellectuals, technicians, cadres, etc. might seem to be inconsistent with the general deemphasis on production that has been analyzed as one of the key ingredients in the ultra-Left line. It could be argued, however, that the sort of production most experts and officials engaged in was largely pointless and was intended as punishment. In other words, it was meant to be ideologically "purifying" rather than truly useful.

123. See, e.g., *GMRB,* Feb. 24, 1979, in *FBIS-CHI,* Mar. 8, 1979, pp. E7–E8; *GMRB,* Mar. 11, 1979, in *FBIS-CHI,* Mar. 14, 1979, pp. E1–E9; also Womack, "Politics and Epistemology."

124. For descriptions of recent changes in Chinese education see Shirk, "Educational Reform and Political Backlash"; on science and technology

see Reardon-Anderson, "Science and Technology in Post-Mao China"; on enterprise management see Fletcher, "Industrial Relations in China: The New Line."

125. See Cornforth, *Materialism and the Dialectical Method*; Lewis, *Leadership in Communist China*, pp. 47–60; Starr, *Continuing the Revolution*, chap. 1; and Schram, *The Political Thought of Mao Tse-tung*, chaps. 1 and 2.

126. See Solomon, pp. 454–63; Starr, *Continuing the Revolution*, pp. 24–27; and Maurice Meisner, *Mao's China*, pp. 301–3.

127. *GMRB*, May 31, 1979, in *FBIS-CHI*, June 12, 1979, p. L7. Actually much of the blame for the original abuse of this slogan in the prelude to the Cultural Revolution and the escalation of an academic question into a political struggle has been laid at the feet of Guan Feng, a member of the "May 16th Group" (a faction purged for its ultra-Left activities during the early phase of the Cultural Revolution) and a close associate of the Gang of Four. Kang Sheng, a former minister of public security and a member of the Cultural Revolution Group, which exercised decisive power within the Party leadership in the late 1960's, has also been implicated in the origins of the struggle over the issue of "one divides into two."

128. *Ibid.*, p. L8.

129. *Ibid.*, p. L7.

130. *Ibid.*

131. *Ibid.*, p. L6; see also Womack, pp. 791–92.

132. For a discussion of the systematic nature of the ultra-Left line see Tsou, "Mao Tse-tung Thought," pp. 521–23.

133. See, e.g., Bettelheim, "The Great Leap Backward."

134. The systematic and logical nature of the ultra-Left line helps explain not only its widespread influence inside China but also its enormous appeal to outside observers, who were greatly attracted by its high idealism. See, e.g., Al Imfeld, *China as a Model of Development* (Maryknoll, N.Y.: Orbis Books, 1979).

135. For an attempt to show the organic ideological links between the line of the Gang of Four and Mao Zedong Thought (with the objective of "proving" that the Gang represented the true revolutionary line in China while the current leadership is on the revisionist road) see Lotta, ed., *And Mao Makes Five*.

Chapter Eight

1. Dittmer, *Liu Shao-ch'i*, p. 344, and Teiwes, *Politics*, pp. 613–15.

2. For details on how both radical and conservative Red Guard factions were able to wave the banner of Mao Zedong Thought for their own political purposes see Milton and Milton, *The Wind Will Not Subside*.

3. Teiwes, *Politics*, esp. pp. 612–14.

4. See Hua Guofeng, "Political Report to the Eleventh National Congress of the Communist Party of China," Aug. 12, 1977, in *Peking Review*, 1977, no. 35, pp. 23–39.

5. *RMRB*, Mar. 8, 1979, in *FBIS-CHI*, in Mar. 16, 1979, p. E7.

6. "Communiqué of the Fifth Plenary Session of the Eleventh Central Committee of the Communist Party of China," Feb. 29, 1980, in *Beijing Review*, 1980, no. 10, p. 9.

7. For one version of an early criticism of Mao see the Hong Kong account of a lengthy talk given by Wang Ruoshui, deputy editor of *Renmin ribao*, on February 13, 1979, at a theory work conference of the Central Committee. The talk, under the title "The Important Lesson of the Great Cultural Revolution Is to Oppose Blind Faith in Individuals" (Wenhuadagemingde zhongyao jiaoxun shi bixu fandui geren mixin), is printed in *Ming Bao Monthly* (Hong Kong), no. 170 (1980), pp. 2–15.

8. *Resolution on Certain Questions*, p. 41. The Resolution also clarified responsibility for the happenings at Lushan by stating that Mao "erred in initiating criticism of Comrade Peng Dehuai and then launching a Party-wide struggle against 'Right Opportunism'" (p. 28).

9. For some interesting comments on how the Gang confused capitalist and socialist relations of production in their view of "bourgeois right" in the early socialist transition see Clegg, p. 2. One might speculate that the lower the level of material development at which the socialist stage (as defined by the revolutionary regime) begins, the more protracted the transitional period will be and the more salient the remnants of "bourgeois right" will be in promoting the development of the forces of production.

10. A systematic study of the dominant lexicon of the Cultural Revolution would reveal a decided bias toward violent and antagonistic terms and phrases. Dittmer's article, "Thought Reform and Cultural Revolution," though not bearing directly on the suggested topic, contains an interesting discussion of how the "polemical symbolism" of the Cultural Revolution affected Chinese politics in the mid-1960's and early 1970's.

11. The rehabilitation of Liu Shaoqi in early 1980 was accompanied by numerous articles citing historical misuse of the term "revisionism" and attempting to offer a clearer definition; see, e.g., *RMRB*, April 3, 1980, in *Beijing Review*, 1980, no. 16, pp. 19–23. See also *Resolution on Certain Questions*, p. 34.

12. *HQ*, 1979, no. 3, in *FBIS-CHI*, Apr. 10, 1979, p. L3.

13. *Ibid.* Retranslated for accuracy; see original, p. 44.

14. *Ibid.*, pp. L3–L4.   15. *Ibid.*, p. L5.

16. *Ibid.*   17. *Ibid.*, p. L2.

18. See Dittmer, "'Line Struggle' in Theory and Practice."

19. See Deng Xiaoping's posthumous eulogies on Peng Dehuai and Liu Shaoqi in *FBIS-CHI*, Dec. 26, 1978, pp. E17–E19, and *Beijing Review*, 1980, no. 21, pp. 9–12, respectively. See also Dittmer, "Death and Transfiguration."

20. *HQ*, 1979, no. 3, in *FBIS-CHI*, Apr. 10, 1979, pp. L6–L7.

21. *RMRB*, Feb. 16, 1979, in *FBIS-CHI*, Feb. 22, 1979, p. E8.

22. *Beijing Review*, 1980, no. 15, p. 3. For a fuller report on the rehabilitation of Li Lisan see Xinhua, Mar. 20, 1980, in *FBIS-CHI*, Mar. 21, 1980, pp. L1–L5.

23. *Beijing Review*, 1980, no. 48, pp. 3–4; see pp. 9–28 for the full text of the indictment.

24. *Beijing Review,* 1981, no. 1, p. 4.
25. See Teiwes, *Politics.*
26. *Ibid.,* p. 616.
27. Dittmer, *Liu Shao-ch'i,* esp. chap. 8.
28. *Ibid.,* p. 351.
29. Communiqué of the Fifth Plenum, p. 10; emphasis added. Wang Dongxing initially retained his seat on the Politburo and his position as vice-chairman of the Party, though he was removed from his posts as director of the Office of the Central Committee, director of the General Office of the Editorial Committee for the Selected Works of Mao Zedong, and commander of Unit 8341, the military unit charged with guarding the high Party leadership. Wu De and Chen Xilian were removed from their respective posts as mayor of Peking and commander of the Peking Military Region, but were allowed, for some time, to retain their nominal positions at the Center. See the two following reports from Hong Kong: *Ming bao,* Jan. 7, 1979, in *FBIS-CHI,* Jan. 12, 1979, pp. E1–E3; *Zheng ming,* 1979, no. 16, in *FBIS-CHI,* Jan. 30, 1979, p. N6.
30. *Resolution on Certain Questions.* p. 48.
31. There has certainly always been diversity and opposition—to the point of irreconcilable differences—within the Chinese Communist Party. But in the new situation this sort of conflict seems less likely to lead to the political draws that have occurred so often in the past. On the question of emerging diversity within a one-party system see Huntington, "Social and Institutional Dynamics of One-Party Systems."
32. The campaign that began in early 1980 to extol the "superiority of socialism" and to defuse the crisis of confidence in Marxism attests to the fact that the post-Mao leadership is well aware of the fragile legitimacy of the ideological basis on which their authority rests. See, e.g., *JFJB,* Jan. 12, 1980, in *FBIS-CHI,* Jan. 15, 1980, pp. L7–L10, and *WHB,* Jan. 13, 1980, in *FBIS-CHI,* Jan. 30, 1980, pp. L9–L11.
33. *GMRB,* Feb. 17, 1979, in *FBIS-CHI,* Feb. 28, 1979, p. E5.
34. *Ibid.* See also another article from the same issue of *GMRB,* in *FBIS-CHI,* Mar. 1, 1979, pp. E10–E11.
35. *RMRB,* Dec. 28, 1978, in *FBIS-CHI,* Jan. 16, 1979, p. E12.
36. *GMRB,* Jan. 23, 1979, in *FBIS-CHI,* Feb. 2, 1979, p. E10. Along the same line, another report referred to "Left revisionism" as "evil ghosts disguised as beautiful women." *RMRB,* Jan. 26, 1979, in *FBIS-CHI,* Feb. 1, 1979, p. E16.
37. The "Seventeen-Year Estimate" was applied mainly to the areas of art, culture, and education, but it can also be said to have been used in the Gang's general appraisal that prior to 1966 "an anti-Party and anti-Socialist line . . . held sway [in the Party] since the founding of New China." *Peking Review,* 1979, no. 51, p. 4.
38. *RMRB,* Feb. 16, 1979, in *FBIS-CHI,* Feb. 22, 1979, p. E10.
39. Xinhua, Jan. 15, 1979, in *FBIS-CHI,* Jan. 19, 1979, pp. G3–G4.
40. *Resolution on Certain Questions,* p. 27. See also *Beijing Review,* 1979, no. 40, p. 15, and *RMRB,* Jan. 2, 1979, in *FBIS-CHI,* Jan. 3, 1979, p. E7. A Hong Kong magazine with close ties to official sources in the Peo-

ple's Republic said in March 1979 that the 1957 anti-Rightist campaign was "basically wrong" and that it was itself a manifestation of the ultra-Left Line. See *Zheng ming*, 1979, no. 17, in *FBIS-CHI*, Mar. 2, 1979, p. N2.

41. See *Peking Review*, 1978, no. 47, p. 3.

42. *GMRB*, Apr. 18, 1979, in *FBIS-CHI*, May 3, 1979, p. L11. The years 1949–53 are considered to be a period of consolidation and rebuilding from the ravages of world war and civil war and come under the rubric "New Democracy." China's socialist construction is said to have begun with the promulgation of the First Five-Year Plan in 1953. A slightly different time span for the dominance of the ultra-Left line was given in an article by Lu Dingyi who suggested an "Eighteen-Year Estimate": "[The] erroneous 'Left' tendency later developed into a line, which was only corrected after the Gang of Four was smashed in October 1976. It lasted for 18 years, from 1958 to 1976." *RMRB*, Mar. 8, 1979, in *FBIS-CHI*, Mar. 16, 1979, p. E7.

In addition to the anti-Rightist campaign of 1957, *Zheng ming* (Hong Kong, see note 40 above) lists the Great Leap Forward ("a truly reckless advance") and the "revolution to overthrow Liu Shaoqi" (i.e., the Cultural Revolution) as the "three great disorders" caused by the ultra-Left line. Another article in the same issue casts the whole idea of the people's communes as a manifestation of ultra-Leftism since it was incompatible with China's level of material and ideological development in 1958–59 (see *FBIS-CHI*, Mar. 14, 1979, pp. N3–N4). For a similar evaluation of the anti-Rightist campaign and the commune movement see Qi Xin, "Zhonggong 'zuo' qing sichao tansuo" (An Exploration into the Chinese Communist 'Left' Deviationist Ideological Trend), *Qishi niandai* (The Seventies), Hong Kong, September 1978, pp. 94–100.

43. *RMRB*, Sept. 7, 1978, in *FBIS-CHI*, Sept. 13, 1978, p. E21.

44. *GMRB*, Feb. 17, 1979, in *FBIS-CHI*, Feb. 28, 1979, p. E5.

45. *Beijing Review*, 1979, no. 40, p. 15.

46. *Resolution on Certain Questions*, pp. 32–33. In the war of words and manipulation of symbols that is so much a part of Chinese politics, the downgrading of the Great Proletarian Cultural Revolution to "cultural revolution" in official translation sources is a conscious part of the thorough repudiation of that period that has emerged from the critique of ultra-Leftism.

47. See the articles by Shirk, Pepper, and Glassman.

48. *RMRB*, June 2, 1979, in *FBIS-CHI*, June 14, 1979, p. L3.

49. Jiangsu Provincial Service, Feb. 26, 1979, in *FBIS-CHI*, Mar. 2, 1979, p. G7; see also *Yunnan Daily*, Mar. 2, 1979, in *FBIS-CHI*, Mar. 5, 1979, p. J4.

50. Among the many "evil practices in society" attributed to "the damage done by Lin Biao and the Gang of Four" are the lack of a serious attitude toward study among youth, idleness and vagrancy, petty crime, the affectation of bourgeois styles of dress and behavior, and the disruptions caused by frustrated youths seeking to redress their grievances with the "down to the countryside" program of rural transfer for middle-school

graduates. See, e.g., *RMRB*, June 8, 1979, in *FBIS-CHI*, June 11, 1979, p. L12.

51. On the origins and impact of the attitude that "Left is better than Right" see *RMRB*, Dec. 12, 1978, in *FBIS-CHI*, Jan. 16, 1979, pp. E11–E13.

52. *ZGQN*, 1978, no. 3, in *FBIS-CHI*, Nov. 15, 1978, p. E3.

53. See Qi Xin et al., *China's New Democracy*.

54. *Beijing Review*, 1980, no. 16, pp. 3–4; Communiqué of the Fifth Plenum, p. 10.

55. For an excellent analysis of the profound differences between the ideologies of the Cultural Revolution and the Four Modernizations see Dirlik, "Socialism without Revolution."

Bibliography

Ahn, Byung-joon. *Chinese Politics and the Cultural Revolution.* Seattle: University of Washington Press, 1976.

Amann, Peter. "Revolution: A Redefinition." In Clifford T. Paynton and Robert Blackey, eds., *Why Revolution? Theories and Analyses.* Cambridge, Mass: Schenkman, 1977.

Anarchism and Anarcho-Syndicalism: Selected Writings by Marx, Engels, Lenin. New York: International Publishers, 1974.

Andors, Stephen. *China's Industrial Revolution: Politics, Planning, and Management, 1949 to the Present.* New York: Pantheon, 1977.

Arendt, Hannah. *On Revolution.* New York: Viking Press, 1965.

Avineri, Shlomo. *The Social and Political Thought of Karl Marx.* Cambridge, Eng.: Cambridge University Press, 1968.

Baum, Richard, ed. *China's Four Modernizations: The New Technological Revolution.* Boulder: Westview Press, 1980.

BBC Summary of World Broadcasts: Far East. London.

Bennett, Gordon. *Huadong: The Story of a Chinese People's Commune.* Boulder: Westview Press, 1978.

———. "Political Labels and Popular Tension," *Current Scene,* vol. 7, no. 4 (1969).

———. *Yundong: Mass Campaigns in Chinese Communist Leadership.* Berkeley: Center for Chinese Studies, 1976.

Bettelheim, Charles. *Class Struggles in the USSR, First Period: 1917–1923.* New York: Monthly Review Press, 1976.

———. *Cultural Revolution and Industrial Organization in China.* New York: Monthly Review Press, 1974.

———. *Economic Calculation and Forms of Property: An Essay on the Transition between Capitalism and Socialism.* New York: Monthly Review Press, 1978.

———. "The Great Leap Backward." In Charles Bettelheim and Neil Burton, *China Since Mao.* New York: Monthly Review Press, 1978.

Borkenau, Franz. *World Communism.* Ann Arbor: University of Michigan Press, 1971.

Brandt, Conrad. *Stalin's Failure in China, 1924–1927.* Cambridge, Mass.: Harvard University Press, 1958.

Bridgham, Phillip. "The Fall of Lin Piao," *China Quarterly,* no. 55 (1973), pp. 427–49.

Brinton, Crane. *The Anatomy of Revolution.* New York: Vintage, 1952.
Burns, Emile, ed. *A Handbook of Marxism.* New York: International Publishers, 1935.
Burton, Barry. "The Cultural Revolution's Ultra-Left Conspiracy: The 'May 16 Group,'" *Asian Survey,* vol. 9, no. 11 (1971), pp. 1029–53.
The Case of P'eng Teh-huai. Hong Kong: Union Research Institute, 1968.
Caute, David. *The Left in Europe Since 1798.* New York: McGraw-Hill, 1966.
Cell, Charles. *Revolution at Work: Mobilization Campaigns in China.* New York: Academic Press, 1977.
Chang, Parris H. *Power and Policy in China.* University Park, Pa.: Pennsylvania State University Press, 1978.
————. "The Rise of Wang Tung-hsing: Head of China's Security Apparatus," *China Quarterly,* no. 73 (1978), pp. 122–36.
Charles, David A. "The Dismissal of Marshal P'eng Teh-huai." In Roderick MacFarquhar, ed., *China under Mao: Politics in Command,* listed below.
Ch'en, Jerome, ed. *Mao Papers: Anthology and Bibliography.* London: Oxford University Press, 1970.
Chiang Hsin-Li. "The Anti–Ultra-Leftist Struggle and the De-Maoization Movement," *Issues and Studies,* vol. 15, no. 12 (1979), pp. 32–51.
Claudin, Fernando. *The Communist Movement: From Comintern to Cominform.* 2 vols. New York: Monthly Review Press, 1975.
Clegg, Jenny. "The Cultural Revolution and the Question of the Capitalist Restoration," *China Policy Study Group Broadsheet* (London), vol. 16, no. 16–17 (1969), pp. 1–4.
Communist China, 1955–1959: Policy Documents with Analysis. Cambridge, Mass.: Harvard University Press, 1962.
Compton, Boyd, ed. *Mao's China: Party Reform Documents, 1942–1944.* Seattle: University of Washington Press, 1966.
Cornforth, Maurice. *Historical Materialism.* New York: International Publishers, 1971.
————. *Materialism and the Dialectical Method.* New York: International Publishers, 1971.
Crook, Frederick W. "The Commune System in the People's Republic of China, 1963–1974." In *China: A Reassessment of the Economy* (Joint Economic Committee of Congress). Washington: U.S. Government Printing Office, 1975.
Current Background. U.S. Consulate, Hong Kong.
"Dalu nongcun gonggong shitangde fazhan" (The Development of the Rural Public Mess Halls on the Mainland), *Zuguo* (Motherland), Hong Kong, vol. 33, no. 13 (n.d.), pp. 300–303.
Daubier, Jean. *A History of the Chinese Cultural Revolution.* New York: Vintage Books, 1974.
Dirlik, Arif. "Socialism without Revolution: The Case of Contemporary China," *Pacific Affairs,* vol. 54, no. 4 (1982), pp. 632–61.
Dittmer, Lowell. "Death and Transfiguration: Liu Shaoqi's Rehabilitation and Contemporary Chinese Politics," *Journal of Asian Studies,* vol. 40, no. 3 (1981), pp. 455–80.

————. "'Line Struggle' in Theory and Practice: The Origins of the Cultural Revolution Reconsidered," *China Quarterly*, no. 72 (1977), pp. 675–712.

————. *Liu Shao-ch'i and the Chinese Cultural Revolution: The Politics of Mass Criticism*. Berkeley: University of California Press, 1974.

————. "Thought Reform and Cultural Revolution: An Analysis of the Symbolism of Chinese Politics," *American Political Science Review*, vol. 71, no. 1 (1977), pp. 67–85.

Domes, Jürgen. *China after the Cultural Revolution: Politics between Two Congresses*. London: C. Hurst, 1977.

————. "New Course in Chinese Domestic Politics: The Anatomy of Readjustment," *Asian Survey*, vol. 13, no. 7 (1973), pp. 633–47.

————. "New Policies in the Communes: Notes on Rural Societal Structures in China," *Journal of Asian Studies*, vol. 41, no. 2 (1982), pp. 253–68.

Dong Chuping. "Lun pingjunzhuyide gongguo yu nongmin zhanzhengde chengbai" (The Merits and Faults of Egalitarianism in the Success and failure of Peasant Wars), *Lishi Yanjiu* (Historical Studies), January 1980, pp. 12–20.

Drachkovitch, Milorad M. *The Revolutionary Internationals, 1864–1943*. Stanford: Stanford University Press, 1966.

Dutt, Gargi. *Rural Communes of China: Organizational Problems*. London: Asia Publishing House, 1967.

Dutt, R. Palme. *The International*. London: Lawrence and Wishart, 1964.

Engels, Friedrich. *Socialism: Utopian and Scientific* (1892). New York: International Publishers, 1968.

Esherick, Joseph. "On the 'Restoration of Capitalism': Mao and Marxist Theory," *Modern China*, vol. 5, no. 1 (1979), pp. 41–78.

Evans, Leslie. *China after Mao*. New York: Monad Press, 1978.

Extracts from China Mainland Magazines. U.S. Consulate, Hong Kong.

Fenwick, Ann. "Chinese Foreign Trade Policy and the Campaign against Deng Xiaoping." In Thomas Fingar, ed., *China's Quest for Independence: Policy Evolution in the 1970s*. Boulder: Westview Press, 1979.

Field, Robert Michael; McGlynn, Kathleen M.; and Abnett, William B. "Political Conflict and Industrial Growth in China: 1965–1977." In *Chinese Economy Post-Mao* (Joint Economic Committee of Congress). Washington, D.C.: U.S. Government Printing Office, 1978.

Fletcher, Martin. "Industrial Relations in China: The New Line," *Pacific Affairs*, vol. 52, no. 1 (1979), pp. 78–94.

Foreign Broadcast Information Service Daily Report: People's Republic of China. U.S. Government, Washington, D.C.

Gardner, John, and Idema, Walt. "China's Educational Revolution." In Stuart Schram, ed., *Authority, Participation, and Cultural Change in China*, listed below.

Gittings, John. *The Role of the Chinese Army*. New York: Oxford University Press, 1967.

Glassman, Joel. "Change and Continuity in Chinese Communist Educational Policy: 'Two-Line Struggle' vs. Incremental Change," *Contemporary China*, vol. 3, no. 2 (1978), pp. 51–70.

Goldman, Merle. "China's Anti-Confucian Campaign, 1973–1974," *China Quarterly*, no. 63 (1975), pp. 435–62.

———. "Teng Hsiao-p'ing and the Debate over Science and Technology," *Contemporary China*, vol. 2, no. 4 (1978), pp. 46–69.

Gottlieb, Thomas M. *Chinese Foreign Policy Factionalism and the Origins of the Strategic Triangle.* Santa Monica: Rand Corporation Report R-1902-NA, 1977.

Gray, Jack. "The Two Roads: Alternative Strategies of Social Change and Economic Growth in China." In Stuart Schram, ed., *Authority, Participation, and Cultural Change in China,* listed below.

A Great Trial in Chinese History. Peking: New World Press, 1981.

Guillermaz, Jacques. *History of the Chinese Communist Party 1921–1949.* New York: Random House, 1972.

Gunneman, John T. *The Moral Meaning of Revolution.* New Haven: Yale University Press, 1979.

Gurley, John G. *Challengers to Capitalism: Marx, Lenin, Stalin, and Mao.* New York: W. W. Norton, 1980.

Gurtov, Melvin. "The Foreign Ministry and Foreign Affairs in China's Cultural Revolution." In Thomas W. Robinson, ed., *The Cultural Revolution in China.* Berkeley: University of California Press, 1971.

Hagopian, Mark A. *The Phenomenon of Revolution.* New York: Dodd, Mead, 1974.

Harding, Harry. "China after Mao," *Problems of Communism*, vol. 26, no. 2 (1977), pp. 1–18.

———. "The Organizational Issue in Chinese Politics, 1949–1975." In *Proceedings of the Fifth Sino-American Conference on Mainland China.* Taipei, 1976.

———. *Organizing China: The Problem of Bureaucracy, 1949–1976.* Stanford: Stanford University Press, 1981.

Harris, Nigel. *The Mandate of Heaven: Marx and Mao in Modern China.* London: Quartet Books, 1978.

Harrison, James P. *The Long March to Power: A History of the Chinese Communist Party, 1921–1971.* New York: Praeger, 1972.

Hinton, William. *Fanshen: A Documentary of Revolution in a Chinese Village.* New York: Vintage Books, 1966.

———. *Hundred Day War: The Cultural Revolution at Tsinghua University.* New York: Monthly Review Press, 1973.

———. *Turning Point in China.* New York: Monthly Review Press, 1972.

Hoffman, Charles. "The Basis of Communist China's Incentive Policy," *Asian Survey*, vol. 3, no. 5 (1963), pp. 245–57.

Hopper, Rex D. "The Revolutionary Process." In Clifford T. Paynton and Robert Blackey, eds., *Why Revolution? Theories and Analyses.* Cambridge, Mass.: Schenkman, 1971.

Howe, Christopher. "Labour Organization and Incentives in Industry Before and After the Cultural Revolution," in Stuart Schram, ed., *Authority, Participation, and Cultural Change in China,* listed below.

Huntington, Samuel P. *Political Order in Changing Societies.* New Haven: Yale University Press, 1968.
———. "Social and Institutional Dynamics of One-Party Systems." In Samuel P. Huntington and Clement Moore, eds., *Authoritarian Politics in Modern Society.* New York: Basic Books, 1970.
Joffe, Ellis. *Between Two Plenums: China's Intraleadership Conflict, 1959–1962.* Michigan Papers in Chinese Studies, no. 22. Ann Arbor: Center for Chinese Studies, 1975.
———. "The Chinese Army after the Cultural Revolution: The Effects of Intervention," *China Quarterly,* no. 55 (1973), pp. 450–77.
Johnson, Chalmers. *Revolutionary Change.* Boston: Little, Brown and Co., 1966.
Joint Publications Research Service. U.S. Government, Washington, D.C.
Kataoka, Tetsuya. "Political Theory of the Great Leap Forward," *Social Research,* vol. 36, no. 1 (1969), pp. 93–122.
Kau, Michael Y. M., ed. *The Lin Piao Affair: Power Politics and Military Coup.* White Plains, N.Y.: International Arts and Sciences Press, 1975.
Kramnick, Isaac. "Reflections on Revolution: Definition and Explanation in Recent Scholarship," *History and Theory,* vol. 11, no. 1 (1972), pp. 26–63.
Kristov, V. I., ed. *Maoism through the Eyes of Communism.* Moscow: Progress Publishers, 1970.
Lampton, David M. *Health, Conflict, and the Chinese Political System.* Ann Arbor: Center for Chinese Studies, 1974.
Lasky, Melvin J. *Utopia and Revolution.* Chicago: University of Chicago Press, 1976.
Lee, Rensaleer W. "The Hsia-Fang System: Marxism and Modernization," *China Quarterly,* no. 28 (1966), pp. 40–62.
Lenin, V. I. *Collected Works.* 45 vols. Moscow: Foreign Languages Publishing House, 1946–67.
Lewis, John Wilson. "Introduction: Leadership and Power in China." In John Wilson Lewis, ed., *Party Leadership and Revolutionary Power in China.* Cambridge, Eng.: Cambridge University Press, 1969.
———. "Leader, Commissar, and Bureaucrat: The Chinese Political System in the Last Days of the Revolution." In Ping-ti Ho and Tang Tsou, eds., *China in Crisis,* Book 1, Part 2. Chicago: University of Chicago Press, 1968.
———. "The Leadership Doctrine of the Chinese Communist Party: The Lesson of the People's Commune," *Asian Survey,* vol. 3, no. 10 (1963), pp. 457–64.
———. *Leadership in Communist China.* Ithaca: Cornell University Press, 1963.
———. "Political Aspects of Mobility in China's Urban Development," *American Political Science Review,* vol. 60, no. 4 (1966), pp. 457–64.
———. "The Social Limits on Politically-Induced Change." In Chandler Morse, ed., *Modernization by Design.* Ithaca: Cornell University Press, 1969.

————, ed. *Major Doctrines of Communist China*. New York: W. W. Norton, 1964.

Leys, Simon. *Chinese Shadows*. New York: Penguin, 1977.

Lieberthal, Kenneth. "Modernization and Succession Politics in China," *Journal of International Affairs*, vol. 32, no. 2 (1978), pp. 239–54.

————. "The Politics of Modernization in the PRC," *Problems of Communism*, vol. 27, no. 3 (1978), pp. 1–17.

————. "Strategies of Conflict in China during 1975–1976," *Contemporary China*, vol. 1, no. 2 (1976), pp. 7–14.

Lippit, Victor D. "The Commune in Chinese Development," *Modern China*, vol. 3, no. 2 (1977), pp. 237–54.

————. "The Great Leap Forward Reconsidered," *Modern China*, vol. 1, no. 1 (1975), pp. 92–115.

Lotta, Raymond, ed. *And Mao Makes Five: Mao Tsetung's Last Great Battle*. Chicago: Banner Press, 1978.

Lowenthal, Richard. "Development vs. Utopia in Communist Policy." In Chalmers Johnson, ed., *Change in Communist Systems*. Stanford: Stanford University Press, 1970.

MacFarquhar, Roderick. "Communist China's Intra-Party Dispute," *Pacific Affairs*, vol. 31, no. 4 (1958), pp. 323–35.

————. *The Origins of the Cultural Revolution: Contradictions among the People*. New York: Columbia University Press, 1974.

————, ed. *China under Mao: Politics in Command*. Cambridge, Mass.: M.I.T. Press, 1966.

Mao Tse-tung [Mao Zedong]. *A Critique of Soviet Economics*. New York: Monthly Review Press, 1977.

————. *Miscellany of Mao Tse-tung Thought*. Joint Publications Research Service, nos. 61269–1, –2 (February 20, 1974), Arlington, Va., 1974.

————. *Selected Readings from the Works of Mao Tse-tung*. Peking: Foreign Languages Press, 1971.

————. *Selected Works of Mao Tse-tung*. 5 vols. Peking: Foreign Languages Press, 1967–77.

Marx, Karl. *The Poverty of Philosophy* (1847). Moscow: Foreign Languages Publishing House, n.d.

Marx, Karl, and Engels, Friedrich. *The Communist Manifesto* (1848). New York: International Publishers, 1968.

Masters, Anthony. *Bakunin: The Father of Anarchism*. London: Sidgwick and Jackson, 1974.

Maxwell, Neville. "Learning from Tachai," *World Development*, vol. 3, no. 7–8 (1975), pp. 477–81.

Mehnert, Klaus. *Peking and the New Left: At Home and Abroad*. Berkeley: Center for Chinese Studies, 1969.

Meisner, Maurice. "Leninism and Maoism: Some Populist Perspectives on Marxism-Leninism," *China Quarterly*, no. 45 (1971), pp. 2–36.

————. *Mao's China: A Political History of the People's Republic*. New York: Free Press, 1977.

————. "Utopian Socialist Themes in Maoism." In John Wilson Lewis, ed., *Peasant Rebellion and Communist Revolution in Asia*. Stanford: Stanford University Press, 1974.

Meisner, Mitch. "In Agriculture, Learn from Tachai: Theory and Practice in Chinese Rural Development." Unpublished Ph.D. dissertation, University of Chicago, 1977.

———. "Dazhai: The Mass Line in Practice," *Modern China*, vol. 4, no. 1 (1978), pp. 27–62.

Milton, David, and Milton, Nancy Dall. *The Wind Will Not Subside: Years in Revolutionary China, 1964–1969*. New York: Pantheon, 1976.

Moody, Peter R. *The Politics of the Eighth Central Committee of the Communist Party of China*. Hamden, Conn.: Shoestring Press, 1973.

Nathan, Andrew J. "A Factionalism Model of CCP Politics," *China Quarterly*, no. 53 (1973), pp. 34–66.

———. "Policy Oscillations in the People's Republic of China: A Critique," *China Quarterly*, no. 68 (1976), pp. 720–50.

Nee, Victor. "Revolution and Bureaucracy: Shanghai in the Cultural Revolution." In Victor Nee and James Peck, eds., *China's Uninterrupted Revolution*, listed below.

Nee, Victor, and Peck, James, eds. *China's Uninterrupted Revolution: From 1840 to the Present*. New York: Pantheon Books, 1975.

Nolan, Peter, and White, Gordon. "Socialist Development and Rural Inequality: The Chinese Countryside in the 1970s," *Journal of Peasant Studies*, vol. 7, no. 1 (1979), pp. 3–48.

Nomad, Max. "The Anarchist Tradition." In Milorad Drachkovitch, ed., *The Revolutionary Internationals, 1864–1943*, listed above.

Oksenberg, Michel, and Goldstein, Steven. "The Chinese Political Spectrum," *Problems of Communism*, vol. 23, no. 2 (1974), pp. 1–13.

Ollman, Bertel. "Marx's Vision of Communism," *Critique* (Glasgow), no. 8 (1977), pp. 4–41.

Onate, Andres D. *Chairman Mao and the Chinese Communist Party*. Chicago: Newton-Hall, 1979.

———. "Hua Kuo-feng and the Arrest of the 'Gang of Four,'" *China Quarterly*, no. 75 (1978), pp. 540–65.

Parish, William L., and Whyte, Martin King. *Village and Family in Contemporary China*. Chicago: University of Chicago Press, 1978.

Peck, James. "Revolution versus Modernization and Revisionism: A Two-Front Struggle." In Victor Nee and James Peck, eds., *China's Uninterrupted Revolution*, listed above.

Pepper, Suzanne. "Education and Revolution: The Chinese Model Revisited," *Asian Survey*, vol. 18, no. 9 (1978), pp. 847–90.

Pettee, George Sawyer. "The Process of Revolution." In Clifford T. Paynton and Robert Blackey, eds., *Why Revolution? Theories and Analyses*. Cambridge, Mass.: Schenkman, 1971.

Prybyla, Jan S. *The Political Economy of Communist China*. Scranton, Pa.: International Textbooks, 1970.

Pye, Lucian. *The Dynamics of Chinese Politics*. Cambridge, Mass.: Oelgeschlager, Gunn, and Hain, 1981.

Qi Xin [Chi Hsin]. *The Case of the Gang of Four*. Hong Kong: Cosmos Books, 1977.

———. "Gongshehua he dayuejinde 'zuo' qing" (The 'Left' Tendencies of

Communization and the Great Leap Forward), *Qishi Niandai* (The Seventies), Hong Kong, October 1978, pp. 30–37.

————. "Wenge 'zuo' qingde jidu fazhan" (The Extreme Development of 'Left' Deviations in the Cultural Revolution), *Qishi Niandai* (The Seventies), Hong Kong, December 1978, pp. 70–78.

————. "Zhonggong 'zuo' qing sichao tansuo" (An Exploration into the Chinese Communist 'Left' Deviationist Thought Trend), *Qishi Niandai* (The Seventies), Hong Kong, September 1978, pp. 94–100.

Qi Xin et al. *China's New Democracy*. Hong Kong: Cosmos Books, 1979.

Reardon-Anderson, James. "Science and Technology in Post-Mao China," *Contemporary China*, vol. 4, no. 2 (1979), pp. 37–45.

Resnick, David. "Crude Communism and Revolution," *American Political Science Review*, vol. 70, no. 4 (1976), pp. 1136–45.

Resolution on Certain Questions in the History of Our Party since the Founding of the People's Republic of China. Peking: Foreign Languages Press, 1981.

Rice, Edward F. "The Second Rise and Fall of Teng Hsiao-p'ing," *China Quarterly*, no. 67 (1976), pp. 494–500.

Riskin, Carl. "Maoism and Motivation: Work Incentives in China." In Victor Nee and James Peck, eds., *China's Uninterrupted Revolution*, listed above.

————. "Small Industry and the Chinese Model of Development," *China Quarterly*, no. 46 (1971), pp. 258–66.

Rue, John E. *Mao Tse-tung in Opposition, 1927–1935*. Stanford: Stanford University Press, 1966.

Salaff, Janet W. "The Urban Communes and Anti-City Experiment in Communist China," *China Quarterly*, no. 29 (1967), pp. 82–110.

Schram, Stuart. "Mao Tse-tung and the Theory of the Permanent Revolution," *China Quarterly*, no. 46 (1971), pp. 221–44.

————. *The Political Thought of Mao Tse-tung*. New York: Praeger, 1970.

————, ed. *Authority, Participation, and Cultural Change in China*. Cambridge, Eng.: Cambridge University Press, 1973.

————, ed. *Chairman Mao Talks to the People: Talks and Letters, 1956–1971*. New York: Pantheon Books, 1974.

Schurmann, Franz. *Ideology and Organization in Communist China*. 2nd ed., rev. Berkeley: University of California Press, 1970.

————. "On Revolutionary Conflict," *Journal of International Studies*, vol. 23, no. 1 (1969), pp. 36–53.

Schwartz, Benjamin I. "Modernization and the Maoist Vision—Some Reflections on Chinese Communist Goals." In Roderick MacFarquhar, ed., *China under Mao*, listed above.

Shirk, Susan. "Educational Reform and Political Backlash: Recent Changes in Chinese Educational Policy," *Comparative Education Review*, June 1979, pp. 183–217.

"Sirenbang" Yanxinglu (A Record of the Words and Actions of the Gang of Four). Hong Kong: Cultural Reference Materials Supply Press, 1977.

Skinner, G. William. "Marketing and Social Structure in Rural China, Part III," *Journal of Asian Studies*, vol. 24, no. 3 (1965), pp. 363–99.

Skinner, G. William, and Wincker, Edwin A. "Compliance Succession in Rural Communist China: A Cyclical Theory." In Amitai Etzioni, ed., *A Sociological Reader in Complex Organization.* 2nd ed. New York: Holt, Rinehart and Winston, 1969.

Sklar, Leslie. "Relations of Production, Productive Forces, and the Mass Line in the Formation of the People's Communes in China," *Journal of Peasant Studies,* vol. 6, no. 3 (1979), pp. 311–41.

Soboul, Albert. *A Short History of the French Revolution, 1789–1799.* Berkeley: University of California Press, 1977.

Solinger, Dorothy J. *Regional Government and Political Integration in Southwest China, 1949–1954: A Case Study.* Berkeley: University of California Press, 1977.

Solomon, Richard H. *Mao's Revolution and the Chinese Political Culture.* Berkeley: University of California Press, 1971.

Stalin, Joseph. *Collected Works.* 13 vols. Moscow: Foreign Languages Publishing House, 1953–54.

Starr, John Bryan. *Continuing the Revolution: The Political Thought of Mao.* Princeton: Princeton University Press, 1979.

————. *Ideology and Culture: An Introduction to the Dialectic of Contemporary Chinese Politics.* New York: Harper and Row, 1973.

Starr, John Bryan, and Dyer, Nancy Anne, compilers. *Post-Liberation Works of Mao Zedong: A Bibliography and Index.* Berkeley: Center for Chinese Studies. 1976.

Survey of China Mainland Magazines. U.S. Consulate, Hong Kong.

Survey of China Mainland Press. U.S. Consulate, Hong Kong.

Sweezy, Paul. "A Crisis in Marxian Theory," *Monthly Review,* vol. 31, no. 2 (1979), pp. 20–24.

Sweezy, Paul, and Bettelheim, Charles. *On the Transition to Socialism.* 2nd ed., enlarged. New York: Monthly Review Press, 1972.

Teiwes, Frederick C. "The Origins of Rectification: Inner-Party Purges and Education before Liberation," *China Quarterly,* no. 65 (1976), pp. 15–53.

————. *Politics and Purges in China: Rectification and the Decline of Party Norms, 1949–1965.* White Plains, N.Y.: M. E. Sharpe, 1979.

Thomas, Paul. *Karl Marx and the Anarchists.* London: Routledge and Kegan Paul, 1980.

Ticktin, Hillel. "Towards a Political Economy of the Soviet Union," *Critique* (Glasgow), no. 1 (1973), pp. 20–41.

Tilly, Charles. *From Mobilization to Revolution.* Reading, Pa.: Addison-Wesley, 1978.

————. "Revolutions and Collective Violence." In Fred Greenstein and Nelson Polsby, eds., *Handbook of Political Science,* vol. 3. Reading, Pa.: Addison-Wesley, 1975.

————. *The Vendée.* London: Edward Arnold, 1969.

Trotsky, Leon, *The Russian Revolution.* Selected and edited by F. W. Dupee. New York: Doubleday, 1959.

Tsou, Tang. "Mao Tse-tung Thought, the Last Struggle for Succession, and the Post-Mao Era," *China Quarterly,* no. 71 (1977), pp. 498–527.

————. "Prolegomenon to the Study of Informal Groups in CCP Politics," *China Quarterly*, no. 65 (1976), pp. 98–114.

Tsou, Tang, Blecher, Marc, and Meisner, Mitch. "The Responsibility System in Agriculture: Its Implementation in Dazhai and Xiyang," *Modern China*, vol. 8, no. 1 (1982), pp. 41–104.

Tucker, Robert C. *The Marxian Revolutionary Idea*. New York: W. W. Norton, 1969.

————, ed. *The Lenin Anthology*. New York: W. W. Norton, 1975.

————, ed. *The Marx-Engels Reader*. New York: W. W. Norton, 1972.

2, 3, Many Parties of a New Type: Against the Ultra-Left Line. New York: United Labor Press, 1977.

Ulam, Adam B. *In the Name of the People: Prophets and Conspirators in Prerevolutionary Russia*. New York: Viking, 1977.

————. *The Unfinished Revolution: Marxism and Communism in the Contemporary World*. 2nd ed. Boulder: Westview Press, 1979.

Union Research Service. Hong Kong.

van Ginnekan, Jaap. *The Rise and Fall of Lin Piao*. New York: Avon Books, 1977.

Vogel, Ezra. *Canton under Communism: Program and Politics in a Provincial Capital, 1949–1968*. New York: Harper Torchbooks, 1969.

Wakeman, Frederic, Jr. *History and Will: Philosophical Perspectives of Mao Tse-tung's Thought*. Berkeley: University of California Press, 1973.

Walder, Andrew. *Chang Ch'un-ch'iao and Shanghai's January Revolution*. Michigan Papers in Chinese Studies, no. 32. Ann Arbor: Center for Chinese Studies, 1977.

Walker, Kenneth R. *Planning in Chinese Agriculture: Socialization and the Private Sector, 1956–1962*. Chicago: Aldine, 1965.

Waller, Michael. *The Language of Communism*. London: Bodley Head, 1972.

Wang Ruoshi. "Wenhuadagemingde zhongyao jiaoxun shi bixu fandui geren mixin" (The Important Lesson of the Great Cultural Revolution Is to Oppose Blind Faith in Individuals), *Ming Pao Monthly* (Hong Kong), no. 170 (1980), pp. 2–15.

Wei Chi. *The Soviet Union under the New Tsars*. Peking: Foreign Languages Press, 1978.

Wheelwright, E. F., and McFarlane, Bruce. *The Chinese Road to Socialism: Economics of the Cultural Revolution*. New York: Monthly Review Press, 1970.

White, Gordon. *The Politics of Class and Class Origin: The Case of the Cultural Revolution*. Contemporary China Centre Paper no. 9. Canberra: Australian National University, 1976.

————. "Politics and Social Status in China," *Pacific Affairs*, vol. 51, no. 4 (1979), pp. 561–85.

Witke, Roxane. *Comrade Chiang Ch'ing*. Boston: Little, Brown and Co., 1977.

Womack, Brantly. "Politics and Epistemology in China Since Mao," *China Quarterly*, no. 80 (1979), pp. 768–92.

Wylie, Raymond F. *The Emergence of Maoism: Mao Tse-tung, Ch'en*

Po-ta, and the Search for Chinese Theory, 1935–1945. Stanford: Stanford University Press, 1980.

Young, Graham. "From Contradictions among the People to Class Struggle: The Theories of Uninterrupted Revolution and Continuous Revolution," *Asian Survey,* vol. 18, no. 9 (1978), pp. 912–33.

———. "On the Mass Line," *Modern China,* vol. 6, no. 2 (1980), pp. 225–40.

Zweig, David S. "A Second Cultural Revolution: Why and Why Not?" *Contemporary China,* vol. 2, no. 2 (1978), pp. 81–91.

Index